Joseph Cottle
and The Romantics
The life of a Bristol publisher

Basil Cottle

ℕ *redcliffe*

First published by Redcliffe Press Ltd in 2008 in association with the Cottle Trust, with the aid and assistance of grants given by the University of Bristol Alumni Association and the Bristol Guild of Kalendars.

Redcliffe Press Ltd., 81g Pembroke Road, Bristol BS8 3EA
Tele: 0117 9737207 web: www.redcliffepress.co.uk

ISBN 978-1-904537-80-9

British Library Cataloguing-in-Publication Data
A catalogue record for this book is available from the British Library.

Typeset by Harper Phototypesetters Ltd., Northampton
and printed and bound by 4edge Limited, Hockley. www.4edge.co.uk

Joseph Cottle

Foreword

The death in 1994 of Dr Basil Cottle (Reader in the English Department of Bristol University) was sudden and unexpected, and the Cottle Trust was formed for the purposes of preparing for publication two ambitious projects he had worked on for many years and which were virtually complete at the time of his death: his comprehensive guide to the cathedrals of France and his biography of the Bristol publisher Joseph Cottle (to whom he was not related). Publication of the former, *All the Cathedrals of France*, was successfully achieved through the Unicorn Press in 2000, and the present volume now brings the latter also into the public domain. Basil Cottle's research interests were primarily in medieval English literature and in the history of English language and literature, and he is best known as the author of *The Penguin Dictionary of Surnames* (1967), *The Triumph of English* (1969), *The Plight of English* (1975), *Names* (1983) and *The Language of Literature: English Grammar in Action* (1985). But he had also a range of other interests. He was, in particular, an expert on Bristol and its history: he was at one time President of the Bristol and Gloucester Archaeological Society and was at all times tirelessly active with tongue, pen and (with regard to guided tours) feet in disseminating information on the architectural, literary and ecclesiastical heritage of Bristol, producing a number of guides, pamphlets and articles on the city and the literary figures (such as Southey, Cottle and Chatterton) associated with it. He had also a special interest in churches, their history, their fabric and their denominational affiliations; he was himself familiar both with the non-conformist persuasion in which he had grown up, and with the Church of England to which his own choice later led him. B. Cottle was, therefore, especially well qualified to tell the story of J. Cottle, a literary man (friend and publisher of the romantic poets Wordsworth, Coleridge and Southey and editor of Chatterton), a Bristol man, and a non-conformist man to whom his church mattered — and who typified that interest in denominational choices which characterized a post-Wesleyan, church-going and sermon-reading generation for whom literary and ecclesiastical passions and loyalties were often interrelated in various ways.

We, the Trust, have altered BC's text as little as possible in preparing it for publication. Some minor local editing was undertaken by Myra Stokes. JC had a portrait collection of which he was proud, and we have included many more pictures of his contemporaries than the two or three to which BC intended to limit himself. We have also included maps, since topographic precision and detail (inside and outside Bristol) is a feature of BC's style. We have, additionally, appended, for the benefit of specialists, a contextualizing survey (provided by Adam Rounce, of Keele University) of such relevant scholarship as has appeared since the 1970s, when the book was written. We have also expanded BC's title (*Joseph Cottle of Bristol*) to one which better indicates to non-specialists the cultural and historical arena which this entertaining, informative and accessible book illuminates. Those documents BC refers to in his notes as in his private possession are now the property of his literary executor, Martin Crossley Evans (Warden of Manor Hall, Bristol).

We close by discharging a pleasant duty: that of acknowledging and expressing our gratitude to the persons and institutions who have contributed the funds, time and/or professional expertise that made possible the publication of both this and the former book. First and foremost must come the many friends and colleagues of BC who responded so generously to our original appeal for funds, that generosity being itself a tribute to BC — for a summary list of his publications, though it may suggest the range and precision of his information, can do little to convey the vigour, clarity and liveliness of his formal and informal delivery (he was in considerable demand as a public speaker) and the warmth and respect inspired in all who became familiar with his distinctive style of learning, as soundly based on scholarship as it was roundly based on his own brand of wit and fun. We thank the Bristol Guild of Kalendars for a substantial subscription and are grateful to the Alumni Association of the University of Bristol for a generous grant to assist us with the costs of the maps and other illustrative material, some of which is here reproduced by permission of the University of Bristol Library, Special Collections, who gave us most valuable and friendly assistance. We would also like to express our gratitude to Adam Rounce for providing his considered and scholarly Afterword; to Marie Fraser for typing the manuscript; and to Jon Cannon for designing and preparing the maps. And of course we thank Redcliffe Press for their initiative and professionalism in helping the Trust to bring this book before the public. Thanks to all of them, Basil Cottle's store of knowledge about the City of Bristol at the time of the birth of the Romantic movement will not be lost by his death.

The Cottle Trust:
Martin Crossley Evans
Don Carleton
Nick Lee
Myra Stokes

Acknowledgements

Joseph Cottle of Bristol has had until now only one secure place in the minds of students of literature: as the publisher of *Lyrical Ballads*. His varied life of eighty-three years has been hard to trace in detail, but my quest has been absorbing and full of surprises. The work in its first form was in fulfilment of the requirements for the Bristol degree of Doctor of Philosophy; in all its stages, it has owed very much to the help, encouragement and inspiration of three scholars – George Whalley, Paul Kaufman and the late Bertram R. Davis of Bristol, whose fine Romantics library is now safely reassembled in Waterloo University, Ontario.

My sources were, largely, unpublished manuscript letters and other papers, in libraries and private collections, including my own. In the years since I began the work, however, a number of these have been published, principally by Kenneth Curry, E.L. Griggs, and the revisers of E. de Selincourt; to their editions – as to Kathleen Coburn's, although again I had already myself extracted the material in the Coleridge Notebooks – I owe a debt for confidence in my own readings or for the discovery of new material. One of the richest sources of minutiae has proved to be the Berg Collection in the New York Public Library, to which I am grateful for permission to make mention of letters not included in Kenneth Curry's *New Letters of Robert Southey*. Finally, I must thank Professor Vivian de Sola Pinto for good advice given long ago, when this book was an academic dissertation.

Basil Cottle

Bristol, 29 June 1974

Illustrations

Abbreviations used in the Notes

1795 Album	Cottle's *Bristol Album, 1795* (at Cornell).
CCS	C.C. Southey, *The Life and Correspondence of Robert Southey* (London: Longman, Brown, Rees, & Longmans, 1849-1850).
Coburn	Kathleen Coburn, *The Notebooks of Samuel Taylor Coleridge* (London: Routledge & Kegan Paul, 1957).
Curry	K. Curry, *New Letters of Robert Southey* (New York and London: Columbia U.P., 1965).
de S	E. de Selincourt, *The Letters .... Later Years* (Oxford, 1938).
EHC	E.H. Coleridge, *Letters of Samuel Taylor Coleridge* (London: Heinemann, 1895).
ER.37	J. Cottle, *Early Recollections: chiefly Relating to the Late Samuel Taylor Coleridge, during his Long Residence in Bristol* (London: Longman, Rees & Co. and Hamilton, Adams & Co., 1837).
FFJ	*Felix Farley's Bristol Journal.*
Griggs	E.L. Griggs, *Collected Letters of Samuel Taylor Coleridge* (Oxford, 1956).
MH.4	J. Cottle, *Malvern Hills, with Minor Poems and Essays*, 4th edn (London: Cadell, 1829).
Moorman	E. de Selincourt, *The Letters .... II: The Middle Years, I, 1806-1811*, 2nd edn, revised by Mary Moorman (Oxford, 1969).
Moorman/Hill	E. de Selincourt, *The Letters .... III: The Middle Years, II, 1812-1820*, 2nd edn, revised by Mary Moorman and A.G. Hill (Oxford, 1970).

R.47   J. Cottle, *Reminiscences of Samuel Taylor Coleridge and Robert Southey* (London: Houlston & Stoneman, 1847).

Shaver   E. de Selincourt, *The Letters of William and Dorothy Wordsworth, I: The Early Years 1787-1805*, 2nd edn, revised by Chester L. Shaver (Oxford, 1967).

Simmons   J. Simmons, *Southey* (London: Collins, 1945).

Contents and Summary

country house; his commitment to religious subjects and to his friendship with Hall and Foster; the Serampore missionaries; he is reconciled with Hannah More; his sister Ann marries, *aet.*48, an old man of wealth, toughness, and piety; Cottle begs Wordsworth to address a poem to him – Dorothy's reply; a piece of Bunyan research; Wordsworth's refusal; *Malvern Hills*, 4th edn; Ann Cottle's husband builds Zion Chapel; Cottle sustains a church secretaryship; Robert Hall dies; Cottle's gift to the Bristol Institution.

Cottle moves out to Bedminster; comfort and prosperity; Coleridge dies; Mrs Southey's madness; further religious tracts; his nieces' wealth; he begins to collect materials for a memoir of Coleridge, to the growing alarm of Poole, Gillman, Green, and the Coleridges; Southey on the whole encourages him; his furious postal quarrel with Gillman and Poole; the Coleridges threaten a suit; he refuses to receive Poole; Crabb Robinson calls and becomes friendly.

Crabb Robinson finds Cottle uncertain; Hartley Coleridge's mockery of Cottle, and Mary Wordsworth's anxiety; Southey comes with his son Cuthbert; Landor comes into Cottle's circle; the *Early Recollections*; correspondence with Wordsworth and Southey; Dorothy Wordsworth's madness; *The Quarterly* makes a savage onslaught on the *Recollections* – individual opinions are no kinder; Hudson Gurney's remarks on it in his copy; the badness of the book; Southey's madness.

Cottle moves to a great mansion overlooking Bristol; Wordsworth finds him not at home; he is prosecuted for libel, but all goes fairly well; his brother Robert founds a sect in Putney called the 'Cottleites'; Cottle helps towards a Chatterton memorial; his printer is prosecuted for libel – a farthing damages, but crippling costs; prolonged religious correspondence with Foster.

KEY TO MAPS

Key to locations on Bristol map
(reading approximately left to right across both pages)
Dates in brackets are for foundation or start of construction of surviving buildings.

1   Bristol Institute (Dowry Sq)
2   Hannah More's school (Park St)
3   Red Lodge (built c.1577 refurbished c.1720)
4   The Assembly Room
5   Merchant's Hall
6   Old Bristol library/City Library (built 1738)
7   Theatre Royal/Old Vic (built 1766)
8   Cooper's Hall (built 1743)
9   Corn St: location of Commercial Rooms; Bush Tavern; Tolzey; Council House
10 Corn St/High St corner: Joseph Cottle's first shop, 48 High St; nearby is former site (until 1733) of Bristol High Cross
11 Broad St: White Hart and White Lion (former coaching inns)
12 Merchant Tailor's Hall (built 1740; Tailor's Ct off Broad St)
13 Wine St: location of Old Dutch House (corner with High St); Corn Market
14 The Bristol Newgate
15 St Peter's Hospital
16 Infirmary (built 1784)
17 Stokes Croft: Bristol Baptist College (1812–1916)
18 North St: Baptist Academy (before 1812)
19 Railway station (Temple Meads: built c.1840 in its first form)

On inset map:
20 Arno's Vale cemetery (1837)
21 Stapleton, home of John Foster
22 Hanham, site of the Henderson School

Homes of Joseph Cottle (in chronological order)
I   Wine St, Cottle's home 1798–1800
II   Gloucester St and Brunswick Sq, successive sites of Cottle's home (and his sisters' school) 1800–1820
III   Dighton St, Cottle's home 1820–31
IV   North St, site of No 1, Carlton Place, Cottle's home 1831–39

On inset map:
V   Belluton Road, site of Firfield House, Cottle's home after 1839

Places of worship (approx left to right across both pages)
Undated buildings are medieval

a   Bristol Cathedral
b   St Michael-on-the-Mount-Without
c   Lewin's Mead Meeting (Unitarian; 1787)
d   St John/St John the Baptist
e   St Stephen
f   St Leonard
g   St Werburgh
h   St Ewen
i   All Saint's (All Saint's Lane with Rummer Tavern immediately to E)
j   St Nicholas
k   Christ Church
l   St Mary-le-Port
m   St Peter
n   St James (Barton Alley behind)
o   Broadmead Baptist chapel
p   St Paul
q   Zion Chapel (Congregational; 1828–30)
r   St Mary Redcliffe/Redcliffe church
s   Temple church

In 1794 Bristol had 4 other Anglican and 18 other Nonconformist places of worship

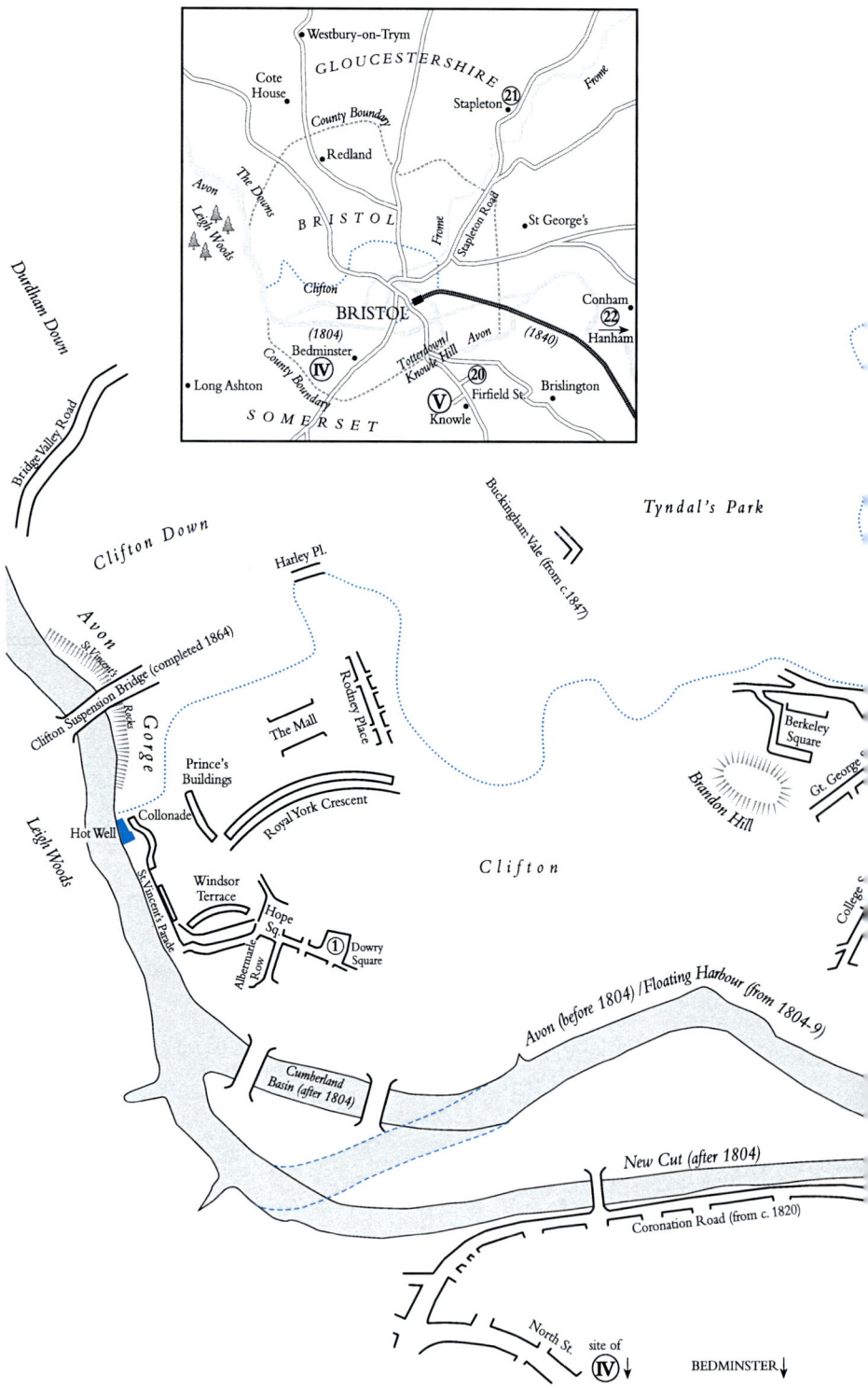

Westbury-on-Trym

GLOUCESTERSHIRE

Cote
House

County Boundary

Stapleton

㉑

Frome

Redland

Avon

The Downs

Leigh Woods

B R I S T O L

Frome

St George's

Stapleton Road

Clifton

BRISTOL

Conham

㉒

Hanham

(1804)

Bedminster

Ⓘ Ⓥ

County Boundary

Long Ashton

Totterdown/ Knowle Hill

Avon

(1840)

㉕

Firfield St.

Brislington

Ⓥ

Knowle

S O M E R S E T

Buckingham Vale (from c.1847)

Tyndal's Park

Bridge Valley Road

Clifton Down

Harley Pl.

A v o n

St Vincent's Rocks

Clifton Suspension Bridge (completed 1864)

Durdham Down

Gorge

Rodney Place

The Mall

Berkeley
Square

Brandon Hill

Gt. George

Prince's
Buildings

Collonade

Royal York Crescent

Clifton

College

Leigh Woods

Hot Well

St Vincent's Parade

Windsor
Terrace

Hope
Sq.

Ⓘ Dowry
Square

Albemarle Row

Avon (before 1804) / Floating Harbour (from 1804-9)

Cumberland
Basin
(after 1804)

New Cut (after 1804)

Coronation Road (from c.1820)

North St.

site of
Ⓘ ↓

BEDMINSTER ↓

XXII

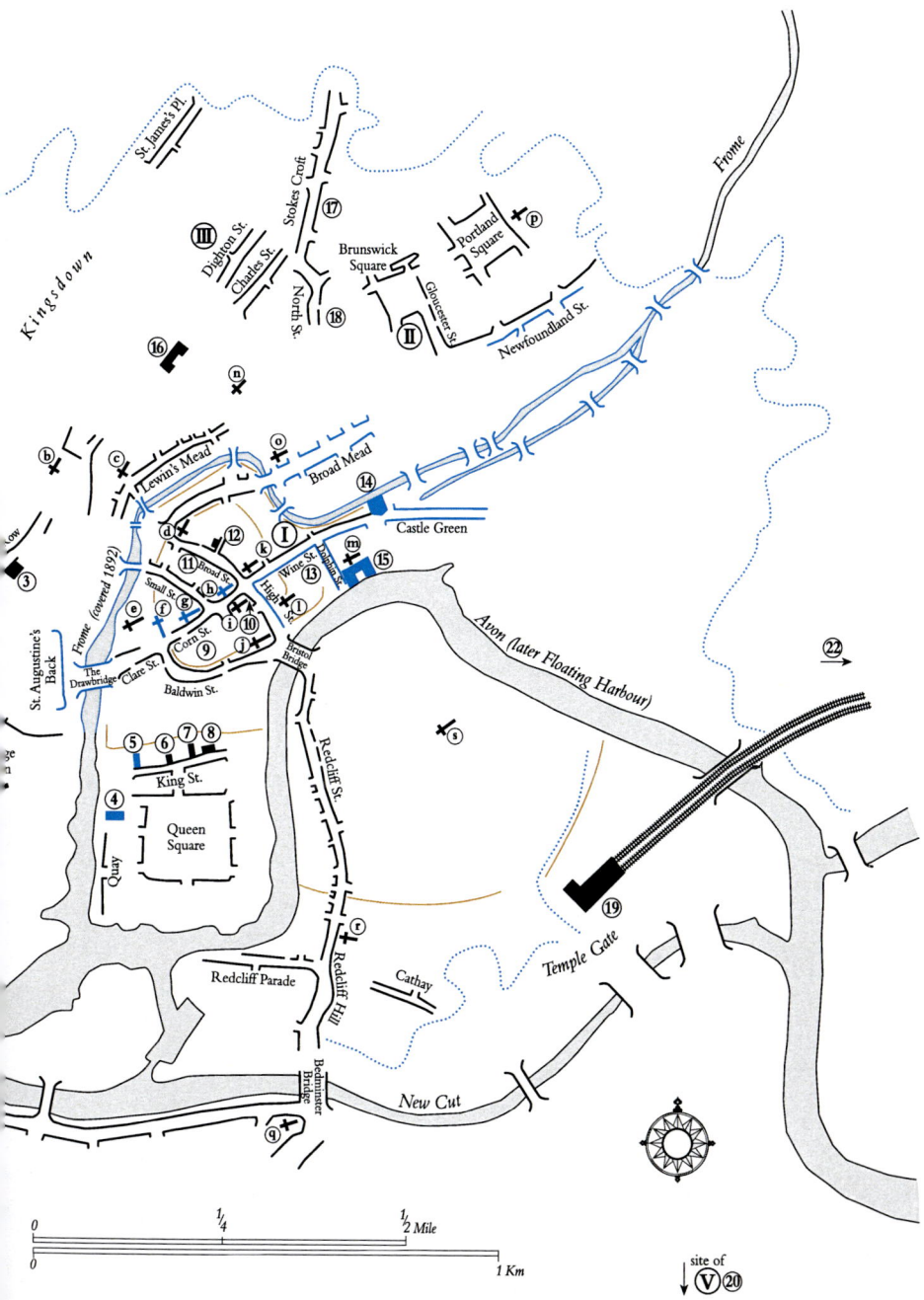

Site now demolished

Approximate limit of built-up area in 1794

Approximate line of medieval city walls, 1581 (largely gone by 1794)

⑪ Location mentioned in the text

Ⓜ Homes of Joseph Cottle

ⓗ Place of worship

↑㉑

St. James's Pl.

Stokes Croft

Frome

Kingsdown

Ⓜ
Dighton St.
Charles St.
North St.

⑰

⑱

Brunswick Square

Portland Square

ⓟ

Gloucester St.

Ⓘ

Newfoundland St.

⑯

ⓝ

ⓑ

ⓒ

Lewin's Mead

ⓞ

Broad Mead

⑭

Castle Green

Low

ⓓ

⑫

ⓚ

Ⓘ

Dighton St.

ⓜ

③

Frome (covered 1892)

⑪ Broad St.

Wine St.

⑮

St. Augustine's Back

ⓔ

ⓕ

ⓖ

ⓗ

High St.

ⓘ ⑩

Corn St.

ⓙ

⑨

Bristol Bridge

Avon (later Floating Harbour)

㉒

The Drawbridge

Clare St.

Baldwin St.

ⓢ

⑤ ⑥ ⑦ ⑧

King St.

④

Quay

Queen Square

Redcliff St.

⑲

ⓡ

Temple Gate

Redcliff Parade

Redcliff Hill

Cathay

Bedminster Bridge

New Cut

ⓠ

0   ¼   ½ Mile

0   1 Km

site of
↓ Ⓥ ㉒⁰

XXIII

Drogheda

Dublin

Killarney

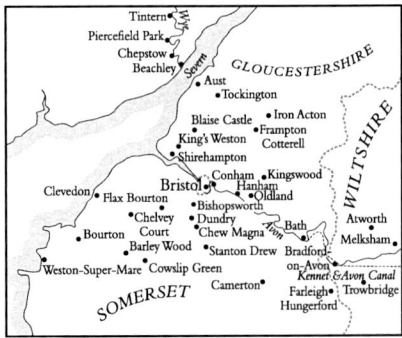

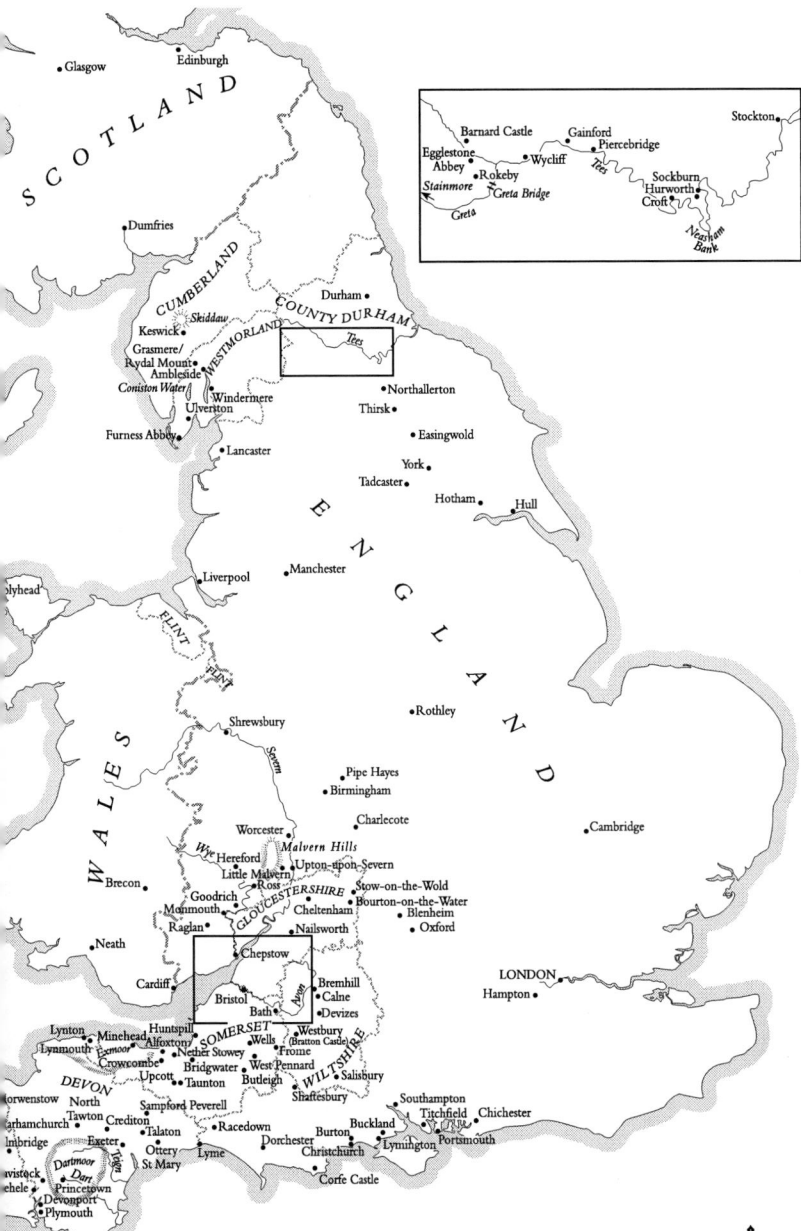
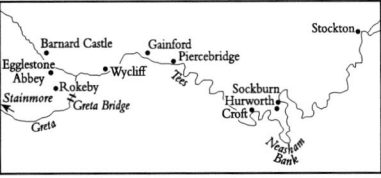

A LITERARY MAP OF BRISTOL

Over the Downs, where Humphry Davy used to walk sniffing N₂O from a green bag so as to bring on poetry; to Westbury-on-Trym, where Wyclif & John Trevisa were Canons, & where the Wedgwoods entertained Coleridge & Southey at Cote House; Southey lived for a time at "Martin Hall", a cottage in Westbury.

Thence on to Henbury, where in 1417 Margery Kempe met the Bishop of Worcester; & to Blaise Castle (see "Northanger Abbey").

(For contemporary accounts of Bristol in the past, see William Wyrcestre in the 15th century, Leland in the 16th, Evelyn in June 1654, Pepys in June 1668, Defoe in his "Tour", & Pope in a letter to Martha Blount of 1739).

Eastward & northward to Kingsdown, where Hartley Coleridge was born; eastward to Charles Wesley's house in Charles St; to Brunswick Square, where De Quincey visited Joseph Castle; to Portland Square, where (at No. 29) died Jane ("Scottish Chiefs") Porter; & at length to Hannah More's birthplace at Fishponds.

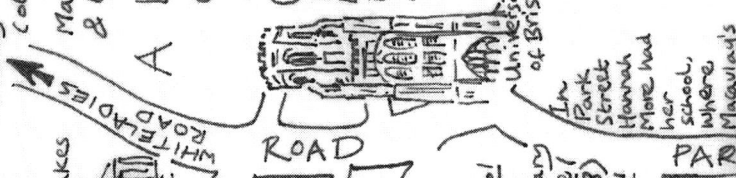

PARK ROW

University of Bristol

In Clifton lived Mrs Piozzi (at 36 Royal York Crescent), John Addington Symonds (at Clifton Hill House), Walter Savage Landor (just by Christ Church), & Humphry Davy & Dr Thomas Beddoes (at 3 Rodney Place, where Thomas Lovell Beddoes was born); Maria Edgeworth & Peter ("Thesaurus") Roget.

Victoria Rooms: Dickens makes ladies faint at a penny reading of Bill Sykes murdering Nancy.

Georgian Clifton

QUEEN'S ROAD

WHITELADIES ROAD

Pupils at Clifton College include Quiller-Couch, Robert Henry Newbolt, Robert Hichens, & Joyce Cary; T.E. Brown ("A garden is a lovesome thing, God wot") was a housemaster. The "Close" where there was a "breathless hush" in Vitaï Lampada was at Clifton College.

At Hotwells, Addison takes the waters (1718), "Ingoldsby" Barham stays at 9 Dowry Square (1845), & Ann Yearsley (the Bristol milkwoman poetess) keeps her circulating library in the Colonnade.

(See also Stanley Hutton, Bristol & its famous Associations, 1907, pp. 44-196; & Dorothy Eagle & Hilary Carnell, The Oxford Literary Guide to the British Isles, 1977, pp. 34-38).

GREAT GEORGE ST

PAR

"The Georgian House", where Wordsworth met Coleridge chez ...

In Park Street Hannah More had her school, where Macaulay's ...

HOTWELLS ROAD

Southey & Coleridge in digs at 54 College St.

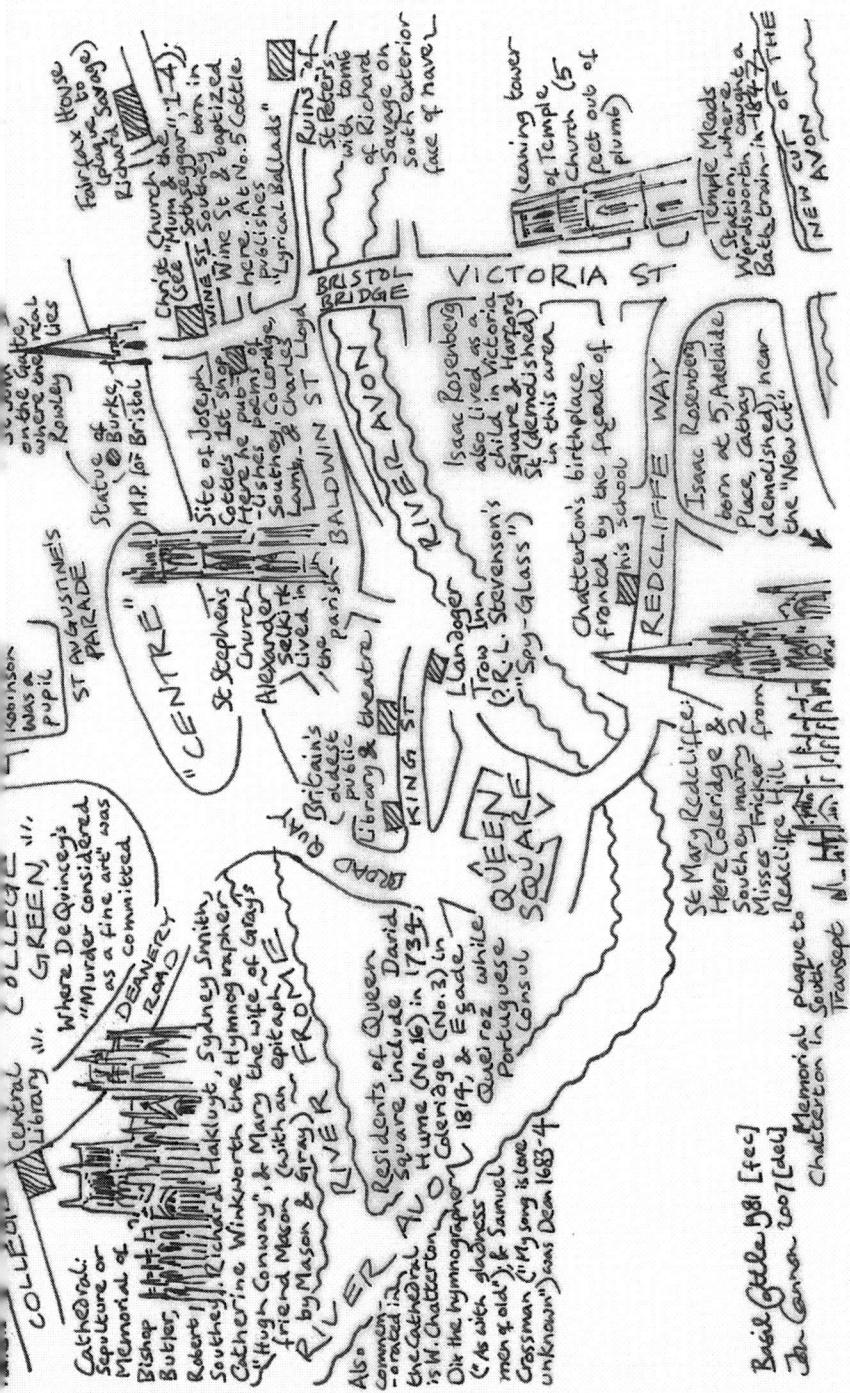

Fairfax House (plaque: Richard Savage)

Christ Church "Mum & sister" Gee born in Wine St & baptized here. At No.5 Castle St Southey, Coleridge & Charles publishes "Lyrical Ballads"

RUINS of St Peter's Church with tomb of Richard Savage on south exterior face of nave

(leaning tower of Temple Church (5 feet out of plumb)

Temple Meads Station where Wordsworth caught a Bath train in 1842

NEW CUT OF THE AVON

St John on the Gate, where Chatterton and friend lies Rowley

Statue of Burke MP for Bristol

BRISTOL BRIDGE

VICTORIA ST

Site of Joseph Cottle's 1st shop. Here he published poems of Southey, Coleridge & Charles

Isaac Rosenberg also lived as a child in Victoria Square & Harford St (demolished) in this area

BALDWIN ST

RIVER AVON

REDCLIFFE WAY

Isaac Rosenberg born at 5 Adelaide Place, Cadney (demolished) near the "New Cut"

"CENTRE"

ST AUGUSTINE'S PARADE

Robinson was a pupil

St Stephen's Church. Alexander Selkirk lived in the parish

Chatterton's birthplace, fronted by the facade of his school

Landoger Trow Inn (?R.L. Stevenson's "Spy-Glass")

KING ST

Old Britain's oldest public Library & theatre

QUEEN SQUARE

BROAD QUAY

St Mary Redcliffe. Here Coleridge & Southey marry 2 Misses Fricke from Redcliffe Hill

COLLEGE GREEN

Central Library

COLLEGE

Where DeQuincey considered "Murder considered as a fine art" was committed

DEANERY ROAD

Cathedral: Sepulchre or Memorial of Bishop Butler, Roberts, Southey, Richard Hakluyt, Sydney Smith, Catherine Winkworth the Hymnographer "Hugh Conway", & Mary the wife of Grays friend Mason (with an epitaph by Mason & Gray)

RIVER FROME

Also commemorated in the Cathedral is W. Chatterton Dix the hymnographer ("As with gladness men of old") & Samuel Crossman ("My song is love unknown") was Dean 1683-4

Residents of Queen Square include David Hume (No.16) in 1739; Chatterton (No.3) in 1814; & Eça de Queiroz Portuguese Consul

RIVER AVON

QUEEN SQUARE

Basil Gotto 1931 [Rec]   Jan Carew Memorial plaque in South Transept Chatterton 2007 [Ded]

Chapter 1
Family and Early Years

Bristol, and the year 1770, made four great contributions to the Romantic Movement in literature. Thomas Chatterton, having escaped from a frustrating life in his native city, encountered worse perils in London and by his suicide on 24 August founded the amazing monument of his fame; William Wordsworth, who would one day enjoy a time of spiritual and financial refreshment in and near Bristol, was born on 7 April; John Foster, who settled on the outskirts of Bristol and became the pioneer critic of the Romantics, was born on 17 September; and on 9 March, in the heart of the city, was born Joseph Cottle, the publisher of *Lyrical Ballads*. In later years he boasted[1] that he had been born not a quarter of a mile from Southey: his father lived, and traded as a tailor, in a small house in Barton Alley, behind the church of St James, City.

Most of Robert Cottle's numerous family received a good education, and the father had a name for citizenship, piety, and hospitality; so that his frequent bankruptcies and his humble status suggest that he had great reserves of energy, or possibly of influence, of which his son Joseph gives us little indication. At all events, his hapless trading illustrates the general decline of the family to which he belonged, a line once influential and knightly in the counties of Cornwall, Devon, Somerset, Wiltshire, and Gloucestershire. Despite the statement of the family historian,[2] it is possible that the name and the line have both two origins: a Norman or Breton family of Cotel who settled in the eastern part of these five counties, and a Cornish family who took their name from their manor of Cotehele (Cornish for 'the wood by the river') on the Tamar. The western branch reached their height about the year 1310, in the person of Sir William Cotehele of Cothele. On his death, a more important manor passed to his son Ralph; his daughter Hilaria inherited Cotehele, and the property was alienated when in 1353 she married William de Edgcumbe, whence descend the Earls of Mount Edgcumbe. At the end of the fourteenth century John Cottell of Yeolmbridge in Devon married into the lines of Carhurta and Malherbe – to which latter family belonged the poet François de Malherbe – and originated a family who held Yeolmbridge for 300 years, and were people of substance at Morwenstow and Marhamchurch in Cornwall, and at North Tawton, Talaton, and other places in Devon; the Civil War, and at least one spendthrift, helped to accomplish their ruin. The eastern branch, however, is more important both in its own status and for our purpose. Sir Robert de Cotel held the manor of Camerton in Somerset as early as 1120, and his three sons were lords of Camerton, West Pennard, and Butleigh in the same county; his great-grandson, Sir Ellys Cotel, became lord of Camerton and of Sampford Peverell in Devon, on his marriage to the daughter of Sir John de Peverell, but he died sonless in 1337, his daughter Editha marrying Sir John de Dinham and thus alienating the property. There were still Cottles in Chelvey Court in Somerset in the nineteenth century, but renting it. In Gloucestershire, the family early owned the manor of Frampton Cottle (now corrupted to 'Cotterell') near Bristol; the last to hold it, John Cotel, died without issue in 1235, and his sister Maud married Sir William Lucy of Charlecote in Warwickshire. In Wiltshire, Sir Roger de Cotel was living at Atworth in 1275; the chapelry and mansion now called Cottles, in that parish, derive their name from this influential branch, who owned great estates in various Wiltshire parishes.

The later Cottles are chiefly interesting in the portion of Wiltshire and Somerset lying just east of Bath. Agnes, Lady Hungerford, of Farleigh Hungerford Castle, was hanged for poisoning her first husband, John Cottle, in 1522;[3] in the parish church of Bradford-on-Avon is a prominent inscription[4] to the memory of Edward Cottle, who died in 1718, and his family; and, above all, in Trowbridge the bankruptcies of 'Thomas Cottle, clothier' (in June 1758) and 'Richard Cottle, clothier' (in March 1760)[5] herald what became almost a habit with Joseph's father. No connection can be proven with Mr William Cottle, 'late a reputable tailor and habit-maker at Bath', who died in October 1793, on the ship *Orange*, while on his way to New York;[6] but Samuel Foote had caricatured him, as 'Billy Button', in his play *The Maid of Bath*, and there is a family resemblance with Joseph's sufferings at the hands of Byron, Lamb, and only too many others.

All these branches of the family bore, in their prosperity, the early, simple, and thus honourable *Or, a bend gules* as the basis of their armorials. The family historian pretentiously cheers the depressed scion by his closing words:[7]

> Through the disposal of their estates, nearly all the members of the various branches of the Cotel family in course of time fell from the degree of Knights and Esquires into lower spheres, in which many of

the descendants now living continue. Perhaps, in years to come, some of future generation may rise to wealth and fame, to whom it may be gratifying to know that, however lowly their immediate ancestors may have been, yet, nevertheless, they descend from those who in the olden time ranked high among the Knights and Gentlemen of the Western Counties of England.

But it is doubtful whether Joseph's family were conscious of this elegant heritage; trade was their métier, and towns their background, and in the time of their eclipse Robert Cottle moved from Trowbridge to Bristol, where by 1754 he was voting among the Freeholders and Freemen of the parish of St John Baptist in the General Election of that year.[8] His mother, Mrs Grace Cottle, was living comfortably with him in 1761, when her cousin, Miss Anne Steele (the 'Theodosia' who wrote *Father, whate'er of earthly bliss* and many more hymns) sent her a letter of congratulation.[9] He was the most respectable of the many Cottles in the city: indeed, one Ann Cottle was transported for fourteen years in 1771, for receiving stolen goods,[10] and in the same year an 'upholder' (furnisher, upholsterer) called Grant Cottle was sentenced to death, but later shipped to Virginia instead, for forcing his aunt into a carriage, gagging her with a handkerchief, taking her to a house in Kingswood under pretence of her insanity, and returning to rifle her house; the judge let him plead his own case, and it was all worth publishing at sixpence a copy, to be had as far away as Taunton and London.[11] In 1786 a malefactor condemned to death 'used to keep company with James Cottle, who was called Charley the Flat'.[12] The more orthodox Cottles were small tradesmen and artisans, and among them Robert moved with some distinction: in 1768 he was President of the Gentlemen Natives of Wiltshire resident in the city, met them on the Tolzey on 18 August, and led them to St James's Church for a fine sermon by the Reverend Mr Popham, after which they dined at the Merchant Tailors' Hall and made a collection to apprentice poor boys.[13]

In the diary of William Dyer, a Bristol citizen who compiled it from 1744 to 1801, we find a note for the morning of Sunday, 18 May 1760: 'Robert Cottle met with my Friends at my House'. Oddly, the very next Sunday is gloomily glossed, 'Our Sunday Mornings Meeting now became useless, being attended with Contention and Controversy'.[14]

Before 1770 Robert had moved from St John's parish to St James's, to the strangely humble surroundings of Barton Alley, a thoroughfare now engulfed by later building; perhaps one advantage of the site was its nearness to Charles Wesley's house in Charles Street, for we shall see that the two families were acquainted. At any rate, by 27 July 1771, 'ROBERT COTTLE, TAYLOR and DRAPER, Hereby informs his FRIENDS and the PUBLIC, That, For the greater Conveniency of carrying on his Business, he is removed from Barton Alley, into a House at the Corner of the BARTON, leading into St JAMES'S-SQUARE; and that he has fitted up a very commodious CLOTH-WAREHOUSE, and laid in a neat and fresh Assortment of the most fashionable superfine BROAD-CLOTHS, SECONDS, LIVERY-CLOTHS, CASSIMERES, WILTONS, and BEAVERS, which he intends to sell on the most reasonable Terms'; the advertisement closes with thanks for past favours and assurance of future service.[15]

Round about these years, his wife Sarah bore him eight children of whom record survives. All of them will play some part in the subsequent narrative: Elizabeth (died in 1789, aged 25), Amos Simon (?1766-1800), Joseph (1770-1853), Robert (1774-1858), Mary (?1772-1839), Ann (?1780-1855), Sarah, (died in 1834), and Martha (died in 1800, aged 15). We shall find that this family was singularly mortal and unmarriageable; there seems to have been something sombre and low-spirited in their whole 'economy', to use one of Joseph's favourite words.

The girls attended the famous, though not fashionable, school kept by Hannah More and her sisters in Park Street.[16] One of them was sufficiently groomed to become a governess in the family of the Earl of Derby;[17] and the survivors later opened in Bristol their own school, which prospered greatly. Joseph shared their admiration of 'Holy Hannah' (as Horace Walpole called her); Southey referred to them as 'very amiable and accomplished women',[18] but Coleridge devised the harsh simile 'doleful as … the Miss Cottles'.[19]

Amos and Joseph entered the school kept by Richard Henderson at Clare Hill, Hanham, on the eastern outskirts of Bristol. This establishment had opened in 1771, under Henderson and assistants, including his son John,[20] then only fourteen. The father had been a notable Methodist preacher for twelve years; the son was a freakish genius who at the age of eight taught Latin at Wesley's school at Kingswood, and at the age of twelve taught Latin and Greek at Trevecca College in Wales. With the initial advantage of a good site on the Bath Road the school combined commodious size and good 'Air and other Conveniences'. Young gentlemen were boarded, and were taught English, French, Latin, Greek; writing, for law and trade; merchants' accounts, by the Italian method; mensuration, surveying, gauging, history, and geography. The fees *per annum* were: Entrance, £1.1.0; Board, Latin, Writing, Accounts, &c., £14.14.0; Entrance for French, 10/6; Ditto per Quarter, 10/6. 'As much Care will be taken of the moral Part of the

Children's Education, so likewise of the right Pronunciation of the French and other Languages'.[21] Amos not only received a classical grounding at Hanham, with seven years under John Henderson, but was enabled to better himself and to proceed for three years to Hull Grammar School, of which the eminent Joseph Milner was then Headmaster;[22] with Milner he 'resided ... For instruction'.[23] It is hard to say how the money was found for this; but Henry Thornton (1760-1815), the anti-slavery agitator, had strong Hull connections (through his mother, his wife, and a Hull by-election), and he was a very dear friend of Hannah More, who also knew the pious circle existing at Hotham, near Hull.[24] He patronized Amos,[25] who was staying with him at Clapham in 1792,[26] and it was probably by his generosity that Amos eventually reached Cambridge.

At all events, the family was for years amicably split between Bristol and London. There was no classical education for Joseph, and certainly no university. He went to the Hanham school when he was eight, and stayed only two years. While Amos reached the top class, with all its advantages of John Henderson's teaching, Joseph remained 'a little urchin ..., with one elbow completely disengaged, being in the lowest seat of the lowest form, very much like a brother urchin in Thomson's *Castle of Indolence*, who minded nought but play, and who easily brought himself to believe that play was the rule, and instruction the exception'. Amos, on the other hand, had an early addiction to poetry, and when he was only twelve covered the walls of his bedroom with his own poems on the different characters in the *Faerie Queen*, a poem to which he was devoted, and which he would expound to Joseph 'for hours at a time'; further, he combined with a subtle wit 'a chaste vein of humour', which his young brother later sought to demonstrate by publishing his fable *The Sparrow and the Gudgeon*.[27]

Otherwise, Cottle's memoirs on his own schooldays[28] concern solely three accidents which befell him, and which he compares with the escapes of Richard Baxter from sudden death. First, he was chased and tossed by a vicious cow; next, he fell from a high sycamore and was unconscious for twelve hours. Neither of these events occasioned any 'permanent inconvenience', but the final disaster closed the school. One afternoon in the summer of 1780, the boys were bathing in the nearby Avon, which they had done 'a hundred times before'. Cottle and Robert Drummond, the ten-year-old son of a Bristol doctor, were standing by themselves in the water when a third boy came up, bent on ducking. He selected young Drummond, and in the resulting struggle the tide carried them out of their depth and drowned them both before the eyes of the whole assembled school. The usher and John Henderson were not near enough to help; but the latter rushed along the bank, with the current, until he saw one of the bodies appearing, and then rushed ineffectually in. He was himself nearly drowned, partly because his pockets were full of books, and he had to be hauled out by Cottle and others. The unfortunate Drummond was buried at Hanham Abbots,[29] and the elder Henderson abruptly closed the establishment.

Whatever further schooling Cottle received, there appears to be no record of it; he kept in touch with the Hendersons, and did some desultory reading. But meanwhile things were not prospering at 21 St James's Barton.[30] The father went bankrupt in 1779,[31] and on 5 June inserted a baleful advertisement in *The Bristol Gazette and Public Advertiser*:[32] 'All Persons indebted to the Estate of ROBERT COTTLE, Taylor and Woollen-Draper, of this City, are hereby required to pay the same forthwith, to said ROBERT COTTLE, or JOHN COOK, his Clerk, who are legally impowered to receive the same. And Notice is hereby given, that the Remainder of the Stock in Trade of the said ROBERT COTTLE, is now selling at and under prime Cost, at his house in St. James's Barton; consisting of a great Variety of Wollen-Drapery, Mercery, and Haberdashery GOODS, which must be disposed of without Delay'. Robert Cottle stayed on in the Barton, and on the evening of Thursday, 9 February 1786, between 8 and 9, a thief stole an iron gate opening into the court in front of his house. 'The thief was met with the gate on his shoulders, in the alley leading into St. James's Square, by a person who instantly informed the family of it. Mr. Cottle, with his son' (who may well have been the 15-year-old Joseph), 'went immediately in pursuit of the man, who was seen by a gentleman a few minutes before; but the villain got off with the booty undiscovered'. Later, Samuel Cox and Richard James were tried for theft, and found guilty.[33]

The Bristol in which Cottle was growing up had changed little from that described so excitingly by E.H.W. Meyerstein in his *Life of Chatterton*.[34] It was the lull before the storm of speculative building, which transformed Clifton from a hilltop village into a magnificent township; but the city itself long remained compact and mediaeval, with many timbered houses at its core and that lovely coronal of steeples sparkling over Bristol Bridge. At the very centre, Christ Church retained its mediaeval spire until 1786, and jostled with the charming cupola of All Saints and with a St Ewen not yet thought redundant; to the east lay St Mary-le-Port and St Peter, not yet charred and derelict from war; behind was, and is, the spire of St John on its gate; westward, St Werburgh had not been whisked away to Stapleton Road, and the gorgeous tower of St Stephen was not half-masked by modern offices; down at the Bridge, St Nicholas received an expensive new body and spire, 'Gothick' covering an interior of reckless rococo, between 1762 and

1769; dominating them all, St Michael-on-the-Mount-Without was likewise rehashed by 1777; and further out, the brave and uncomprehending spire of St Paul rose after 1789. Thus far, Gothic held the field; but elsewhere the city was Georgian, its well-mannered roof-levels not to be outdone by the truncated spire of St Mary Redcliffe or the dumpy Cathedral shorn of its western limb. The spectacular Quay, which has been steadily receding, still nodded with masts; and no great public buildings went up in Cottle's first twenty years, the last having been the Theatre Royal in 1766. But these years were prolific of great terraces of domestic buildings: parts of Albemarle Row, of Brunswick Square, of Park Street, and of Redcliffe Parade; College Street, where Southey and Coleridge would soon be living, the Colonnade at Hotwell, Berkeley Square, Great George Street, Portland Square; and the design or execution of the Mall, Prince's Buildings, St Vincent's Parade, the giddily-placed Windsor Terrace, and the enormous conception of Royal York Crescent, all round about 1790.[35] Amid all this new splendour, the Barton must have remained a backwater, a place of little promise; of all its houses, only No. 12 was really monumental, and still survived in worn dignity until the 1950s, when it was scandalously razed. The Cottles were neither rich nor fashionable, and the failing merchant who presided over them derived his strength from respectability and the unity of his family.

In what Cottle calls 'this earlier, and most important period of my life',[36] the shaping influence was certainly that of the astounding John Henderson; and no better training can be imagined for subsequent acquaintance with Coleridge. Henderson's voracious reading, his profundity, and his eloquence, evaporated in a short life that produced nothing; he never embarked on the journey for which he had packed, and his friends remembered only the squandering of his talents. His eventual recourse to opium was a gloomy foretaste of Coleridge; but perhaps the most striking resemblance lay in the long conversations – or, rather, monologues – to which he treated his former pupil, and which prepared the boy for similar feasts when Coleridge would be around. At first, Cottle revered him from a distance, but at fourteen he was admitted almost to the great man's friendship; Henderson was by now in Johnson's old rooms at Pembroke College, Oxford, and their many meetings must have taken place during his vacations. Cottle's adulation of his tutor, which was printed in the *Poems* of 1795, expanded into the first essay in his *Malvern Hills*,[37] and later condensed in the *Recollections* of 1837 and the *Reminiscences* of 1847, clearly states one side of a very bizarre case. Admittedly, others besides Cottle marvelled at Henderson's powers; the Reverend William Agutter of Magdalen, who preached Henderson's funeral sermon, pointed out that as a baby he 'was never known to cry, or to express any infantine peevishness'; his patron Dr Tucker, Dean of Gloucester and Rector of St Stephen's, Bristol, always felt in his company like 'a Scholar in the presence of his Tutor'; he conversed for several hours one evening with Dr Johnson himself, in '*hard words*', and beat him at his own game; Burke and Boswell and Hannah More had the highest opinion of him, and Johnson, on his own annual visit, always insisted on the inclusion of the young under-graduate in the company; 'many of the Heads of Colleges and other eminent characters habitually attended his *evening parties*'; his tutors, in fact, wondered why he had come up, and 'were soon contented to learn, where they had been accustomed to teach'. Yet we become a little incredulous of Cottle's almost unqualified praise: his ten foreign languages, in most of which he conversed fluently (and they included 'Saxon'!); the fact that his 'favourite studies' were Philology, History, Astronomy, Medicine, Theology, Logic, Metaphysics, and *all* the branches of Natural and Experimental Philosophy; his skill in the 'mechanic arts', and in mimicry of 'the dialect of every foreign country [and] the particular tone of every district of England'; his belief in the science of Physiognomy, by which he could read anyone's thoughts; his virtue, his 'Spartan frugality of words', his forbearance in sparing the pygmies with whom he argued, his benevolence – so great, that he sold his precious Polyglot Bible to obtain funds for donations and drugs during an epidemic, in which he worked ceaselessly among the stricken poor of Oxford.

In the first place, this paragon had a more human side. At Hanham, says line 40 of Cottle's *Malvern Hills*, he would (ambiguously) 'roll the school-boy's marble on his knee'. The portrait made by William Palmer, which Cottle afterwards owned, and which was used for the frontispiece of *Malvern Hills*, shows a plump, mild, complacent young man of twenty-five with wavy hair and a fringe; he leans on two tomes, and generally looks like the 'firm tory and churchman' that Johnson found him.[38] Hereafter his mind and body declined, with irregular hours of sleep, what is now called chain-smoking, eccentric clothes, the use of opium, deliberately sleeping in a wet shirt, abstention from food for as long as five days, and an addiction to wine and spirits. His panegyrist Agutter was honest enough to mention his intemperance, and Cottle versified it, very charitably, in his oft-printed *Monody on the Death of John Henderson*:

> 'Tis true, the midnight bowl he lov'd to share,
> Yet never cloud it rais'd, or maniac glare;
> But, only made, with stimulation kind,
> The body wakeful to the unsleeping mind;

John Henderson: engraving from a painting by William Palmer, 1787 (from University of Bristol Library, Special Collections: Fry Portrait Collection)

But only (till unmechaniz'd by death)
Kept the pipe vocal to the player's breath.

Refusing to adopt a profession, and shunning society, he gave himself up to studying Lavater, believed in communication with the dead, and dabbled in spiritualism, astrology, alchemy, and magic; it is possible that Cottle knew little of these circumstances, though he has to excuse the opium by saying that Henderson took it to relieve pain. Hannah More, who had helped him financially, visited him and found him uncouth and solitary; her remonstration, and her comment that he had untidy hair and no shoe-buckles, made him protest against her feminine scheming 'for new modelling me that I may be made like a gentleman ... Are you not my friend? Then do not command me to be genteel. It will trouble me, for it in no way suits me'.

One fact recorded in Cottle's memoir may help towards an understanding of Henderson's peculiarities. He and his mother loved each other intensely, but she died when he was eighteen, 'and her name, through life, was never uttered by him without a tear. She was buried at St. George's, Kingswood, two miles from Bristol, in the direct road to Hanham; and when arrived at man's estate, John Henderson once told me, in a confidential moment, that, in the summer months, when returning of an evening, from Bristol to his home, he has often repaired to the churchyard, and lain *all night on his mother's grave!*' This was not the only confidence that Henderson entrusted to his young admirer; Cottle was regretting that Henderson had not written, to the benefit of mankind, some tangible result of his researches, and he received the reply, 'More men become writers from ignorance, than from knowledge, not knowing that they have been anticipated by others. Let us decide with caution, and write late'. Joseph says that Henderson had a high esteem for Amos, and quotes a pious passage from a letter in which Henderson urges Amos to govern his passions; from what we know of Amos, it is doubtful whether the warning was needed, and his correspondent seems quite happy about him. Somehow, too, Joseph obtained, and partly quotes in his *Essay*, a letter[39] which Hannah More wrote (from her then residence with the Garricks at the Adelphi) to the declining Henderson on 11 April 1788; alarmed by rumours of some dark practice, saddened at his estrangement from her family, and anxious to rescue him from his 'unprofitable way of life', she urges him to go and ask Mr Wilberforce's advice at Bath.

He had only seven months to live. But, before this final break up, he had done what was perhaps his one great service to posterity: his deep understanding of his fellow-men, which Cottle praises, enabled him to train for its best use the limited talent of his pupil. After Cottle had reached fourteen,

Henderson helped him constantly with books and advice; he regretted that Joseph, unlike Amos, had received no classical education, and advised him at least to read the standard authors in English. Thus, having a mind 'naturally ardent' and industrious, Cottle had read, before he was twenty-one, 'more than a thousand volumes of the best English literature'; one wonders what these could be, since he cannot have started with *Widsith*. Once, he had a fortnight's holiday with the Hendersons at Hanham; and on this occasion, as on all others, he had the benefit of advice that could form his judgment, resolve his difficulties, and inspire him to imitation. His one example of Henderson's joviality leaves us unconvinced. He tells us that 'In an *unbending* season, John Henderson would sometimes condescend to *pun*, but then his puns were *good!*' After borrowing a book on witches, Cottle asked him his views on the Witch of Endor, whereat he replied, 'Joe, you could not have applied to a better person, for I am *Hender-son*'. Above all, he discussed Cottle's plans, and recommended that he be a bookseller; the youth wisely followed this momentous advice, with its tinge of condescension, and became apprenticed to the bookseller William Bulgin.

The evening before Henderson last left Hanham for Oxford, Cottle was privileged to sit up with him until three in the morning, 'unconscious of the waning hour, from the flow of his animated conversation'. But now 'Death called him to graduate in a sphere more favourable to the range of his soaring and comprehensive mind', as Cottle foolishly puts it in his *Essay*. He died on 2 November 1788, of inflammation of the bowels, and his friend Agutter followed the corpse to the church of St George. *Felix Farley's Bristol Journal* printed a tribute to him;[40] and Agutter's funeral sermon, delivered at St George on 23 November and at Temple Church, Bristol, on 30 November, was printed and sold by Bulgin and his partner, Rosser.[41] These two Sunday services, no doubt, were among the very few that saw the nonconformist Cottle inside an Anglican church. Amos wrote the epitaph of four lines, which was engraved on the tombstone and is trite enough;[42] by 1792, the broken-hearted father had joined his wife and son in the same churchyard.

Four months after the funeral, Wesley at the age of eighty-six walked from Kingswood to Hanham, though his friends thought the distance too far for him; he wanted to comfort Richard Henderson, who had ordered the grave to be reopened to satisfy himself that John was dead: 'I spent some time with poor Richard Henderson, deeply affected with the death of his only son, who, with as great talents as most men in England, had lived two and thirty years and had done just nothing'.

John Henderson has had no greater memorial than Cottle's *Monody*. The couplets are passable (Coleridge afterwards wished that Cottle had stuck to rhyme), and Lamb praised the climax of the fourth line, 'Shall I not praise thee? Scholar! Christian! Friend!' But, more strikingly, through Cottle's grief shine his gratitude and his resolve; some time had passed since the first shock of bereavement, and he had met the great and the learned – 'Yet Memory turns from *little men* to THEE'. All the sentiments have an obvious sameness, and so have the couplets; but the awe at this 'mind of daring flight' is sincere. After all, Cottle tells us in lines 85-92 that he had attended faithfully on Henderson's sick-bed, weeping nightlong and eagerly listening to his doomed wisdom; despite his diffidence that this transcendent genius should 'Depend for fame on Cottle's artless line!', he saw that it was his sacred duty to commemorate his benefactor. He envisaged the scepticism with which this very chapter has been coloured –

> One generation doubts, the next denies,
> And, robbed of oil, thy trembling taper dies!

The resultant urn may be a little too storied, but we must remember that Bulgin's young apprentice had passed through an apprenticeship to more than bookselling; he had learnt to observe a just admiration for genius, and to keep his own place in relation to it. His life had not yet known its little reflected triumphs, or its relentless file of disasters and disappointments; but it had known loss tangled with inspiration, and the closing lines[43] of the *Monody* move resolutely:

> If friendship be a flower whose am'ranth bloom
> Endures that heavenly clime beyond the tomb,
> I, haply I, thy honour'd form may see;
> And thou, perchance, not sad, remember me:
> E'en thou mayst hail my freedom from life's chain,
> And be my loved Instructor once again,
> Dispel the mists upborne by error's rays,
> Unfold the doors of Wisdom to my gaze,
> And teach my eyes to grasp, with nobler sense,
> The dark, mysterious rounds of Providence.

> Upon the thought with solemn joy I dwell.
> Till that blest hour, GREAT MIND, again, farewell!

Before Cottle reaches twenty-one and his chosen career, we must consider what other influences had equipped him for it, apart from Henderson and the thousand volumes. At home, the cultural and religious life of the family was adorned by the Reverend James Newton, classical tutor at the Bristol Baptist Academy (at this date in North Street), who lodged at Robert Cottle's for twenty years and died there in 1789.[44] Cottle, with his gift for vile phrasing, says that 'His learning was his least recommendation'! He befriended the boy, and taught him much; besides which, he and Henderson amazed Cottle many an evening by their Latin arguments. He also taught Hannah More Latin; and, since she used to submit her effusions to him, Cottle 'preceded the public' in seeing her *Bas Bleu* and her poem on the slave trade. His funeral eulogy, preached by Dr Caleb Evans to a congregation in tears, said that 'He never made an enemy, nor lost a friend'. Another important connection with the heroes of nonconformity was that Sarah, the unmarried and only surviving daughter of Charles Wesley, was a frequent visitor at Robert Cottle's house. She was ten years older than Joseph, and, though she lived until 1828, he was never a Methodist, and his move from Baptists into the Independents may have moved him further and further from her society; at any rate, he does not mention her later life, or her death in Bristol.

Then there was William Gilbert,[45] the mad author of *The Hurricane*. His father, the philanthropist Nathaniel Gilbert of Antigua, had given religious instruction to slaves; the son, however, was so obviously odd by 1787 that he was put into the elder Henderson's asylum at Hanham. Young John occasionally brought him into Bristol, and he would meet Cottle and his brother; Cottle particularly remembers one afternoon when Gilbert's volubility lasted for two hours and 'was only suspended by sheer physical exhaustion'. After a year, a partial cure took him from Bristol; but he reappeared in 1796 and, as we shall see, Cottle introduced him to Coleridge and Southey. Paul Kaufman, in a stirring article[46] of 1970, exhibits Gilbert's inspiration of Wordsworth and possibly of Keats, and his position in the history of Theosophy; there were disciples of Boehme active in Bristol in the seventeenth and eighteenth centuries, and these may have stimulated both Gilbert and Coleridge. Kaufman wonders whether the 'strange poem with the provocative title is a call to enhance our own conception of romanticism in the light of the theosophic vision'.

From all these influences it is clear that Cottle emerged no unlettered booby awaiting the condescension of talent, but a young man who worked hard to fit himself for an enlightened career. He was already writing verse, and two little stanzaic pieces are marked as 'Juvenile' in the *Malvern Hills* volume. In *Ellen and Edward*, the heroine imprudently waits on a rock liable to the tide and apostrophizes her seafaring and apparently faithless lover, until the sea gets her and she discovers, in the arms of his wraith, that he is faithful and already drowned; one wonders why children write such things. *Emma* may be 'juvenile', but it is not a little forward; in her roses-and-cream cheek Emma has a dimple, the 'Soul of Love' is in her eyes, and Cottle asks as his only boon that she will always smile on him. Alas! – it is the first and last sign of a tender passion in his life; very soon, his broken physique, and the seeming melancholy of his family, deprived him of a free and ample manhood, and doting sisters hastened round to close the ranks and make everything comfortable for him. The stanzas *On the Death of a Young Lady*, also appended to *Malvern Hills*, sound middle-aged and avuncular; her mourners are very plural, and, though she had youth and beauty, everyone now draws salutary conclusions from her immanent worm and clay. Yet this dead girl may be the same that figures mysteriously in another poem in the volume, the second of two written in an arbour (Contents, page x: *Harbour!*) at Tockington, a Gloucestershire village just north of Bristol; the pair were written twenty years apart, and the earlier sounds like a youthful piece, full of dreamy confidence and tumbling in quatrains of trochees. The later, 'On re-visiting the same Arbour', appears at first to be in the same metre, but is iambic – and all else is changed besides. Twenty years before, he had written his musings on the wall, in time of balmy weather; the place was covered with roses, and 'oft in youth' he paused there. *Now* all is in ruin, the garden deflowered and the orchard fruitless; the former owner of the mansion, where Cottle had been so welcome, is dead, and

> The loveliest form of human nature
> There ran her angel-like career;
> But she hath pass'd to joys unfading,
> And fragrant is her memory here!

There is one poem in the anthology which can be approximately dated to his twentieth year, and which derives its force and its failure from real grief: the twenty-one quatrains of his *Elegy on a Beloved Sister* (*who died, aged 25, 1789*). This is Elizabeth, then living with her father in the Barton, whose death on Wednesday, 9 December 1789, is recorded in *Felix Farley's Journal* of the following Saturday. Cottle makes no mention of this elder sister's beauty; she had endured a short and 'stormy' life, and she was meek and saintly. He uses Caleb Evans's remark on James Newton, 'She never made a foe, nor lost a friend', and his poignant sadness, so often renewed at midnight by his thought of her, is consoled by his certainty of their future reunion; as it is, at night he loves 'to seek one lonely tomb, And o'er the holy tablet bend, and weep'. She had helped to train him to pity and generosity, cancelling the silly fears and hopes of childhood; here again, then, one crucial stanza shows his proper reverence for those who formed him. No 'other loves', he says, will tear her image from its place deep in his heart; and, for whatever reason we may assign, it is a fact that Cottle appears throughout his long life as a dedicated bachelor.

In the *Gazette* of Tuesday, 14 December 1790, Robert Cottle, 'merchant-taylor, dealer and chapman', was declared bankrupt. *Felix Farley's Journal*, on the next two Saturdays,[47] gives this melancholy fact to the Bristol public; and the Attorney, Mr Thomas Morgan, of Dolphin Street, summons creditors to three meetings. These are to take place at 11 am on Monday and Tuesday, 27 and 28 December (a glum Christmas for the Cottle family), and on Tuesday, 25 January 1791, all in the Bush Tavern, Corn Street. At these times, the bankrupt is to surrender himself to the Commissioners for his examination, and there fully disclose his estate and effects. Those indebted to him are not to pay save to whom the Commissioners appoint, and must give notice to the Attorney.

Worse followed: the sale of his house, his furniture, and his stock. In *Felix Farley's Journal*, on the first day of 1791,[48] is the notice ('By Order of the Assignees') of an auction sale to be held at the bankrupt Robert Cottle's house in St James's Barton from 10 am to 3 pm on Wednesday and Thursday, 12 and 13 January. Here they would sell all his

HOUSEHOLD FURNITURE, PLATE, LINEN, CHINA and BOOKS
... bedsteads with stuff damask, Manchester stripe and check furniture; very good feather and millpuff beds; mattrasses; quilts, blankets, &c. mahogany bureau; lady's ditto; chests of drawers; escrutoire; dining, pier, card, and pillar tables; chairs and elbow ditto to match; night-stools; bason-stands; easy chairs; pier, swing and dressing glasses; painted floor-cloth, floor carpets, &c. bed and table linen; a variety of kitchen and brewing utensils; a good eight-day clock, &c. &c.

The Cottles had evidently known comfort, and perhaps taste.

The lease of the premises had six years unexpired on the next Lady Day, and would be sold at 12 noon on the Thursday; Thomas Morgan the Attorney would give further particulars of it. Finally, on Monday and Tuesday, 17 and 18 January, all his stock would be auctioned on the spot '(unless disposed of by private contract, of which notice will be given)'; anyone thus wishing to treat for it privately was to apply to the Assignees of the estate, Mr John Maddick (of Clare Street) or Mr John Prideaux (of Wine Street); persons indebted to the estate are again reminded to pay the

Assignees or whom they appoint – indeed, this reminder is repeated in the *Journal* throughout February and into March. The stock was of woollen-drapery and men's mercery: 'superfine broad, narrow, & fancy Cloths, Cassimeers, Beavers, Thicksets, Velverets, Velvateens, Sattinets, &c. – A large assortment of fashionable Buttons, with a variety of other Articles in the above branches'. The auctioneer was D. Cherry, of 10 Small Street. A last meeting was held in the Bush at 10 am on Friday, 26 August, to make a dividend, which would be paid by Maddick any day after 15 September; creditors were to prove debts if they had not already done so, and debtors must pay or be sued.[49]

It is hard to see how the family recovered from this plight. But the sisters had perhaps already opened their young ladies' school, Amos was provided for, and a probable kinsman, Robert Cottle, a linen-draper at 26-27 Shoreditch, London, was important enough at this very season to witness the payment of huge prizes offered by the Royal Union Bank, Shergold & Co., 50 Lombard Street, London; the other sixteen witnesses are all Londoners save for (significantly) two from Trowbridge.[50] Whatever the means of recovery, it is astonishing to see Joseph's confident advertisement, not three months after the last melancholy sale. William Bulgin had married Martha Snook, youngest daughter of a Broad Street wine merchant, on 20 January[51]; and his apprentice, who had been living with him,[52] was out of his time. In *Felix Farley's Journal* for Saturday, 9 April 1791, Joseph Cottle inserted his first advertisement as Bookseller, Print-seller, Stationer and Binder, at the corner of High Street and Corn Street, facing the Council House and the Old Dutch House. He would be selling new books and periodicals; a 'very large and beautiful Assortment of MODERN PRINTS'; first impressions, to be sold at London prices; account books, opening free and ruled to any pattern; Macklin's Bible; and Prints of the Poets' Gallery, of which the first and second numbers could be seen as specimens. *Sarah Farley's Bristol Journal* repeats the advertisement a fortnight later. He had chosen a superb site, a corner shop, 48 High Street, at the very Palladium of Bristol, the High Cross where its four chief business streets met;[53] at the site of the Dutch House, opposite, the war-time ruin of Bristol began, but Cottle's shop was burnt out as early as December 1819. Nor had the luckless father been quite crushed; *the New Bristol Directory* for 1792, and *Matthew's New Bristol Directory* for 1793-4, both show him continuing as a tailor at 21 Barton.

From the time when Cottle opened his shop, the Bristol papers contain fairly frequent advertisements of books printed for him and sold by him. The *Bristol Mercury and Universal Advertiser* carries some of these; but they are best studied in *Felix Farley*, as follows.[54] On 16 April 1791, Ann Yearsley's

View (engraving) from Wine Street, showing the Corn Street corner site of Joseph Cottle's shop (from University of Bristol Library, Special Collections: from *Bath and Bristol, with the Counties of Somerset and Gloucester, Displayed … from Original Drawings*, by Thomas H. Shepherd, with historical and descriptive illustrations by John Britton (1829))

historical play *Earl Godwin*, just published, is being sold by Bulgin, Norton, Cottle and Johnson, all at Bristol; and they can supply her earlier works. On 25 June, W. Lane (at the Minerva, Leadenhall St, London) announces his twenty-five new novels, to be obtained at Cottle's, who will also get subsequent ones as soon as they leave the press, many being 'on the eve of publication'; those who want to buy to sell again, or to enrich their public libraries, may get them from Cottle on exactly the same terms as if they applied to the publishers. The novels in question are:

1. Cypher, or the World as it goes.
2. Duchess of York, an historical tale.
3. Persiana, or the Nymph of the Sea.
4. Monmouth, a Tale.
5. Bansay, A Tale of Incidents in Life.
6. Lidori, a Tale of Chivalry.
7. Charles Mandeville, Sequel to Lady Julia.
8. Charles Altman, a son of Nature.
9. Fair Cambrians, a sentimental Novel.
10. British Knight Errant, a Tale of Chivalry.
11. Laurentia, an interesting Story.
12. Charlotte, a Tale of Truth.
13. Indian Courage, a Tale.
14. Tancred, a Tale of Antient Times.
15. Delia, a pathetic and interesting Tale.
16. Victoriana, an interesting Tale.
17. St Alma, a Story to the Heart.
18. Edmund, or the Child of the Castle.
19. Laura, or Original Letters, a Sequel to Rousseau.
20. Foscari, a Venetian Tale.
21. Baron of Manstow, from the German.
22. Radzivil, a Romance from the Russian.
23. Hermione, or the Orphan Sisters.
24. Semphronia, a Tale to the Heart.
25. Errors of Education, by Mrs Parsons.

All this could be a quotation from *Northanger Abbey*, but most of the books offered are of a more serious kind. On 16 July, we are told that a genuine letter in English by a native of Malabar in Indostan (employed by the Honourable Company at Masulipatam), addressed to a Protestant missionary living at Cuddalore, has been printed in London for a London dealer and for Cottle, price 1/6; in the same number of the paper, it is announced that the

third edition of Thomas Marryat's *Sentimental Fables*, Designed chiefly for
the use of Ladies, has been printed at Bristol for Cottle. Politics first appear
on 27 August, in *A Mirror for the Times*, or, *A complete Detection and
Refutation of the Pseudo-Philosophy of Levelling Sophisters*; it is 'A REJOINDER
to MR PAINE'S Pamphlet, entitled RIGHTS OF MAN; or, A reply to
Mr BURKE'S Attack on the FRENCH REVOLUTION. By an
ENGLISHMAN. London: Sold by C. and G. Kearsley, bookseller; and by
W. Bulgin, and J. Cottle, Bristol' – price, 2/-. In memory of his friend, the
Reverend Caleb Evans, Cottle was selling on 29 October the sermon
preached at his funeral by Samuel Stennet, D.D., entitled 'The Mortality of
Ministers contrasted with the Unchangeableness of Christ'. Or Cottle
would join with others in selling some volume in demand; on 7 January 1792
he and a dozen more booksellers will be selling the *New Bristol Directory*.
And his simple piety, and his disapproval of slavery, are seen on 19 May 1792
in his sale of the shilling 'Letter from de Negro Alkmond to de Rev. Mr H.E.
Holder'; he is also selling Mr Holder's publications. His first specific advertisement for prints is on 2 June 1792, for James Hogg's engraving of William
Palmer's portrait of John Henderson (7/6) – a portrait that Cottle himself
owned; on 25 August 1792 he is receiving (along with various Londoners)
subscriptions for a Thomson's *Seasons* with twenty-two engraved illustrations.
On 7 December 1793 he announces a Sermon preached at St Nicholas,
Worcester, for the benefit of the Severn Humane Society. The first volume
resembling his future work is advertised on 21 December 1793 – Volume I
(Chaucer, Surrey, Wyatt, Sackville) of *Poets of Great Britain*, the whole to be
of eleven volumes; it was printed by J. & A. Arch of 23 Gracechurch Street,
who will figure in our story again.

There was other profitable business besides literature and prints. We observe
with surprise, and perhaps with distaste, that Cottle (in common, admittedly,
with other stationers and booksellers) ran a little counter of quack remedies; he
called it 'the Medical Warehouse, corner of High-Street'. From 1792 to 1798
Felix Farley[55] advertises his sale of 'Howard's Pills for the Venereal Disease', 2/9
a box wrapped 'in printed Papers minutely *describing* the different Symptoms of
the Disease, in both Sexes'; the British Ointment for Corns and Sole Treads,
made by W. Naylor, Chemical Colour-maker to His Majesty; Jackson's Infallible
Ointment for the Itch – it will be 'Infallibly CURED at *twice rubbing*'; Simson's
Infallible Ætherial Tincture (for toothache); Young's Dew Balls (for blacking
shoes against wet); Thomas's Tolu Essence (for consumption); and Dr
Wheatley's Remedies for the Itch, which cure in four hours.

Most of his advertisements, however, suggest that he specialised in books
of a pious tendency; and he might well have gone on prospering in a goodly

and pedestrian trade, turning into a mere fussy little provincial shop-keeper, if he had not been jolted into new life by the strange events of his black and white years 1794 and 1795. Meanwhile his mind was broadening by contact with the sufferings of others; and, being now in a position to dispense a modest charity, he began his succession of benefactions for which, even alone, his name should be honoured.

The first subject which agitated his mind was slavery, and there were extant two kinds from which to choose: that of the blacks, and that of the white factory children in England. His own tender heart, and Amos's acquaintance with Henry Thornton, interested him in the movement for abolishing slavery and in the foundation of the ideal colony of Sierra Leone, with its company of which Thornton was chairman.[56] From here came the attractive and unfortunate African prince, H.G. Naimbanna,[57] who was invited to Thornton's house at Clapham while Amos was staying there. (The name 'Naimbanna' had been prominent among the local kings since the accession of Naimbanna I in 1680.[58]) Amos showed him round the chief buildings of London, and the prince, having gone on to Rothley to study, did Amos the honour of sending him his first attempt at an English letter. Instead of enjoying its *gaucherie*, Joseph prints it, with the excuse that there is 'a touch of nature' in the postscript.

Dear Sir

I hope you are well as I am this present and how you go on and how you do in England and how your family do Cottle in London

I am humble Savent

Naimbanna

April 15 1792

Sierra Leone is only one million miles from England.

In the next few months Naimbanna's faculties developed, and a second letter to Amos from Rothley on 5 December 1792 is well composed: he has written before, through Thornton, is happy at his studies, and agrees with Amos that *Pilgrim's Progress* is very entertaining; will Amos send him any news he may hear from Sierra Leone, and also let him have his 'universal Traveller'? (Both these letters Cottle obtained at Amos's death.) High hopes were entertained for the youth, that he would be able to promote 'religion and civilization' on his return to Africa; but he died of smallpox in sight of his native land. Apart from a kind-hearted notice in *Malvern Hills*, Cottle indirectly wrote poor Naimbanna a memorial poem, some time before 1795; on reading Keate's *History of the Pelew Islands*, he was struck by the pathetic true story of the Prince Lee Boo, who came to England to be educated, showed great promise, and succumbed to smallpox; the two stories thus come together in his poem *Lee Boo*, printed and copiously annotated in his 1795 volume of poems. No doubt in the choice of subject we may also see the influence of Coleridge, who had early grieved over Lee Boo's fate, as he mentions in a poem that Cottle published.[59] Cottle's picture of the impact of civilization on a primitive Eden is well-reasoned and touching, though he invents a fiancée for Lee Boo and, with an infinitely wide range of choice, calls her 'Dorack', as if to vie with the cacophony of her lover. He argues that, after all, 'it was morally impossible that a King's son, so elegant in his manners, and with such mental endowments, should have lived in that country to the age of eighteen without feeling a personal attachment'.[60]

But this is an idyll. Cottle's graver feelings on the treatment of the black races come out in lines 715-880 of *Malvern Hills*; and although, by this time (1796), he had retreated to blank verse, the poor, jerky lines, with their quite artificial *enjambement*, still tell a moving tale. He casts his protest into the form of a narrative, sharply conceived: the magnate 'Who deals in bones and sinews'; the captain, his hired creature, with his frightful ship, its gags and chains; the African landscape, mockingly beautiful; the raid on a village, whence the captives are dragged off with no more heed for 'their pungent agony' and their entreaties 'than though they were all gnats of evening grey'; the ship thriftily crammed to capacity; the black-skinned and black-souled chieftain at appalling Benin; the bargain sealed by kegs of spirits. From this filth Cottle turns to apostrophize Wilberforce, his compeers like Thornton, and politicians like Brougham and Russell, all of whom detected the hypocrisy of a nation's prizing freedom yet denying it to others; later names, like that of Fowell Buxton, were added in Cottle's various revisions of the poem – he was prouder of it than of any of his other works, and kept tinkering with it.

In 1793, his mind was 'deeply impressed' with the enormities 'of the Factory system', when a wagon-load of children, aged between six and eight, left the hospital at Bristol for a factory in the North. The children, with child-like excitement at a morning ride, were marched two by two out from the iron gate and loaded into the wagon until it was as packed as a slave-deck, their parents in the crowd weeping at the sight. It had been promised that these waifs would be well fed and clothed and cared for, given recreation and further education, and not overworked; but, more than thirty years later, when hapless little London milliners were being forced to work eighteen hours a day for the whims of fashion, Cottle wondered just what had happened in the grim, early mills of the North. His indictments of the system are finely eloquent;[61] that in *Malvern Hills* is full of scorn for the 'butterflies' whose exactions keep poor dressmakers sitting daylong round the table, 'Like statues, permanent; like statues, pale!' Work continued on the Sabbath, and these poor 'half-forgotten instruments Of Ball-room splendour' woke to unwelcome bells that would merely recall them to their slavery: 'They must not learn Of Better Worlds!' From them Cottle goes on to the worse horrors of the huge outwardly handsome factories, where infants work on until midnight,

> Assailed by languor, loathsomeness, disease,
> Till death, the friend of misery, close the scene!

– while their employers 'Loll at their boards' and live a jolly life. He emphasizes that the children's moral well-being is as much in danger as their physical; and, with a bold disregard for many 'church-going' persons, he calls on Britons to see 'all mankind/ As offspring of one Sire', and to redeem these orphans, these parish children carted round like lumber, 'nipp'd by the frost of gain'.

He was moved by individual suffering, too, as well as by these national abuses. In 1793, the fiftieth anniversary of the death of Richard Savage, he visited the room in Bristol Newgate where the poor poet had died, and wrote in pencil on the wall twenty-six lines of heroic couplets in his memory.[62] The act, and the sentiments, are charitable: he admits Savage's vicious life, but exhorts the reader to remember how the boy was cast on the world and found 'one long and stormy day'; let the reader search his own conscience and

> if some virtues in thy breast there be,
> Ask, if they sprang from *circumstance*, or *thee*!

Coleridge once told Cottle in a postscript[63] that he liked the lines; and they anticipate Cottle's later services to the memory and family of Chatterton. It is pleasant to add that, near Savage's burial-place, a tablet was later fixed to the outer wall of St Peter's, and survived the bombing of that church.

In this same year, 1793, Cottle had the opportunity of championing Mrs Ann Yearsley, the Bristol milk-woman and poetess. 'Lactilla' had long since quarrelled with Hannah More, who had given her poems to the world but had invested the proceeds — £600 — beyond the woman's control. The strife of these two headstrong women makes ugly reading:[64] 'Holy Hannah' had the greater resources behind her, but even she had incurred the ill will of such as Horace Walpole, who no doubt rejoiced at the mud splashed on her 'dainty blue hose'.[65] Cottle records the whole affair, but his tone is gingerly; by the time he came to look back, he had discovered how badly Hannah More could treat her inferiors, a personal experience which he told to de Quincey.[66] He says flatly that funds collected in this way from the labours of 'ingenious individuals', or out of pity for them, should be handed over to them – then no-one but the beneficiary is to blame for ensuing disasters, and dissatisfaction and ingratitude will not arise. Well, emerging with the money, triumphant but discredited, Mrs Yearsley opened a circulating library in the Colonnade at the Bristol Hotwell; the business was too small, and the location not central, but a novel, a play, and other books of verse kept her going. In 1793 'an imposition was attempted to be practised upon her, and she became also involved in temporary pecuniary difficulties, when by timely interference and a little assistance' Cottle 'had the happiness of placing her once more in a state of comfort'.[67] In gratitude she sent him a handsome volume of her poetry. But the comfortable state was short-lived; her two sons died, and she retired to Melksham, whence her body returned in 1806 for burial in Clifton churchyard. Cottle observes that he merely wishes 'to rescue her name from unmerited obloquy, and not in the remotest degree to criminate Hannah More';[68] but the milk-woman certainly wins the encounter as he tells it.

Felix Farley[69] affords its readers some account of his new little importances and charities. On Wednesday, 2 October 1793, a meeting of the inhabitants of All Saints Ward met in the Rummer Tavern, in view of the recent rioting, to consider the state of the police; the twenty-nine present, including Cottle, resolved to support the magistrates to the utmost of their power. On 14 December 1793 we are told that he has given one guinea to the local subscription for Distressed Spitalfields Weavers, and so has 'A.B.' *per* him. On 1 February 1794 we hear that Bath ladies are collecting for shoes for the militiamen at home, and the place to subscribe at Bristol is Cottle's bookshop; he has given the sum of 10/6 – an average for the list, where even Hannah More has given only two guineas. And on 29 November 1794 he is seen giving another fair subscription, two guineas, to an asylum for fifty poor orphan girls; he, and a few others, are also receiving subscriptions.

It is now within his scope, at the age of twenty-four, to be a philanthropist and a patron of the arts. Everything must have seemed very satisfactory: plans were working out, a leisured competence was assured, life was progressing discreetly – and suddenly it was gravelled. In 1794 (or, as he adequately dates it,[70] fourteen years after the Hanham drowning and thirty-five years before the 1829 edition of *Malvern Hills*) he was riding in the country to visit a friend, with the Baptist ministers Dr Ryland and the Reverend Joseph Hughes, Secretary of the Bible Society, when he was thrown out of his gig; his ankle was dislocated, and this proved to be the start of a persistent lameness. For his remaining sixty years he walked painfully with two sticks; we shall see that this comparative immobility brought on other disorders. But, static and reliable in his invalid state, he and his shop became more and more of a pivot for literary men, especially those in youthful need of encouragement. His verses and patronages up to now had been only indirect offerings to the Muse; he was about to be touched more nearly.

1   Letter to Southey of 1 Nov. 1814, in 'Original Letters from Joseph Cottle to Robert Southey', Bristol City Library MS.B 20877 (*olim* Bristol Museum and Art Gallery MS.G 1375).

2   W.H. Cottell, *A History of the Cotel, Cottell or Cottle family of the Counties of Devon, Somerset, Cornwall and Wilts* ... (London: Taylor, Little Queen St, Lincoln's Inn Fields, 1871; for private circulation only), *ad init*. The outline history that follows in this paragraph is based on Cottell's account, though he makes Hilaria de Cotehele an only child.

3   *Wiltshire Archaeological and Natural History Magazine*, Vol.44 (1927-1929), p.484.

4   Quoted in *Miscellanea Genealogica et Heraldica*, 2nd Ser., Vol.III (1890), p.149.

5   *Wiltshire Notes and Queries*, Vol.II (1896-1898), pp.55, 116 (quoting *Gentleman's Magazine*).

6   *Gentleman's Magazine*, Vol.LXIII (1793), ii.1149.

7   W.H. Cottell, *op.cit.*, *ad fin*.

8   Bristol Poll-Book for 1754: Freeholders and Freemen, p.43.

9   *1795 Album*.

10 *FFJ*, Vol.XX, 31 Aug. 1771.

11 *FFJ*, Vol.XX, 2 March, 6 April, 29 June 1771; and *Sarah Farley's 'The Bristol' Journal*, Nos. 2864, 2870, 2871 of 2 March, 13 April, 20 April 1771.

12 *FFJ*, Vol.XXXVII, No.1956, 22 April 1786.

13 *FFJ*, Vol.XVII, 20 Aug. 1768. The Tolzey marks the original site in Corn Street of the mercantile court of that name. The Merchant Tailors' Hall was in Merchant Tailors' Court (off Broad Street).

14 Wm. Dyer, *Memorable Events; extracted from my Memorandums & Diarys* (Bristol City Library MS.B 20095), Vol.I, p.100.

15 *FFJ*, Vol.XX, 27 July 1771, repeated in the next six issues.

16 *R.47*, p.53.

17 Robert Southey, letter to Grosvenor Bedford; CCS, I.258-260.

18 Letter to Grosvenor Bedford, 12 June 1796 (Bodleian MS.Engl.Letters, c.22).

19 Letter to J.J. Morgan, 2 June 1814, in Griggs, III.502, No.935.

20 *Dictionary of National Biography*, Vol.XXV (1891), p.401, 'John Henderson'; MH.4, II.349 ff.; and Dorothy Vinter, 'John Henderson of Hanham', *Stories of the King's Wood* (Kingswood: The Central Press, 1950), pp.9-12.

21 *FFJ*, Vol.XX, 5 Oct. 1771; advertisement.

22 J.A. Venn, *Alumni Cantabrigienses*, Part II, Vol.II (Cambridge, 1944), p.147, *sub* Cottle, A.S.; and *Dictionary of National Biography*, Vol.XXXVIII (1894), p.17, 'Joseph Milner'.

23 MH.4, I.228.

24 W. Roberts, *Memoirs of the Life of Mrs. Hannah More* (London: Seeley, 1836), II.208, 380.

25 Robert Southey, letter to Grosvenor Bedford, 12 June 1796 (Bodleian MS.Engl.Letters, c.22).

26 MH.4, I.124.

27 *ER.37*, I.108-134.

28 MH.4, II.365-367.

29 Burial Register, Hanham Abbots Church (kindly communicated by Mrs. Dorothy Vinter of Kingswood).

30 The number is given in Sketchley's *Bristol Directory* (1775), where Robert Cottle appears as 'taylor & woollen draper'.

31 *Gentleman's Magazine*, Vol.XLIX (1779), p.216.

32 Vol.XII, No.618, 24 June 1779.

33 *FFJ*, Vol.XXXVII, Nos.1946, 1977, 1978 of 11 Feb., 16 and 23 Sept. 1786.

34 E.H.W. Meyerstein, *A Life of Thomas Chatterton* (London: Ingpen and Grant, 1930), pp.13 ff.

35 The many building schemes of the 18th century are amply dated in W. Ison, *The Georgian Buildings of Bristol* (London: Faber, 1952).

36 MH.4, II.368.

37 MH.4, II.349 ff.

38 *Dictionary of National Biography*, 'John Henderson'.

39 *1795 Album*.

40 *FFJ*, Vol.XXXIX, No.2089, 8 Nov. 1788.

41 *FFJ*, Vol.XXXIX, No.2093, 6 Dec. 1788.

42 MH.4, II.371.

43 I have tidied up the punctuation a little; but Cottle's *'errors'* may be the intended reading.

44 Cottle's account of him is in *R.47*, p.53.

45 Cottle's account of him is in *R.47*, pp.42 ff.

46 Paul Kaufman, '"The Hurricane" and the Romantic Poets', *English Miscellany* 21 (Rome, 1970), pp.99-115.

47 *FFJ*, Vol.XLI, Nos.2198 and 2199, of 18 and 25 Dec. 1790.

48 *FFJ*, Vol.XLII, No.2200, of 1 Jan. 1791; repeated in the next issue.

49 *FFJ*, Vol.XLII, No.2233, of 20 Aug. 1791.

50 *FFJ*, Vol.XLII, No.2202, of 8 Jan. 1791. The movements of Joseph's brother Robert are mysterious; it is quite likely that he was already a Shoreditch draper.

51 *FFJ*, Vol.XLII, No.2204, of 22 Jan. 1791.

52 Letter of Robert Southey to his brother Tom, 21 March 1795 (British Museum MS.Add.30927); Curry, I.92.

53 The High Cross stood at the top of Corn Street.

54 *FFJ*, Vol.XLII, Nos.2215, 2225, 2228, 2234, 2243; Vol.XLIII, Nos.2253, 2272, 2274, 2286; and Vol.XLIV, Nos.2334, 2336.

55 *FFJ*, Vol.XLIII, No.2268; Vol.XLIV, Nos.2325, 2326, 2332; Vol.XLVIII, No.2499; and Vol.XLIX, No.2581.

56 For the honourable principles on which the company was founded, see F.W. Butt-Thompson, *Sierra Leone in History and Tradition* (London: Witherby, 1926), pp.80 ff.

57 Cottle's account of him is in *MH.4*, I.124-125.

58 Butt-Thompson, *op.cit.*, pp.38 ff.

59 S.T. Coleridge, *Poems on Various Subjects* (London: G.G. and J. Robinson, and Bristol: J. Cottle, 1796), p.37 and note.

60 J. Cottle, *Poems*, 2nd edn (London: G.G. and J. Robinson, 1796), pp.lv-vi.

61 In *ER.37*, II.319 ff.; and *Malvern Hills*, lines 881 ff., with its interesting later note.

62 *R.47*, pp.132-133. The Bristol Newgate was located within the gatehouse of the old walls near the junction of Wine Street and Castle Green.

63 *R.47*, quoting a letter from Stowey.

64 See especially R. Southey, *The Lives and Works of the Uneducated Poets*, ed. J.S. Childers (London: Humphrey Milford, 1925), pp.125-134 and 195-198; and *R.47*, pp.47-52.

65 Childers, *op.cit.*, p.195.

66 See below, Chapter 13.

67 *R.47*, p.48.

68 *R.47*, p.52.

69 *FFJ*, Vol.XLIV, Nos.2326, 2335; and Vol.XLV, Nos.2342, 2385.

70 *MH.4*, II.366.

Chapter 2

Southey, Coleridge, and Pantisocracy

There was assembled at Bristol in the year 1794 a group of young intellectuals fired by quaint revolutionary dreams. Two of them, Robert Southey and George Burnett,[1] the son of a farmer from Huntspill in Somerset, had met at Balliol. The third, whom Southey had met at Bath, was a little older – Robert Lovell,[2] the son of a rich Bristol Quaker; he had inherited no liking for commerce, and his marriage with the beautiful Mary Fricker, who had been on the stage, estranged him from his family. Yet, despite her calling, Mary was a respectable and talented girl, even though her dead father had unsuccessfully manufactured sugar-pans; her sisters Sara and Edith were soon the wives of Coleridge and Southey – the one disastrously, the other blissfully – and another sister, Martha, was intended for Burnett.[3] The revolution, of course, was to be taken out of the country; there is little doubt that Pantisocracy began in Southey's restless scheme of emigrating, and that the name and shape were given by Coleridge. They had first met at Oxford, probably on 11 June 1794, and Burnett says that the plan was sketched out in Matthew Bloxam's rooms at Worcester College.[5] Southey, Coleridge, Burnett, Lovell, Edmund Seward and Robert Allen (two men in no particular way connected with Bristol) formed the party which would emigrate, together with wives existing or hypothetical; and Bristol was clearly the place to recruit wives. Later, the young men were to be limited in number, twelve only. By the time Southey wrote to his brother Tom on 20 September 1794, the party had lost Seward (who was suffering from prudence) and gained a Bristol apothecary called Heath; and various Southeys, Frickers, and Lovells made the number up to about twenty. In mid-October it had risen to twenty-seven,[6] still predominantly Bristolian.

Pantisocracy and its train reached Cottle[7] through Lovell; and he says frankly *why* he was permitted to share such confidences and 'be generally surrounded by men of cultivated minds' – simply because he was a bookseller. Much of the myth of his vanity vanishes in the light of this self-knowledge. We cannot now be sure where all these momentous meetings took place, but we can assume that it was in his bookshop at the High Cross. At any rate, towards the end of 1794 the young bridegroom Lovell told him of the proposed site on the Susquehannah, the unselfishness of its economy, its incorruptible adherents, their application of 'sound principles' in an 'unrestrained' manner, and their exclusion of 'all the little deteriorating passions'; and he invited Cottle to join the party. At first Cottle was bewildered with 'images of patriarchal and pristine felicity', but a moment's thought reminded him of the 'old and intractable leaven in human nature', and he saw the fallacies in the scheme; also, perhaps, his lameness was poignantly brought home to him, and his natural caution won the day. He asked Lovell how they would be going, to which Lovell replied that they would freight a ship and take ploughs and such things with them; it occurred to Cottle that they would be more economically bought in America, but he did not want to worry Lovell with all the probable difficulties, so he asked merely who formed the party, and when they sailed. He did, however, point out that they would need money to 'sail out in the high style of gentlemen agriculturists'. But Lovell just said, 'We all contribute what we can, and I shall introduce all my dear friends to you, immediately on their arrival in Bristol'. Whether this charming *non sequitur* is a piece of Lovell's frankness or tactlessness, or merely a piece of Cottle's notorious editing, it is now impossible to say.

Lovell, he adds, was a poet himself; but the abject sonnet *Stonehenge*, which he quotes in proof of this, is a poor witness. Cottle, at the time, had his own 1795 *Poems* in the press, and he was therefore all the more interested when Lovell read him some manuscript poems by his two eminent friends. If all the Southey poems were still in manuscript only, this meeting may be dated before Cruttwell's Bath edition, in the autumn of 1794, of poems by Southey and Lovell. Wistfully, Cottle records how eager he felt to meet two men who had enjoyed the advantages that he, of course, had lacked – talents and learning and the classics. And he was sorry for them, too, in their voluntary exile; he does not add that he felt any envy.

It is strange that he did not preserve the date of his meeting with Southey, save that it was 'one morning shortly after' Lovell had called.[8] It must surely have been some time after the crazy night of 17 October 1794, when Aunt Tyler threw Southey out of her house in College Green, and he tramped to Bath in a gale of rain;[9] Cottle so swiftly became generous and hospitable to Southey that the latter would surely have turned to him for shelter, had their friendship already begun. It is probable, therefore, that they met after Southey's enforced residence in Bath, his journey up to London in January 1795 to bring Coleridge to Bristol, and his own final return to Bristol at the beginning of February. Before the 8th of that month he had joined Coleridge and Burnett in their lodgings in College Street,[10] and it is significant that Cottle describes both him and Burnett for the first time on the same page. Southey was introduced by Lovell, and immediately captivated the young Maecenas more than anyone in his life had done or ever did afterwards. The secret was what is now called 'personality', and this, combined with his obvious rectitude, gave him an unfair advantage over competitors like Coleridge in gaining Cottle's regard; the lame little bookseller, looking up at his bland and bright-eyed face, at once shook hands with him, and sealed a friendship which neither seriously betrayed. Yet, even at this juncture, Cottle realised that poets, his life's heroes, had 'eccentricities' as well as 'vicissitudes'; he had seen a real poet at last, but the poet was being silly – and Cottle in the next couple of lines calls Pantisocracy a wilful and 'epidemic delusion'.

At the same time, presumably, he met Burnett, but was merely struck by his honest face, modesty, and good temper; he assumed that the farmer's son was of no great talent, but Burnett was afterwards a Milton editor, an anthologist of early prose, and a commentator on Poland.

The next to arrive at Cottle's shop was Coleridge, whom Lovell introduced 'at length'.[11] The little shop-keeper was impressed, as he had been with Southey: he 'instantly descried his intellectual character; exhibiting as he did, an eye, a brow, and a forehead, indicative of commanding genius'. The two began to come often; they accepted his invitations, read their works to him, and assured him of their good opinion until his heart was warmed and he was devoted to their interests. By Cottle's introductions to 'several intelligent friends', and by their own winning ways, they soon moved in admiring circles; the more comfortable this popularity seemed, the further off lay the consummation of Pantisocracy, yet they talked incessantly of it. The subject was 'barren' enough, says Cottle; but Lovell was even sillier, estimating that they would have to work for only two hours a day, most of the other twenty-two thus being available for reading, writing and talking. The bookseller in Cottle prompts him here to a sharp remark: they wished to write just for their own pleasure in creating, and not necessarily with a view to publication; and he quotes, against this view, an unpublished letter of Cowper which he possesses.[12] From the start, too, Coleridge's flow of good intentions afforded Cottle some indulgent amusement and a few little qualms – at least, if we are to trust his memories in the 1837 and 1847 volumes; in compiling these, he knew that he must be frank about Coleridge's defects, as the great man could 'so well afford deduction without serious loss',[13] but it is possible that he early saw Coleridge as another Henderson – a resemblance soon pointed by obesity, opium, and plans unfulfilled.[14]

It is uncertain where Burnett and the two poets lived during this period. Cottle says that they all lodged at 48 College Street, which still survived in 1955, re-numbered 54 and bearing an unworthy iron label; but a Southey letter of 21 March 1795 says plainly, 'Direct me at Mrs Savier's, 25 College St, Bristol'.[15] To complicate matters, it has long been assumed that Coleridge, in a huff with Southey, eventually migrated to this very Number 25 – a house destroyed even before Number 48/54 was scandalously demolished in 1955; he was certainly there by 31 July 1795, when he wrote Cottle a facetious letter from his 'one pair of stairs room'.[16] It seems that the numbering of lodging houses in College Street must aptly remain of mere academic interest. From Number 48, at any rate, Coleridge early sent a note which gratified Cottle immensely; he wanted to borrow £5 – *not* for passage or freight on the absurd expedition, but for these highly convenient lodgings. Cottle does not print the date of this note, and his chronology is sadly hazy. But Coleridge owes for seven weeks, and Burnett (who had moved in before) for twelve, their total bill amounting to £11. (If they 'all lodged'[17] together, why is Southey's bill not mentioned also? Was he not 'pooling' with his fellow Pantisocrats?) To tally with Coleridge's known movements, a date near 7 March 1795 will fit this turning-point in Pantisocracy and in Cottle's relationship with the poets; on receipt of this note, he says, the spectre of a ship faded from his thoughts, and, strangely relieved to find them so poor, he began to cast around for 'means by which the two poets might advantageously apply their talents'.[18]

'Soon after' (for what Cottle's methods of dating are worth), the opportunity came. He found Coleridge glum, and tried to rally him by urging him to publish a volume of poetry; the poet replied that all the London booksellers had refused his collection, except for one who had insulted him with an offer of six guineas for the copyright. Cottle pounced: he would give him twenty guineas, by way of encouragement. Even as Coleridge's face lit up, he increased it to thirty: 'Others publish for themselves, I will chiefly remember you'. Further, Coleridge could have the money when he needed it, before the work was complete; in silence, they shook hands, showing (says Cottle, clumsily) that 'at that moment one person was happy'. Cottle – who records his generosity with a show of reticence[19] – next met Southey, told him of the proposal, and offered him the same for a similar volume of *his* poems; to this Southey gladly agreed, and also to his offer of fifty guineas, and fifty free copies, for the honour of publishing in quarto *Joan of Arc*, of which Southey had one evening read him several books.[20] Southey's record of the offer suggests that it was made on the occasion of the reading; Cottle's, that there was a lapse of time. At all events, the offer was made before 5 March 1795, when Cottle wrote off to Messrs G.G. and J. Robinson in London:[21] he has bought the copyright, and is going to print in quarto, at a guinea a copy. Will they allow their names to be inserted in the proposals for receiving subscriptions, and as the London vendors on the title page? He adds a recommendation of Southey's mature judgement, despite his youth, and couples his classical education with his obvious promise. With an eye to his own future as a poet, he also asks them if they will publish 'a little volume of poems nearly ready on the plan of Pleasures of Memory'; though any affinity between Samuel Rogers's anonymous poem and the resulting *Poems, by Joseph Cottle* is now hard to see. To both these requests they agreed by return of post, and Cottle set to work on his proud venture. Southey is full of praise for his care;[22] few books were being printed in the provinces, least of all those in quarto. 'A font of new types was ordered for what was intended to be the handsomest book that Bristol had ever yet sent forth', and Southey's misgivings over his own composition were soon assuaged by the luxury of 'fine wove paper and hot-pressing'. The young poet, and the 'bookseller as inexperienced and as ardent as himself', had begun their lifelong partnership with a fine regard for standards.

In these early, unclouded days Cottle helped the pair in three ways of which he leaves us interesting record:[23] by introductions to people of influence or interest, by organizing lecture-courses for them, and by taking them on a memorable trip to Tintern. The lecture-courses were intended to raise money for the expedition, though Coleridge's lecturing activity was prompted by another ambition; he wished, or imagined he wished, to marry Sara Fricker. Cottle sold tickets at his shop, as did another bookseller; and, though his works show no violent political feelings, he was perhaps courageous in standing by Coleridge in his anti-Pitt, anti-slavery, pro-French campaign. He kept all the prospectuses, and gives a desultory account of Coleridge's political and moral lectures from the end of February 1795 to late in the summer, which he doubtless attended and which he found well-argued, witty, and archly spoken, but *not* inflammatory. Possibly the lectures did not all have the same status; they were given variously at the important Corn Market in Wine Street, at the Assembly Coffee-House on the Quay, and at a room in Castle Green, mostly at eight in the evening. Cottle gives little space to Southey's course of twelve historical lectures, but crams his account with flattering reports of the huge and discriminating audience, and the self-possession, delivery, and reasoning of the young lecturer; Wordsworth, seeing him with different eyes, called him a coxcomb, but in Cottle's regard he was a fit recipient of Henderson's copy of Sidney's *Arcadia*, handed to him in this year.[24]

It was in this season that Cottle realised that Pantisocracy need never happen; apart from its inherent challenge and risks, all was not well with its adherents and their brotherhood. Coleridge and Lovell were the first whom he observed to drift apart;[25] they ignored each other, and Coleridge called Lovell a villain for opposing his marriage with Sara. Cottle patched up the quarrel, assuring him that Lovell would be proud to have him as a brother-in-law – it was just that he wanted the marriage put off 'from prudential motives'; and in a few days they were 'as sociable as ever'.

But, clearly, a rift between the two leaders would soon make mute for ever the far music of the Susquehannah, and Cottle[26] is our authority for the first real quarrel; he tells the story with humour and shrewdness, and has been praised for it.[27] The fourth lecture in Southey's course was to be on the *Rise, Progress, and Decline of the Roman Empire*, and would be given on Tuesday, 3 March; Coleridge particularly asked to be allowed to give it, since he had studied the subject, and Southey agreed. The room was crowded, and they waited over half an hour for the lecturer, who, at Cottle's guess, was probably smoking his pipe at 48 College Street, the whole engagement having slipped his memory. (He treated in the same way a Bristol doctor's invitation to dinner, and naturally these lapses lost him subscribers to his lectures.) For the next two days, Cottle had arranged an excursion to the River Wye, whence they would return in time for Southey's next lecture on Friday the 6th: he had invited the two poets and their Fricker fiancées, and the morning of the 4th proved fine, with even Coleridge punctual. They were aiming especially at Piercefield Park, with its woods and cliffs, and Tintern Abbey, neither of which any of the party had seen; all five were excited at the rich prospect in buildings and scenery, and they set off cheerfully for the Old Passage at Aust, crossed by the ferry to Beachley, and so reached Chepstow. First they visited the great castle, and then arrived at the Beaufort Arms in time for a good dinner, which sounds a jolly affair, with references to Homer. So far, so Pantisocratic; but after dinner Southey, 'whose regular habits scarcely rendered it a virtue in him, never to fail in an engagement', improved the satisfied minutes of relaxation by regretting aloud that *his* audience had been let down by Coleridge's forgetfulness. Coleridge said he thought it hardly mattered; Southey remonstrated, and got his answer. Cottle tried to conciliate, but in vain; the two sworn brothers showed their fundamental lack of concord, of sound principles, and of unselfishness, and fell to quarrelling. Such was 'the rope of sand to which they had confided their destinies!' He left them to it, and went to the other end of the room, amazed and grieved; but the argument only extended its range, since the two Frickers sided with their beaux, until a general exhaustion let Cottle slip in and suggest that, at any rate, the cause of the trouble would not happen again. Though Southey shook his head and thought otherwise, Cottle urged them to think only of the pretty scenes now before them, and, the ladies concurring, he put the two men's hands together and they all made friends.

Since his lameness made him a poor walker, he had hired a horse, and the others, two on each side of his 'Rosinante', escorted him through the parkland of Piercefield and so on to the superb view from the Wynd Cliff. But their tarrying at Chepstow, and the time they gave to this eminent scenery, confused them, and, almost benighted, they reached a junction where their directions had seemed to tell them to turn right. Doubt 'threw ice into some hearts', but they plunged into what proved a mere lane, a tunnel of trees, which the young moon could not penetrate, and where Cadwaladr and Taliesin might have trodden. Everything went black; they 'floundered over stones, embedded as they appeared in their everlasting sockets, from the days of Noah', and in the gully alongside a stream gurgled warningly. Fearful for his limbs, Cottle dismounted and led his trembling steed; Coleridge, the ex-dragoon, thereupon mounted without a word, 'determined to brave, at all hazards, the dangers of the campaign'. He led the perilous way down storm-channels, Southey marching valiantly on with a lady on each arm, and Cottle haplessly tottering behind without even a stick. They began to sympathize with the Babes in the Wood; and the ladies, 'with all their admiration of disinterested pity', hoped to put off the 'kind robins with their sylvan pall'. Then, either because the moon had broken from cloud or because their sight had grown accustomed, they began to see a little, though there was little to see that was cheering. Coleridge urged them on, and they beguiled the time by trying to find a suitable name for this 'horrible channel of communication between man and man'; after they had thought of various caustic titles, Southey censured them for their lack of charity and suggested 'Bowling-green-lane'. But they had little cause to smile: they had just reached a spot where three roads diverged, and in the growing darkness a reasoned choice was impossible. In the hope of attracting some woodman, they shouted – the ladies shrilly and harmoniously – and were answered by an ominous silence and by that inexorable choice of finding themselves back at Chepstow, or half way to Raglan, or successfully at Tintern. Someone said, 'Of what service is it to boast a pioneer, if we do not avail ourselves of his services?'; Coleridge took the hint, and crept away as fast as he could. He was gone for so long that they began to think of a search-party for *him*, when they heard his horse's hoofs on the stones. Not that his report was good – the first path led to a disused quarry, and his steed had only just stopped in time! He next explored the second path, 'like a well-disciplined orderly man', and came back with his cheeks scratched by thorns, the proof that the way was impassable. Thus, says Cottle, by using the syllogism, 'If the right road must be A, B, or C, and A and B were wrong, then C must be right', they struck boldly forward and reached Tintern Abbey rejoicing.

They were hungry, and asked a rustic for the hotel, but Tintern had nothing to offer but a homely inn called the Tobacco Pipe; still, anything was better than what they had just escaped, and after supper they became sight-seers once again. Cottle proposed to show them the Abbey by torchlight, and there was a crescent moon to assist them. He may be said to have started the Tintern cult, though he cannot be blamed for the commercialism which has entered it, or for the shift of emphasis to a moon of harvest dimensions; in his lifetime, the Duke of Beaufort provided a better road than that which got them so way-wildered, and the loud motor-coaches of our own time are in the tradition. We shall see later that Cottle was linked with the most fruitful of all visits, that of William and Dorothy Wordsworth.

Perhaps through his upbringing in Gothic Bristol, he writes excitingly of Tintern, but vaguely; it is hard to identify the turrets in his account, which succeeds in being horrid in the approved manner of the Gothic Revival. The whole party

> set off to view the beautiful but mouldering edifice, where, by an artificial light, the ruins might present a new aspect, and, in dim grandeur, assist the labouring imagination. At the instant the huge doors unfolded, the horned moon appeared between the opening clouds, and shining through the grand window in the distance. It was a delectable moment; not a little augmented by the unexpected green sward that covered the whole of the floor, and the long-forgotten tombs beneath; whilst the gigantic ivies, in their rivalry, almost concealed the projecting and dark turrets and eminences, reflecting back the lustre of the torch below.

Disturbed jackdaws, rising in thick flocks from their nests in the ruins, screamed maledictions over the visitors. Even when they returned to their inn, Cottle had not supped deep enough of the horrid, and told them that there was nearby a big iron foundry, best seen at night. Coleridge would not move again, feeling he had had enough exercise for one day and being quite content by the inn fire; the ladies were replete, too, but Southey and the indefatigable Cottle set out at midnight and found the sight sublime, though they had to skirt an ugly mill-pond in the gloom.

Next day, 5 March, they safely returned to Bristol. This gave Southey time to prepare for the 6th lecture on the *Rise, Progress, &c.*, to make up for the one Coleridge had missed, and Cottle immediately wrote his business-like letter to Messrs Robinson; work had begun again. On 21 March Southey wrote to his brother Tom that Cottle was buying the copyright and would print 'more elegantly than the last' (Cruttwell, presumably); Cottle, when he lived at Bulgin's, knew Tom as a customer, and was now asking after him.[28] On 1 July Southey, in a letter to Grosvenor Bedford, called his bookseller 'a good man and one whose liberality might rescue the fraternity from all obloquy'; Cottle was 'soon coming up to town – chiefly to get a good frontispiece engraved',[29] but there is no other record of this visit. It is plain that Southey was working hard at his lodgings, while Coleridge sat and disturbed him with his plans and pipe-dreams; with his sensible, second-rate brain, Southey wrote for Cottle saleable articles, and would be the only author who brought his publisher a profit. He had been using the Bristol Library since 1793, and on 13 July 1795 borrowed the three volumes of the *Edda Sæmundar hinns Fróda* (Copenhagen, 1787), which he returned on 29 July and borrowed again in October;[30] this is perhaps his first interest in Norse, and it links him with his respected acquaintance Amos Cottle, whose sole claim on the literary historian is his verse translation – a pioneer work, bad as it is – of the *Edda*. Amos, now in his thirtieth year, had just been admitted sizar at Magdalene College, Cambridge; he is mentioned as scholar in the same year, and matriculated in Lent, 1796.[31]

On 25 May 1795 Cottle began to circulate among his friends a big album in which they must write specimens of their art. Southey first obliged with *English Dactylics, to a Soldier's Wife*; next day 'Hurricane' Gilbert put in *The Aurora of Human Happiness*, and on 30 May Lovell added his *Stonehenge*. Thereafter it moved as follows: Amos, *Extempore Lines on the Vale of Oldland*, which has been scored out; 5 June, an insane man at Dr. Fox's asylum, *Evening*; 6 June, Coleridge, *Lines Written at the King's Arms, Ross*; 14 July, Beddoes, *Verses on a Cornish Lady*; 4 August, John Rose, *Sonnet: To Contentment*; then, after a long break, 27 June 1796, Charles Fox, *To Selima*, and, from the same hand, in July, verses in Persian and English (two of each); July, Coleridge, *To the Princess of Wales*; 30 July, Southey, *Specimen of English Sapphics*; Amos, *A Fable: The Glow-worm and Grasshopper*; 20 October, Charles Lloyd, *Dirge Occasion'd by an Infant's Death*; 22 October, George Catcott, Poem by Thomas Skone; 29 March 1797, Wordsworth, *Written on the Thames near Richmond*; finally, Sir C.F. Williams, *On a faded Cowslip presented me by Anna*. After this, Cottle used the album to stick in letters, poems, and other holographs, of Coleridge, Southey, three of the

Wordsworths, Cowper, de Quincey, and many more, with dates from the 18th century to 1844; the whole precious volume was exported to Cornell in 1955.

All the time, Coleridge was being awkward. His dirty stockings, his haphazard social life, and his other odd manifestations of genius, must have shocked Cottle at the time, though by 1837 and 1847 he could smile at them. But it went too far; Coleridge wrote so tartly of Dean Milles, Chatterton's editor, that Cottle had to warn him that their acquaintance, Captain Blake of the small stature and huge sword, was the Dean's son-in-law.[32] And Cottle, through his financial relationship with Coleridge, was the chief victim of his irregularities; he is careful to tell us all what he had to put up with, though he pretends that he wishes only to 'amuse the reader'.[33] After all, he had paid Coleridge in advance, and late in July he asked for some of the poems so that the printer could make a start; Coleridge sent a note promising a copy by Monday morning – a sheet a day, if the printer could work it – and 'a day or two after', on 31 July, he followed this with a teasing and facetious letter affirming his desire to smoke, offering to write 'a panegyrical epic poem' to Cottle with as many books as there were letters in his name, and promising to write out in the copy book by the next morning enough for a sheet and a half.

Very little came of such promises, though Coleridge promptly complied with Cottle's part of the bargain and pocketed the money. Cottle tolerated all this, but when the printer grumbled at the inconvenience, he at length sent Coleridge a mild note explaining the printer's point of view; Coleridge, without real justification, wrote to Wade[34] behind Cottle's back, calling the note an 'unkind act', but saying that he would bear in mind all Cottle's services to him – it was just that his own 'present brain-crazing circumstances rendered this an improper time' for any reproof. As the summer wore on, he despatched various reassuring notes: there would be some copy tomorrow, *Religious Musings* would be with Cottle by Thursday, 'a very devil' was giving him agony on the left side of his face and shoulder. Although he could sign himself 'Your Affectionate Friend and Brother', he tactlessly preferred the claims of others to Cottle's: he is busy doing something important at Lovell's, so could Cottle's servant buy a pound of bacon and two quarts of broad beans in the market, ask the maid at College Street to cook them, and tell her he will be home at three? – then Cottle must come and have tea with him, and he will try to get the copy ready. They met every day; Cottle, with a smile, would ask if there was anything ready, and would get a promise, or a dozen lines, or even a few pages. Yet Coleridge had at various times recited to him nearly all the poems in the volume, save for the new *Religious Musings!* When excuses were exhausted, he would admit that he had little 'finger industry', though at any rate his mind was working hard. By 1837, Cottle remembered Coleridge as reading him every forty or fifty lines he had ready, even condescending to ask for criticism; when he brought Cottle a dozen or twenty lines for the printer, Cottle preserved the precious strips – like the six different beginnings for *Religious Musings* – and bound them up with manuscripts of Coleridge's lectures.[35] Finally, 'My dear very dear Cottle' prints the letter that marked the end of the task: Coleridge is invited to dine with Michael Castle, but he will be at Cottle's at 6.30 sharp – if not, Cottle can summon him by note; then, if provided with a dish of tea, he will write the notes and the preface by 11 o'clock, and Cottle can lock him in until everything is finished.[36]

Cottle felt (or by 1847 believed that he had felt) that he must not spoil the poet's pleasurable task by turning it into an urgent duty, and he really let him take his own time. Since the marriage with Sara Fricker seemed certain, he offered him a guinea and a half for every hundred lines of rhyme or blank verse, after the projected volume should be complete; when a common friend asked the straitened Coleridge how he proposed to keep the pot boiling, he replied that this new offer had set his mind at rest on that score. By the end of August, the College Street *ménage* had broken up, and Coleridge was renting a cottage at Clevedon preparatory to his marriage, the banks of the Susquehannah having yielded to those of the Severn (to borrow Cottle's image). Southey was making up his mind to waste in Portugal the time before his annuity, from the generous young Wynn, should start to be paid. The two Pantisocrats were drifting apart, though Cottle (or perhaps Cottle's purse) adroitly retained the friendship of both. Coleridge, some time before 4 October 1795, congratulated George Dyer on his forthcoming book, and wrote that he had ordered ten, which Cottle had sent for;[37] it seems a generous order, and it would be interesting to know who finally paid. On 1 September Southey wrote to Grosvenor Bedford[38] that his poems would not be out until January, so as to suit Cottle, 'a most worthy little fellow ... whom you must know and love, a poet himself'; for Cottle's own *Poems* would be published on Tuesday the 8th, and be available in London at Robinson's. There is a little gentle mockery in this warning – the volume has elegant typography, on fine paper hot-pressed, and Bedford should buy it for the sake of the author; but the *Monody on John Henderson* includes some beautiful lines, and friendship has inspired in Cottle a poem that Southey would not have identified as by the same hand as the rest. 'Coleridge has used the pruning knife with me over them ...' This first edition is anonymous; a second edition followed quickly, in 1796, likewise published by the

Robinsons and with additions, though the 1795 preface was omitted and Cottle's authorship was acknowledged. A scribble in Southey's hand,[39] of a much later date, says that 'Poems were formerly pointed in Spain according to metre – not syntax … Cottle once thought there ought to be a comma at the end of every line, and so was printing his first poem but I corrected the proof'.

Southey's faint praise is just; apart from the *Monody* and the curiously touching *Lee Boo*, the only poem in the 1796 collection that Cottle continued to value is *John the Baptist*, whose decent couplets, compared with Cottle's later blank verse, lend weight to the argument that Pope did far less harm to our poetasters than did Milton. Its 230 lines are neat, sometimes sonorous, rarely pregnant. Most of the phrases we have heard before, but in a metaphorical passage on the out-going soul, 'O'er the black wave the eye reluctant toils' (line 167), and the Jews are told 'Your race full long sustain'd a ritual chain' (line 40); otherwise, the poem has all the tedious resources of inversion, including the admired chiasmus of 'A stone his pillow, and his bed the ground', but it is not doggerel, and it is devout.

The Moral Tale of *Ricardo and Cassandra*, however, illustrates the strange paths taken by the muses of the uninspired and, in that respect, is a cautionary tale in a sense other than the one intended. Its trite, tinkling couplets read like a parody of their *genre*, but Cottle is fatuously serious in this attack on 'INTEMPERENCE! King of Death's aye hov'ring train'. Ricardo's mother has brought him up nicely; she has taught him to pray, has 'Enlarged his mind with scientific lore', and has advised him against prejudice, splendour, pomp, and meretricious glare. Above all, 'by tears obstructed', she has shown him that the best way to live to be seventy is to avoid VICE, and she seems to recommend Humility as the best antidote. He is a good-looking young fellow, too, with a breast not 'damp'd' by nasty suspicions, and it is a 'melody divine' to hear him talk about Truth. All the more regrettable, therefore, is the slight ambiguity of 'No interest sway'd the friendship he profest', and the yawning *double-entendre* of the next line, 'No little cunning clos'd his full-orb'd eye'. Ricardo is moved by a virtuous passion for one Cassandra, who sounds a little as Mona Lisa *looks*:

> Pride of her sex, CASSANDRA liv'd to please,
> Polite with dignity, reserved with ease.

They used to walk hand-in-hand through 'flow'ry vale' and 'forest glade', when their dialogue was severally protestation, accusation of flattery, and deprecation combined with renewed avowal and with imprecations on

Ricardo's own head if he should ever love anyone else. But – 'RICARDO yet of life had little known'; his friends urged him to go abroad and learn what he could not find in books (and, indeed, he did; though not in the way they meant). In an evil hour they found him a TUTOR to escort him; a man soft-spoken but stormy at heart, content to read of the virtues of classical heroes and sages, base, deceitful, unsympathetic, selfish and – not surprisingly – unpopular. With these curious qualifications for moral tutorship, he takes Ricardo to GALLIA, of all places, and then passes out of the picture; Ricardo meets some gamblers, loses his money, learns their bad language, and (after twelve lines of youth as a storm-tossed boat) takes to singing, tobacco (or, at least, he 'extends the circling fume'), wine and women. The two last are woven into the delicious line, 'And fills his BUMPER to – he cares not whom'. Naturally, 'CASSANDRA now no longer fans his flame', but after two of these foolish years 'The youth resolves to visit home again', and in his altered shape, 'With hectic cough' and with whispered joke, he approaches his mother, who well-nigh repudiates him. Cassandra has been consoling herself with listening to roundelays; she hastens to greet him, finds him on his death-bed, and so little recognizes him that she is given an eight-line Homeric simile of a shepherd trying to identify a dead lamb. She upbraids his altered look, and he dies in her arms. She chooses a tomb for herself beneath a yew, but lasts fifteen years longer, and is buried with him; the rustics sigh when they pass the spot, and even the old SEXTON, who is not given to pause or reverie at the normal kind of grave, is uncommonly moved, and tells the children the whole story.

The other three poems in the book give less warning of Cottle's future. The greatly extended *Paraphrase of the Eighteenth Psalm* is, in its metre (heroic couplets) and its heavy music, nothing like his poor later versions of the Psalms. The Scottish tale of *Sir Malcolm and Alla* is in ballad metre, and tells a fair story of love and war, but its 648 lines at length become unendurable; as with many of Cottle's other encomiums, the good characters are all incredibly good, and the heroine's song could even stop 'The well-tun'd bagpipe'. But she is a warrior, too, and her change from 'the Fair', of best eighteenth-century style, into the blaster of proud Edward's banners, is utterly incongruous. *War, A Fragment*, is more important, if only for its revolutionary hint that war is not the best corporate expression of a nation's will; we know now, of course, that the Pantisocrats and Wordsworth forgot this early ardour, but it is interesting to see that Cottle shared so much of it – and, in fact, in his humbler position he could retain far more of it than they. The story of *War* is absurdly conceived and told; a great city has long defied a British siege, until she is beaten by famine; this setting, alone, would hardly make the poem popular in the 1790s in patriotic Bristol. A kind young citizen named Orlando sneaks out at night to talk to the dying on a gory battlefield, and is first detained by a British youth clutching the picture of a girl. Nothing, clearly, can be done for him, so Orlando gives him a political lecture on the cause that tore him from his far home and set his hand against his fellows. And here Cottle writes sharply:

> Perchance some statesman's pique, some shrine profan'd,
> A flag insulted, or a skiff detain'd;
> These blow the blasts of war.

The youth admits his folly, saying that he left the plough because he was dazzled by the uniform and opportunities of some soldiers – who make a most unlikely speech about their motives and their solid satisfaction with the military life. After the youth's dying words, Cottle turns to more general invective, and (at line 190) to the fate of Poland and Kosciusko; his praise of this 'most-injur'd Patriot' moves surely, and it is good to know that Kosciusko read the lines and thanked him for them in a letter. Here, as with *Lee Boo*, we may detect the influence of Coleridge, whose Effusion VIII in *Poems on Various Subjects* is in Kosciusko's honour. Then the angry words swell to a denunciation of so many heroes,

> Scourgers of earth, and Heralds of dismay,
> Pests of mankind, and whirlwinds of their day;
> From whose example blushing History rakes
> Her nest of Scorpions, and her brood of Snakes.

Let those who admire war and its pageantry think of the putrid plain of corpses, and remember of every victim that some

> blazon'd warrior led him to his doom,
> To gain, he knew not what, to fight, he knew not whom.

The starving children and widowed women whom Cottle invokes are commonplaces, and he admits that he may be criticised for sentiments so womanly and so essentially inglorious; but the glory is tinsel, the gain is hollow, and all praise of war is rooted in falsehood, the only exception being when one's land is invaded and one's fellows are enslaved. The thesis and its illustrations are all rather obvious and pre-Napoleonic; but, at that date, the frank and ill-tempered lines must have been thought daring.

1   *Dictionary of National Biography*, Vol.VII (1886), p.411.
2   *Dictionary of National Biography*, Suppl.III (1901), p.111.
3   E. Dowden, *Southey* (London: Macmillan, 1909), p.37.
4   The meeting is so dated in Simmons, p.232, note 52.
5   Simmons, p.232, note 56.
6   Simmons, p.47.
7   Cottle's own lively and not unfair account of the group is in R.47, pp.2 ff.
8   R.47, p.5.
9   Simmons, p.48.
10 Simmons, p.51.
11 R.47, p.6.
12 R.47, p.7. It is curious that this was still unpublished in 1847, since Southey had brought out the Works of Cowper (including his correspondence) in 1833-1837, and Cottle would surely have helped him with the loan of any manuscript that he possessed.
13 R.47, p.9.
14 See Coburn, I.Notes, item 174(5), for the fascinating conjecture that Henderson's piercing eye was the original of the Mariner's.
15 To Tom Southey, British Museum MS.Add.30927; Curry, I.93.
16 R.47, p.36.
17 R.47, p.10.
18 R.47, p.11.
19 R.47, p.12.
20 R. Southey, introduction to *Poetical Works* (London: Longman, Brown, Green and Longmans, 1837-1838), I.xviii.
21 Bodl.MS.Montague d.6, fol.462.
22 Introduction to *Poetical Works*, I.xix.
23 R.47, pp.13-19, 25-35.
24 Coburn, I.Notes, item 1011.
25 R.47, p.20.
26 R.47, pp.25 ff.
27 e.g., in Simmons, p.54.
28 Curry, I.92.
29 Bodl.MS.Engl.Letters, c.22; Curry, I.97.
30 G. Whalley, 'The Bristol Library Borrowings of Southey and Coleridge, 1793-8', *The Library*, 5th Ser., Vol.IV, No.2, Sept.1949, pp.121-122.
31 J.A. Venn, *Alumni Cantabrigienses*, Part II, Vol.II (Cambridge, 1944), p.147.
32 R.47, p.24.
33 R.47, pp.35-39.
34 Griggs, I.190, No.110.
35 ER.37, II.52.

36 Cottle (*ER.37, I.56*) dates this letter in April 1797, but Griggs (I.193, No.113n) puts it in March 1796.

37 Griggs, I.152, No.81.

38 Bodl.MS.Engl.Letters, c.22; Curry, I.99.

39 Now in the possession of Mrs Annabel Bracher, and deposited in the library of Waterloo University, Ontario.

Chapter 3

Wordsworth: Weddings and Holidays

On paper, at least, Coleridge took Southey's defection equably; and a letter to Cottle of mid-August, 1795, is chiefly pleased that Southey is not taking Orders. Coleridge slept at Cottle's on the night of 1 October, on which day Cottle was to send off some of their old prints to Miss Fricker's, whence a 9 a.m. cart would take them and the rest of their goods to the honeymoon home.[1]

Meanwhile, Cottle had met Wordsworth, probably late in August; he confuses the whole issue of this momentous meeting, and the whole pattern of this wonderful year, by stating in his *Reminiscences*[2] that they were introduced at Stowey in 1797, and this careless memory illustrates the slighter impact that Wordsworth made on him after his first delighted impressions of Southey and Coleridge. He no doubt found Wordsworth less communicative, less tolerant of city life, less willing to flatter him. It would be pleasant for a Bristolian to be able to say that Bristol was a great inspiration to Wordsworth, that he settled here for a goodly period with no thought of moving, that he kept returning here gratefully and expectantly, and that the city was the motive power of some of his best verse; but all this, alas! would be quite untrue, and Cottle perhaps sensed and resented the fact. Although Bristol saw Wordsworth a number of times between 1795 and 1841, it was never for long; perhaps his first feelings about it were when he came under the spell of Chatterton, whom he certainly imitated in a schoolboy ballad, followed years later by the great tribute in *Resolution and Independence*. Cottle's shop had a picturesque and suggestive site, with the black and white of the Dutch House opposite and the spire of Paty's Christ Church glittering in new-built glory. And Wordsworth (who later boasted that he had seen every English and Welsh cathedral save Llandaff and St David's) was not indifferent to medieval architecture, as Coleridge was; but he disliked noise and congestion, which brought on nervous headaches, and he avoided cities when he could. His association with Bristol was a purely business relationship, and much the same might be said of his friendship with his chief acquaintance there, Joseph Cottle. It was the longest

View (pen and ink) from near Joseph Cottle's Corn Street shop, showing Christ Church and the Dutch House (in the possession of Martin Crossley Evans)

friendship of Cottle's life, limping on from 1795 to 1850; between bouts of neglect and even meanness, Wordsworth occasionally showed that he appreciated what Cottle had done for him. Southey was uniformly tolerant and thoughtful towards his benefactor; Coleridge was often sweepingly friendly, and their disagreements are more easily understood when it is realised that Cottle, admittedly bigoted and of inferior intellect, had no means of appreciating Coleridge's maddening pain and frustration; but the fifty-five years' friendship does not show Wordsworth in a good light, and Cottle may have found him, as the scattered evidence now finds him, selfish and tactless. Cottle judged the three in this order of merit, an order which the judgement of posterity would precisely reverse.

In any case, Wordsworth had come to the West Country to fulfil a practical plan. At long last, he and his sister Dorothy could set up house together, and on very favourable terms. The rich Bristol merchant, John Pinney, owned a house in Dorset called Racedown, which he had given to his elder son, John Frederick Pinney, to do as he pleased with. This son had hitherto kept a couple of servants there as caretakers; but he and his younger brother were pupils of Wordsworth's admiring friend, Basil Montagu (son of the Earl of Sandwich and a murdered actress), and through Montagu he met Wordsworth. He seems to have shared Montagu's feelings immediately, and offered Wordsworth the house rent free, with everything thrown in except linen. Strangely, the elder Pinney was under the impression that Wordsworth was paying rent for Racedown. But even a rent-free house would not keep the poet and his sister, since they had nothing but Raisley Calvert's legacy of £900; so they were going to look after two infants — the motherless son of Basil Montagu, and the natural daughter of their cousin Tom Myers. They thus hoped for a total income of nearly £180 per year, and young Pinney was going to stay with them from time to time *and* pay for his board! If Wordsworth was given another little Pinney as a pupil, he hoped to get '200 a year with him'. By August 1795 Wordsworth was in Bristol, staying at the Pinneys' – what is now the 'Georgian House' in Great George Street, and gratifyingly open to the public. Here he met Southey and Coleridge; his acquaintance with the former was long and light; the gain, and the mutual gain, of his friendship with the latter, let warring critics determine. In a letter of 2 September 1795,[3] Dorothy Wordsworth, left alone while William is away at Bristol with the Pinneys, outlines their schemes and adds, 'Bye the Bye I must not forget to tell you that he has had the offer of ten guineas for a work which has not taken him up much time, and half the profits of a second edition if it should be called for. It is but a little sum but it is one step and promises that something may be done'. In other words, he had met

Cottle, either at the Pinneys' or in the shop, and Cottle had offered him ten guineas for *Guilt and Sorrow*; it may seem little, but the poem, in its various states and with its wavering title *Salisbury Plain*, bears signs of the four separate years in which Wordsworth tackled it, and it is not among his best works. To Dorothy, obviously, the offer was a real beginning of better things; Cottle, neither awed by the patent moral excellence of a Southey nor blinded by the conversation of a Coleridge, tells us nothing at all of the first months of his acquaintance with one whose morals were less obtrusive and whose genius was less approachable.

But is the gap in Cottle's record just carelessness? Harper,[4] a hostile witness, uses a later but undated letter of Dorothy's to suggest that he deliberately falsified. She tells Jane Marshall, 'William is going to publish a poem. The Pinneys have taken it to the booksellers'. Harper's reconstruction of the story is that Cottle in 1795 made an offer for *Guilt and Sorrow*, withdrew it or had it rejected, and, when no London publisher came forward, was again asked about it by the Pinneys. And, as nothing came of it in Cottle's hands, he may well have suppressed 'the evidence of a false start' with one of his valued trio.

The beginning of October 1795 afforded Cottle some social joys. Through his sisters, he was accepted at the home of Hannah More (though we shall see that her snobbery imposed limits); the eldest 'Mrs' More invited him and Southey down to Cowslip Green (Hannah More's Somerset home near Wrington) for the whole of Monday, 5 October, and the poet's conversation and manners charmed all five Mores. He was so 'brim full of literature', one of them told Cottle later.[5] Southey, too, told Bedford[6] that he had enjoyed the day; the ladies had praised Horace Walpole, and had made him like Wilberforce better.

The day before, 4 October, the Reverend Benjamin Spry had married Coleridge and Sara Fricker in a quiet ceremony at St Mary Redcliffe; the couple then slipped away to the cottage which Coleridge was already occupying in Clevedon, and where their honeymoon and early married life would be spent. But two days afterwards Cottle received from Coleridge a letter, the contents of which were hardly related to an idyll; can Cottle send, in all haste, 'A riddle slice; a candle box; two ventilators; two glasses for the wash-hand stand; one tin dust pan; one small tin tea kettle; one pair of candlesticks; one carpet brush; one flour dredge; three tin extinguishers; two mats; a pair of slippers; a cheese toaster; two large tin spoons; a bible; a keg of porter; coffee; raisins; currants; catsup; nutmegs; allspice; cinnamon; rice; ginger; and mace'? Cottle sarcastically ascribes to philosophy the fact that these articles had not already been laid in; besides, since Clevedon was soon to be exchanged for the banks of a primeval river, present comfort would have been a mockery. Yet it is certainly a surprising list, from the essential Bible through the agreeable (shared?) slippers to the luxurious catsup. Cottle was a willing victim; he collected the articles from the appropriate tradesmen, added a few more, and sent them off at once to the not unpractical bridegroom. Next day, 7 October, he rode down to pay his respects and, instead of mere cake and wine, was received with 'hearty congratulations'. He liked the cottage. It was at the west end of the village, and had only one storey; the house at present labelled with Coleridge's name fits neither description, and is surely suspect. He admired the little garden, and the rose tree at the window; and the annual rent was so small that the poet could have paid it with verses in one hard-working week. The only thing wrong, to Cottle's taste, was the parlour white-wash, which was neither becoming nor recent; he therefore, on his return to Bristol the same day, sent down an 'honest upholsterer, (a Mr W. a good little weak man) … with a few pieces of sprightly paper'. (We are told more of this weak little paper-hanger: he wanted to be a Baptist Minister, and confided this to the Reverend Robert Hall, adding that he did not want to bury his talents in a napkin; Hall, surely to his own discredit, suggested a pocket-handkerchief instead.[7])

Further proof of Coleridge's business-like honeymoon is seen in the letter[8] he wrote on the same day, for Cottle to bring back and post to Thomas Poole of Nether Stowey. He has given up the idea of *The Provincial Magazine*, two of his six reasons being that it will cost Cottle £100 in buying paper and so forth, 'all on an uncertainty', and that Cottle has engaged to pay him one-and-a-half guineas for every hundred lines (enough for his maintenance) and to buy his prose works. Poole is told to write c/o Cottle, who will then forward.

On his next meeting with Cottle after the honeymoon, Coleridge enthusiastically read him his tender lines on Sara's soft cheek,[9] but Southey must have been excluded from these confidences; there was another of the six reasons more cogent that the rest, and listed first: a magazine would involve collaboration with Southey, and this would now be intolerable. They must have met very rarely; Southey was officially living at Bath by the autumn, but was merely week-ending there and spending the other five days with Cottle, so as to be near his Edith. He wrote to Bedford on 9 October, 'Cottle offered me his house in a letter which you shall see when we meet, and for which he will ever hold a high place in your heart'.[10] One day when both he and Coleridge were in the city, they 'cut' each other, and Coleridge sent Cottle a letter[11] of unwarranted remarks about Southey. When Southey renounced Pantisocracy, and told Coleridge that he was going to Lisbon instead, the last link was severed; Coleridge (who, Cottle thinks, had already abandoned the scheme in his own mind) turned furiously angry at this defection and, realising that all their calculations were a bubble, turned his self-upbraidings against another. Southey, says Cottle, was 'the safety-valve of feeling'; he had been honest, and he now acted on the defensive, returning argument for opprobrium and remonstrance for epithet. Cottle, as always, saw Southey's point of view more easily, and went from one to the other[12] in this puzzling situation, whereby Coleridge could actually accuse Southey of something. But his mediation was in vain, and Coleridge finally blotted out the old friendship by his 5,000-word letter[13] to Southey on 13 November, written in the morning and delivered by hand to Southey on this, his wedding eve. It is all vituperation, regret, and farewell; the Chepstow incident had warned him, even to tears, of the betrayal; in the walks of Piercefield, thereafter, Southey had allayed his suspicions; but a strawberry party at Long Ashton, and a walk together towards Bath, had put matters wrong and clear again. He had not publicized Southey's seductive letter from his uncle, but 'To Danvers indeed and to Cottle I spoke more particularly — for I knew their prudence, and their love for you —: and my Heart was very full'.

But Southey had plenty of other things to think of. Next morning, Saturday, 14 November, he quietly married Edith Fricker at St Mary Redcliffe, with Cottle and his sister Sarah as witnesses. Cottle paid for the ring and the marriage fees. The two Southeys parted at the church door; she went home for the night, he 'slept as usual at Cottle's',[14] and they took another leave of each other on the 15th. Edith, with her wedding-ring suspended round her neck, and still calling herself Fricker, came to live with Cottle and two of his sisters as a parlour boarder; and by the 19th her secret husband had left for Falmouth and Portugal, buoyed up with at least one constructive thought: that Cottle had offered, on handsome terms, to publish any volume of his travels. Before he left, Cottle noticed that he had no stick, and lent him a stout holly of his own; it nearly had an adventure in Spain, since the sight of it intimidated a would-be robber, but Southey brought it back next year, and Cottle treasured it ever after. Late in November, while still waiting for the packet, Southey wrote to Cottle from Falmouth;[15] he had heard from Lovell that his marriage was known in Bristol, but he was indifferent. He added, for Cottle's benefit, a further reason why the marriage had taken place: he might not come back, and then his relatives would forgive Edith and receive her — but Cottle must not show her this bit. It seems that he was at least easy in his mind about her present situation, if we judge by a letter[16] of 29 November to Bedford; the two Misses Cottle are 'women of elegant and accomplished manners ... And you will have some opinion of them when I say that they make even bigotry amiable'. The elder (probably Mary) is only 23; she has been a little while a governess in Lord Derby's family. They are very religious, and this one, especially, urges him to read good books and tempers her admiration of him with the fear that he be irreligious, as he speculates 'beyond reason' and attends no place of worship.

With Southey out of the way, Coleridge had a monopoly of Cottle, who was using Rose to print for Coleridge three of the political lectures;[17] one of their first joint activities was to become members and borrowers at the Bristol Library in King Street.[18] This fine society, a closed subscription association, had been founded in 1773, and charged an entrance fee and an annual subscription of one guinea each until 1798, when the fee went up to four guineas; it was six in 1801, and went on rising, and the subscription went up to a guinea and a half in 1806. The membership rose from 137 in 1782 to 198 in 1798; in that year there were 5,000 books, along with the custody of 2,000 belonging to the city. Until 21 March 1796, you could borrow one book for a month; then, up to 20 March 1797, two of a set; thereafter, two. The 'overdue' fine was rarely enforced in the early days, but was used after 1806 so as to release new books; you were sent an elegant printed 'reminder' on pale blue paper. If two members wanted the same book, the dispute was settled by lot; you could reserve books that were 'out', but a book could not be transferred to you without its first being returned to the library. Scarce and valuable books were normally confined; if you sent someone for a book, he must bring your signed and dated order, and any book sent out or brought back must be wrapped in paper. You were not eligible for membership if you kept a lodging-house, inn, tavern, coffee-house, place of public entertainment, or circulating library. The exterior of the handsome building [now, in 2007, housing a Chinese restaurant], repaired and cleaned, can still be seen in King Street; and the lovely panelled library room is incorporated in the present library on College Green.

It is as well, for our purpose, to know the rules and conditions of the oldest public library in the country, since from now on we know more of Cottle's movements to and from it than of any of his other restricted physical activities. The rich and fascinating library register, where great men dart in and out in their own autographs, shows him as a regular visitor, very often signing last of the day, as if he had hurried from his shop after closing-time; for the library was closed on Saturday and Sunday. He normally came himself, though he occasionally commissioned his servant. Several of his circle were members: they all signed a register subscribing to the rules, and

Lovell was member No. 235 (borrowing thick and fast from 7 September 1790), John Pinney 246 (from March 1792), Southey 278 (from 25 November 1793 until his marriage), Coleridge 295 (from 2 March 1795), Joseph Cottle 310 and Amos Cottle 326. Other early borrowers who were, or would be, Cottle's friends include Dr Beddoes, James Tobin, members of the Bowles family, the father of the drowned Robert Drummond, and Humphry Davy in 1799; occasionally a Countess or an Admiral enlivened the scene, but all the mighty are departed by about 1810. As Cottle's own published works became more and more prolific, he gave copies of them to the library; though they do not much occupy the borrowing columns afterwards.

His first visit to the library was on Wednesday, 25 November 1795, with Coleridge; he borrowed Volume III of James Burgh's *Political Disquisitions* – but Coleridge had just taken out the first two volumes, and even signed for him! If this had remained the pattern of Cottle's visits, it would bear out the charge made against him, and especially by Professor George Whalley,[19] that he borrowed books for others to read, and not for himself; that when Coleridge withdrew his membership, he went on using Cottle's; that every Coleridge visit to Bristol caused a flurry of Cottle borrowings; that Wordsworth did not spend the money on becoming a member, simply because Cottle was willing to borrow for him on his own subscription; that Cottle, in fact, got out books for any clever friend in the hope of publishing the works that they inspired. Even Amos is said to have benefited from his brother's borrowing of the *Edda*; and it is not conceded even that Cottle may have read hard to keep abreast of his friends' reading and to bring a fuller understanding to their works, which he so obviously enjoyed. This relegation of Cottle to the rank of mere messenger-boy may be substantially true, but another interpretation is possible. In the first place, there are many periods of heavy borrowing when none of the poets was at hand to reap the benefit. Secondly, the sheer bulk of his verse is enormous; he is a very Lydgate, three of his poems alone totalling 39,000 lines. I think he must be allowed either great originality (which I should hesitate to grant) or voracious reading; his signatures in the library register, and his own good collection of books, bear out the latter way of looking at this well-documented problem.

The rest of the year 1795 was irradiated for him by his publication of *Joan of Arc*, fixed for 1 December. Southey had been revising it in the late summer and the autumn, and radically altered it at the proof stage. The first 452 lines of Book II were by Coleridge, apart from 97 by Southey stirred in; the poet was thus including a silent tribute to his lost friend. These lines were omitted in the second edition, but Cottle surely blunders when he says that Southey had warned Coleridge of this 'as early as the autumn of 1795'.[20] Why plan for the second edition before the first was out, and why include the lines when their excision had been determined? The *Joan* is a particularly handsome volume, and Cottle's care over it was justified by its good sale. On 9 December he wrote[21] to Messrs Cadell and Davies of London, enclosing an invoice for twelve copies, on sale or return, at 16/- apiece; they were to receive them on the night of Wednesday the 16th, by Wiltshire's wagon, with more to follow in a few days. He assures them that the book will sell well, and hopes that they will do all they can to promote this; at the time it left the press, he had 168 subscribers to it, so highly is it thought of in the poet's native city. He adds that Southey is at present travelling in Spain and Portugal; but he had, in fact, left Falmouth only the day before, and after a shocking passage wrote a gay, grumbling letter[22] to Cottle from Corunna on the 15th, all about fleas, filth, sea-sickness, custom-houses, and the corrupt Spanish court and priesthood. Cottle finished this astonishing year with a second visit to the library in company with Coleridge on 23 December; he returned the Burgh, and signed in his own hand for Caesar's *Commentaries*.

1796 was necessarily something of an anti-climax, a period of quiet prosperity and of marking time. His reading (or other people's), as far as it may be gathered from the Bristol Library Register, may be conveniently tabulated here:

4 Jan. – 8 Feb.	G. Keate, *An Account of the Pelew Islands*
5 Feb. – 8 Feb.	W. Hodges, *Travels in India*
8 Feb. – 29 Feb.	D. Hartley, *Observations of Man*, Vol. I
11 Feb. – 29 Feb.	*ditto*, Vol. II
16 Feb. – 22 Feb.	J. Moore, *Zeluco: Various Views of Human Nature*, Vol. I
29 Feb. – 7 Mar.	*ditto*, Vol. II
1 Mar. – 7 Mar.	G. Chalmers, *An Estimate of the Comparative Strength of Britain* ...
4 Mar. – 29 Mar.	Lord Kaimes, *Sketches of the History of Man*, Vol. I
29 Mar. – 9 May (after a reminder on 6 May)	G. Keate, *An Account of the Pelew Islands*
9 May – 9 June	J. Locke, *Works*, Vol. III
8 June – 18 July (after a reminder on 13 July)	W. Smellie, *Philosophy of Natural History*
11 July. – 19 Aug.	Bishop Burnet, *History of his own Time*, Vols. I and II

5 Aug. – 19 Aug.	Keate, *Pelew Islands* (The Lee Boo story is still haunting him)
18 Aug. – 23 Aug.	W. Guthrie, *Cicero*, Vol. II
23 Aug. – 17 Oct.	Samuel Johnson, *Works*, Vol. VIII
22 Sep. – 4 Jan.	J. Nott, *Select Odes from the Persian Poet Hafez, translated into English Verse*

('renewed' on 26 Oct., returned after letters on 7 Dec. and 4 Jan.)

1 Nov. – 5 Dec.	*Treatise on the Police of the Metropolis*
21 Dec. – 12 Jan. 1797	E. Gibbon, *Decline and Fall*, Vol. I

The year began with a pleasant token of the newest friendship; Wordsworth wrote[23] on 7 January, and Cottle proudly endorsed the letter, 'Wm. Wordsworth, 1st Letter'. It is a very friendly beginning to their correspondence: Wordsworth is unusually flattered by Cottle's gift of a *Joan*, sent through Mr Pinney, and would have thanked him at once, had he not been hoping to include a manuscript of *Salisbury Plain* as well. Engagements have prevented this, but he is now at leisure, and hopes to send it in a few days; would Cottle convey his compliments to Coleridge, and say that Wordsworth wants to hear from him? (The poem finally reached Cottle before 25 March, when Azariah Pinney wrote telling Wordsworth that he had delivered it; Cottle was to hand it to Coleridge for inspection.[24])

Meanwhile, Coleridge's true character was beginning to show itself. He had brought his wife back from Clevedon late in the previous November, and they settled in Mrs Fricker's tedious household on Redcliffe Hill. Fortunately, Poole invited the Coleridges down to Stowey, and there could be thoughts of poetry again, and of the long-promised Bristol edition. Cottle prints[25] a letter, and a scrap of others, which he received from Stowey at this time, the close of 1795. Coleridge is sorry that, with all his brotherly love for Cottle, he always has to write on business, and with so many excuses and apologies; the time he spares from gardening and reviewing he devotes to *Religious Musings*, but it progresses slowly, since he spends far more time altering it than writing it. He had read the poem to Cottle, who had criticized it; it has now changed 'monstrously', but it *will*, with its prefaces, occupy the number of pages that he had promised. He wants it to be perfect; and it cannot be, if it has to be finished at once. Cottle never saw three poems which Coleridge mentioned in another letter to him (the long *Nativity*, an epistle to Tom Poole, and a 300-line ballad); he suspects that they got no further than Coleridge's mind. After the holiday with Poole, Coleridge returned to Bristol – to project, to be near the press (says Cottle), and to start his wanderings. Cottle tells various stories to illustrate

Coleridge's habit of projecting schemes that came to nothing; to another characteristic, procrastination, Cottle attributes the failure of *The Watchman*, since Coleridge could never stand up to the recurring demands of a periodical. Very late in 1795, or very early in 1796, Coleridge convened a meeting in the Rummer (in All Saints Lane) to outline his plans for this lively journal. Cottle was not invited, possibly because Coleridge thought him too stick-in-the-mud politically, though his excuse was that all present were expected to subscribe, and Cottle had been bled enough already. In Bristol, Cottle obtained 250 subscribers, and Reed the bookseller, 120. The printing of the ten issues cost only £35; the paper cost more, and was paid for entirely by Cottle.[26]

1796 began with Coleridge unwell, and breaking engagements with Cottle and Beddoes, through drinking the New Year in;[27] but on Sunday, 3 January 1796, before he started on his sensational canvassing and preaching tour of the big cities, he was invited by the Reverend David Jardine (whose *Sermons* Cottle published in 1798) to preach at the Unitarian chapel in Bath. Cottle's account[28] of the visit is amusing and may be true, but he detested 'the sentiments of Socinus', and did all he could to win Coleridge from them; so that we must allow for exaggeration and for his wilful sense of humour. This was to be Coleridge's inaugural sermon, and would test his qualification to enter their ministry. No conveyance had been provided, so Cottle (out of curiosity) and Charles Danvers took him over from Bristol in a chaise, and they arrived in time for the morning service. Someone asked them where the Reverend Mr Coleridge was preaching, and Danvers hopefully replied 'Follow the crowd'. When they reached the chapel, Coleridge played his first unorthodox trick: he insisted on wearing his blue coat and white waistcoat, and would not put on the black gown, despite Jardine's protests. It was the smallest congregation that Cottle had ever seen, and a very dull service – a stiff prayer, 'languid' singing, and then the sermon … The text was tactless, since it mentioned that hungry people shall 'curse their king' – in a year of great scarcity! – but it all developed into a mere political lecture on the Corn Laws, which Coleridge had already used at the Assembly Room (on the Quay) in Bristol. So to a dinner in a tavern, where the preacher continued his theme and added that he would be willing to preach again that afternoon. Hoping for an improvement, they encouraged him, and he rang the bell and sent the waiter to Jardine, offering to give a sermon on the Hair Powder Tax. Cottle assumed that the minister would have had enough, but the waiter returned with an acceptance, and they hurried back to the 'concourse'; Cottle claims that, apart from himself, Coleridge, Danvers and Jardine, there were present men, women, and children numbering only seventeen. Coleridge's friends had heard it all before; he kept glancing at them, and Cottle had to hold his head down for fear of smiling; half way through the sermon, a pew-door banged and a man walked out, two more escaping soon after … Cottle hoped that they would not be left alone.

It was a gloomy ride back; Coleridge felt that Jardine had been offhand with him, and his companions considered it 'a Sunday desecrated'. Not long before, Cottle had heard Coleridge in conversation with the great and saintly Baptist preacher, the Reverend Robert Hall; *then* they had been evenly matched, but now Coleridge's inferiority in the pulpit was all too obvious, and Cottle hoped that he would never see him in one again.

It is not to Cottle's purpose, of course, to say much the arduous, and not unsuccessful, tour of the northern cities; apart from rather facetious praise, he just prints in *Reminiscences* some passages from the wanderer's letters to Josiah Wade. It is clear that Coleridge was proving thoroughly tiresome. Before setting out, and perhaps as early as October 1795, he sent[29] Cottle further instructions about printing his perfected sheets, with a request for Burnett to help with the annotation; then Cottle shall have the rest of the poems by 9 on Saturday morning. (The Unitarian minister Estlin was to do some checking also.) In the same letter, he asks Cottle to pay Mrs Fricker a guinea that Sara owes her, and put it to Coleridge's account, 'if it prove convenient'; and, perhaps to mollify Cottle for this, he mentions *The Silver Thimble*, which Sara (heavily aided by her husband) had addressed to him. The story is the prettiest that has survived from these days of their friendship, before Coleridge's duplicity, Cottle's prejudices, and Sara's moaning combine into a picture of ruin. Sara had lost her thimble, and Cottle, hearing of this, sent her four to choose from; she chose a silver one relieved with blue enamel, and in her (or, rather Coleridge's) poem of thanks she evokes Ariadne and also gives a pleasantly preposterous reason why the thimble was an apt gift from Cottle: his verse, and especially the *Baptist*, the *War*, the *Alla*, and the *Henderson*, as recited to her by her husband, is so 'thought-bewildering' that she might easily prick her finger! Coleridge now wished to include this with his own poems, and it actually figured in the first edition. In another matter, however, there was a change of plan. Coleridge here announces that the shorter pieces will occupy Volume I, and Volume II will have nothing under 300 lines. But the poems as published are in one volume only. The postscript of the letter shows that he was still at Stowey; the promised preface will have to come 'by some conveyance or other', and he has been sea-bathing. Indeed, this latter fact is reported in the waggish way that Cottle must have laughed at: 'I smoked yesterday afternoon – and

Samuel Taylor Coleridge: lithograph from a drawing by Robert Hancock, 1796 (reproduced from *Early Recollections* 1837)

then imprudently went into the Sea – the consequence was that on my return I was taken sick – and my triumphant Tripes cataracted most Niagara-ishly'.

Likewise, when he returned from his tour, he went on sending delaying letters to his patient publisher. From one,[30] we learn that George Burnett was apparently domesticating with them, and his temporary absence, and Sara's 'Spirits', have prevented Coleridge from keeping an appointment with Cottle on the previous Saturday; but he will be in the next day, to dine with Mr Coates. Then – again as if to placate Cottle – he adds that Cottle may certainly print his own name on the poem which Coleridge had addressed to him, with Sara's *Thimble* poem as a further compliment. Coleridge's tribute,[31] in Spenserian stanzas, begins with the apostrophe 'Unboastful Bard!' and asserts that Cottle has wandered effectively in the mild meadow at the foot of the poetic mount, though soaring with the inspiration of Henderson's death; besides this monody, the poem praises the *War* and the *Baptist*, but it is hard to believe that Coleridge's big words of approval and advice are anything more than flattery. Cottle perhaps did not detect that Coleridge often avoided his company, though producing an elegant excuse … 'I shall consult my poetic honor and of course your interest more by staying at home than by drinking Tea with you. – I should be happy to see my Poems out by the conclusion of next week – and shall continue in stirrups – that is – shall not dismount my Pegasus till Monday morning'.[32] Or, with a promise of some delayed copy, just 'What a dreadful night!'[33] Eventually, since text and preface and notes were not forthcoming, Cottle decided not to bother the poet further, but to let him take his own time; and on 22 February 1796, having a friend who wanted to meet Coleridge, he innocently invited them both to dinner, sending his manservant (his brother, according to Coleridge's reply) off to Redcliffe Hill with the invitation. The man found that Coleridge was out, and stupidly brought the note back; and when Coleridge returned from 'composing in the fields', and learned of the undelivered message, he assumed that it could relate to only one subject – that it was a 'dun' for some verses. He at once sat down and dashed off a petulant and self-pitying letter[34] to Cottle, on the thanklessness of an author's life, Sara's miserable company, and the prospect (seven months before the birth even of his first child!) of 'the thin faces of them that want bread, looking up to me!' Then, with ill-concealed venom, he assures Cottle that he need not worry about being out of pocket on Coleridge's account; he loves Cottle, quite apart from gratitude, and in fact he had just come home from the fields to write the preface. The letter was the first positive sign of the nastiness which Cottle was soon suffering at the hands of a contemptuous genius. Patiently, he at once sent some money, corrected Coleridge's misapprehension, and renewed the invitation; the dinner-party was a great success, and Coleridge (who should have felt foolish) was as expansive as ever.

But before the poems could be published, the promised *Watchman* must be given to the world. When the first number came out on Tuesday, 1 March, the two of them took four hours arranging, counting (Coleridge checking Cottle's figures), packing and invoicing the 3d copies for the London and provincial customers. Every eighth day this labour was repeated, Cottle willingly giving his time for Coleridge's sake. Everyone was disappointed in the journal; the subscribers felt that they had been promised too much, and their author was weary of the whole venture before *they* were. From time to time, he wrote to Cottle complaining of the slavish routine that attended the preparation of each issue; he cannot accept an invitation because of 'Watch drudgery'; he cannot stir out because his eye is inflamed and because Burnett has abridged the parliamentary debates so carelessly; he really cannot call until after 9 in the evening (and should he come to the Barton or the shop house?), because he is 'on "Watch"' until then, but he can accept for Wednesday, though he is sorry to keep causing Cottle the expense of entertaining. In any case, by April the *Poems on Various Subjects* were out, and they diverted his mind from its sorry hebdomadal task; at the tenth number, says Cottle, 'the Watchman at the helm cried, "Breakers", and the vessel stranded!' Tom Poole's brother Richard had only just asked for two copies to be sent weekly, his newsman to call at Cottle's;[35] but the decision that the Wakeman waketh in vain was a blessed relief to author and publisher, even if it caused bitterness among them and Biggs the printer.

It is probable, indeed, that Coleridge behaved churlishly towards the worthy Biggs, even though Cottle's evidence[36] for this is slightly suspect. (He takes gross liberties with a Coleridge letter, omitting or changing vital sentences.) Coleridge, it seems, was 'vexed' because Biggs was providing the paper for *The Watchman* at a profit; but, says Cottle, this was not happening at all – Biggs was merely choosing the best paper for Cottle's benefit, out of various samples. Coleridge is also ungracious in his schemes for saving himself no end of money; whereas, in fact, Cottle let him have the paper at cost price, was occasionally but incompletely reimbursed, and, by making himself responsible to Biggs for the printing, 'reduced the price per sheet, as a bookseller, ... from fifty shillings to thirty five shillings'. Cottle lost heavily on the whole deal; and he was indignant when Coleridge, in *Biographia Literaria*, told the story that Biggs had refused to wait a month for his payment and threatened to throw Coleridge into gaol for £80 or £90.

Nor did Coleridge's *Poems on Various Subjects* (with some by Lamb) bring Cottle any reward save later reverie. They were published on 16 April by the Robinsons and Cottle, and were fairly well received and reviewed; on the 15th, Coleridge had written on the blank leaf of one volume a touching tribute to Cottle, to whom 'the world owed them', and without whom 'none perhaps of them would have been published, and many not written'. But Cottle lost by the grand schemes of salesmanship that Coleridge formulated: to send 25-30 copies and half-a-dozen guinea *Joans* to Parsons of Paternoster Row, with similar consignments being variously dispersed, Cottle to pay the carriage for London and Birmingham destinations, Coleridge for other cities. This is all very well; but Parsons, after making further orders, paid not a farthing. Coleridge also had an impressive list of complimentary copies, with a sonnet written on every fly-leaf – for Lamb, for Wordsworth, for Dr Beddoes and even for Mrs Barbauld; but it is here that Cottle so naughtily mauls the letter he is quoting, since he altogether omits the promise, 'I will not give away *one* at your expense, except for your interest'. Another of his plans was broached in a persuasive but ingenuous letter[37] to Cottle; they had been talking about the possibility of 'Rumfordizing' Bristol's hospitals and workhouses into garden cities, and now Coleridge had an idea for pamphlets, priced at a shilling, to be addressed to the citizens on this subject. After that, the wording could be slightly altered to suit Manchester and Birmingham; 750 copies would be enough, and Cottle could either print it and share the profits, or give Coleridge three guineas for the copyright. Only the last item materialized; Cottle 'presented Mr C. with the three guineas, but forbore the publication'.

All this time, Southey was languishing in Lisbon, and on 1 February wrote[38] to Cottle earnestly entreating one letter to cheer his exile. Cottle had been neglecting him, and he badly wanted news of his Bristol friends, and of the sales of *Joan*; Coates had sent him good news of it, and he was planning a second edition, with a new preface, an amplified last book, and all Coleridge's lines omitted. This last stipulation gave less hope of the reconciliation that Cottle had set his heart on. The enormous letter is a first-rate hostile account of life in the Portuguese capital – its earthquakes, its filth, its unburied carrion, its unhygienic friars, its flooded streets, its dogs and rats feeding at the same dunghills, its swarms of red ants, its worse swarms of priests. Southey here lets loose all his loathing of the superstitions of the Roman Church, a loathing which Cottle always shared; his two best illustrations are the image that knocked on the doors of two churches, and the burning of the Jews. He promises that he will be with Cottle the third day after his landing at Falmouth, or earlier, if he can get a post-chaise. Will

Cottle see to it that he is sent *The Watchman*, and Coleridge's lectures and poems? There seems to be one good feature of Lisbon for Southey: the climate is pleasant, and the air is so clear that the new moon caries the old moon as a perfect 'O' in her arms; Joseph and Robert must look for it one fine night.

On 24 February, Southey wrote to Bedford[39] to ask if he had had the original *Joan*, 'written at Brixton, bound decently, &c.? I left it with Cottle, to send with your copy: he has the transcript of it himself, which he begged with most friendly devotion, and, I believe, values as much as a monk does the parings of his tutelary saint's great toe nail'. He gives Bedford an example of Cottle's lovable clumsiness: Southey had written a climax,

> With jealous eye,
> Hating a rival's look, the husband hides
> His miserable meal,

which Cottle, after Southey had corrected the proof and left town, changed to '... each man conceals', because he was sorry for the husband! He is the kind of man who could not 'hide a morsel from the hungry ... I was very much vexed, and yet I loved Cottle the better for it'.

At Whitsun Cottle took an important little holiday in the Malvern district of Worcestershire, and early in the morning of Whit Monday, 16 May, he began a lame and laborious climb;[40] the 1600-line *Malvern Hills*, which arose from this, shares something of its two qualities, but it was his favourite poem and, I suppose, his best. We have seen something already of the full canvas that he uses here – his condemnation of all slavery, foreign and domestic; but the poem wanders amiably through musings on Chatterton, a mountain thorn (which sounds very like Wordsworth's later Thorn), the history of the district, lovers killed by lightning, local ruins of castle and priory, materialism, papist wickedness in withholding the Bible, the Christian's welcome of death, village bells and merriment and music, and James Crichton (to whose work he may have introduced Coleridge[41]). Indeed, his visionary field is as full of folk as was Langland's when *he* wandered on the same hills, though the resemblance ends there.

He was alone on the hills, in fresh though misty weather, and conscious of the holy season of Pentecost. He must have been staying in the 'one large Inn' near the healing well, and he praises it; it accommodated all the visitors to the well, including some quite healthy people, and they shared a common table. He apparently knows the district already (line 28), though there is no record of a previous visit. The mist clears, and he gains the top of the

Beacon, with a dazzling view around him: Upton-on-Severn, the orchards and Malvern Chase, the sequestered priory of Little Malvern (still as hushed and forgotten as he knew it), and the hundred churches which a telescope will reveal. The poem often plunges to 'Stuffed owl' lines like the notorious

> How long, and steep, and dreary, the ascent!
> It needs the evidence of close deduction
> To know that I shall ever reach the height.   (lines 33-35)

But let it be remembered that Wordsworth paid Cottle the supreme tribute of borrowing lines 1579-1583, lines utterly peaceful and sweet and sympathetic, and embedding them in the glorious setting of his own *Prelude*, Book VIII:

> A cheerful smile unbends the wrinkled brow,
> The days departed start again to life,
> And all the scenes of childhood reappear,
> Faint, but more tranquil, like the changing sun
> To him who slept at noon and wakes at eve.

1   Griggs, I.159, Nos.88 and 89.

2   R.47, p.182.

3   Shaver, p.149, No.50.

4   G. McL. Harper, *William Wordsworth* (London: Murray, 1916), I.277.

5   R.47, p.13.

6   CCS, I.250.

7   R.47, pp.39-42.

8   Griggs, I.160-161, No.91.

9   R.47, p.63.

10 CCS, I.248-249.

11 Cottle, letter of 9 April 1836, in Bristol City Library MS.B 20877.

12 R.47, pp.104-106.

13 Griggs, I.163-173, No.93.

14 Curry, I.102.

15 R.47, p.190n.

16 CCS, I.258-260.

17 Griggs, VI. Appendix B, p.1003, No.93A (?Nov.1795).

18 For the Library rules, members, and signatures, see the many volumes of the Registers preserved in the present Library on College Green, Bristol – A

Catalogue of the Books, belonging to the Bristol Library Society ... (Bristol: Gutch, 1814) – and G. Whalley, *op.cit.*

19   *op.cit.*, especially pp.128-129.

20   *R.47*, p.129.

21   Bodl.MS.Montague d.4, fol.118.

22   *R.47*, p.191.

23   Shaver, p.163, No.57. The footnote makes Cottle meet Southey and Coleridge a year too early.

24   F.W. Bateson, *Wordsworth, a Re-Interpretation* (London: Longman: 1954), p.15n.

25   *R.47*, pp.65-66.

26   Cottle's seemingly exaggerated story of *The Watchman* and the *Poems* is in *R.47*, pp.74-83.

27   Griggs, I.174, No.96, letter to Cottle, who in *ER.37*, I.184, particularly states that he cannot remember its date (that is, the year – since he puts 'January 1st.'); it is now in the Berg Collection, New York Public Library. Its mention of Beddoes dates it before the Doctor's death in 1808, but why is it addressed to 'Brunswick Square'? – the family were not there until 1807. The fact is that Cottle has assigned it to a period eleven years too early.

28   *R.47*, pp.93 ff.

29   Griggs, I.162, No.92. Cottle, in *R.47*, barbarously chops this letter into two (pp.66, 157) without notice of the fact, and mutilates the parts.

30   Griggs, I.186-187, No.106.

31   E.H. Coleridge ed., *Complete Poems of Samuel Taylor Coleridge* (Oxford, 1935), pp.102-104.

32   Griggs, VI.1005, No.111.

33   Griggs, VI.1004, No.105A.

34   Griggs, I.185, No.105; Cottle's version is in *R.47*, pp.68-69.

35   Mrs Henry Sandford, *Thomas Poole and his Friends* (London and New York: Macmillan, 1888), I.137.

36   *R.47*, pp.81-83. See Griggs, I.201, No.118.

37   Griggs, I.205, No.123.

38   *R.47*, pp.193-199.

39   CCS, I.267, 271.

40   The year, month, and day can be fixed, in Cottle's usual haphazard fashion, by footnotes on pp.72, 11, and 1 of *MH.4*.

41   Coburn, I.Notes, item 294.

Chapter 4
Lamb: The Bliss of the Dawn

Southey was back at Portsmouth by 15 May 1796, made straight for Bristol, collected Edith from the Cottles, and settled with her in lodgings; his address for a time was c/o Cottle.[1] The quarrel with Coleridge ceased to smoulder, and leapt to flame; Cottle again mediated, begged Coleridge to 'soften his asperity', and wrote to Southey with the hope that at least he would not look daggers at Coleridge when they met. But all in vain.[2] (Yet Coleridge, in a business letter to Cottle which the latter never published, expressed delight at Southey's return.[3]) It was, in any case, a time of break-up; on 3 May Robert Lovell, brother-in-law of both the poets, died of a fever, and Coleridge was all the while in a ferment over his wife's ailments and the necessity for moving on and making some money. Early in July he was offered the assistant editorship of the *Morning Chronicle*, which would involve moving to London; he was torn, called on Estlin, but found that he and Danvers and Wade were all away, and so had no-one to consult but Cottle, who naturally told him to accept. In letters to Estlin and Poole,[4] on 4 July, he poured out this problem and his longing to stay in Bristol. Southey, in huge relief at being back, was more pleasantly employed until the time when he must settle to a career in Law; in a letter of 12 June to Bedford,[5] he says that he means to go down to Hannah More's on Saturday, the 18th, and spend the day there. Amos was going down on the Friday, and they would return together; it seems that Amos is a talented young man, patronized by Thornton the friend of Negroes, and about to take orders. But a note, added on the following Sunday, says that Southey did not go after all. We know that Amos gave up this idea of the Church, and briefly had recourse to Law also; he was apparently in Bristol during the latter part of 1796, the infallible library Register establishing his movements and his reading:

21 June – 11 July	Guy, *Voyage Littéraire de la Grèce*
16 Aug. – 15 Sept.	d'Anacharsis (Jean Baptiste de Cloots), 1st and 1st Vols, 1 English and 1 French

22 Aug. – 26 Oct.	M. Madan, *New and Literal Translation of Juvenal and Persius*, Vol. I
30 Sept. – 26 Oct.	*ditto*, Vol. II

On 8 June, enter Charles Lamb; not that he and Cottle had yet been introduced, but he had received his gifts of *Joan* and of Coleridge's and Cottle's *Poems*, and his long letter[6] from London to his friend Coleridge is devoted entirely to criticism. Cottle comes off well: 'The "Monody on Henderson" is *immensely good*; the rest of that little volume is *readable and above mediocrity*'. When he continued the letter next day, he cited certain lines from the *Monody* as 'superlatively excellent. That energetic one, "Shall I not praise thee, Scholar, Christian, friend", like to that beautiful climax of Shakespeare "King, Hamlet, Royal Dane, Father". "Yet memory turns from little men to thee!" "and sported careless round their fellow child". The whole, I repeat it, is immensely good'. These remarks are very different from the spiteful things Lamb was soon saying about Cottle's epics; but, in each case, Lamb spoke accurately, and we must regret that Cottle deserted his real genre for themes far beyond his competence.

In this year 1796 Cottle was able to undertake two other charitable schemes. Mrs Newton, Chatterton's sick and poverty-stricken sister, had been swindled out of her brother's manuscripts by the surprisingly reverend and baronetted Herbert Croft. She showed his letters to Cottle, who advised her to write for more remuneration than the £11.10s. he had given her; on 4 August she wrote again, saying that, if he did not compensate her, his methods would be made public, and his brutal reply of 1 September almost suggested that she was blackmailing him. While Southey was living in Bristol, Cottle told him of all this, and they called on Mrs Newton, who confirmed the whole story, adding that she had nothing left but her brother's last pocket-book, which she would never part with. Cottle wrote to Croft, 'urging him, by a timely concession, to prevent that publicity which, otherwise, would follow'. When no answer came, Southey decided not only to expose Croft in the *Monthly Magazine*, but to print all Chatterton's works, by subscription, entirely for Mrs Newton's benefit; it was this undertaking, in which Cottle was his partner, that came to a really triumphant conclusion in 1802.[7]

After Robert Burns's death on 21 July 1796, Cottle spoke to Coleridge about raising a fund for the widow and five children, who 'had little more than their father's fame to support them'. Coleridge promised to write a poem for a Bristol newspaper, and Cottle inserted in the same paper an appeal for subscriptions, stating how much had been collected in Dumfries,

Charles Lamb: lithograph from a drawing by Robert Hancock, 1798 (reproduced from *Early Recollections* 1837)

Edinburgh, and Liverpool, and expressing his willingness to receive donations at his shop. (The final sum, he says, did credit to the citizens of Bristol.[8]) The poem, though centred on Burns, took the curious form of an address 'To a Friend who had declared his Intention of writing no more Poetry'. This was Lamb; and the verses must have been written just after Lamb's agonized letter of 27 September, outlining to Coleridge his sister's murderous brainstorm.[9]

In 1796 the mad William Gilbert, whom we last saw being discharged in 1788 from Henderson's asylum at Hanham, reappeared in Bristol. Since he was a man of talent and of winning manners, he was introduced by Cottle to Coleridge and Southey, and got on well with each of them; their own solid genius so impressed him that his opinions and conversation were moderate and wise in their presence, and Coleridge's staying powers of speech no doubt dammed the spate of Gilbert's verbiage. This was the year of publication of his *Hurricane, a Theosophical and Western Eclogue*, whose free and wriggling blank verse is, in a few patches, well worth discovering. Cottle, as if to see what would happen when you mixed two unlike substances, introduced him also to Robert Hall (whom Cottle madly admired). And the expected argument set in, on the merits of More *versus* Yearsley; there were 'felicitous torrents of eloquence' from both, 'yet without the introduction of the least indecorous expression'. Then, because Gilbert was an astrologer, Cottle invited him to supper with a doctor who was very hostile to horoscopes: Cottle warned him first that the doctor was going to be kind enough to cure him of 'all his astrological maladies', but Gilbert said grimly, 'The malady is on his side. Perhaps I may cure him'. And so it proved; it cannot have been a very peaceful supper-party, since they fell to argument at once and it ended with 'the man of sense vanquished by the man of words'. There was eventually an end to these noisy threesomes at Cottle's; Gilbert left Bristol early one morning and vanished for ever, until they heard that he had died at Charleston, in the United States.[10]

For Cottle, probably the happiest feature of the end of 1796 was the partial reconciliation of his two poets. Since Southey had settled in lodgings almost opposite Coleridge, their continued feud must have seemed rather inconvenient, or perhaps Edith and Sara were weary of their divided loyalties; at any rate, Southey made the first move in a note, Coleridge answered encouragingly, they met at a relation's, and they were suddenly in each other's arms. After these embracements, they broke the delicious news to Cottle. That the renewed friendship was an empty and insincere affair is shown by what Coleridge wrote to Thelwall on 31 December, and by Southey's contemptuous references to Coleridge when he looked back on those early days; but, at the time, Cottle believed – and was probably meant to believe – that a genuine partnership had started again. Early in the autumn, after a jolly walk in the country, they called on him arm in arm; their benefactor was appeased, and they 'seemed to relish the surprise and the delight which it was impossible for me to conceal'. But Cottle 'had reason afterwards to think, that this sprightly scene was a preconcerted arrangement to heighten the stage-effect'.[11] Evidently, it was still worth Coleridge's while to keep Cottle's approval; but the *Poems on Various Subjects* were selling well, and by mid-October a second edition was called for. In this unlooked-for position, it was a nuisance for the poet that his bookseller owned the copyright, and there was an interchange of contrasting views. Cottle, under no obligation at all, offered Coleridge twenty guineas on the sale of the second edition of 500 copies; this was not lavish, perhaps, but it was precisely twenty guineas more than he needed to give. Coleridge's reply,[12] on 18 October, is ugly behind its dignity. He is not mercenary, and he could not think of bartering with Cottle, who, he realises, will get nothing for his twenty guineas unless there be a third edition. But, to think of himself, he will get no more, and perhaps less, from Cottle for the sale of the poems than if he published them on his own account; it is the choice between his keeping the copyright for ever, or losing it after two editions. One facetious piece, and the sonnet to Lord Stanhope, are to be omitted as 'unworthy' of Coleridge; and the best pieces are to be in the front of the volume. Of course, by this time Coleridge was worried not only by his own ill-health and his uncertain position, but also by the ill-health of his paying guest, Charles Lloyd, who was an epileptic. In refusing some invitation by Cottle in early November,[13] he wrote in the maddening pain of neuritis that he was sorry to disappoint, but he was seriously ill – from '*mental* causes', said his doctor; he had a blister put under his right ear, and he was taking twenty-five drops of laudanum every four hours. Cottle has scribbled on the back of this letter, 'Oh, that S.T.C. had never taken more than 25 drops each dose!'[14] Coleridge's frantic longing to settle at Stowey, to rest in the strength and calm of Tom Poole, was now approaching hysteria; in letters[15] to him of 12 and 13 December he wailed out his fears that Poole had turned from him, and his anguish that there was a conspiracy to send him off to Iron Acton near the city. At Bristol, true, Cottle and Estlin were willing to serve him, but what could they do for him? At Stowey, he would not have to ask anything of Wade or Cottle; save that Cottle had promised to correct his proofs for him. This savage yet pathetic letter conquered Poole's misgivings, and the Coleridges (with Lloyd to follow) moved into the Stowey cottage on the last day of 1796, whereafter parcels of books, etc., were to reach him *via*

Cottle's shop; but, if Mrs Sandford[16] is right, and Cottle and the other Bristol worthies had urged Poole against Coleridge's settlement at Stowey, and if Coleridge realised this, he may have remembered Cottle with resentment against the background of these terrible weeks. Early in 1797 Southey, too, had departed, to study Law in London; Cottle was ominously alone.

He saw little of his heroes during 1797, save by spending holidays with them; on the other hand, his business and family life continued uneventfully. His father is still noticed in *Matthews's New Bristol Directory* for 1797, as a tailor, and his sister Mary is there shown as keeping a *Ladies' Boarding School* in Portland Square, then a new and fashionable locality. The younger brother, Robert, was associated with printing; as a 'Stationer, Wine St', he served in the First of the ten Companies of Gentleman Volunteers of Bristol, who were founded in this year 1797.[17] Amos was flourishing at Cambridge. The father is one of thirty-eight Master Tailors mentioned in *Felix Farley* for 9 April 1796 and the next four numbers as having met in their hall on the evening of 30 March and resolved that, despite the efforts of their Journeymen, they would pay 'by the Piece only'; the public would thus be better served, and industrious workmen would be able to increase their wages by their industry, being assured of constant employment if they apply to any of the thirty-eight masters. Joseph was advertising various goods in *Felix Farley*: in the issue of 4 July 1795 (along with twelve other Bristol booksellers), an improved Ruling Machine for ruling paper for account-books; on 26 December 1795, Jones's *English System of Bookkeeping*, at one guinea to subscribers and one-and-a-half to others; on 28 January 1797, tickets for Clarke's course of twelve Natural and Experimental Philosophy lectures at the Coopers' Hall (which now forms the front of the Theatre Royal in King Street), with another on the eye, at one guinea for thirteen lectures or half-a-crown each; on 25 March 1797, Estlin's *Discourse delivered at the Chapel in Lewin's-Mead, Bristol, on the Nature and the Causes of Atheism*, printed by Biggs; and on 30 December 1797, guinea subscription tickets for Messrs Bowles and Smith's lectures at the Red Lodge (in Park Row) on Animal Oeconomy, to begin on the first day of the coming year. One of his most eminent publications during 1797 was an unusual work by the Persian scholar Charles Fox, who had finally settled in Bristol: *Poems, containing the Plaints, Consolations, and Delights of Achmed Ardebeili, a Persian exile, with notes historical and explanatory*. New and interesting as the book was, it was worth nothing to Longman by the time Cottle came to sell his copyrights.[18]

Knowing that Cottle's trade declined in 1798, we may see a sign of the collapse in his absence from *Felix Farley's* lists of tradesmen's signatures on petitions to the King, Volunteer propaganda, anti-war petitions, subscriptions to the Bristol Infirmary, appeals for the Camperdown widows and orphans, etc., throughout 1797, and beyond. Almost every month of the year, he paid from one to four visits to the library, and it must be stated that his borrowings bear little relation to Coleridge's needs.

4 Jan. – 9 Jan.	Monstrelet, *Chroniques* (Coleridge *had* used this in 1796; and Cottle can have had little French)
9 Jan. – 12 Jan.	J. Strutt, *View of the Manners, Customs, Arms, Habits, &c. of the Ancient Inhabitants of England*, Vol. I
12 Jan. (returned same day)	Gibbon, *Decline and Fall*, Vol. II
12 Jan. – 13 Jan.	J. Strutt, *View*, Vol. II
13 Jan. – 3 Apr. (after reminder of 13 March)	Saxo Grammaticus (probably because he and Amos were growing interested in the *Edda*)
10 Feb. – 9 Mar.	Roland, *Appeal to Impartial Posterity*, Pt. I
31 Mar. – 24 Apr. (renewed 13 Apr.)	*Observations on Rowley* (he was beginning his charitable work for Mrs Newton)
13 Apr. – 24 Apr.	*Observation on the three first Volumes of* (Warton's) *History of English Poetry*
24 Apr. – 16 May	Murphy, *Works of Tacitus*, Vols. I and II
5 May – 6 June	Gibbon, *Decline and Fall*, Vol. II
16 May – 29 May	Rousseau, *Confessions*, Vol. I
29 May – 3 July	*ditto*, Vol. II
12 June – 19 June	Gibbon, *Decline and Fall*, Vol. III

Hereafter, Amos appears on the scene again as a borrower; and it is possible that the library distinguished him from his younger brother by calling him 'Mr Cottle'. At all events, 'Mr Cottle's' movements are as follows (and his borrowing of the *Edda* would seem to identify him with Amos):

1 Aug. – 16 Nov (renewed 11 Sept. after letter of 8 Sept.; renewed again 13 Oct.)	*Edda*
10 Aug. – 14 Aug.	J Strutt, *Complete View of the Dress and Habits of the People of England*, Vol. I
17 Oct. – 19 Oct.	Sinclair, *Statistical Account of Scotland*, Vol. 8
19 Oct. – 23 Oct.	*ditto*, Vol. 9

(returned on the same day as an Amos signature, which perhaps means that

'Mr Cottle' = Amos; and Amos's own signatures give further proof of this for the following items)

18 Sept. – 23 Oct.	Froissart, Vol. I
(after letter of 20 Oct.)	
23 Oct. – 27 Nov.	Sinclair, *Statistical Account of Scotland*, Vols. 6-7 (continuing 'Mr Cottle's' reading)

Joseph's certain borrowing is renewed with:

15 Nov. – 22 Jan. 1798	*Works*, Vol. I.
(renewed 29 Dec. after letters of 6 and 22 Dec.)	
27 Nov. – 8 Jan.	*Statistical Account of Scotland*, Vols. 3 and 4
(renewed 12 Jan. after letter of 10 Jan.)	

Of course, Amos may have acted as his messenger, or may even have read to him, since we shall see that this year he suffered much from ill-health and sore eyes.

The three poets were now separated from Bristol and from each other; but Southey, in particular, wrote assiduously to Cottle and published two more 'best-sellers' in Bristol. His letters show a measure of content at setting off on what he calls his 'race', and Cottle proudly edits many paragraphs of the series, wrongly assigning the impossible date 1796 to several of them. Accepting his law studies as a dull necessity, and happy to have Edith with him, Southey writes gaily throughout the spring. In the first of these letters,[19] written soon after his admission to Gray's Inn on 7 February 1797 (but headed by Cottle 'Nov 1796'), he expresses his manly wish for independence, and thanks Cottle 'for the comforts of my later time'. Edith comes on Monday, they settle in on Tuesday, and he starts his legal studies on Wednesday morning and *Madoc* the same evening; but Cottle must say nothing about the poem – Southey 'must have the character of a lawyer'. This is his busy programme; and he has declined to make his wife a Literary Club widow, although he has been elected to such a gathering at the Chapter Coffee-house. He promises that his next letter will be all about the famous people whom he has met in London and of whom they have heard in the provinces.

So, on the day that his books were 'organized' at last, he wrote another letter,[20] which must have been about people's physiognomies, though Cottle prints only the latter part of it: you can judge a man by his love of prints, and his own at college, especially his Claude Lorraines, have afforded him many a happy day-dream; they have a ghost in the house – a fallen girl, who perished miserably, and whom he hopes to see, since these things are 'part of the poetical creed'. From 20 Prospect Place, Newington Butts (a house, in fact, with no prospect even of a city that afflicted Southey), he also wrote to Amos at Cambridge;[21] he says that he is not getting on badly at Law, while Amos is amusing himself with Mathematics –and the world is tumbling, a fact which Southey regards with indifference and tranquillity. It says much for the Cottle brothers that Southey, intensely busy and ambitious, was willing to compose good, long letters to them; but it seems that Cottle was no better at writing than when Southey had been in Portugal, and on 6 March Southey sent a grumbling letter[22] pointing out that Cottle had more leisure than he to sit by his fire and write 'huge' missives. Not that he sounds angry; George Dyer (who will recur in our story) is going to introduce him to various London *literati*, and Cottle shall have an account of their faces. Already Southey hated London, and when the letter[23] of 13 March about 'phizzes' arrived it found something wrong with the looks of all these lions – especially Godwin's hateful nose, though the ladies are let off more lightly. Southey asks for copies of *Joan* (and someone has scribbled on the letter in a tiny hand, 'Rob. has sent the books with a civil note'), and broaches the idea of a Chatterton volume to help Mrs Newton; he wants to be remembered to Robert, and wishes that Cottle were within a morning's walk. By now Cottle was bringing out two more of Southey's works, and on 5 April the poet wrote[24] that he was running a race with his London publisher, Cadell, to translate Necker's *Revolution*, Vol. II, from the French, at the rate of sixteen pages a day; despite these claims on Southey's time and proof-reading, Biggs had printed for Cottle the 220-page duodecimo *Poems*, an edition of only 500 copies, which were gratifyingly sold out by July; another edition of 1,000 more was out in the early autumn, and was largely gone by Christmas. Things went similarly with Cottle's edition of *Letters written during a short Residence in Spain and Portugal*, published before 26 April and out of print by November; Southey had put the finishing touches to them on 2 January.

Cottle obliged with a letter on 20 April, and on the evening of the 26th Southey thanked him for the box he had sent to the 'Swan', and composed a letter full of news.[25] From it we also learn a little of Cottle's affairs: he had hurt his hand, he had decided to cease doing business with Hazard, who had told him 'huge lies', and he had written to Herbert Croft. Southey promises that in a dozen years Cottle shall eat potatoes of Southey's digging – apparently a last glance at Pantisocracy – and tells him of his new acquaintances, Thomas Park the versifier and the coarse Flower (of Cambridge).

Joseph Cottle at the age of 49: from the lost miniature by Nathan Branwhite (from University of Bristol Library, Special Collections: from Priscilla Fry's extra-illustrated copy of John Latimer, *Annals of Bristol in the Eighteenth Century*)

There is some genial nonsense about the physiognomical tribunal, of which Cottle will be one of the jury, and which will transport all ugly fellows, in naval vessels, on the evidence of their own faces. Cottle is further flattered by being told that he and Danvers and Burnett are Southey's only correspondents; but he is to remember Southey to William Reid the bookseller, to 'Hurricane' Gilbert, and to the Cottle sisters. This lively letter, with its many intimacies, is a proof of Southey's trust in him; and the only business discussed is the possible splitting of the next edition of the *Letters* into two volumes.

In a succeeding letter the remarks on people's faces continue. We may well wonder whether Southey and Cottle were entitled thus to criticize other men's looks, and what they made of Wordsworth. But Southey, of course, had a striking profile, and Cottle's appearance seems to have been pleasing. He was little and lame, but Nathan Branwhite's 1819 portrait of him shows a fine, though rather querulous, face; big, mild eyes; a high, broad brow; and a weak, cleft chin. During these years he laid the foundation of his valuable collection of portraits – valuable mainly as documents, and a priceless record of the appearance of his great associates. He seems to have commissioned the best portrait painters in Bristol, and all his life he was proud to exhibit Robert Hancock's *Southey* (1796), *Lamb* (1798) and *Wordsworth* (1798); Peter Vandyke's *Coleridge* (1795); and William Palmer's *Henderson* (1786) and – a little masterpiece – *Amos Simon Cottle* (1787), with other portraits by that group of painters and by Branwhite and Miss Eden. Amos has a gentle, sensitive face with well-cut features and a girlish complexion; he wears a green coat with metal buttons, and a frilly white cravat. Palmer's admirable pastel (now in the National Portrait Gallery) has been given deserved fame for quite the wrong reason, by its publication in a cheap collection of good coloured reproductions,[26] where it is ascribed to the great Samuel Palmer, born five years after Amos died!

In May 1797, after a letter of 2 May making fun of Godwin's nose (which Southey longs to cut off) and mentioning that he is about to meet Opie, Southey sent an unflattering account[27] of Opie's bluntness and harsh voice, and of Chatterton's fat biographer, Gregory, a good candidate for the 'phiz' tribunal. Southey and Cottle were now working out their plans for the Chatterton volume, and Cottle wrote to Herbert Croft a letter which Southey praised later in May.[28] Southey was at Gregory's last night, and heard a curious piece of old scandal: the Gregory family had known Charles Wesley's daughter, with whom Southey had once dined at Cottle's; and she had declared that she was to have married John Henderson, only he died prematurely. Southey wants to know if this is true, and Cottle's footnote

a house with two bedrooms, and he invited[45] Cottle to occupy one of them as soon as he could, provided he let them know the time of his arrival, so that Southey could meet him; there would be claret to drink. Plenty of rowing-boats are available, on lovely waters; and he has made friends with Rickman (who afterwards conducted the first census, that of 1800; the second was Poole's). Southey is envious at having missed Kosciusko's visit to Bristol; only to have seen him would be something to talk of ever after. This admiration links Southey with Coleridge's sonnet, Cottle's lines in *War*, and Keats's later sonnet to the hero. Kosciusko had just been staying (from 13 to 19 June) with the American consul at 37 Queen Square; a deputation of citizens waited on him, and gave him plate worth 100 guineas, accompanied by an address, which must have affected him.[46]

Early in July, and just before the 11th (when Southey wrote to John May that Cottle had left[47]), Cottle spent a few days at Christchurch. He brought with him a copy of the handsome second edition of Coleridge's poems, just published, and Southey told May that he knew 'no volume that can be compared to it'. They discussed the Chatterton project; Cottle would be the publisher, would get the paper at prime cost, and would not take the usual profits from the sale; the accounts would be published in full. When they started work, Southey contributed a preface and advice; it may seem strange that it all took until 1803, but the lion's share of the work fell to Cottle, and the years between were busy, worrying, and even tragic, for him. On this holiday, he was introduced to Rickman, whom Southey found 'sensible enough, and blunt enough, and seditious enough; that is simply anti-ministerial'; and Rickman told Cottle a farcical story of a volunteer officers' feast given by Sir George Rose, the local magnate and colonel, of the anti-Jacobin toast and three in a row to Lady Rose, and of a jolly chorus that one officer-poet had composed. Another result of Southey's friendship with Cottle was that Tom Southey's gallant French enemy and rescuer, Captain Boutet of the *Zoe*, was released from imprisonment at Plymouth by the good offices of Birt, a friend of Cottle's.[48]

Amos came to Burton, too, and he and Southey spent many cheerful hours together, panting up the friable cliff, pausing in the cool breeze, and gazing out over the sea – Southey also fell in a bog; they examined the ruined castle of Christchurch together, and saw the great tower of the priory. Cottle was 'very happy', and the Southeys 'were as happy in making him so'.[49] Southey wished, later in the year, that Amos and Joseph, who held almost a brother's place in Southey's heart, might meet again in 'that low abode' where the Southeys spent so many happy months.[50] When Southey visited Bristol in the autumn, he found Amos, on long vacation, engaged on translating the *Edda of Sæmund* for Joseph's benefit; he had started a prose version, but on Southey's advice turned over to verse, and within six weeks the book was half printed. This was a pioneer work, in the mere fact of its presenting remote and pagan Norse poetry to English readers; and, though Southey had borrowed the *Edda* from the Library in 1795, there is every reason to suppose that Amos had taken up the study of his own accord. Not that he tried to become a Norse scholar: he simply translated, without acknowledgement of sources, the Latin version printed parallel with the Icelandic in the 1787 Copenhagen edition. Southey, being a good scholar, disapproved of the haste in rendering it, and wrote to William Taylor, on 4 January 1799, that he would like 'to build up a Runic song'. But he hoped that it would do good, and he at once wrote an interesting poem to Amos, which the latter published along with his translation; Southey recalls the happy times at Burton, and goes on to display his interest in Norse mythology. Amos's own preface of 1 November, intended to be critical, is worthless; but in the actual translation there is some pleasure to be got out of the varied metres. Perhaps less mealy-mouthed than Joseph, he left in a lot of the improper bits – one in Latin, for the benefit of the initiated. The *Edda* was printed in Bristol by Biggs for Joseph, and sold in London by the Robinsons. It came out on about 11 November, and within a month a copy from Joseph was passing through Coleridge's hands on its way to Wordsworth; Coleridge borrowed the Copenhagen edition from the Library and kept it through most of December, and to the end of March 1798.[51] It is even possible that the *Edda* was a powerful influence on *The Ancient Mariner*.[52]

The series of long letters from Southey, written from various addresses between February and July 1797, and so stupidly mutilated and shuffled by Cottle in his *Reminiscences*, is not very attractive, being devoted largely to the technical and financial sides of book-production; but it has some lively humour, considerable tenderness towards Cottle, and provides proof of his equality and familiarity with Danvers and the rest of the group. Thus after the holiday Southey wrote with varied news of Croft's prison sentence, Birt's intercession for the French captain, books read or searched for, and the arrival of his twenty-odd drawings from Lisbon, which Cottle just missed by being in such a hurry to depart; did he return via Corfe Castle?[53] And how is his bad eye? – if he cannot see well enough to reply, let Robert do so instead.

Three of Southey's 1797 letters are among the twenty-six from him, and two from Coleridge, proudly calendared by Cottle in his letter-book now in the Bristol City Library; they range from this year right down to 1836, and

Cottle has numbered them from '17' (with '67' crossed out) to '105', not getting them in quite the right order. This series is now in the Henry W. and Albert A. Berg Collection, in the New York Public Library, and Kenneth Curry has edited fourteen of the best; once the business matter in them has died down, they are a series of some kindness and gaiety, and it is again a great shame that Cottle so abused them when he pressed them into his memoirs. One, dashed off in minutes on a 'Thursday night', apparently at Bath, weaves personal touches in and out of printing instructions and the request to lend Lloyd's poems to Mrs Estlin without telling Lloyd; Cottle is hastily invited to come at the weekend '& make the map', but this is as hastily altered to the following weekend, since Southey remembers a dinner invitation to Bradford-on-Avon; he likes Cottle's elegy on his sister, apart from one false passage, and he can judge of the loss from the remaining sisters, who should render their brother 'in love with life'. Another, also from Bath and after the death of Mary Wollstonecraft Godwin, asks for her book on Norway and Sweden, to help Southey with the poem he is writing for Amos – who, along with Robert, obdurately doesn't come and visit him; and he invites himself and Lloyd over, some time in the next week, arriving early enough for breakfast with the Misses Cottle. Mary Wollstonecraft had died on 10 September, and it is in an October letter that he thanks Cottle for the book; his plan to breakfast in Bristol is renewed, and he will bring the finished epistle himself to Amos 'in the Irish way'.

While the Southeys were at Christchurch, Coleridge told Cottle of his plans to work hard at *Osorio* and, when he had finished it, to walk to Shaftesbury for a few days' stay with the poet Bowles, thence to go on to Salisbury, and thence to Christchurch. But the Southeys left by mid-August, and nothing came of the whole expedition until Coleridge left Stowey for Shaftesbury on 6 September.[54] The visit cannot have been a success. Cottle remembers how Coleridge had praised Berkeley and Hartley and Bowles, 'whose sonnets he delighted in reciting', but the first two dwindled in his regard, and, after the visit to Shaftesbury, he had almost nothing to say of Bowles. Cottle, with no further comment, is therefore recording Coleridge's escape from a not very salutary influence,[55] though Professor Fruman in *Coleridge: the Damaged Archangel* states the case for Bowles's sonnets as worthy exemplars.

This summer Cottle suffered the first attack of a persistent eye-trouble, and was in low health; Wordsworth ('Your affectionate friend') expressed his grief at this, and hopes of recovery, in a pleasant letter[56] of 18 August, marking the renewal of their friendship. Cottle had sent him a 'convenient' two guineas – for what service it is hard to say – and had proposed a draft which Wordsworth might use; luckily, this was unnecessary at the time, but whenever Wordsworth needs any pecuniary help, he will 'take a pleasure in applying'. They are now settled at Alfoxton, and Cottle is always welcome – and any of his friends he chooses. Wordsworth was slow in answering Cottle's reply, with its renewed offer of financial help; but on 13 September he apologized,[57] assured Cottle that he would bear the offer in mind, and then turned affably to personal affairs. He will be in Bristol before three weeks, and will want to talk about books and so forth; but can Cottle come over to Alfoxton *before* that? He hopes Cottle's health is now quite better; Dorothy sends her regards.

Coleridge was also afflicted with Cottle's sickness, and in September wrote[58] asking for news to be sent by Milton the carrier; he tells Cottle that Herbert Croft is now in gaol at Exeter, that Wordsworth is well, and that little Hartley (with another tooth) 'sends a grin'. Could Joseph's brother Robert put on his hat and run to the inn where Parsons's Bath wagon stops in Bristol, and intercept a trunk of Thelwall's addressed to Coleridge at Stowey?

Southey's works were still selling; on 12 September Cottle wrote[59] to Messrs Cadell and Davies in London asking them to deliver to the Robinsons (who are nearly out of the books in question) any unsold copies of *Joan*, the *Letters*, and Fox's *Achmed*, and to pay them the balance due to Cottle. Southey, on the eve of being painfully parodied in the *Anti-Jacobin*, wrote two strangely intense blank-verse poems to Cottle's sister Mary.[60] The first accompanied the gift of *Joan*, and urged her to remember him as he struggled on his way to independence and to the emancipation of mankind, even as he would remember *her*. The second, written on 6 November 1797, longs to be away from insincerity and with her, seated by her fireside; in the evening, when one thinks particularly of old friends, and when he has just given a self-satisfied reading to his latest composition, he wishes she could be present. The world is so different from her! But his visions of 'blessed solitude' and of the foretaste of heavenly joys always conjure up, near their own peaceful home,

> A little Dwelling, whose white lim'd walls
> Look comfort, and I think that it is yours.

To these the scribe of Bodley MS.Engl. misc. c.36 has added a proof that Robert Cottle, too, was versifying, as were his brothers: the 'petition of the Chess King to Charlotte S. (now Mrs Stack) by Robert Cottle Esqr.'.

The old ranks were opening out; the group of lads were now in their early and middle twenties, and their youthful loyalties were receding. When

Coleridge ridiculed Lloyd and Lamb, and even himself, in the 'Nehemiah Higginbottom' sonnets for the November issue of the *Monthly Magazine*, he not only offended Lloyd but even made Southey huffy, thinking that *he* was being burlesqued. Coleridge explained[61] the poems to Cottle, the older man, as intended to help 'our young bards'; but, though Cottle finds them amusing, he suspects that it was Mr Higginbottom who started the quarrel which separated Coleridge from his fellow-anthologists. For all Cottle knew, the two greater men of his circle were thinking principally of their unsaleable tragedies, since a Coleridge letter of November, rather critical of Southey's lines to Amos, and one from Wordsworth on 13 December, gave him news of their failures with the London promoters; he could not know that *The Ancient Mariner* had already been planned, in November weather, Dorothy trudging by their side. Coleridge was in Cottle's shop on the evening of Saturday, 2 December, and sent Poole kind regards from Estlin and Cottle and Wade;[62] on 6 December Cottle gave him a nice red notebook, which became 'my Cottle Book' and Notebook No. 21 in the British Museum set. Professor Kathleen Coburn, in fact, sees it as a desk-book for entries directly bearing on projected works, as if Cottle were impelling him to industry.[63] Wordsworth warned[64] Cottle from London that he and his sister would be in Bristol on the night of Friday, 15 December, presumably to put up at Cottle's. He takes this opportunity to thank Cottle for a copy of Amos's *Edda*, though he is sorry about the inaccuracies! To complete this little round of reunions in Bristol, Southey was in the city until he returned to London, whence he wrote[65] on 14 December to thank Cottle for a parcel. He has been working on *Joan*, and has borrowed some fine old books for it from Dr Williams's Library in Redcross Street; he tells Cottle of a plan for a 'Convalescent Asylum' wherein poor persons discharged from hospitals could get thoroughly well again – Dr Beddoes is to be consulted about it. But he was perhaps not feeling very satisfied with the progress of the new *Joan*; he wrote[66] to his brother Tom on 24 December that it was 'scandalously delayed at Bristol. I have had only five proofs in all'. This was the second edition of two little duodecimos, published in July 1798, an anti-climax after Cottle's splendid quarto of 1796.

In addition to sending Southey parcels of 'treasures',[67] Cottle was useful in other and subtler transactions; when old Mrs Southey became confused and distressed over relinquishing her house in Bath, her son wrote to Cottle begging him to go over and manage the affair, which included paying off debts by the sale of the furniture.[68]

1   CCS, I.272.

2   R.47, p.106.

3   Griggs, I.217, No.128.

4   Griggs, I.222-226, No.134, and I.226-227, No.135.

5   Bodl.MS.Engl.Letters, c.22.

6   E.V. Lucas ed., *The Letters of Charles Lamb* (London: Dent and Methuen, 1935), I.15-16.

7   R.47, pp.144-147; and Meyerstein, *op.cit.*, p.491.

8   R.47, pp.138-139.

9   E.V. Lucas, *op.cit.*, I.39 ff. Cottle (in ER.37, I.245) says that the friend was Charles Lloyd.

10   R.47, pp.43-46.

11   R.47, pp.106-107.

12   1795 *Album*; Griggs, VI.1005-1007, No.145.

13   Another note, speaking of the 'very devil' that grips him, but including business-like directions, is in the 1795 *Album*; Griggs, VI.1007, No.148.

14   Griggs, I.248-249, No.150.

15   Griggs, I.269-276, Nos.162, 163.

16   Mrs Henry Sandford, *op.cit.*, I.194.

17   See *The Rise, Progress & Military Improvement of the Bristol Volunteers* ..., ed. James Brown (Bristol: W. Matthews, 1798; reprinted 1916).

18   *Dictionary of National Biography*, Vol.XX (1889), pp.91-92; and ER.37, II.26-27.

19   R.47, pp.199-200.

20   R.47, pp.201-202.

21   R.47, pp.200-201.

22   R.47, p.202.

23   Bristol City Library MS.B 20877; printed in part in CCS, and mauled by Cottle in R.47, pp.203-204.

24   CCS, I.307n.

25   L.N. Broughton, *Some Letters of the Wordsworth Family, Now First Published* (Ithaca, N.Y.: Cornell U.P., 1942), p.114.

26   W. Léon Soldes, ed., *Masterpieces of British Art* (London: Foyle, 1940).

27   CCS, I.306; and R.47, pp.211-212. But Cottle's editing of this group of Southey's letters, written in the spring and summer of 1797, is worthless; the survivors of the series are presented in Curry, I.125-127, 127-129, 129-131, 131-132, 138-140, dated 2 May, 4 May, May, 26 May, 28 July.

28   R.47, pp.212-213.

29   Griggs, I.296-300, No.172; the letter is mostly printing instructions. Cottle made three of it, and added a postscript.

30   Letters wrongly dated 1796 in R.47, pp.100-101 and 107-108.

31   Griggs, I.309, Nos.177, 178.

32   Griggs, I.312-314, No.180.

33   This last remark is the one personal touch in a letter of 15 March 1797 (Griggs, I.315-316, No.181).

34   Cottle's conceited memoirs of this poem occupy pp.118-126 of R.47.

35   Griggs, VI.1007-1009, No.184; Cottle (in R.47, pp.102-103) not only garbles and falsifies, but puts the letter in 1796.

36   Griggs, I.190, No.110.

37   Letter published piecemeal in R.47, pp.117 and 136-137; and complete in Griggs, I.324, No.188. In E.L. Griggs, *Unpublished Letters of Samuel Taylor Coleridge* (London: Constable, 1932), it was unfortunately headed 'JOSIAH COTTLE', with Amos glossed as 'bookseller and author'.

38   R.47, pp.133 ff.

39   Griggs, I.325, No.190; and haphazardly in R.47, pp.142-143. Racedown (in Dorset) was where Wordsworth was then living.

40   Griggs, I.328-329, No.193.

41   Griggs, I.330-332, No.195.

42   R.47, pp.149-151.

43   Catherine M. Maclean, in *Dorothy Wordsworth: The Early Years* (London: Chatto and Windus, 1932), p.53, quotes this as evidence of the bliss of that dawn, but seems wrongly to associate Wordsworth and his sister with the party, adding the comment that their acquaintances sensed their new happiness, 'even though its sources were not understood'.

44   R.47, p.213; and CCS, I.313.

45   R.47, pp.214-215.

46   FFJ, Vol.XLVIII, No.2520, 24 June 1797.

47   CCS, I.318-320.

48   Curry, I.133n.

49   Curry, I.136.

50   Southey versified this holiday in lines to Amos affixed to Amos's *Edda*.

51   MH.4, II.260 ff.; Whalley, *op.cit.*, p.125; H.G. Wright, 'Southey's Relations with Finland and Scandinavia', *Modern Language Review* XXVII (1932), pp.149-150.

52   Coburn, I.Notes, item 170.

53   Curry, I.138. Corfe Castle is in Dorset (above the Isle of Purbeck).

54   L. Hanson, in *The Life of S.T. Coleridge: The Early Years* (London: Allen and Unwin, 1938), p.469, note 33, forgets this delay, and dates Coleridge's letter to Cottle, about his plans, in September.

55   R.47, pp.21, 133.

56   Shaver, I.191-192, No.73.

57 Shaver, I.192, No.74.

58 *R.47*, pp.144-148. But Croft was abroad in 1797, and in prison in 1795; here, again, Cottle has been 'editing'.

59 Bodl.MS.Montague d.4, fol.120.

60 Bodl.MS.Engl.misc., c.36, fol.27; copy of first in *1795 Album*, dated 1796.

61 Griggs, I.356-358, No.212.

62 Griggs, I.358, No.213.

63 Coburn. I.Notes, xli.

64 Shaver, I.196, No 79.

65 *R.47*, pp.215-216.

66 CCS, I.327.

67 Curry, I.144.

68 Curry, I.154-155.

Chapter 5

Annus Mirabilis: Davy

1798, which would be an Annus Mirabilis for some, was for Cottle a period of declining fortunes in his chosen career. He was proud, and remained proud, of the daring publication which has made his name remembered, *Lyrical Ballads*, but financially even this was a losing venture, and the time was approaching when he would have very few guineas to bestow on genius. He entered into partnership with Biggs, which at least pleased Southey, since Biggs was his printer and there was no man alive 'of simpler and purer heart, or of more real benevolence', than Cottle;[1] and this, says Southey, was Cottle's motive for selling *Joan* to Longman, 'as wanting ready money to enter the printing business'.[2] As yet, the ruin that had attended his father was not importunate, and waited until the close of the century, when illness and much bereavement sprang out on him also; meanwhile, Coleridge's great year gave Cottle one sparkling summer holiday for which the world may be grateful. He used the Library only until June; and this fact, coupled with the departure of Wordsworth and Coleridge for Germany in September, does admittedly lend weight to the idea that he borrowed on their behalf. At all events, he had borrowed some of the volumes before:

12 Jan. – 2 Feb.	Rousseau, *Confessions*, Vol. I
15 Jan. – 19 Feb.	Middleton, *Life of Cicero,* Vol. II. (From 8 to 15 Jan., Coleridge had Vol. I 'out')

(Whalley[3] affirms that Cottle at the same time made the first entry for Mrs Lovell (widowed since May 1796), borrowing Cartwright's *Journal*, Vols. II & III. I am sure that this is not his handwriting. Nor is this the first entry for her; on 18 December 1797 the same hand writes 'Mrs Lovell' for Vol. I of the *Journal*.)

2 Feb. – 26 Feb.	Rousseau, *Confessions*, Vol. II
21 Feb. – 9 Mar.	Middleton, *Life of Cicero*, Vol. III
12 Mar. – 19 Mar.	Shirley, *Plays*, Vol. I

19 Mar. – 20 Mar.	*ditto*, Vol. II
20 Mar. – 27 Mar.	*Philosophical Transactions*, Vol. 86, Part I
20 Mar. – 29 Mar.	*ditto*, Vol. 86, Part II
27 Mar. – 29 Mar.	*Origins of Laws, Arts and Sciences*, Vol. I
30 Mar. – 3 Apr.	*Philosophical Transactions* (?Vol.), Part I (Coleridge borrowed Vol. 75 on 23 April 1798)
11 May – 18 May.	Blair, *Lectures*, Vol. II
1 June – 14 June.	Strutt, *View* ... Vols. I & II
6 June – 14 June.	Strutt, *Chronicle of England*

His own *Malvern Hills* was published this year, and, with various increases in size and with new companion pieces, proved his most popular volume, running to four editions by 1829. The *Gentleman's Magazine*[4] found the chief poem 'a vehicle for many sentiments favourable to the poor' and thought it strange that Dr Booker had written one on the same subject, which they reviewed in the preceding article. But, for the time being, the letters of Cottle's friends make no mention of the book. Southey, through staying in Bristol and then wandering in search of health, seems to have written very little; and Cottle is almost silent about him. He temporarily fades from our story after 19 January 1798, when he wrote[5] a letter to Cottle (the last part of which survives) on the back margins of a proof sheet of the Argument to *Joan*, with Southey's corrections for the second edition. As befits such a setting, the letter is a business-like affair, though he congratulates Cottle on some news (perhaps of a complete recovery). He thinks the Wordsworths have been 'very unhandsome' to Lloyd, displaying a 'mean and overbearing ... act of vanity'. Since Cottle has said nothing of the printer Rose and the second volume, Southey reminds him that he wants it begun by another printer, if only 'to let Biggs know that I think he behaved very ill to us'. He also gives Cottle his plans for various works, and a list of the books he has reviewed.

The early part of the year was dominated by the worry of getting Coleridge settled. On 5 and 6 January Coleridge wrote to Wade, Estlin, and Cottle, explaining why he had refused the Wedgwoods' offer of £100 to save him from taking a Unitarian pulpit at Shrewsbury (by which action, only Estlin could be really pleased). He reached Shrewsbury on 13 January, and the Wedgwoods' compelling offer of £150 a year started out from Penzance on the 10th and chased him through Stowey to Shrewsbury and on to Wem. This time there could be no refusing; but, while the matter was still in the balance, Cottle wrote to him hoping that the rumours of a rejection of this liberality were unfounded. This letter was prompted not by Cottle's common-sense alone; it will be remembered that he detested 'the doctrines of Socinus'. Coleridge cheerfully reassured him in a letter of 24 January,[6] adding that he hoped to see Cottle at the end of the next week. John Rowe, the Unitarian minister, delivered it by hand; by 30 January Coleridge had reached Cottle's shop in High Street,[7] where he wrote to Thelwall.[8]

But there were still monetary troubles. He wrote to Cottle on 18 February[9] with plans for further publications; he has finished his ballad of 340 lines (*Christabel*, Part I?), his *Visions* are progressing, and two fragments from his tragedy will make up a total of 1,500 lines. Shall he add his tragedy, so making a second volume, or insert 1,500 more lines in the third edition? And, if Cottle advises a second volume, would he also 'wish – i.e. find it convenient – to be the purchaser?' He wants Cottle to understand his financial situation: the Wedgwoods have done nothing yet, he cannot borrow again from Poole or Estlin, and he owes £5 to Biggs the printer and another £5 to old Mrs Fricker for the last quarter. This dismal letter begins on a note of cross humour: could Cottle write '*one* line at least' when he sends a parcel? – because Coleridge always has to 'pay like damnation'. Cottle's footnote in his 1837 *Recollections*[10] adds, 'It is hardly necessary to say, this £10 I immediately paid for Mr C'. Coleridge expressed his gratitude in a letter of 8 March;[11] he will repay in a few weeks with money or verses, just as Cottle wishes. The letter was probably written in a mood of dejection; one of his rotten teeth, which caused him so many years of pain, had brought him to bed with a fever, and he has lost sleep because 'dear Mr Estlin' has not written to him. Cottle can do what he likes with Lloyd's poems, provided they are not republished with Coleridge's! 'The Giant Wordsworth – God love him!' – has written 1,200 marvellous blank-verse lines, which Poole greatly admires. As for his own plans, he is going to lengthen *Religious Musings*, 'and I should think it would answer to you in a pecuniary way to print the third Edition *humbly* and cheaply'. Cottle must have been advertising Poole's house, since he is now asked to do nothing further about it.

But Cottle had worries of his own. On 14 March 1798 the elder Robert Cottle, no doubt exhausted by unsuccessful tailoring, was appointed Master Corn-Measurer to the City of Bristol.[12] On 7 March, Joseph moved to a house last inhabited by Wade, in Wine Street; Southey, staying above in Kingsdown near the 'Montague', adds that 'In consequence of this revolution he gives up the house in the Barton'. And in *Felix Farley's Journal* for 24 March Joseph suddenly announces the penumbra of his own financial eclipse; he thanks his friends and the public for their past favours, and says that he has moved from the corner of High Street to a commodious shop,

No. 5 Wine Street, formerly Mackinder's, where orders will be dealt with, etc. He had thus exchanged a commanding corner site for an unobtrusive position – though the new shop was larger – in a packed street (now utterly destroyed by war). Thirty-five years later, in a letter to Quillinan,[13] Wordsworth recalled the move as disastrous, and used it to qualify Rogers's kindness to Moxon: '… but I remember with some apprehension that when my good friend 'Joseph of Bristol, the brother of Amos' went from just such a pigmy shop as Moxon's late one the change did not prove advantageous, an instance that Ambition in small matters as well as great is apt to play false with her Votaries'. Cottle's benefactions were dwindling too. In *Felix Farley* for 3 March, under a huge list of Bristol Voluntary Subscriptions to the Bank of England for the defence of the country, his one guinea is among the smallest of the twenty-two gifts from All Saints' Parish, gifts which include sums like twenty guineas 'for the duration'; on the other hand, in the next issue his sister Mary gives a guinea under St Paul's Parish – and, indeed, her school saved the situation for him when ruin came. Besides his own works and those of Southey, Coleridge, Wordsworth, Lamb, Lloyd, Charles Fox and Amos, he had published, before the end of his short career, sermons by the Unitarians Jardine and Estlin, and a medical lecture by Dr Beddoes, the father of the poet. His advertisements in *Felix Farley* are by now few and unimpressive: he is selling, on 30 June, J. Bicheno, *A Glance at the History of Christianity and of English Nonconformity*; on 27 October, R.K. Hutcheson's book on excise laws; and on 17 November, tickets for the anatomy lectures of Messrs Bowles and Smith. He also ran a little agency by which, for example, on 8 September, anyone with an estate for sale in Gloucestershire or Wiltshire should direct to A.B., care of his shop.

Late in March, Coleridge wrote[14] with alternative plans for the third edition, and expressing utter indifference over what happened to Lloyd's poems. If the edition is wanted immediately, it must merely be rearranged, with the juvenilia at the end; but if it can wait ten weeks, Coleridge will make it worthy of himself and cast out half of it 'to pitch black Oblivion'. Cottle primly observes that you can't do things like this if you are an influential author; the public have seized the bad with the good, and it can never be completely withdrawn. 'So much the more is circumspection required'. Whichever Cottle chooses, Coleridge will repay him his money, in money, in a few weeks; or, if the press *can* wait ten weeks, let Coleridge pay for the additions, however big, to make up for the omissions. Now Wordsworth has asked him to put two questions to Cottle. What could he and would he 'conveniently and prudently' give them for their two tragedies – 6,000 lines of print in all, with brief prefaces? They would be delivered within a week of Cottle's answer, and he would pay them at the end of four months. Again, what about a volume made up of *Salisbury Plain*, the *Tale of a Woman*, a few other pieces by Wordsworth, and notes? This could arrive three weeks after Cottle accepted it, and, as before, he would pay after four months. Coleridge finally begs Cottle not to be rashly generous from any illusions about the poems. Dorothy added a note[15] to her guest's letter, wishing that Cottle 'were of the party', promising to send *Malvern Hills*, a greatcoat, and a waistcoat, and thanking him for some books – presumably the *Zoönomia*, which had been borrowed from Mr Pinney. Then the two would-be playwrights waited; Cottle offered them thirty guineas each, which they stupidly refused through hopes of having the stuff staged. The volume of poems was left for the time being.

A little after this proposal, in answer to a letter from Cottle, Coleridge wrote graciously,[16] absolving him from almost all blame for the trouble with Lloyd and Lamb: 'I never involved *you* in the bickering – and never suspected you, in any one action of your life (except that of *"our poems"*) of practising guile against any human being except yourself'. Cottle's letter had supplied a link of information; and Coleridge would be writing to Lloyd that day. (But Cottle, in fact, emerges mysteriously guilty from this affair; when Lamb dedicated his Works to Coleridge in 1818, he suggested that 'some ungracious bookseller' had caused the rift – which may help to explain his later ill-treatment of Cottle.) Cottle had apparently invited Coleridge to come to Dr Beddoes's chemical lectures at the Red Lodge, but Sara is a month off her confinement (Berkeley was born on 14 May), and he cannot leave her. At present he is at Alfoxton; 'and my new and tender health is all over me like a voluptuous feeling'. Coleridge's next letter[17] is a wordy affair, with some signs of duplicity. Both Wordsworth and he would have felt uncomfortable if anyone but Cottle had been given the first offer of the tragedies and the poems; but they realised, at the time, that he would not be able to advance the sum they needed. And now they do not want them published; it would be a shame to throw away 'for a mere trifle' the chance of staging them; after all, Coleridge strained all his 'thoughts and faculties for six or seven months' and Wordsworth put more of everything into *his*. What they had in mind was the acquisition of the whole sum immediately (there is no mention here of the four months' grace), but now they have decided to get the money some other way. The offer of the poems is still open, and the money can be handed over in the last fortnight of July. Of course, Cottle ('dear fellow!') must consider himself only, must think as a bookseller, must remember that they need money to go to Germany, but are able to scrap the whole plan. In any case, Wordsworth could sell the poems to someone else, or they could raise the money without selling them … So Coleridge entreats Cottle, 'again and again, in your answer, which must be immediate, consider yourself only'. (It is hard to determine whether Cottle accepted this invitation to selfish materialism; whatever his motives, the outcome was the *Lyrical Ballads* – perhaps he considered posterity as well.) Coleridge tells Cottle of the trouble Wordsworth has had at Alfoxton; he hopes that, with Poole's help, a house can be found at Stowey – 'for the hills, and the woods, and the streams, and the sea, and the shores, would break forth into reproaches against us, if we did not strain every nerve, to keep their Poet among them'. And, as the agreement expires before Midsummer, Cottle must come down before then … 'and we will procure a horse easy as thy own soul, and we will go on a roam to Linton and Linmouth, which, if thou comest in May, will be in all their pride of woods and waterfalls, not to speak of its august cliffs, and the green ocean, and the vast Valley of Stones, all which live disdainful of the seasons, or accept new honours only from the winter's snow'.

Before this invitation could be accepted, there was a slight estrangement. In April, Cottle seemed almost to throw in his lot with the intriguers, and did a very tactless thing: he published Lloyd's novel, *Edmund Oliver*. Written by Lloyd, published by Cottle, dedicated to Lamb, its title projected by Southey,[18] and its narrative devoted to heavy gibes at Coleridge's lady-loves, sloth, cavalry career, and opium-taking, it involved all four men in Coleridge's resentment. As Lloyd spread his mischief further, by repeating what Coleridge had said in confidence of Southey and Lamb, these two became further alienated; and Lamb sorely wounded Coleridge by his ebullient letter of bitter wit, headed 'THESES QUAEDAM THEOLOGICAE', which Coleridge gave to Cottle with the remark, 'These young visionaries will do each other no good'. Cottle (the hero of the narrative as he tells it[19]) assured him that Lamb's feelings 'would soon subside' – as they did; and, concerned by Coleridge's loss of Lloyd as a lodger, he wrote Lloyd 'a conciliatory letter'. These altercations had apparently limped through April and May, for it was not until 7 June that Lloyd wrote to Cottle from Birmingham, thanking him for his 'pleasing intelligence respecting Coleridge', exonerating himself from all blame, and promising to write to Coleridge that very day; 'I love Coleridge, and can forget all that has happened'. Cottle had obviously tried to induce him to move back to Stowey; but he says he cannot leave his parents so suddenly. He mentions, too, that Lamb has just left after a fortnight's holiday, and Lloyd has 'been much interested in his society'; the letter makes it clear that Coleridge is his idol no more.

It was high time that Wordsworth fully availed himself of Cottle's services. Up to now, Cottle had helped with reading-matter, since Racedown and Alfoxton were bookless regions. This was Wordsworth's source of periodicals; for instance, he can write to James Losh on 11 March[20] to say that he has not yet seen any numbers of *The Economist*, though he had asked Cottle to transmit them. On 12 April, however, Wordsworth addressed to Cottle a very friendly but very unpoetical remark:[21] 'I have gone on very rapidly adding to my stock of poetry. Do come and let me read it to you, under the old trees in the park'. They were not staying much longer, and the country was at its loveliest. On 28 February or 7 March, in a letter headed 'Wed. morn.' and wrongly dated 1797 by de Selincourt,[22] Wordsworth thanks him for a £10 note, and says they will ask for more if they want it; could Cottle get Erasmus Darwin's *Zoönomia* (he writes *Zonoomia*) for him at once? – if he cannot borrow it, could he ask the Wedgwoods at Cote House (in Westbury-on-Trym) for it, for ten days?[23] Wordsworth was determined to get Cottle down to Alfoxton, and wrote again on 9 May,[24] urging him to come, and bring one of his sisters, and stay a week or more. Wordsworth will not say anything about *Salisbury Plain* until they meet; he had another plan, but that must await the same event. He thanks Cottle for Lloyd's works, three volumes of Massinger, and £13.6s.6d; with the Darwin, they are returning the poems, which they have enjoyed, but only Dorothy has read the novel, and with mixed feelings. They had meant to send Lloyd's poems, but the volume is at Stowey; could Cottle send all the numbers of *The Economist* as soon as possible?

Being thus pressed by both the poets, Cottle spent a week's holiday at Alfoxton in May. In his *Reminiscences*,[25] he absurdly makes two holidays out of it, but the facts can be sorted out. Wordsworth was in Bristol, and asked him to come down at once; since Cottle 'drove him down in a gig', the invitation was not without its advantages for Wordsworth. At Nether Stowey they called for Coleridge, Dorothy, and Betty the servant, who all went on to Alfoxton, while Wordsworth apparently stayed put. They proposed to dine at the house, on simple 'philosophers' viands': brandy, a loaf, a large piece of cheese, and lettuces from the garden. On the road, however, they gave some money to a sturdy beggar, who rewarded them by stealing the cheese as they gazed at the cloudscape – or so they presumed when they found it missing. As they entered the courtyard, Coleridge pointed out that no-one need starve with bread and brandy; but, as he unbuckled the horse and jerked the shafts down, the bottle rolled from behind them on the seat and was dashed to pieces on the stones – there was nothing to reward them save the aroma. While the rest stood miserably around, Cottle led the horse into the stable, removed the harness, and tried to get the collar off; failing, he called for help, and Wordsworth did no better; Coleridge, the acknowledged expert, nearly strangled the horse, and said it must have developed gout or dropsy after the collar had been put on. At that, Betty came up, and with a 'La, Master!' turned the collar upside-down and slipped it off at once.

The dinner table thus had an admirable brown loaf at the top, a dish piled with cos lettuces in the centre, and an empty plate at the other end; they drank 'fine sparkling Castalian champagne' – Cottle, who later advocated temperance and cold water, should surely have been gratified. Someone asked for salt to make the lettuce more palatable, but Betty had quite forgotten to buy it, and they all just laughed, including Wordsworth their host. Dinner continued in the greatest good humour, but for the next meal they resorted to the village a mile away.

Thereafter, part of the holiday was occupied with reading poems in manuscript; it was decided that the joint volume should be called *Lyrical Ballads*, that the bulk of it should be made up of short and recent poems, and that *Peter Bell* and most of *Salisbury Plain* should not appear in it. Cottle had wanted two volumes, but they were determined on one, to be published anonymously. They took him, as promised, to the wildly beautiful region which had engendered so much of their best poetry – Lynton and Lynmouth and the Valley of Rocks; unfortunately, at this point Cottle repents of having said so much about the Tintern trip, and says he must not digress again. He returned to Bristol on Wednesday, 30 May,[26] clutching his greatest prize, *The Ancient Mariner*, which would let the printer make a start; he perhaps just missed Hazlitt, another visitor, but a Coleridge letter[27] pursued him closely, and showed that business was the aftermath of pleasure. The day after Cottle left, Coleridge walked over to Lynton again, and returned on the Saturday; now he has proposals to make, which he will argue with Cottle when he sees him 'in a week or two'. After discussion with Coleridge, Wordsworth does not object to the publication of *Peter Bell* or *Salisbury Plain* singly, but he will emphatically not have his poems brought out in two volumes. Coleridge feels that his own tragedy is a poor thing compared with Shakespeare's or Wordsworth's, but 'it rises' when compared with other contemporary ones; so he will reconstruct it. He is against dedication to the Wedgwoods (which Cottle perhaps recommended); and he thinks that Cottle is wrong in opposing anonymity: 'Wordsworth's name is nothing – to a large number of persons mine *stinks*'. So let Cottle get on with *The Ancient Mariner*. Hancock the artist was then at Stowey, and had drawn Wordsworth; Coleridge promises Cottle that the picture will be sent – and it became one of his treasures. They thank him for 'love-gifts and book-loans'; *Joan* is so beautifully produced, and opens so 'lovelily', that Coleridge hopes that Cottle will print a few of their own poems in such format. If only he had time, Coleridge would write him an Essay on the Metaphysics of Typography, but he can only give some practical hints here, on the number of lines, the ink, the wide margins: 'That is *beauty* – it may even under your immediate care mingle the sublime!'

Before Wordsworth leaves Alfoxton on 25 June, it will be apt to discuss the one mark which Bristol left on his poetry. At Alfoxton, some time in 1798, he wrote a harrowing poem of 100 lines, beginning 'Her eyes are wild, her head is bare'; and it was published in the same year. At first the title was *The Mad Mother*, but in the 1815 and subsequent editions it was identified by its four opening words. The Fenwick note simply says, 'The subject was reported to me by a Lady of Bristol who had seen the poor creature', and no-one has identified the subject further. But I have a feeling that it is Louisa, the Maid of the Haystack, who (like William Gilbert) lived for a time in the elder Henderson's asylum at Hanham. Her story, outlined in Latimer's *Annals of Bristol*,[28] is as strange and romantic as that of Wordsworth's heroine.

In 1776 a girl, young, pretty and well-mannered, but obviously crack-brained, entered a house at Flax Bourton near Bristol and asked for some milk. She then wandered about the fields, slept for four nights under a haystack, and decorated the nearby hedge with trinkets. Some good ladies of the district fed her, and tried to induce her to occupy a bed in one of their houses; but she would not sleep inside four walls, and it is pleasant to find that the ladies, respecting her independence, clubbed together and bought her the haystack! She became sillier, and was removed to St Peter's Hospital, Bristol;[29] but they were unable to hold her, and she returned to her haystack for four years. The neighbouring gentry kept her in food, and she acquired the name of Louisa, or 'The Maid of the Haystack'. Hannah More took her up in 1781, and had her removed to the Henderson Asylum at Hanham. The circulation of Hannah More's *A Tale of Real Woe* in the *St James's Chronicle* led to a spate of continental pamphlets (it was translated into French and German), and especially to G.H. Glasse's *A Narrative of Facts... translated from the French* (London, 1785). These sensational writings asserted that she was a natural daughter of the Emperor Francis I, and a half-sister of the Queen of France, and that she had kept up a princely establishment at Bordeaux. She was probably a gipsy.

She had a Queen Anne half-crown sewn on a black ribbon, which she wore on her arm and kissed, saying it was like mama. Her story eventually was that her father had confined her in a Schleswig convent for not marrying the man of his choice, and she escaped with her lover. She also said that her father's country was Bohemia, and that he had a carriage drawn by eight horses. Certainly, a young man from abroad visited her at the asylum; he gave her one look, she screamed, and he sprang horrified into his carriage. The 'Mdlle.la Frëulein' (sic) of *L'Inconnue: Histoire Véritable* was finally abandoned at Quiévraing near Mons in 1769,[30] which would then involve seven lost years if she were Louisa.

Being friendly with Henderson, John Wesley thrice visited her at Hanham between 1782 and 1785, and found that she seemed to know German.[31] Horace Walpole wrote to Miss Hamilton on 7 October 1783, to ask how he could help Louisa, and whether they could discover her religion.[32] Hannah More's humble friend Cottle knew Henderson, of course, through having been at his school; he is bound to have heard of Louisa before 1798, and he (as well as the 'Lady of Bristol') may have mentioned her to Wordsworth. Certainly he owned a portrait of her, executed in 1786, an oval twelve inches by nine, by the same William Palmer who drew the pictures of young Henderson and Amos in Cottle's collection.[33] Another of Cottle's friends, Ann Yearsley the milk-woman, wrote pityingly about her in her poem *Clifton Hill* (lines 205-301);[34] in her tour, Mrs Yearsley reaches the actual haystack, and discourses on the inconveniences of wind and lightning, and on the girl's madness and dishevelled mien. As for Hannah More, the poor girl was much in her thoughts; in 1782 she twice wrote[35] to her sisters from Hampton on the subjects of subscriptions and pamphlets in Louisa's interest. She believed all the grandiose claims, and kept Louisa until the latter's death in 1800.

Even if Hannah More be not the 'Lady of Bristol' in the Fenwick note, one of Cottle's sisters (whom the Wordsworths knew) could have supplied the information. Wordsworth keeps the girl mad, gypsyish in colouring, and 'underneath the haystack warm', and of provenance 'far from over the main'; but, in addition, she has a baby, which becomes the theme of her addled song. If Wordsworth's piece is really indebted to the Scots Ballad, *Lady Anne Bothwell's Lament*, we can see further why the poet strayed somewhat from his actual human subject. It is perhaps not surprising that he did not quote her name; his *Louisa* (of which his sister is the subject) is three years later than our poem, but the name may already have been in use as a pseudonym for Dorothy. In the late autumn of 1836, Wordsworth, replying to John Kenyon, wrote[36] that it must be left quite clear in the poem that, though she was from afar, English was her native tongue; Kenyon had objected that 'It was in the English tongue' was superfluous.

Thus, at Midsummer, 1798, Wordsworth and his sister set out for Bristol with *Lyrical Ballads* and the haziest plans. After a week with Coleridge they

William Wordsworth: lithograph from a drawing by Robert Hancock, 1798
(reproduced from *Early Recollections* 1837)

proceeded on foot and arrived at Cottle's on 2 July; they put up there, whence Wordsworth could all the more conveniently 'superintend the printing' of the poems. But they had no intention of staying in the city; when Dorothy wrote to Mrs Rawson next day, 'in a front room in one of the most busy streets of Bristol', she expressed (not very gratefully) her hatred of the noise and of cities in general.[37] So as to be in the same village as James Losh[38] (with whom Wordsworth and Amos Cottle had supped on 12 June[39]), they took lodgings in Shirehampton lower down the Avon, a place which she describes as 'beautiful'. But they had crossed the Bristol Channel before the week was out. Their four-day tour (with nights at Tintern, Goodrich, and again Tintern) ended as they entered Bristol at evening, Wordsworth still composing the immortal *Lines written a few miles above Tintern Abbey*; tradition says that the poem was completed in his head as they walked down Park Street towards Cottle's shop, and this would be the end of their route from the Aust Ferry and over the Downs. Back in Cottle's parlour, Wordsworth at last wrote the *Lines*, and they were ready for publication in *Lyrical Ballads*. The Wordsworths stayed in Bristol for some weeks. It was at this period that Cottle let James Tobin, brother of John Tobin the dramatist, have a peep at *We are Seven*, with its first line remembering him as 'dear brother Jem'; whereat Tobin earnestly (and in vain) implored Wordsworth to suppress the whole poem, as the Fenwick note amusingly tells us.

Coleridge came down to work out the arrangements for their German tour; on 3 August he wrote to Poole, enclosing the 'best love' of the Wordsworths, Wade, and Cottle. But Cottle, on the eve of his greatest undertaking, had begun to lose heart and to meditate his retirement from the publishing trade. Before 14 July, when Southey wrote rather grumblingly to his brother Henry, Cottle transferred to Thomas Norton Longman, for £370, the second edition of *Joan* and Southey's 1797 *Poems*; as Simmons points out,[40] 'he was simply disposing of his assets in the ordinary way', and this must be borne in mind when we come to consider his behaviour over *Lyrical Ballads*.

Southey, despite his happiness at 'Martin Hall', his converted ale-house out at Westbury-on-Trym, where he settled in the summer of 1796 (his books arriving from Cottle's in July[41]), started his wanderings again, through Herefordshire and later through South Wales, in August. He visited Cottle on Tuesday, 21 August,[42] and he also wrote to him from Hereford,[43] with sumptuous plans for poems leading up to the destruction of Domdaniel, and with an invitation for Cottle to come by the daily Welsh mail-coach to Ross, where Southey would meet him, and then they could go to Goodrich,

Monmouth, and Raglan, and perhaps revisit Tintern; Cottle must just let him know the day. But there is no record that this holiday ever took place; Cottle's time and crippled strength must have been fully occupied in 1798.

As for Coleridge and the Wordsworths, they had flown. By various vehicles they left Bristol, visited Blenheim and Oxford, and so reached London on 27 August, never returning to Bristol for long. Next day Wordsworth wrote Cottle a letter[44] asking for all sorts of help; their box has not come, or any letter from Cottle about its dispatch; they have forgotten the letter of introduction to Longman, and Wordsworth has omitted to mention a draft for £23, which has not been accepted – what should he do about it? Can Cottle help him to sell two expensive Gilpin's *Tours*? And can he write about the boxes *and* to Longman on the same sheet, thereby saving Wordsworth double postage? ... It is all hardly a cordial farewell.

On 16 September they all sailed for Germany. Dorothy had written (to an unknown correspondent[45]) on the 13th that the poems were 'printed, but not published ... Cottle has given thirty guineas for William's share of the volume'. If we may start with the traditional story (which has been seriously challenged from 1938 onwards), it may be said that the momentous book was printed and published in Bristol, on or about 1 and 14 September respectively, in an impression of 500 copies, with the title-page: 'LYRICAL BALLADS,/WITH/A FEW OTHER POEMS./ BRISTOL:/ PRINTED BY BIGGS AND COTTLE,/ FOR T.N. LONGMAN, PATERNOSTER-ROW, LONDON./ 1798'. Of this first form, with the Bristol imprint, the slippery Wise[46] claimed to identify only six survivors, calling it 'an elusive rarity, to be dreamed about but seldom possessed', and quoting Swinburne: '... the black tulip of that sort of literature ... I do break the tenth commandment into shivers when I think of that book!' And so, until 1938 (when Professor R.W. Daniel[47] began the final process of robbing Cottle of the credit), the *Lyrical Ballads* was held to be of Cottle's publication, and quite his greatest achievement; yet he does not even figure as the publisher on the title-page. Whence this reticence? Harper[48] offers a choice of two explanations, and obviously prefers the second. Either Cottle was loyally helping the two poets to preserve their anonymity, which would have been compromised if their known friend's name had appeared; or (a murkier motive) he did not wish to suffer by the ill-repute of the two, whereas he could publish for the immaculate Southey openly and with confidence. The next chapter of this disappointing story is even sadder: within a fortnight, and probably as early as 17 September, he sold off the bulk of the impression to Messrs J. & A. Arch of Gracechurch St, London – all 500, apart from the few that had been distributed (his recent detractors are not willing to concede that any had been *sold* or even offered for sale). We have already seen that his retirement was looming, and that even with Southey's works he was 'disposing of his assets', yet the haste seems indecent. His own excuse for it[49] is not even plausible; he says that the sale was slow, 'most of the reviews' were severe, and his good opinion of the poems looked like being unrewarded. But why did he despair of sales after only a week-and-a-bit? – after four days, by Professor Daniel's computation. And *what* reviews could have been issued so soon? He is, in fact, lying (or forgetting after fifty years, and inventing), and the one piece of truth which he inserts helps to show his deceit: on 15 September, the day before they sailed, Wordsworth wrote asking him to make over his interest in the volume to Johnson of St Paul's Churchyard – and Cottle could not do so, because *already* the deal with Arch had been clinched. His word 'reviews' perhaps gives the clue to the truth, and Harper makes the most of it: Southey, nettled with Coleridge and indifferent to Wordsworth, was preparing a hostile review of *Lyrical Ballads*, did not wish to hurt Cottle, and influenced him to part with his stock, though Cottle retained his thirty-guineas'-worth of copyright. Even Harper thinks this interpretation 'almost too bad to believe', but it makes a kind of sense, and goes well with Southey's lordly and ill tempered article on the poems, in the October *Critical Review*. Cottle says that he sold to Arch at a loss, and this we may well credit.

However, my friend Mr David Foxon, of the British Museum, had built up by mid-1953 a hypothesis which I found far more attractive than either of these theories. He argues, first, that Cottle had to print some sort of title-page by the end of August, so that the first issue would be ready for the Wordsworths to take it with them to London. Not knowing who would accept the volume, but regarding Longman as his first chance (since Longman had bought his editions before), he printed 'for T.N. Longman'; and, if they would *not* take it, he would just have to print a new title. He inserted their name in advance, and in hopes. Secondly, is Harper right in thinking that the curious Bristol imprint in any way protected the poets from discovery, or Cottle's reputation from smirch? Mr Foxon sees Cottle as determined to have his cake and eat it, to be on the title-page without apparent responsibility; if he really wanted to be out of things, he could have retired utterly – as did both his *name*, and the name of Bristol, in the second title-page. Thirdly, Mr Foxon sorts out Southey's curious behaviour; Cottle's deal with Arch was through by the time that it took for Wordsworth's parting letter to reach him (say, 16 or 17 September), and Dorothy could write on the 13th that the poems were 'printed, but not published'; yet Southey wrote to Taylor on the 5th asking him if he had 'seen a volume of

Lyrical Ballads', and slating the book. Now Southey had page proofs of the poems, which have reached the New York Public Library; but the first title-page is later than these – printed after the realisation that *Lewti* must be cancelled. Presumably, in mid-August, before the title-page was run off, Southey warned Cottle how bad the poems were and what a bad review they would get; presumably, too, he was not privy to Cottle's scheme of not publishing at the beginning of September but of trying to sell to a London publisher – and so, when he wrote to Taylor on the 5th, he thought that the original plan had gone through and that copies were available. Well, Cottle had to get copies ready before the German trip began, and so the Wordsworths took them with Longman's name on them; meanwhile, Longman refused the book, and Wordsworth, knowing that it could not yet have been published, flirted with Johnson!

By 17 November 1954, when he read to the Bibliographical Society his admirable paper on the 'Printing of *Lyrical Ballads*', Mr Foxon had hardened still further towards Cottle, and was ready to twitch the book almost out of Cottle's hands. He admits that his reconstruction is 'highly speculative'; but I find it too consistent and coherent to reject, however much (*pietatis causa*) I may deplore it. And so, having accepted Professor Daniel's mere four days during which the Bristol issue could have been on sale, we are led to Mr Foxon's calamitous conclusion: 'Indeed, it looks very much as though the Bristol issue was never published, but merely circulated to friends. Since Cottle had a large circle of friends in Bristol' (like Beddoes, who was obliged with a droll copy that had bits of Beddoes inserted), 'and since Wordsworth and Coleridge presumably wanted a number of copies, it would not be difficult to visualize some twenty-five copies circulating in this way, of which twelve are known to be extant'. Is this, then, the famed Bristol edition, the brightest jewel in our hero's crown? At all events, he had sponsored the poems, and bought them, and printed them, and distributed twenty-five of them; I believe that he even appreciated them. This is evidently not quite the same as publishing them; but we shall see that they were still on his conscience, and it was not long before he owned and wielded the copyright again.

Yet can Richard Wordsworth[50] be blamed for putting a 'very unfavourable interpretation' on Cottle's letter of 2 October to Johnson, and for saying that if he had received such a letter from an attorney he would think 'very meanly of him'? Cottle writes that Wordsworth wants him to give up his interest in *Lyrical Ballads* to Johnson; Cottle can 'perceive clearly' from 'the tenor of his letter' that he is worried about the sale's not answering Cottle's purpose in publishing – but, then, he had bought them so as to publish them, and this is still his intention, so he has sent them to his agent. Perhaps Wordsworth has assumed that Cottle will comply, and thus may have received some money from Johnson; but Cottle doesn't want to be influenced by Wordsworth's motive, so may he just hear whether any money has changed hands, and how much? From another of Cottle's letters, written to James Tobin just before 8 February 1799, we learn that he was at Plymouth Dock when Wordsworth's request arrived in Bristol, so he couldn't reply in time before Wordsworth went abroad; Wordsworth had sold him the copyright, but when last in London was worried lest 'the undertaking might be prejudicial' to Cottle's interest (from Cottle's 'not residing in London'), and '*entered* into something like *an engagement* with Johnson', without waiting for Cottle's answer. So could Tobin tell Cottle whether 'Wordsworth *received any Money of his Brother* upon the presumption of being reimbursed from Johnson'. Southey, writing to C. W. Williams Wynn on 17 December 1798[51] (and saying that *The Ancient Mariner* is 'nonsense'), shows us how touchy the publisher now was on the subject of copyrights; faced with the question of what should be done with Southey's 'Ballads', of which he owned the copyrights, he 'referred it entirely' to Southey, 'but seemed convinced that to let them be printed elsewhere would injure the sale materially'.

The departure of the two poets left Southey the master of Cottle's limited field. If Cottle had any doubts about his hero's candour, they were dispelled in this year by a conversation with Southey's mother,[52] who assured him that even in her son's infancy, 'whenever any mischief or accident occurred amongst the children, which some might wish to conceal, she always applied to Robert, who never hesitated, or deviated from the truth, though he himself might have been implicated' – a fine period sentence rounded off with a delicious concessive clause. Cottle still had the reputation, even if not the competence, for charity, and some time after 21 April Southey sent him an urgent application:[53] on his brother Tom's ship, *Mars*, there had been a midshipman called Bligh, now killed in battle and leaving a widow and children. Thus Cottle spells his name; but James, in his *Naval History of Great Britain*,[54] gives it as James Blythe, and the engagement in which he died, and in which Tom was wounded, was that with *Hercule* on 21 April 1798. Is Cottle thinking of Captain Bligh, and is this another faint echo of the theory that Fletcher Christian secretly inspired *The Ancient Mariner*? Blythe sounds a kind of Tom Bowling, and Tom Southey loved him for his purity and for his husbandly devotion: 'Surely, Cottle, there will be no difficulty in sending his poor wife some little sum. Five guineas would be much to her …'

But now another great mind was at work in Bristol, and Cottle was soon admitted to some of its secrets. The young Humphry Davy's reputation reached the city in April 1798, when Dr Beddoes, who had already met him while geologizing in Cornwall, began to consider him for the post of super-intendent at his Pneumatic Institution. Beddoes – whose elder son would write *Death's Jest Book* and illustrate it with his own suicide, and whose younger son became the grandfather of Gerard Manley Hopkins – was a leading figure in the scientific and literary life of Bristol, or at least of Clifton, and Cottle was among his friends. He showed Cottle the glowing testimonial sent by his friend Davies Giddy on behalf of the young Penzance chemist, and asked his opinion about engaging him. Cottle urged him to act on so decisive a letter, and he replied to Giddy on 4 July. As usual, the 1847 *Reminiscences*[55] fog the real date by saying that Giddy's letter was produced 'a month or two after Mr Coleridge had left Bristol for Germany', and that Davy appeared 'two or three weeks after'; thus a conversation that happened in, say, June is post-dated to September or later, and Davy's arrival on 5 October is made to follow far too swiftly on Beddoes's decision. Otherwise, there is no reason to doubt Cottle's narrative, and he is our chief authority for the human side of Davy's stay in Bristol. As soon as they were introduced, he was struck by Davy's intellectual face and his ingenuousness; the boy was only nineteen, and had no friends in Bristol yet, so Cottle 'encouraged and often received his visits', Davy sometimes spending the whole afternoon with him.

Davy at first stayed with Beddoes in Rodney Place, Clifton; but in November Beddoes took the lease of 6-7 Dowry Square, Hotwell, in the north-west corner of that handsome square, and altered the interiors to suit his Institution. Here, of course, 'the road to painless surgery had its commencement',[56] and Cottle must have helped by his patronage and encouragement. Literary men had not been serving him very well, and a scientist was just the tonic he needed. When they met, Davy would tell him of his life and his many chemical experiments, or would recite his poems, giving him several which Cottle proudly kept. He used to invite Cottle to attend his experiments at the Institution, and was so eager to make converts that he bought his new enthusiast 'a box of chemical tests, acids, alkalies, glass tubes, retorts, blow-pipe, trough &c. &c.', and helped him in his first experiments. Cottle was still using the trough in 1847, but his only tangible contribution to the advancement of science was that he was still experi-menting with an efficacious varnish for oil-paintings when he was over eighty!

The Institution was worrying the medical world, and causing a stir in Bristol. Beddoes had acquired a great reputation, and at his house Cottle would see the two young Lambtons, one of whom became the first Earl of

Durham, and their consumptive father, who entrusted the boys to Beddoes's care and helped to endow the establishment. One of the Wedgwoods had given £1,000, and Davy had met them in Penzance, so that Cottle's mention of his friendlessness is not quite accurate. Further, his interest in writing verse soon admitted him to a circle whose pursuits were mainly literary: Poole, with whom he long kept in touch; Southey, who, as Poet Laureate, would one day be, like Davy, the official head of his profession; Tobin the dramatist; Beddoes's wife, sister of the novelist Maria Edgeworth; and later, on Cottle's introduction, Coleridge. He enjoyed great privileges at Hotwell, and it was a time of splendid happiness and fulfilment; he already had the backing of James Watt's son, Gregory, and the great Joseph Priestley's son came to Hotwell to study under him. He was given the 'genteel maintenance' that he had demanded, his quarters and his laboratory were thoroughly satisfactory, and he had abundant time for research. Though he stayed only until March 1801, and though his greatest work (including his miners' safety-lamp) was produced elsewhere, Bristol was the first place to give him his chance, and he was still in his first freshness before the bestowal of those honours, riches and adulation which he later pursued to the detriment of his character and life-work. It is of this period that Cottle writes with gusto and some understanding; and three achievements stand out from it. First, he began 'galvanic' experiments, and wrote papers on the subject of electricity. Secondly, Cottle was present when Mr W. Coates told Davy how his boy had just rubbed together two bonnet-canes in the dark, and found that they produced light; Davy, by listening attentively to the story, and by experiment and analogy, proved that 'all canes, as well as straws and hollow grasses, have an epidermis of silex'. Cottle gives the matter three pages, and poses a dozen questions on the origin of this silex; he remained interested in the subject, and some years later, when a large mow had been burnt near Bristol, he secured part of the 'stratum of pure, compact, vitrified silex' in 'one continuous sheet, nearly an inch in thickness', and found that he could strike sparks from it with a steel.

Thirdly and principally, Davy, who was at Hotwell to study the effect of gases, made in this connexion his most 'popular' discovery. He was taking the gravest risks, and Cottle used earnestly to warn him against some of his experiments, half despairing 'of seeing him alive the next morning'. At Penzance they had said, 'He will blow us all into the air!' But now he willingly inhaled gases whose powers were quite unknown, and his friends attributed the early break-up of his health to his rash courage at this time. He nearly killed himself with three respirations of water-gas, sending his pulse to over 120, yet murmuring, 'I do not think I shall die'. In breathing nitrous gas he was unable to expel all the air in his lungs, and the resulting *aqua-fortis* severely injured his palate, tongue, and teeth. Because, after three quarts of pure nitrous oxide, he could not tell whether it was stimulant or depressing, he took four, and eventually sixteen; he also combined these inhalations with a whole bottle of wine. The thrill which attended these experiments was soon shared with his friends; and, since Beddoes was planning a publication on the subject, Southey, Coleridge, Lovell, Edgeworth, Tobin and others breathed from the green bag in which the 'laughing gas' was kept. One laughed, one danced, one hit Davy with his fist; Cottle, ever prudent, was pressed by Beddoes to record his testimony, but declined the honour, 'being satisfied with the effects produced on others'. Beddoes also wanted to try it on a lady, so a female volunteer (whom Cottle coyly and uselessly calls 'Miss —-') became the first of her sex to take a few sniffs; she dashed out of the room and down the Institution stairs, raced along Hope Square, jumped over a big dog, and was secured only after a hot pursuit. With all these merry moments, the laboratory became a 'region of hilarity and relaxation'; but when no cures were forthcoming, the number of patients declined, and even a reward of sixpence a day could not tempt them to attend and to submit to the gases. Davy found laughing-gas a useful anaesthetic when he was cutting a wisdom-tooth, but his findings were not seriously followed up for many years, and Cottle writes the Institution's epitaph when he says that 'by its failure, it established the useful negative fact, however mortifying, that medical science was not to be improved through the medium of factitious airs'. It is pleasant to think of Davy walking happily on the Downs at Clifton with his green bag, inhaling from it so as to improve his poetry; the result is more clinical than poetical:

> Not in the ideal dreams of wild desire
> Have I beheld a rapture-wakening form:
> My bosom burns with no unhallow'd fire,
> Yet is my cheek with rosy blushes warm;
> Yet are my eyes with sparkling lustre filled;
> Yet is my mouth replete with murmuring sound;
> Yet are my limbs with inward transports fill'd,
> And clad with new-born mightiness around.[57]

Still, Southey encouraged him as a poet, and even tried to turn his mind from science; warning him, however, that there was no-one in his circle at Bristol who knew anything of poetry, Beddoes's taste being pessimistic and Cottle liking only what he and his friends wrote.[58]

1   Curry, I.170.

2   Curry, I.171.

3   *op.cit.*, p.129.

4   Vol.LXVIII (1798), ii.703.

5   Bristol City Library MS.B 20873.

6   Griggs, I.380, No.226.

7   L. Hanson, *The Life of S.T. Coleridge* ... p.243, makes it Wine St.

8   Griggs, I.382-383, No.230.

9   Griggs, I.386-287, No.233.

10 *ER*.37, I.309.

11 Griggs, I.390-391, No.235.

12 Revd. A.B. Beaven, *Bristol Lists* (Bristol: Taylor, 1899), p.247.

13 de S, No.1040.

14 Griggs, I.399-400, No.239.

15 Shaver, I.214, No.86.

16 Griggs, I.400-401, No.240.

17 *R*.47, pp.176-178.

18 CCS, I.286; letter to Grosvenor Bedford.

19 *R*.47, pp.168-171.

20 Shaver, I.212-214, No.85.

21 Shaver, I.215, No.87.

22 E. de Selincourt, *The Early Letters of William and Dorothy Wordsworth* (Oxford, 1935), No.62; Shaver, I.198-199, No.82.

23 Cote (now a home for the elderly) is off the top of Parry's Lane.

24 Shaver, I.217-218, No.90.

25 *R*.47, pp.178 and 182 ff.

26 Shaver, I.220n.

27 Griggs, I.411-413, No.250.

28 J. Latimer, *Annals of Bristol* (Bristol: Arrowsmith, 1906), IV.425-426.

29 This was located behind St Peter's Church. It was destroyed in the war.

30 H. Thompson, *The Life of Hannah More* (London: Cadell, 1838), pp.48 ff.

31 Nehemiah Curnock, ed., *The Journal of the Rev. John Wesley, A.M.* (London: Kelly, 1909-1916), VI.343, 482, and VII.115. Jane Bowdler's poem, *Louisa*, to which Curnock refers (VI.482n), is on a totally different subject.

32 Lady Llanover, ed., *Autobiography and Correspondence of Mary Granville, Mrs. Delany*, 2nd Ser. (London: Bentley, 1862), iii.145.

33 *ER*.37, I.317.

34 Ann Yearsley, *Poems on Several Occasions* (London: Cadell, 1785), a volume to which Amos Cottle subscribed.

35 W. Roberts, *Memoirs of the Life of Mrs. Hannah More* (London, 1836), I.182, 194.

36 de S, No.1185, pp.812-813.

37 Shaver, I.219, 222, Nos.91, 93.

38 I am indebted to Mr F.W. Bateson for this information, found in a MS. in Tullie House, Carlisle.

39 Shaver, I.225n.

40 *op.cit.*, p.79.

41 Curry, I.169.

42 Letter to Tom Southey, in CCS, I.347-348.

43 *R*.47, pp.217-218.

44 Shaver, I.226-227, No.96.

45 Shaver, I.227, No.97.

46 T.J. Wise, *Two Lake Poets: A Catalogue of Printed Books, Manuscripts and Autograph Letters* ... (London: for private circulation, 1927), pp.3 ff.

47 R.W. Daniel, 'The Publication of the "Lyrical Ballads"', *Modern Language Review* XXXIII (1938), pp.406-410.

48 *op.cit.*, I.356.

49 *R*.47, p.257.

50 Shaver, I.673-676, Richard to William Wordsworth, enclosing Cottle's two letters to Johnson and Tobin, both now at the Wordsworth Library, Grasmere.

51 Curry, I.176-178.

52 *R*.47, p.419.

53 *R*.47, p.217.

54 W. James, *The Naval History of Great Britain* ... (London: Bentley, 1837), II.107 ff.

55 Cottle's version of Davy's activities in Bristol is in *R*.47, pp.260 ff.; for the authentic dating, see F.F. Cartwright, *The English Pioneers of Anaesthesia (Beddoes: Davy: Hickman)* (Bristol: John Wright and London: Simpkin Marshall, 1952). Cartwright's authoritative attitude is needed as a corrective to Cottle's rather idle and flippant reminiscing; Davy, after all, became a laughing-gas addict.

56 Cartwright, *op.cit.*, p.103.

57 Cartwright, *op.cit.*, p.232.

58 Cartwright, *op.cit.*, p.182.

Chapter 6

The Break-Up

This new interest, centred on Davy, must have been for Cottle the most cheerful feature of 1799, which saw his financial collapse in the summer. Most of his activities were connected with the settlement of his affairs, but the year had its pleasanter side; Amos graduated B.A. at Magdalene College, Cambridge, and Cottle found himself in print again, in the first issue of Southey's *Annual Anthology*. This brave anthology was intended as an English 'Almanack of the Muses' for minor poems more neat than significant; half of the first number was by Southey, and the rest was made up of poems by Davy, Lloyd, Lovell, Beddoes, Taylor, Amelia Opie, Grosvenor Bedford, Cottle, and others.[1] Amos submitted *The Hermit Boy*, an ugly thing of prancing anapaests (or amphibrachs) in five-verse stanzas all about a boy whose widower father brought him up in a secluded wood, until the day when he saw 'two females' while going to get simples for the old man's ailments; at this, 'Unusual commotion then shot thro' his frame', and as soon as he was an orphan he stepped out into the last stanza.

Cottle's contributions are, for the most part, already familiar. *Ellen* still clings to the rock and apostrophizes her Edward, and the worthwhile lines on Savage are printed without a signature. The rest are sorry things. *The Affectionate Heart*, eight quatrains of anapaestic trimeters (a flattering description), asks for an affectionate friend and sets below him, or her, fame and wit and learning; because, at the end of time, affection

> shall stand on its permanent base;
> It shall last till the wreck of the mind.

It had the honour of being quoted in *The Stuffed Owl*, that merry anthology of 1930, so hostile to Southey and Protestants and anti-Jacobites that it actually ascribed the Roman Catholic Tom Moore's fatuous *By that Lake* (all about the revered St Kevin) to the anti-Roman Southey!

Under the pseudonym CITELTO (an anagram of 'I. Cottle') appears *The Spirit*, in the same jogtrot metre as Amos's poem. May we call it a *jeu d'esprit*?

– The ghost turns out to be 'old Gaffer's grey mare' in the last line, but not before an old crone has given us some impressive words:

> They are Night-Ravens
> That pick the dead-men's eyes;
> And they cry qua, with their hollow jaw;
> Methinks I one this moment saw!
> To the banquet at hand he flies.

Destiny, which acknowledges his authorship, is just a string of platitudes in five ten-verse stanzas, condemning physical and aesthetic pleasures and trying to soar on 'Religion's pinion'. *Age and Youth*, also under his name, is an angry colloquy in octets between a crabbed and cynical old man and an idealistic and rather likeable youth, who wins the debate. Finally, there is Cottle's *The Killcrop*, which appeared anonymously and was thus published as Southey's in Galignani's 1829 Paris edition; we shall see that Cottle thought a lot of this dialogue in blank verse about a diabolic changeling child in a German village, but Luther's version has the real *diablerie* which this derivative quite lacks.

The Library register for 1799 shows how greatly the pleasures of reading (or, at any rate, borrowing) cheered this difficult year, though he did not visit the building until March:

1 March – 24 May	W. Barrett, *History and Antiquities of the City of Bristol* (renewed on 10 Apr., reminder on 17 May)
11 March – 26 March	*Life of Catherine II*, Vol. III
26 March – 9 April	*ditto*, Vol. II
9 April – 2 May	Sully, *Memoirs*, Vol. I
2 May – 9 May	*ditto*, Vol. II
2 June – 14 June	Pontoppidan, *Natural History of Norway*
10 June – 1 July	R. Henry, *History of Great Britain*, Vol. II
14 June – 21 June	Hon. Daines Barrington, *Naturalists' Journal*
21 June – 1 July	Whitaker, *History of Manchester*, Vol. II
1 July – 5 July	Strutt, *Chronicle*, Vol. I.
1 July – 3 July	Strutt, *View ...*, Vol. I
3 July – 5 July	Henry, *History of Great Britain*, Vol. I
5 July, returned same day	Strutt, *Regal and Ecclesiastical Antiquities of England*
5 July – 8 July	Strutt, *Dress ...*

5 July – 8 July	*Biographia Britannica*, Vol. I
8 July – 12 July	T. Hearne's Continuation of Dugdale, Vol. I
8 July – 10 July	*ditto*, Vol. II ('not permitted to be taken out of the library')
10 July – 11 July	Borlase, *Antiquities of Cornwall*
11 July – 12 July	Potter, *Enquiry into some Passages in Dr. Johnson's Lives of the Poets*
12 July, returned same day	Martyn and Lettice, *Antiquities of Herculaneum*
12 July, returned same day	Albin, *Natural History of English Insects*
12 July – 15 July	Hon. Daines Barrington, *On the Probability of reaching the North Pole*
15 July – 16 July	Beattie, *Dissertations Moral and Critical*
15 July – 16 July	Beattie, *Essay on the Nature and Immutability of Truth*
16 July – 17 July	*Runic Poetry: Five pieces, translated from the Icelandic Language (1763)*
16 July – 17 July	Verstegan, *Saxon Antiquities* (one of Chatterton's sources, and surely borrowed in connexion with work on Chatterton)
17 July – 18 July	Pennant, *Tour in Scotland*, Part I
17 July – 24 July	*ditto*, Part II

Whalley[2] calls the subsequent books 'a flurry of borrowings' and links them with Coleridge's return from Germany; but Cottle's fourteen or more visits to the Library during July may also reflect the added leisure resulting from his retirement from bookselling in this month.

18 July – 24 July	Pennant, *Tour in Wales*
25 July, returned same day	Pennant, *British Zoology*, I and II
25 July – 26 July	A. Gordon, *Lives of Pope Alexander VI and his Son Caesar Borgia*
25 July – 5 Aug.	R. Robinson, *Ecclesiastical Researches*
26 July – 2 Aug.	Lord Kaimes, *Elements of Criticism*, Vol. II
2 Aug – 5 Aug.	Pennant, *Arctic Zoology*, Vols. I and II
5 Aug. – 6 Aug.	W. Hutchinson, *View of Northumberland*, 2 Vols. (perhaps for his North-Eastern holiday)
6 Aug., returned same day	R. Wood, *Essay on the Original Genius and Writings of Homer*

6 Aug., returned same day	Webb, *Remarks on the Beauties of Poetry*
6 Aug. – 9 Aug.	Kaimes, *Sketches of the History of Man*, Vols. I & II
9 Aug. – 15 Aug.	Crantz, *History of Greenland*, Vols I & II
15 Aug. – 22 Aug.	Hutchinson, *History and Antiquities of Cumberland*, Vol. I Pt. i, Vol. II Pt. iii (as he had been invited to Lakeland, too)
22 Aug. – 26 Aug.	T. Broughton, *Dictionary of all Religions*, 2 Vols.
26 Aug. – 27 Aug.	P. Newcome, *History of the Abbey of St Alban*
26 Aug. – 27 Aug.	Ogilvie, *Observations on the Nature, Character and various Species of Composition*, Vol. I
27 Aug. – 16 Sept.	Beckmann, *History of Inventions and Discoveries*, Vols I & II
10 Sept. – 16 Sept.	D. Williams, *History of Monmouthshire*
16 Sept. – 3 Oct.	Duc de Sully, *Memoirs*, Vol. 5
3 Oct. – 10 Oct.	*ditto*, Vol. 6
11 Oct. – 22 Oct.	*Historical Memoirs of Voltaire*
22 Oct. – 23 Oct.	Voltaire, *Histoire de Charles XII*
29 Oct. – 8 Nov.	*Life of Garrick*, Vol. II
8 Nov. – 15 Nov.	Count Benyowsky, *Memoirs and Travels*, ed. W. Nicholson, Vol. I
(borrowed 'by W. Osman', presumably a servant)	
12 Nov. – 11 Dec.	*Encyclopaedia Britannica,* Vol. 6 Pt. I
13 Nov. – 6 Dec.	Lewis, *Philosophical Commerce of Arts* (so by now he had three books 'out')
6 Dec. – 17 Dec.	Hakluyt, *Voyages*, Vols. I and II in one
11 Dec. – 6 Jan. 1800	Benyowsky, *Memoirs*, Vol. II
17 Dec. – 18 Dec.	Whitaker, *History of Manchester*, Vol. I
18 Dec. – 10 Mar. 1800	*ditto*, Vol. II
(after letters of 5 Feb & 5 March)	

In *Felix Farley* for 30 March 1799, it was announced that the dividends of 'Robert Cottle of Bristol, merchant-taylor', would be declared at the Bush Tavern on 16 April. In the issue of 27 April, the solicitor Thomas Morgan advises creditors of Robert Cottle, declared bankrupt in 1790, that they may get the final dividend by applying to Prideaux, Thorne, & Co. any morning after 5 May. The elder Robert is at last missing from the Bristol directory for 1799-1800, but his daughter Mary continues her school in Portland Square.

The great men who were Cottle's friends did nothing to relieve his financial tension: in fact, they added to his worries. On 13 May 1799, Southey said in a letter to him that Arch expected to lose on the first edition of *Lyrical Ballads*, which he had bought. Southey's report may be spiteful, and Cottle's repetition of it[3] self-righteous, though he adds that Hannah More admired the book when he presented it to her, and on his next visit to Barley Wood (her Somerset home near Wrington) he had to read out of it to the ladies, to their great 'amusement'; she now put Wordsworth before his other young friends, and insisted on hearing *Harry Gill* twice over – which is no great tribute to her taste. It is interesting, in view of Cottle's bungling of financial matters for Wordsworth, that he was behaving efficiently for Southey, who praises him in a letter to Edith of 15 May[4] for his prompt forwarding, with a covering letter, of £20 drawn on S. Hamilton, the editor of the *Critical Review*; in his plans for reunion with Edith, Southey would return to Bristol on the night of Monday, 27 May, and call on Cottle, 'however late it might be', though having warned him, for news of her.[5] Southey also had Amos in mind, rejoicing that he was to write the monograph on Southey for Richard Phillips's 'dirty book of *Public Characters*', because 'there will be no lies' and Southey 'can object to any thing objectionable';[6] since Amos is bringing out a poem on Owen Parfit in the *Monthly Magazine*, he is 'in full employ'.[7]

Wordsworth, on returning to England and settling at Sockburn-on-Tees, lost no time in writing to Cottle on business. In a letter of the end of May,[8] he reminds him that, the day before leaving for Germany, he had written asking that Cottle's right to *Lyrical Ballads* should be transferred to Johnson; this would have been advantageous to Wordsworth. Cottle was also to draw on Wordsworth's brother in London for any money that Wordsworth owed him. There had been no time to get Cottle's answer, so Wordsworth still does not know how the poems were disposed of; could Cottle write quickly and inform him? Coleridge tells them that Cottle is well. (Since Coleridge was still in Germany, this must mean that Cottle wrote more often to him than to Wordsworth.) Dorothy joins 'in kind remembrance to your Mother &c.', and in love to Cottle himself.

Yet Cottle had incurred his displeasure, and when he wrote to his brother Richard Wordsworth on 13 May[9] he said that he had not heard from Cottle, but feared that there had been 'some sad mismanagement'. Richard must tell him what he has had for the poems, and from whom. Richard's harsh letter[10] of the 15th, with its enclosure of the two Cottle letters and its censure of his brother's fecklessness, must have made Wordsworth wince; in a letter of 23 May,[11] he apologized for the trouble that Richard had been caused, and put his views on Cottle's behaviour. A letter of Cottle's had improperly used the word 'purchase'; now Wordsworth had 'expressly told him' that he had not mentioned 'any *positive* agreement' between them to Johnson, so Cottle 'out of delicacy' should not have mentioned it to Johnson either. Also, since Cottle had kept reiterating that he was publishing the poems only for Wordsworth's benefit (which was why Wordsworth 'suffered' him to have them), it was blameworthy on his part not to surrender his claim into Johnson's hands. And, further, in his letter to Johnson he lyingly says that Wordsworth wants to relieve Cottle of the book because 'it will not answer for' Cottle, when all the time Wordsworth had told Cottle by letter that he would like him to resign his claim for Wordsworth's benefit alone. He has written to Cottle, and expects an answer in a day or so; and, if it isn't satisfactory, he will write again. Richard must not worry about his brother's use of the word 'mismanagement' – none of it could be ascribed to *him*.

This irritation prepares us for a rather nonplussed letter[12] of 2 June to Cottle, whose letter, being inadequately addressed, had arrived only the day before: so Cottle could not have complied with his request, having already 'entered into a treaty with Arch'? But it is a pity, since Wordsworth loses his chance of a connexion with Johnson, since the poems would sell quicker in Johnson's hands, and since they will now have to be separated from anything else that Wordsworth may publish. Cottle should not have told Johnson that the poems had been *sold* to him; had not Wordsworth virtually asked him not to? Are the poems likely to sell? And what happens to the copyright when Cottle quits bookselling? They hope that he 'will be rich enough, and very happy' once he is out of his shop; is Robert going to succeed him? Wordsworth calculates that Cottle owes him £21.10s., has paid him £10 and was to pay him 30 guineas, but Wordsworth bought paper long ago from him, and still owes for it; so could Cottle deduct the last item from what he owes Wordsworth, and send the remainder as soon as possible? *How many poems have been sold? And what are they to do with the copyright?* Cottle must remember to answer this, especially as, if sales are good, Wordsworth will substitute some poems for *The Ancient Mariner*. Wordsworth then remembers to express appropriate sentiments about Cottle's good and bad news: he was remaining in the printing trade, which was going well; but his lameness was increasing – Wordsworth tells him, 'you must live in the country if possible when you are no longer "imprisoned" in Wine Street'. After Dorothy's love, a postscript returns to business: if Cottle cannot remit the whole, let him send Wordsworth £5 and remit the rest, as soon as he can, to Richard in Staple Inn. Wordsworth wants three volumes of the poems to bestow on friends; how can he get them? – apparently Cottle did not reserve to himself the disposal of any of them, and now Wordsworth has to pay for them.

This letter must have left Cottle smarting, harassed as he already was with the winding up of his business. Years later, he took his own quiet kind of compensation for it. In his *Reminiscences*[13] he edits the document quite out-rageously, leaving out all the tart bits, and even omitting Robert and his own lameness; ending it with the end of Wordsworth's *last* letter; and stuffing it with praise of the *Annual Anthology*, and especially of his abject *Killcrop*, which they 'liked better than any' – if only he could have saved the poor baby's life by the efficacious workings of nature! (Incidentally, Cottle 'obliged' with a happy ending in the Appendix to the 1837 *Recollections*.) It is clear that Cottle would not manufacture this praise in 1837-1847, during Wordsworth's lifetime; but he is our only authority for this passage, and Wordsworth, whenever he wrote it, certainly did not write it on 2 June 1799.

However, he replied by sending the £5, and Wordsworth thanked him on 24 June,[14] asking for the other £15 direct and quickly, instead of through Richard; this assumed that Cottle's calculations were accurate – Wordsworth's had been based on a rather hazy recollection on Dorothy's part. So 'the poems have not sold ill'? – '*what number* have been sold'? (Cottle must often have been an infuriating correspondent.) And then Wordsworth says a melancholy thing: it seems to him that *The Ancient Mariner* has done the damage (of course, this is due to 'the old words and the strangeness of it'!), and a second edition would have, instead, 'some little things which would be more likely to suit the common taste'. (Cottle did not fail to report this bad opinion; the off-hand treatment which *he* suffered was thus merged into the many little hostilities which were part of the Romantic comedy.) He begs Cottle to read this bit twice, and to answer it. When Cottle sends his parcel to Lloyd, could he enclose three *Ballads* for Wordsworth? He and Dorothy are touched by Cottle's wish to see them again in Somerset; but they have no plans at all. It has been kind of Cottle to look after their box, and they do not need any of its contents yet. They are worried at not having heard from Coleridge since they arrived in England.

Cottle's last advertisement appeared in *Felix Farley* for 8 June 1799: Romaine Joseph Thorn's *Lodon and Miranda, a Poem*, to which was added *The Poor Boy, a Tale*, all at 6/-, printed by Biggs and Cottle and to be sold by all booksellers. On 6 July *Bonner and Middleton's Bristol Journal* announced his forced retirement: 'Book-Selling Business/ To be disposed of/ Joseph Cottle being about to/ decline the Bookselling business/ will be willing to treat with/ any Gentleman for his House/ and Stock./ This will be found an/ advantageous offer to any active/ person who may be disposed to/ enter upon the above concern./ No.5 Wine Street, Bristol'. He was, in fact, near to ruin; he did not mention this at the time in any surviving letter, and pride made him suppress it when he compiled his *Recollections*, but a letter to Cadell the publisher on 3 June 1823[15] tells the sadder side of the story and puts him with Sir Walter Scott in his long and plucky fight to raise himself. He could pay his creditors only 10/- in the pound, through 'bad debts and losses in the Kennet and Avon Canal'. Thereafter, for over twenty-five years, he struggled to repay all liabilities, which he had now *'legally* ... but not *morally'* discharged; by 1823 some debts were completely paid, including one of £200 for money that he had borrowed, and he was devoting to the same end whatever he made on publications. His apprentice, C. Carpenter, succeeded to his working stock and moved to the offices of Messrs Biggs and Cottle, opposite the Drawbridge; he put his first advertisement in *Felix Farley* on 9 November 1799, saying that he would be available there as a working stationer and bookbinder. Thus Cottle 'quitted the business of a bookseller', an occasion which by 1847 had grown so dim that he dated it[16] at the departure of the two poets for Germany in 1798. He was only 29, and he had done wonders unwittingly; now a door had slammed, and the new room in which he found himself was narrow and chilly and drab.

At first, through his own reticence, his friends cannot have understood the nature of his 'retirement'; Davy soon sent him, at 'Wine Street or Gloucester Street', a charming letter (now in my possession) with a little word of envy for his new status:

> Dear Cottle,
>   My experimental business and the badness of the weather have prevented me from calling on you in your new habitation, to behold you the man of Leisure and of science. – I hope however to do it in two or three days. – I have written a long owed letter to Southey; but I know not where to send it to him. Will you be so good as to direct it and forward it by the post of today. – I have got some chemical things at the glass house for you: but before you get them you must come and spend a day with me.
>   Adieu and believe that H Davy is yours very sincerely
> Tuesday Morning

Cottle's reply to Wordsworth's letter must have mollified the poet, who on 27 July thanked him[17] for a draft received the previous evening and assured him that he was not poor enough to 'take interest for a debt from a friend, paid eleven months after it is due'. In fact, he adds frankly, 'If I were in want,

Note from Humphry Davy to Joseph Cottle (1799) (in the possession of Martin Crossley Evans)

I should make no scruple in applying to you for twice that sum'. He is afraid that Cottle is deceiving himself, and just trying to give pleasure, in reporting so favourably on the sale of the *Ballads*. The blessing, and the signature, of this letter are very affectionate, and it ends with an honest P.S.: he grows so averse to publication that he will never go to press again – except for money! He has heard of a notice in *The Monthly Review* (for May), and in another letter to Cottle[18] he bitterly asks why Southey, who knew he had published the poems for cash, accepted the job of reviewing them when he had so poor an opinion of them. By 20 August, when Wordsworth wrote to Richard,[19] the mood of cross resignation was abating; he hopes that he will not have to trouble his brother much more, and has had thirty guineas from Cottle, in part payment for the book.

Then Wordsworth made a friendlier gesture; he urged Cottle to take a holiday in the North, and in a letter of 2 September[20] promised to conduct him on his tour. Cottle was to write in advance, and come to Greta Bridge, on the Tees, about twenty miles from Sockburn, and Wordsworth and Dorothy would meet him; she would then return to Sockburn, and the two men could explore that region, whereafter they would go into Cumberland and Westmoreland. Obviously the poets had mistaken ideas about Cottle's new-found leisure, and associated wealth with it. Southey could write quite gaily on 22 September,[21] 'I congratulate you on being out of book-selling; it did not suit you. Would that we authors had one bookseller at our direction, instead of one bookseller directing so many authors!' – it is not surprising that Cottle did not print this sentence when he put the letter into his *Reminiscences*. Southey was writing from Exeter, in hopes that Cottle would soon be sending some of his own poems, and some of Davy's, for the second *Annual Anthology*; he would have liked to include Mrs Yearsley's, too, if she had been well (Cottle perversely prints 'living' instead of 'well', seven years before she died.) He recommends Cottle to read *Gebir*, which a Gilbert half as mad might have written; the poem was anonymous, so that Southey could not yet know that the author was Landor. Exeter he finds politically bigoted and quite filthy, but it has good books for sale, especially at the shop of one Dyer – 'not Woolmer, whose catalogue you showed me'. He has noble plans, including a *History of Portugal*, but his present servile toil is like 'Columbus serving before the mast'.

Coleridge was also back from Germany, and after short stays in Stowey, Ottery, and Exeter, and with the Wedgwoods at Upcott, came to Bristol; he had already announced this intention in a letter to Southey of 30 September,[22] and added that he would then leave some verses at Cottle's to be sent on in any parcel for Southey. The valuable feature of his visit was that he met Davy, and on this point, again, Cottle's record[23] does its best to mislead us; he claims to have introduced them – which may be true – on Coleridge's 'return from the north'. They had looked forward to meeting, and were not disappointed in the fulfilment. They often met under Cottle's roof, and between passages of brilliantly intellectual conversation would exchange details of their past lives, which Cottle heard and collected into his memoirs:[24] how Davy's theories of 'mind over matter' were refuted when a crab bit his toe in Mount's Bay (at St Michael's Mount, Cornwall); and Coleridge's adventures in Hesse, at Cambridge, and as a soldier. For that curious interlude in the dragoons Cottle is the best authority, and he tells us that the account is compiled chiefly from what Coleridge told him and Davy; it comes partly from other friends like Lovell, but to make a more continuous narrative he will tell it as if it all came from the former source. Granted that Coleridge exaggerated, and that Cottle wrested it all a little more, these pages are still among the most amusing Coleridgeana that survive, culminating in the poignant story of the poor trooper in the sick-bay, fascinated by Coleridge's account of the twenty-seven years of the Peloponnesian War, who exclaimed, 'There must have been famous promotion there'.

Cottle takes advantage of this context to give us two pieces of literary information. First, he refutes Bowles's statement that *Religious Musings* was written 'in the tap-room at Reading', and can prove that it was written at Stowey, on Redcliffe Hill, and in his own parlour, where Southey, too, sometimes composed his verses. Secondly, at about this time Coleridge gave him some of his versions of German poets – including Lessing, whom he said he intended to translate in full. Cottle 'smiled. Mr C. understood the symbol, and smiled in return'. Perhaps from this transitional period, too, come a string of little incidents mentioned in *Reminiscences*:[25] how Cottle urged him to go to Ottery and visit his relations, or to dedicate some poems to his brother George; how he asked Coleridge about a nicety in hexameters, and on producing a sheet of paper was immediately rewarded with English specimens and introductory remarks to them; how, in an argument on similes, Coleridge said he hated bull and bear ones, but Cottle reminded him that he had added a *wolf* one to Southey's *Joan*.

Alarmed by news of Wordsworth's health, Coleridge was planning, in the autumn of 1799, to hasten north and see him. Cottle really meant to go to London, to wind up his affairs by a discussion with Longman; but Wordsworth's previous invitation, and the prospect of Coleridge's company on the journey up, made him change his arrangements, and he postponed his London visit until after the tour.[26] They therefore set out together from

Bristol on 22 October, in a post-chaise, on what Coleridge called 'my most important Journey to the North'. There is no record of their travels until Tadcaster, where Coleridge feelingly noted a sheep-boy and his dog with a sick sheep two hundred yards behind the rest of the flock; the same day, he observed some sheep going round and round, and leaping on and off a bank. Of his companion he records little; he calls him 'poor Cottle', and is possibly referring to him when he says 'Taste for Paradox in my man of Roads – always preferred cold water in shaving – and turned the Glass and looked steadily at its Back while shaving, &c. &c.' (Cottle later recommended cold water as an aid to longevity.) They stopped at York, and after breakfast at the inn Cottle went off to inspect the Minster – alone, as he saw that Coleridge was engaged; but a bookseller's shop detained him, and meanwhile Coleridge set out to look for him. He assumed that he would be at the Minster, but when the porter told him that no-one of Cottle's description had entered, he did not even trouble to peep inside, but went off in further search. Cottle, instead of taking this as flattering friendliness, denounces it as 'high treason against all architectural beauty!' He points out that Coleridge had no interest in buildings, and on his later return from Italy had nothing to say to Cottle of the antiquities of Rome.

By the 25th they were at Easingwold in the North Riding, where Coleridge noted a house with so many weeds in the thatch that it looked like a 'Hill-bank', which he thought he would put into verse, and, on the same day, a light yellow aspen; after this they must have proceeded by Thirsk and Northallerton, though their manner of eventually reaching Sockburn on the 26th is not recorded. The Wordsworths and Hutchinsons were delighted, but it was a fatal meeting: for the first time, Coleridge saw Sara Hutchinson. After tea Cottle asked Mary Hutchinson what she thought of Coleridge's first appearance.[27]

Asra or no Asra, the visitors certainly did not stay there long. On the afternoon of Sunday, 27 October, Wordsworth and Coleridge and Cottle set out on a tour of the Tees, mostly on its County Durham bank; the two poets walked, and Cottle, 'his Legs hugely muffled up', rode on a mare called Lily. From Sockburn they descended a 'miry lane' by Neasham Bank, which overlooked the peninsula formed by the Tees, and so to Hurworth, where Coleridge found interest in the dials on all the houses, the Hebrew on tombstones in the churchyard, and the fact that the mathematician Emerson had lived there. After another mile, by a footpath on the east side of the river, they reached the pretty village of Croft, where they discussed polytheism, monotheism, and roadside and churchyard tombs; it is unlikely that Cottle was the protagonist – and did he not feel uneasy about these excursions on the Sabbath? The same day they got to Piercebridge with its 1789 bridge, and spent the night at the George Inn, where 'the handle of the bell rope in the parlour was made of a shell'; Coleridge's further Notebook 5 entry, 'Landlady & Alfred', suggests some farcical scene involving Cottle. On Monday, 28 October, they covered the three miles to Gainford, where the exceedingly interesting church detained them only in so far as they read the churchyard epitaphs. They were at Barnard Castle by the end of the afternoon, which is poor going, though they turned aside to look at Egglestone Abbey; they should at least have gone a little south to Wycliffe-on-Tees, the birthplace of the Morning Star of a Reformation which, to Cottle at least, was a very real thing. Barnard Castle (lacking the Bowes Museum!) saw the last of them next day, Tuesday, 29 October, when they went three miles south-east along the Tees past Rokeby to the main road and the bridge over the Greta. Coleridge's Notebook No. $5^{1}/_{2}$ speaks rapturously of the little river, and how he 'hung over the Bridge', and when I saw the place in 1953 it was still defying the efforts of main-road traffic to spoil it. But to Cottle it suddenly meant something else; transport for the south was obtainable there. Either because the journey with Coleridge had been too energetic, or because Wordsworth was morose over *Lyrical Ballads*, he let them catch alone the coach over Stainmore to the Lakes. He says that the book was mentioned once, 'casually, and only to account for its failure! which Mr W. ascribed to two causes; first the "Ancient Mariner", which, he said, no one seemed to understand; and secondly, the unfavourable notice of most of the reviews'. Perhaps Cottle talked importunately of it, and Wordsworth grew testy; at any rate, at Greta Bridge, on the morning of Wednesday, 30 October 1799,[28] Cottle rode amiably out of their lives – finally, it might have seemed. Something else was ending for him besides the eighteenth century.

Coleridge was glad that he had left them – 'His timidity is indeed not greater than is easily explicable from his lameness and sedentary STATIONERY occupations; but it is extreme, & poor dear fellow! his self-involution (for Alfred is *his* Self) O *me that Alfred!* William and I have atchieved one good Thing – he has solemnly promised not to publish on his own account'.[29] The same feelings must lie behind Coleridge's remark in Notebook 5, 'Jo Cottle's angry Blow with the down of a Goose'.[30]

Cottle turned, not towards Bristol, but to London.[31] To settle his account with Longman and Rees (Owen Rees, who had been his neighbour in Wine Street), he called on the firm in Paternoster Row and sold them all his copyrights, which a third party valued as one lot. But when he next met Longman, he was told that the copyrights of *Lyrical Ballads* and Fox's *Achmed* were 'reckoned *as nothing*'. He made the astute or obvious answer that as the authors were personal friends of his, he would like the copyrights back, and then he could have the pleasure of returning both to them. Longman, 'with his accustomed liberality' (or, one might say, 'caught'), said that Cottle was welcome to them; so that when Cottle was back in Bristol he gave Fox his receipt for twenty guineas, and when Coleridge was back from the north he gave him Wordsworth's receipt for thirty. Thus 'whatever advantage has arisen, subsequently, from the sale of this volume of the "Lyrical Ballads", I am happy to say, has pertained exclusively to Mr W.'. This happens to be true, but the story can be filled out from the Copyright Book at Longman's, where (under a heading *Cottle's Copies*) appears among other things 'Lyrical Ballads' deleted. For all his books and copyrights, Longman paid Cottle a total of £210; but no books are mentioned in the case of *Lyrical Ballads*, and the deletion must reflect the later return of the copyright. So Cottle must have sold all the copies to Arch, retaining only the copyright. As for the copyright of *Achmed*, bought by Longman with 108 copies, it is not deleted from the Copyright Book, and it figures in two subsequent volumes; Mr W.J.B. Owen guesses that Longman would not part with it until he had sold the stock of 108.[32] By 15 December, when Southey wrote to Coleridge,[33] Cottle was 'busy', and would be adding just 'one short piece' to the *Annual Anthology*.

Two letters written on Christmas Eve of this year sneer at the hapless Cottle. Wordsworth, writing to Coleridge from Grasmere,[34] describes their journey thither from Sockburn – he was mounted on 'Lilly, or Violet as Cottle calls her'; later he adds, 'take no pains to contradict the story that the L.B are entirely yours. Such a rumour is the best thing that can befall them. Poor Cottle! Of this enough.' Coleridge, writing[35] in reply to Southey's news that Longman had paid Cottle £150 for the second edition of *Joan*,[36] assures him that Longman regrets the bargain, but that he is very eager to secure the property of Southey's works 'at almost any price'. In case Cottle hasn't told him, *he* can tell Southey what Cottle has arranged in London: the sole copyright of *Joan* and the first volume of Southey's *Poems* (quite apart from what Longman had given already) was taken up by Longman at £370. 'You are a strong Swimmer & have borne up poor Joey with all his leaden weights about him, his own & other people's. – Nothing has answered to him but your works. By me he has lost somewhat – by Fox, Amos & himself *very much*'.

Coleridge's last extant letter before a very long silence had reached Cottle at the beginning of December; he asked urgently if Sara were at 17 Newfoundland Street – if so, she was to write by return, and he would send her travelling and other expenses. They must live in London for the next four months.[37]

The present-day reader might feel that Cottle's 'importance' now ceases, that only Cottle the publisher has any lasting significance. But there is full justification for witnessing the rest of his crowded life; and it is a pleasure to quote from a very encouraging letter which Professor George Whalley sent to me in 1968:

> Cottle is a very real person, compassionate and sensible, and upright in the face of disability and disaster. I don't feel that he needs any apology or case made for him. The accident of his brilliant acquaintance doesn't diminish him; it puts him under a stronger light. By treating him with a sort of Hogarthian gravity you can do what STC, WW, and Lamb never did – see him straight. They treated him as a butt, were often unkind; and Lamb's letter on Amos's death would be unpardonable for its cruelty if it were not such pure fun and devoid of malice. I find Cottle fascinating more for what he was than for what he did.

Among provincial typographers and publishers his name should stand high; without the splendours of Baskerville at Birmingham, or the daring range of McCreery at Liverpool, he nevertheless braved risks such as the *Lyrical Ballads* and Fox's *Achmed*, and brought out handsome or pretty volumes such as the great *Joan* and the Coleridge-Lamb *Poems* of 1796. But the authoritative S. Morison in his *Four Centuries of Fine Printing* (1924), though admitting that 'the years 1770 to 1820 represent the finest period of English typography',[38] uses no specimen of his work; and it has been generally held that it was Bulmer, Bensley and McCreery who together 'played the major part in creating the classic period of English printing'.[39]

1   See Kenneth Curry, 'The Contributors to the Annual Anthology', *Papers of the Bibliographical Society of America*, Vol.42, 1st Qr., 1948.
2   *op.cit.*, p.139.
3   R.47, p.260n.
4   Curry, I.186-189.
5   Curry, I.192.
6   Curry, I.189.
7   Curry, I.192.
8   Shaver, I.259, No.113.
9   Shaver, I.257-258, No.111.
10   See Chapter 5, note 50.

11 Shaver, I.259-261, No.114.

12 Shaver, I.262-264, No.116.

13 R.47, p.258.

14 Shaver, I.264-265, No.117.

15 British Museum MS.Add.34486, fol.26.

16 R.47, p.185.

17 Shaver, I.267, No.119.

18 Shaver, I.267-268, No.120.

19 Shaver, I.268-269, No.121.

20 Shaver, I.269, No.122.

21 R.47, pp.219-220; for the fuller version see CCS, II.25.

22 Griggs, I.533-536, No.294.

23 R.47, pp.274 ff.

24 R.47, *loc.cit.*; but doubtless much of the Coleridgeana came to Cottle's ears at other times, as he admits.

25 R.47, pp.72, 126, 141.

26 The holiday will be seen from Cottle's point of view in R.47, pp.259 and 314n; and from Coleridge's in Notebooks 2, 5, 5¹/₂ and 21 (British Museum MS.Add.47518).

27 Coburn, I.Text, items 571 and 1537.

28 Shaver, I.271, No.124.

29 Griggs, I.543, No.299.

30 Coburn, I.Text, item 503.

31 R.47, p.259.

32 W.J.B. Owen, 'Costs, Sales, and Profits of Longman's Editions of Wordsworth', *The Library*, 5th Ser., Vol.XII, No.2, June 1957, p.93.

33 Curry, I.207.

34 Shaver, I.273-281, No.126.

35 Griggs, I.551-553, No.305.

36 Curry, I.209-210.

37 Griggs, I.546-547, No.301.

38 *op.cit.*, p.xxii.

39 J.R. Barker, 'John McCreery: A Radical Printer', *The Library*, 5th Ser., Vol.XVI, No.2, June 1961, p.82.

Chapter 7
Paulo Minora Canamus

The disappointments of the closing century were followed in 1800 by tragedy, the departure of his friends, and something near to financial ruin. He was still at Wine Street on 31 August 1799, when he advertised in *Felix Farley* for a house to rent near Durdham Down, any applicant to send a post-paid letter; but having left Wine Street, he went to live with his family in Gloucester Street, at its intersection with the new, fashionable, and handsome Brunswick Square. Consolations were few, but even without Coleridge to read for him he (or, to begin with, his man Osman) paid thirty-odd visits to the Library, at regular intervals:

6 Jan. – 30 Jan.	*Encyclopaedia Britannica*, Vol. I, Part 1
30 Jan. – 21 Feb.	*ditto*, Vol. I, Part 2
21 Feb. – 2 Mar.	*ditto*, Vol. II, Part 1
20 Mar. – 2 Apr.	Harwood, *Abauzit's Miscellanies*
2 Apr. – 8 Apr.	*Manuscripts in the Library of the King of France*, Vol. I
8 Apr. – 15 Apr.	*ditto*, Vol. II
(all the foregoing were borrowed by Osman)	
14 Apr. – 15 Apr.	T. Hearn's *Continuation of Dugdale* ('Does not circulate. v. Catalogue')
14 Apr. – 15 Apr.	Bentham, *History and Antiquities of the Cathedral Church of Ely*
15 Apr. – 16 Apr.	Pennant, *British Zoology*, Vol. I
16 Apr. – 22 Apr.	Lord Kaimes, *Sketches of the History of Man*, Vol. I
16 Apr. – 22 Apr.	Strutt, *Regal and Ecclesiastical Antiquities of England*
22 Apr. – (returned same day)	T. Broughton, *Dictionary of all Religions*, Vol. I
22 Apr. – 12 May	Hutchinson, *Northumberland*, Vol. II
22 Apr. – 23 Apr.	Pennant, *Scotland*, Part II

23 Apr. – 12 June (after letter of 30 May)	Henry, *History of Britain*, Vol. II
12 May – 12 June	Pennant, *Arctic Zoology*, Vol. I (connected with the writing of Cottle's *Markoff*)
21 May – 18 June	*Runic Poetry*
27 June – 15 July	J. Dryden, *Prose Works*, Vol. I
27 June – 15 July	G. White, *Natural History and Antiquities of Selborne*
15 July – 18 July	*Life of Catherine II*, Vol. I
18 July – 25 July	*Life of Lewis XV*, Vol. I
23 July – 11 Sept.	Camden, Vol. I (connected with Cottle's visit to Westbury in this year)
25 July – 11 Aug.	*Life of Lewis XV*, Vol. II
1 Aug. – 11 Sept.	Boswell, *Life of Johnson*, Vol. I
11 Aug. – 19 Aug.	*Life of Lewis XV*, Vol. III
19 Aug. – 26 Aug.	*ditto*, Vol. IV
26 Aug. – 18 Sept.	Rushworth, *Historical Collections*, Vol. I
11 Sept. – 19 Sept.	*Runic Poetry*
18 Sept. – 10 Oct.	Rushworth, *Historical Collections*, Vol. II
10 Oct. – 28 Nov.	*ditto*, Vol. III
1 Dec. – 23 Dec.	Wraxhall, *Remarks in a Tour through Copenhagen, Stockholm, and Petersburgh*
23 Dec. – 13 (?15,?18) Jan. 1801	Mrs Piozzi, *Anecdotes of the late S. Johnson, LL.D.*

(From September on, he had to be sent four reminders; he seems to have been more dilatory than most of the members)

The great men continued to use him and Biggs as printers. Early in the year, Wordsworth was arranging with them for a second edition of *Lyrical Ballads* in two volumes. On 1 January Coleridge writes to the Pneumatic Institution[1] that Longman wants Davy to publish a volume and will settle 'all the tradesman part of the Business' with the two printers. Davy stood in a position of greater trust than Cottle: Wordsworth told him on 29 July[2] that in future he would send the manuscripts 'to Biggs and Cottle with a request that along with the proof sheets they may be sent to you'; and Coleridge, writing from Greta Hall on 25 July,[3] hopes that Wordsworth will be writing to the two at once, but says that the poems must not be handed over to them yet, since *The Brothers*, which Coleridge has forgotten to give to Davy, must begin the volume.

In this year the second volume of the *Annual Anthology* came out,[4] with two contributions from the Cottle family. 'C', whom Southey's copy at Harvard notes as 'A. Cottle', submitted *An Elegy written in a London Churchyard, A Parody*; and Joseph himself had written *Markoff, a Siberian Eclogue*, which was printed in his name. This is a rather foolish poem in couplets, with its circumstantial details based on Pennant, about a contented Cossack in Siberia, with a wife and family, who was suddenly afflicted with wanderlust and resolved to brave the snows – in fact, to 'gaze on Nature in her rudest form'. After a daring ride through a ferocious *paysage*, his faithful reindeer all died and he was rescued by a band of SABLE HUNTERS; a footnote, as long and garrulously interesting as others with which Cottle relieves his verses, corrects our first surprised impression that they were negroes. The poem was eventually bound up with the *Malvern Hills* volume; and one of its phrases, 'caves of ice', finds an echo in *Kubla Khan*. It must be in connexion with this *Anthology* that Cottle was 'threatening' Southey 'with a packet from Trauma' (their unkind name for James Jennings).[5]

The only holiday of which we hear in 1800 took him to Westbury in Wiltshire, where he 'visited the Roman Camp, lying on the brow of the hill';[6] this is in fact an Iron Age fort called Bratton Castle, above the White Horse. He had been reading Camden on the subject and, suspecting that Camden's account of human remains in an oblong barrow was based merely on tradition (since there were no signs of excavation), he obtained permission from the proprietor and the incumbent of the parish to open the barrow. The workmen cut a trench lengthwise, and two transverse ones, and after ten or twelve feet reached a thin layer of charcoal and then immediately a great quantity of human bones. Cottle made notes on the stratification, went down into the trenches, and then had them filled up again. He was thus acquiring a new pursuit, archaeology, which would occupy his mind – never very profoundly – to the end of his life.

Southey was, as usual, the nicest person to know. On 6 April he sent to Cottle's new address in Gloucester Street a playful verse note:[7]

> Lend me Coleridge's second edition,
> Which is just now in requisition
> For I want a passage to quote,
> And have not got it by rote.
> And the volume shall be returned duly
> By Robert Southey, yours truly.

Perhaps of the same period are two slips among the same Southey miscellanea formerly in the Bristol Museum and now in the City Library;[8] they have been pasted on paper in a book, and then ripped out. They consist of large and small Greek letters, their English equivalents, and (on one) names and pronunciations like 'Upe-silon'; one slip has an example on its second page. They are partly in Cottle's hand; he heads them '118', '119', and writes 'Greek Alphabet, for writing English written by Robert Southey for J.C.'. Why Cottle coveted this curious piece of knowledge it is hard to say, and there is no evidence that he ever used it as a code or otherwise; it would have opened his eyes if he had ever picked up Coleridge's jottings in the Sara Hutchinson period.

Before 24 April, Southey wrote to him from Falmouth, where he and Edith were awaiting their boat to Portugal. So uncertain was their future, and so worried was Southey over his health, that these cheerful letters[9] do credit to him and to his correspondent. He disapproves of everything in Cornwall – inns and rain and rogues and food and horses, no favourable wind, and the lack of pilchards and white ale and squab pie. Cottle is to tell Davy that his birth there is the only thing in its favour. So with Devon; travellers who overpraise it must have slept through Somerset. Coleridge in a letter has spoken of 'fleaing (Cottle prints *flaying*) Sir Herbert Croft – which may not be amiss'. Southey is filching time from *Thalaba* to write to Cottle; when they meet again, he hopes to be stronger, with 'a trunk full of manuscripts'.

Eight days after landing at Lisbon he wrote again,[10] in tumbling Skeltonics, about the alarming voyage, his sea-sickness, Edith's fleas (he also rimes her with 'readeth'), and the lovely scene from their window; they will be glad to hear from him. Southey will write in prose next time, 'But in rhyme or prose,/ Dear Joseph knows/ The same old friend in me'. In July, when they had moved up to the cool of Cintra, he wrote yet again[11] – in haste, because his dear friend Miss Barker Congreve was leaving and could take the letter. He is in good health now, *Thalaba* is rapidly coming to an end, and he has amassed materials for his great work on Portugal. Cottle must 'abuse' Danvers, who has not written; nor have Edith's sisters written to her. And Cottle must write, too; Southey longs for Bristol news and society – if only he could transport this weather over! A postscript speaks of Methodist zeal, but says that the wide arms of the Church will soon absorb it, a sentiment which Cottle probably did not share. The Roman Church has the makings of a lasting political system, but is largely a 'pretty puppet show, with the idols, and the incense, and the polytheism, and pomp of paganism'; here Cottle would be heartily in agreement. Cintra, it seems, was all very pleasant, but Southey wrote to his mother on 21 August[12] that he wanted her, Danvers, Davy, Rickman, Cottle, some fresh butter, and the newspaper; just as he had written to Rickman on 2 May[13] asking to be remembered to George Dyer, 'the friend of every body', and to Amos and Robert Cottle, then both in London. But Rickman, we know, was hostile to Joseph's epic project; in a letter to Southey on 28 May he says that 'J. Cottle is vigorously printing unfortunate Alfred. I look with melancholy to his future disappointment. Amos Cottle dines with me on Saturday. We shall drink your health … I hear that R. Cottle (whom I do not know) is going to commence a bookselling business'. By 23 December he could write to Southey that a wicked wit in his rooms was calling Cottle the 'Epic Owl'.[14]

While Wordsworth was nettled over *Lyrical Ballads*, Coleridge in April estranged himself from Cottle by his own clumsiness. Cottle was in money difficulties and, stung by mean and frank things that Coleridge had said about his rising epic, had started pressing for payment of an old debt of £20. When the bill stood thus four years before, Cottle was 'in prosperous and promising circumstances', rich and indulgent, and promised that Coleridge would never be in his debt until he was a richer man than Cottle himself. So he had never sent the bill. But now his affairs had 'fallen to rack and ruin', and he sent Coleridge an importunate letter on the subject. The poet's method of payment was characteristic: he had no money, but was expecting more than £20 from his bookseller, so he gave Cottle a draft on Wedgwood, not to be presented for three weeks; and *then* he was going to write to Wedgwood, explaining, and send the money before the three weeks were out. Cottle (not, we hope, in revenge) anticipated him by presenting the draft before the time-limit – and Wedgwood wrote for an explanation. Coleridge was staying with Wordsworth at Grasmere, and on 21 April, upset by his own indiscretion, he sent off to Wedgwood his own wheedling excuse: he is sure that Cottle dunned him only in anger about his epic, when all the time Coleridge had advised him for his own good, to save him from publishing it at his own expense! – and his letter has shown 'a wounded & angry mind'.[15]

The dangerous Charles Lloyd makes a brief final entry into Cottle's life this year, with an affable letter (now in my collection) suggesting that with Cottle, at least, he had no quarrel; it also shows that Cottle was still known to have not only literary influence but active business interests in the form of his partnership as a printer with Biggs:

Olton near Birmingham
4th July, 1800.

Dear Cottle

I still expect to be in Westmorland in September, when I intend to make a point of duly transmitting to you an account of E. Oliver. Mrs. Lloyd and I are at present at a Country House of my father's; where we are likely to stay till after her confinement; which she is now expecting to take place every day. I sent a blank verse poem to R. Southey from Cambridge which he *talked* of inserting in the *next years Anthology* – I had *much* rather that it should not appear there, will you therefore be so good as to forbid its introduction.

If it would not seem obtrusive, I would request you to thank Mr Davy for the pleasure which I have received from his poem in the last Anthology – but you will consult your own discretion in this.

I have written a good many poems lately – I have also been engaged in a defence of Christianity – but I have no thoughts whatever of publishing. I feel myself obliged to you for your intention of sending me your "Alfred". Indeed, Cottle, on many accounts you are entitled to my friendly remembrance and gratitude.

With best regards to Miss Cottles, & your brothers, if they be in Bristol – I remain your obliged & affect.

C. Lloyd Jr.

P.S. if you write to Southey soon – pray give my love to him. I intend to send him a letter as soon as Mrs Lloyd is confined. I have lost your letter in which you sent your address – I shall therefore direct to you, in your *mercantile* capacity ──────

On Thursday, 15 May, Cottle's youngest sister Martha died at their Gloucester Street home in her sixteenth year.[16] It was the first of three deaths that rocked the family during 1800. All the time, he was scribbling away at his epic, *Alfred*. Eventually the twenty-four books, which in later versions reached over 13,500 dreary lines, were complete, and came out in 1801. His retirement from bookselling was a sad thing in itself; and nothing makes us regret it more than does the added leisure which let him write *Alfred*. On 1 August he penned at Bristol the astonishing Preface, which sounds like the clarion-call of some new poetic school. It attacks the epic machinery of slaughter, supernatural intervention, and 'the most flagrant violation of physical laws'. He feels that the time is drawing near when poetry will be freed from its ornamental appendages, which too often bring it under the ban of Philosophy; and in this poem he is concentrating on the feelings and passions of his readers, trying to find 'an avenue to the heart'. The dramatic poet has an advantage over the epic, who must declare the catastrophe without using suspense; but the latter *can* develop a sub-plot, 'where the result cannot so well be anticipated' – and this is where Alfred's Queen, Alswitha, comes in. In the first book, he admits, he has broken his own rules and let his imagination rip, because of the scope afforded by 'Gothic superstitions'; and in Book XXIII (*The Vision of the Guardian Angel*) he is so glad to be able to express the sentiments in 'the perceptive part' that he excuses the halt in the general narrative. If he is to be criticized, he expects 'candor'; but the reader will observe that the poet has had a hard task: skipping from Saxon to Dane, moving feelings of marvel, keeping 'the simple voice of Nature' going through so long a poem, 'preserving a necessary elevation of style', and so on. Of course, in his own passages of description he has used a loftier tone than he ascribes to the high speeches of simple men, which might else sound like bombast. But, whatever defects there are, he hopes it will be conceded 'that the tendency of the following poem, is decidedly in favour of morality'. If he had all 'the aggregate genius of all the poets that ever lived', he would still burn all his writings rather than publish a line against Virtue or Religion.

No poem of Cottle's earned and won such obloquy as *Alfred*, yet he learned nothing from the 'candor' he had invited. *The Fall of Cambria* – when, in due time, it lumbered up in all its twenty-four books – was wisely ignored; and *Messiah*, as bad as the rest, was protected by its theme. But friends, enemies and outsiders fell on *Alfred* with glee. Phrases like 'Cheer thou up' (III.462) provided a bathos that made the whole thing almost readable. Yet it suffered three more editions in 1804, 1816 and 1850, and an American edition at Newburyport in 1814. We shall see that Canning, Moore, and Byron, lumping Cottle with Jacobins and Lake Poets and such, used *Alfred* as a weapon; but Southey, Coleridge and Lamb were no kinder. We may assume that Wordsworth never read it, though as late as 1820 Dorothy, penned with her brother in a hot and smelly boat on the Lake of Lucerne, remembered the dismal poem: 'some of the party (to use the words of an Epic Poet, the Author of *Alfred*, on another occasion), "suffered grievously from heat"'.[17] The first broadside came from Lamb, who perhaps got no further than the horrific first book, and made the most of it. In a letter to Coleridge on 26 August, he wrote,[18] in a mood more frolic than gentle:

> Now I am touching so *deeply* upon poetry, can I forget that I have just received from Cottle a magnificent copy of his Guinea Epic. Four-and-twenty Books to read in the dog-days! I got as far as the Mad Monk the first day, and fainted. Mr Cottle's genius strongly points him to the *Pastoral*, but his inclinations divert him perpetually from his calling.

He imitates Southey, as Rowe did Shakespeare, with his "Good morrow to ye; good master Lieut[t]." Instead of *a* man, *a* woman, *a* daughter, he constantly writes one a man, one a woman, one his daughter. Instead of *the* King, *the* hero, he constantly writes, he the king, he the hero – two flowers of rhetoric palpably from the "Joan". But Mr. Cottle soars a higher pitch: and when he *is* original, it is in a most original way indeed. His terrific scenes are indefatigable. Serpents, asps, spiders, ghosts, dead bodies, stair-cases made of nothing, with adders' tongues for banisters – My God! What a brain he must have! He puts as many plums in his pudding as my Grandmother used to do; and then his emerging from Hell's horrors into Light, and treading on pure flats of this earth for 23 Books together!

Southey wrote scathingly to Danvers from Cintra on 13 September,[19] pressing into the service of his wit even the pallor of the invalid's face:

Never did Authors friends deal more honestly with him! And if his Enemies are as blunt – luckily the loss, if loss there be, will fall upon the London Cormorants – I have no bowels of compassion for them. And to sum up the merits of the book we shall have it flavoured with Essence of Tabernacle! I gave Cottle credit for more sense. If he really does swallow this miserable cant, we shall have him disgorge it in more ways than in Alfred, and Joseph will perhaps end in a Methodist Parson. Vexed and mortified as I should be – yet I should laugh to see his white face wax warm in the pulpit with a glowing description of the Great Furnace, charitably ordained for the ungracious like you and me!

In a later letter to Danvers, on 6 November,[20] Southey shows himself motivated by annoyance as well as contempt:

I have read *Alfred*. You remember my annotations upon the Poem made at your house; you remember too that as they were written in pencil Cottle rubbed them out but you will perhaps be surprized to hear that most of the passages which I then marked as nonsensical or bad are unaltered. The very Contunder which he knows to be sheer nonsense is there. I can give you the history of this incomparable piece of no-meaning. Thors weapon was a mall — mallet — or hammer. Poor Amos [Southey had recently heard of the death by consumption of both Amos and the Pantisocrat Hucks] in his Edda called this with propriety a Contunder from the verb *contundo*. Joseph did not know the meaning of the word, and what idea he annexed to it would puzzle Hartley to explain – however the word tickled his ear – and there it is

P.299. I fear the Reviews will half induce him to hang himself. About the Poem I am most orthodoxly calvinistic and believe it will be condemned to eternity.

Lamb's next chance for mockery came very soon, but it was an inappropriate occasion. Amos Cottle, now 34, died at his chambers in Clifford's Inn, London, on 28 September. Dorothy Wordsworth saw the announcement in *The Morning Post*, and just noted it in her Journal for Friday, 3 October.[21] Literature, mathematics, the Church, and now finally the Law, had been his little loyalties, and his unfulfilled life finds its poor memorial in his rashly venturesome *Edda*, in Southey's friendly lines to him written in 1796, and in the nine poems of his that Joseph published in his own *Malvern Hills* volume. His rimeless *Sonnet I* is to a nightingale, and may well have been written in the present 'Nightingale Valley' of Leigh Woods, facing Bristol across the Avon Gorge, since *Sonnet V* has this setting named. *Sonnet II*, of Shakespearean type, is a playful affair to his 'Dear bard' of a brother, whom he imagines sitting on a three-legged chair by a hawthorn, or 'Wooing the muses in ecstatic fit' under an oak, while cow or foal or cock or bees enrich his 'soft mellifluous lay'; soft are his lays, indeed, Amos repeats – as soft as the mole burrowing below him, but he must beware that no she-elf twitch his chair away. In the Miltonic *Sonnet III* he is in the Gorge again, in a solitary cell within St Vincent's Rocks, which had been among his 'youthful haunts'; the cave still exists in our own day, under the tower of the Observatory. *Sonnet IV* is to Poverty, which had been the lot of Spenser, Otway, Butler, and Burns; Amos imagines her squalid cot, and Independence passing by it 'with elastic foot'; as with the first of the series, this is a sonnet only in having fourteen lines. *Sonnet V*, like the other rimed ones, ends with an Alexandrine; one Edwin is addressed, and urged to lie during hot weather in the shade of Leigh Woods, where linnet and thyme will variously charm him and St Vincent's Rocks will front his view – but then Amos realises that, for poor Edwin, 'Not Tempe's self would please, were Rosalind away'.

The sixth poem, *On the Milton Gallery*, can be dated in the last year of Amos's life, since Henry Fuseli's Milton Gallery was opened in London in 1799; Amos gives some praise to Lawrence, Hoppner, Barry and Opie, but reserves his wonder for the daring flights and plunges of Fuseli's strange interpretations of Milton. The eccentric line 'Or sad Ulysses on the larboard steer' became notorious, since 'steer' (a noun) was taken as implying a young ox. In six-verse iambic stanzas, the seventh poem, *On the Vale of Oldland, Gloucestershire*, depicts the village (north of the Avon, on the way between

Bristol and Bath) where his feet used to stray 'In life's gay morn' – mill, 'decent church' and old yew, cottages and sheltering trees, nightingale and village green; Amos hopes that he is destined to dwell in a quiet vale, and not to be shaken in his mind by storms. The only other poem, apart from the uninspired Latin of *Italia Vastata*, is *On my Venerable Grandfather*; the old man had stuck at every post to which duty had assigned him, and like a brave warrior welcomed home from a last campaign departed for heaven after fighting the good fight, while angels escorted him joyfully.

Amos, who later suffered posthumously from the careless venom of Byron and others, had perhaps come under censure in his life on account of his association with 'Jacobins'. At any rate, *The Anti-Jacobin* in 1799 claimed that 'there exists at this moment, in some corner of the English literary world, an ode, Sapphic in metre, and Jacobin in sentiment, beginning with this line, "Amos, how oft, when we have been at Highgate"'; *they* will certainly read it if it comes their way.[22] This ludicrous piece cannot definitely be ascribed to Southey, or referred to Joseph's brother, but the existence of Southey's known Sapphics makes both conjectures likely.

Cottle went up to London for Amos's funeral, and Lamb, accompanied by George Dyer, who had been Amos's neighbour at Clifford's Inn, visited the house of mourning. Lamb's description of the scene, with Robert Cottle, Junior, also present, is contained in a letter of 9 October to Coleridge,[23] and is in a sparkling style of comedy; but it is surely too mocking for the circumstances:

> I suppose you have heard of the death of Amos Cottle. I paid a solemn visit of condolence to his brother, accompanied by George Dyer, of burlesque memory. I went, trembling to see poor Cottle so immediately after the event. He was in black; and his younger brother was also in black. Every thing wore an aspect suitable to the respect due to the freshly dead. For some time after our entrance, nobody spake till George modestly put in a question, whether *Alfred* was likely to sell. This was *Lethe* to Cottle, and his poor face wet with tears, and his kind eye brightened up in a moment. Now I felt it was my cue to speak. I had to thank him for a present of a magnificent copy, and had promised to send him my remarks, — the least thing I could do; so I ventured to suggest, that I perceived a considerable improvement he had made in his first book since the state in which he first read it to me. Joseph, who till now had sat with his knees cowering in by the fire-place, wheeled about, and with great difficulty of body shifted the same round to the corner of a table where I was sitting, and first stationing one thigh over the other, which is his sedentary mood, and placidly fixing his

Amos Cottle: lithograph from a painting by William Palmer, 1787 (reproduced from *Early Recollections* 1837)

benevolent face right against mine, waited my observations. At that moment it came strongly into my mind, that I had got Uncle Toby before me, he looked so kind and so good. I could not say an unkind thing of *Alfred*. So I set my memory to work to recollect what was the name of Alfred's Queen, and with some adroitness recalled the well-known sound to Cottle's ears of Alswitha. At the moment I could perceive that Cottle had forgot his brother was so lately become a blessed spirit. In the language of mathematicians the author was as 9, the brother as 1. I felt my cue, and strong pity working at the root, I went to work, and beslabber'd *Alfred* with most unqualified praise, or only qualifying my praise by the occasional politic interposition of an exception taken against trivial faults, slips, and human imperfections, which, by removing the appearance of insincerity, did but in truth heighten the relish. Perhaps I might have spared that refinement, for Joseph was in a humour to hope and believe *all things*. What I said was beautifully supported, corroborated, and confirmed by the stupidity of his brother on my left hand, and by George on my right, who has an utter incapacity of comprehending that there can be anything bad in poetry. All poems are *good* poems to George; all men are *fine geniuses*. So what with my actual memory, of which I made the most, and Cottle's own helping me out, for I *really* had forgotten a good deal of *Alfred*, I made shift to discuss the most essential parts entirely to the satisfaction of its author, who repeatedly declared that he loved nothing better than *candid* criticism. Was I a candid greyhound now for all this? Or did I do right? I believe I did. The effect was luscious to my conscience. For all the rest of the evening Amos was no more heard of, till George revived the subject by inquiring whether some account should not be drawn up by the friends of the deceased to be inserted in Phillips's Monthly Obituary; adding, that Amos was estimable both for his head and heart, and would have made a fine poet if he had lived. To the expediency of this measure Cottle fully assented, but could not help adding that he always thought that the qualities of his brother's heart exceeded those of his head. I believe his brother, when living, had formed precisely the same idea of him; and I apprehend the world will assent to both judgments. I rather guess that the Brothers were poetical rivals. I judged so when I saw them together. Poor Cottle, I must leave him, after his short dream, to muse again upon his poor brother, for whom I am sure in secret he will yet shed many a tear. Now send me in return some Greta news.   C.L.

Much of Lamb's mockery reached Josiah Wedgwood, since Coleridge quoted it in a letter to him on 1 November,[24] with the introduction, 'Poor Alfred! I have not seen it in print'. Cottle coolly put Coleridge's letter into his own

Reminiscences,[25] leaving out the part about himself, and adding the usual litter of mistakes.

Robert Cottle the elder was ending his unequal fight with Fortune. In *Felix Farley* for 4 October, we are told that the commissioners in a renewed commission of bankruptcy against him, since his bankruptcy in 1779, intend to meet at the Rummer Tavern, All Saints Lane, on Friday, 10 October, to make a final dividend of his estate and effects; and creditors with debts contracted earlier than 4 December 1798 (the date of the first commission) must come and prove them, if they have not done so, or be finally excluded from the dividend. He died on 25 November; *Felix Farley* calls him 'corn-meter, of this city', the office to which he had recently been appointed and which was abolished in 1862.[26] Thus Joseph Cottle found himself surrounded by women-folk only, his brother Robert being apparently resident in London. The printing occupied some of his time, and a series of fifteen cold, pragmatic letters[27] from Wordsworth to the firm of Biggs and Cottle, between mid-July and 23 December, contain instructions about the reprinting of *Lyrical Ballads*; though Wordsworth was the source of them, they are as often in the hand of his sister, or of Coleridge, or even of Sara Hutchinson. Wonderfully interesting as they are to us, with their rewordings and their stress on some particulars, they are so off-hand as to be meant for Biggs's attention only, even though Cottle's name is in the address and 'Dear Sirs' often in the heading; in fact, Cottle is not mentioned in their text, though 'Mr Biggs' is, and the few that start 'Sir' or 'Dear Sir' or 'Mr Biggs,/Sir' prove that in the poet's eyes Cottle was the sleeping partner. And, of course, they really represent the strangely selfless labours of Coleridge, who not only arranged the business side of the printing at Bristol, and of the publication by Longman, but worked solidly on the presentation of what were mainly Wordsworth's poems. Wordsworth's last letter to Cottle, for many years, was written on 18 or 19 December,[28] with news that Mrs Coleridge and the baby were with them, and Coleridge at Keswick; Wordsworth is sorry that he cannot give Cottle a copy of *Lyrical Ballads*, but he foolishly forgot to stipulate with Longman for any copies for himself – so the few he has must go to people who would otherwise be offended. (This might have been better put.) The second edition, to which Wordsworth here refers, had been printed for Longman and Rees by (as it says on the last page of the *Notes*) 'Biggs and Cottle, St Augustines-Back, Bristol'. On the 18th, also, as well as rounding off his correspondence with Cottle, Wordsworth in a letter to Longman[29] pointed out that 'by some unaccountable mistake, Mr Cottle sold the Copyright of the first volume when he had no more right to do so than to sell the house which I now inhabit'.

Freed from the pleasing pain of writing *Alfred*, Cottle was beginning to think of the worthier work of assisting Chatterton's sister; he must have had it in mind in October, when he invited W.H. Ireland, the Shakespeare forger, then visiting Bristol, 'to insert specimens of his ability at the end of one of the Burgum copy-books, then in Cottle's possession' – all this, Meyerstein adds,[30] 'with a sad lack of fitness'.

After a year so tragic and disastrous, 1801 must have begun a period of recruitment. He visited the Library only until June, and thereafter did not return until 1805; perhaps he could not even afford the subscription. His borrowings are of no great interest:

16 Jan. – 2 Feb.	W. Coxe, *Travels into Poland, Russia, Sweden, and Denmark*, Vol. II
2 Feb. – 20 Feb.	*ditto* Vol. I
4 Feb. – 7 Feb.	N. Drake, *Literary Hours*, Vol. II
6 Feb. – 19 Mar.	*Letters of a Hindoo Rajah*, Vol. I
20 Feb. – 24 Feb.	W. Coxe, *Travels into Poland, &c.*, Vol II
24 Feb. – 5 Mar.	Poiret, *Travels through Barbary*
5 Mar. – 26 Mar.	*Encyclopaedia Britannica*, Vol. VI, Pt. 1
19 Mar. – 23 Mar. (after letter of 21 April)	*Letters of a Hindoo Rajah*, Vol. II
26 Mar. – 7 Apr.	*Encyclopaedia Britannica*, Vol. VII, Pt. 1
7 Apr. – 30 Apr.	*ditto*, Vol. VIII
9 Apr. – 27 May (after letter of 19 May)	*Life of Catherine II*, Vol. I
4 May – 24 June (after letter of 15 June)	Boswell, *Life of Johnson*, Vol. II

There was another sadness on the way. Davy left Bristol for his triumphs in London, and on 9 March 1801, when just about to go from Hotwell, sent Cottle as a farewell gift Currie's edition of Burns. He had been so busy for six weeks that he could not call; even that morning he had meant to come and say goodbye, but engagements had prevented him, and the letter must suffice. If ever Cottle were in London, he would be welcome at the Royal Institution. Davy put a very affectionate subscription on the letter, and Cottle proudly inserted bits of it in *Malvern Hills* and the *Reminiscences*.[31]

The Cottles were Baptists, and Joseph was for some time a member of the Baptist College Committee. In 1801 we first have record of the family in the highly interesting archives of the venerable Broadmead Baptist Church (Union Street). On Tuesday evening, 5 May, Cottle's sister Sarah (named after her mother), being of well-attested character, was proposed and recommended as a member at Broadmead, and made her profession of faith and repentance; next morning she was baptized at the church with ten others, by the Reverend J. Ryland.[32]

Alfred was now published – for, presumably, the same reason that the tolerable *John the Baptist* would soon be available in a separate volume: to make money and to save the fortunes of the house. The epic gave Coleridge a fine opportunity to express himself, which he did in a letter to Southey on 22 July:[33] 'Poor Joseph! he has scribbled away both head and heart. What an affecting Essay I could write on that Man's character. — Had he gone in his quiet way, on a little poney looking about him with a sheep's eye cast now & then at a short poem, I do verily think from many parts of the Malvern Hill, that he would at last have become a poet better than many who have had much fame – but he would be an Epic, & so

> Victorious o'er the Danes I Alfred preach,
> Of my own Forces Chaplain-General!'

It is some tiny tribute to Cottle that Coleridge here bestowed on him a piece of his soundest, yet most charitable, criticism. Three days after, Southey replied to Coleridge:[34] Cottle had told him that Coleridge's poems 'were reprint*ing* in a *third* edition'; Southey had not yet read a number of wretched-sounding poems, including the Laureate Pye's *Alfred* '(to distinguish him from Alfred the pious)'. In fact, at Grasmere and at Greta Hall, says Coleridge, bits of slang were quoted whenever they talked of 'poor Joey, George Dyer, and other Perseverants in the noble Trade of Scriblerism'.[35]

I think it is important to stress here that until Professor Kenneth Curry's publication of the *New Letters of Robert Southey* we were unaware of the extent of Southey's betrayal of Cottle's simple trust; his protestations to his admirer (and confused imitator) were many, but behind his back he scattered remarks that were often harsh, hostile, and flippant. From most of these Cottle was mercifully screened; those few that reached him must have affected him cruelly in his lameness, lung-trouble, near-blindness, financial straits, religious questings, and loneliness. His inability to cope with the events of the day is perhaps summed up in Southey's 'Poor Cottle I can taste the bitter', unless this is just an anticipation of what the reviewers would do with *Alfred*; in the same letter[36] (from Portugal, on 20 January 1801) he asks Danvers to pay three guineas to his cousin, poor Peggy Hill, now in consumption and poverty, 'and as in Cottles circumstances he must find it inconvenient to pay her the guinea a month with which the Anthology account was chargeable, do you be her paymaster for this monthly sum – how can he have managed so ill? Did you not tell me that he had set up a one-horse chaise? And the poor fellow is utterly unfit for any situation – as there happen to be no convents in England. He would make an excellent monk'. Ten days later, in a letter to Rickman,[37] he couples 'Poor Amos' (presumably for being dead) with 'poor Joseph! and alas for Alfred the long, and his most inimitably original similes! I quake for Cottle when the reviews come at him – bunglers and block heads as they are'.

Back in England, he wrote to his Burton friend Charles Biddlecombe on 17 August[38] warning him not to buy *Alfred*, and tattling that Cottle is busy 'berhyming King Davids psalms – foolishly in my mind – but Death has made such havock in his family that he is turnd Calvinist again, and will one day be immersed in the mind and mire of methodism'. On the other hand, Southey is missing Amos, 'a pleasant companion, and a man whose knowledge and powers were daily increasing'. Assuming that Cottle had not remembered to get some copies of the *Anthology* for John King, Southey informs Danvers on 19 November[39] that he has himself obtained them. The same denigrating remarks continue into 1802. In January he tells Rickman[40] that 'Cottle – he who brayed thro the epic trumpet and played afterwards upon the Jews-harp, hath committed another work, an anonymous satire named the Methodist, quite as long and rather more fanatical than the extempore sermon of his own Angel in *Alfred*. Methodism has been very hurtful to him. His head has lost something – but such a head it matters not what becomes, but since he has taken to faith he has taken leave of good works'.

However, the review of *Alfred* in *The Gentleman's Magazine*[41] was surprisingly lenient. The reviewer feels it strange that, Alfred being so eminent a man, our 'first-rate poets' have sought other themes. Save for d'Urfey, in his *Historical Ballad of Alfred*, Cottle is the first to treat the subject; he has done so 'with great ability, and, in many instances, with success. It would not be fair to judge him by the rigid rules of epic poetry, which he has, in our opinion, very justly rejected, on a theme that would bear him out without them'. There follows a quotation from the *Preface* on this matter. The writer adds that it is a pity that Cottle has not written a new life of Alfred, since so many materials are available in the Bodleian and Harleian collections. There are some inequalities. Of course, 'Many of the sentiments are domestic, and such as will be felt by every British bosom'; and he quotes at length Alfred's speech to his men before battle – not, apparently, to carp at it.

The Reverend Robert Hall was deeply moved by the poem, which Cottle had sent him as a present. He found in it the true spirit of poetry, original

The Reverend Robert Hall: engraving (in the possession of Martin Crossley Evans) from a painting by Nathan Branwhite

images, exact descriptions, touching sentiments, proofs of the author's Christianity, a good psychological examination of Alfred's mind, and much to soften and improve his own. He wrote and told Cottle all this in a letter of 30 April from Cambridge,[42] and unfortunately Cottle hung on to the letter and let it inspire him to rewrite the poem for the 1850 edition. Hall was saddened at the death of Amos; 'untoward circumstances' had interrupted their friendship, but Hall still respected him and blamed only his 'connexions' for his 'coolness'.

Cottle spent ten months of 1802 in London,[43] staying at a printing-office in Crane Court, Fleet Street, and researching at the British Museum (which he misprints the 'Bristol Museum') and at the College of Heralds, where Garter, Sir George Naylor, had the 'urbanity' to let him use the library, and where officials told him Burgum had brought his 'pedigree' to be verified – with mortifying results. The subject of his studies was the Chatterton controversy, and he was greatly assisted by J. Haslewood, who had collected a copy of every relevant book, and who let him see them. Southey treated the work as a co-edition, and made Cottle put 'J.C.' against his own contributions, which chiefly concerned the authenticity of Rowley. We are glad to see that Cottle, by sifting the documentary evidence and through knowing so many of the boy's personal friends, including Thistlethwaite, made the right choice and vindicated Chatterton's authorship in four 'essays'. These were, in fact, a conclusive proof of Chatterton's forgery and his genius, and they mark an important stage in Chatterton scholarship. Cottle continued to acquire fresh matter, and enlarged his thesis in the 1829 *Malvern Hills*. The joint work does both men great credit, though the general arrangement fell to Southey.[44] Skeat, in his compromising and respelled edition of the works (1890), makes fun of Cottle's versions of Chatterton's Latin and Old French, but retains at least one of his mistakes, *Guateroine* for *Gualeroine*.[45]

Among Chatterton's acquaintances, old George Symes Catcott was probably the most helpful. Cottle was in touch with him from London, and when he wrote back on 18 March 1802 he had already called on poor Mrs Newton and told her the necessary portions of Cottle's letter. She was full of approval, and of gratitude to the two editors; Catcott promised all the help he could give in Bristol, and praised the two men's charity towards the widowed and fatherless. But he had consulted the most influential friends, and all were agreed that the filthy and libellous (and, incidentally, so asterisked as to be meaningless) *Exhibition* should be suppressed; and so it was, until the British Museum manuscript was edited in 1930. The object of their charity wrote to Cottle on 25 March,[46] approving the publication but asking for a few pounds before the sum should be settled in 'annuitys'; the last two years had been very difficult, she added, and she wanted to place her daughter to a mantua-maker. One happy story survives from this time: Cottle told her that he had proved her brother to be the author of all the Rowleiana; brightening, and with a very arch smile, she replied, 'Aye, to be sure: any body might have seen that with half an eye'.[47] In the 1795 *Album* is a copy of her 'candid account' of what she knew; it is only slightly illiterate, and Cottle appears in the third person. In August, Southey sent him an enthusiastic letter[48] praising his handling of the notes, assuring him that he was not offended by anything Cottle had taken on himself, and urging him to initial his own paragraphs; he had seen Catcott and talked to him about Chatterton's suicide threat. Cottle's reply found Southey away from home negotiating for a house eight miles from Neath, where he might have settled for ever instead of in the Lakes; and his explanatory letter to Cottle[49] was posted in London in September.

During this long stay in London, Cottle became friendly at last with Lamb, whom he had known before only from 'one casual visit', though Coleridge had kept Cottle informed of him; now they often met, a circumstance of which Cottle was no doubt proud when he wrote his *Reminiscences*.[50] Of their meetings we have only Lamb's whimsical description. Little did Cottle know that, behind his back, Lamb was again expressing an opinion of his Muse, in a letter to Thomas Manning of November 1802:[51]

… *Now*, as Joseph Cottle, a Bard of Nature, sings, going up Malvern Hills,
> How steep! how painful the ascent!
It needs the evidence of *close deduction*
To know that ever I shall gain the top.
You must know that Joe is lame, so that he had some reason for so singing. These two lines, I assure you, are taken *totidem literis* from a very *popular* poem. Joe is also an Epic Poet as well as a Descriptive, and has written a tragedy, though both his drama and epopoeia are strictly *descriptive*, and chiefly of the *Beauties of Nature*, for Joe thinks *man* with all his passions and frailties not a proper subject of the *Drama*. Joe's tragedy hath the following surpassing speech in it. Some king is told that his enemy has engaged twelve archers to come over in a boat from an enemy's country and way-lay him; he thereupon pathetically exclaims –
> *Twelve*, dost thou say? Curse on those dozen villains!
Cottle read two or three acts to us, very gravely on both sides, till he came to this heroic touch, – and then he asked what we laughed at? I

had no more muscles that day. A poet that chooses to read out his own verses has but a limited power over you. There is a bound where his authority ceases …

The tragedy seems to be lost, mercifully; perhaps Cottle, for once, listened to criticism and destroyed this curious offshoot of the drama.

As for the new *John the Baptist*, Southey effectively summed it up in a letter to Danvers on 23 March:[52]

> As for Mr Cottell
> He's exceedingly well
>   And another *poem* he has writed,
> About John the Baptizer,
> Twill not make you wiser
>   Nor will you be over-delighted.
> It was you may guess
> The first fruits of his press –
>   To me he presented a copy –
> Some bards ere they sing
> Quaff from Castaly spring,
>   But Joseph takes syrup of poppy.

We know something of the Cottle ladies in this year. On 17 January 1802, his sisters Ann and Mary sign, as 'Hearers' and after the members, the call of Brother Henry Page to be Assistant Minister at Broadmead.[53] That is, they were not members of the church, but 'constant Attendts on divine Worship, at the Baptist Meeting-house, in Broadmead, Bristol, & Subscribers to the Support of the Gospel'. Indeed, the Συνγραφη (Συγγραφη would be better) Σκκληιας[54] for 1802 has no male Cottles, but only the two Sarahs, mother and daughter.

On 24 April 1802 a sad little transaction occurred within the bereaved family. Old Mrs Cottle had long before given a little fat Bible of 1775 to one of her daughters (probably Elizabeth), who died. The mother had it rebound and wrote on an inset page:

> S: Cottle to her son Amos *This* was your dear Sisters Bible I have had it new Bound and now present it to you She made it her daily study and delight. May it be yours also O! that you like her may take it as the way of your counsal in every step thro Life.
> You will find it an unerring guide. A pleasant companion A Faithful counsallor and Sure Source of instruction & comfort under all the

difficulties and Troubles of Life. And may ye Lord the Spirit enlighten your Mind to understand it and direct your Heart into the Knowledge and love of it

> Here is ye Field where hidden lies
> The pearl of price unknown.
> That merchant is divinely wise
> Who makes that Pearl his own.

But now Amos, too, was dead, and the mother wrote on the next page:

> The dear Hands into which this Book was once given being now laid low in the dust I give it the third time (at her request) to my dear Daughter Ann. Hoping she will esteem it not only for its intrinsick worth which is far beyond mountains of Gold but also for the sake of her dear departed Sister & Brother and *not yet departed* Mother
>
> April 24th 1802

Another hand has written in it stanzas of hymns, including the whole of Anne Steele's *Father, whate'er of earthly bliss*, and Ann Cottle carefully signed her name; in the 1840s she had it rebound, and signed her married name on the fly-leaf. After its many adventures, this Bible came into my possession in 1949, by the kind gift of Major Ernest Dawson of Sidmouth, whose paternal grandmother was a Cottle.

On 12 September 1802, Mary Cottle changed her status at Broadmead, moving from the 'Hearers' into membership of the Independent Paedobaptist (or πβ) Church assembling therein.[55] This she did by a written declaration of her religious 'Exercises' in a letter to the Pastor, read to the Church, and she became 52nd in a list of members which ended at 80.

In London (at 46 Conduit Street, Hanover Square), Joseph Haslewood was behaving charmingly.[56] He was, after all, an eminent antiquary, and at first George Dyer (who knew so little of poetry!) acted as go-between – any *Life* of Chatterton was to be sent either to Dyer or to 'Cottle & Biggs, Printers, Crane Court', and Cottle 'thought himself authorized to open' such parcels as arrived. Dyer was keeping Haslewood informed; though in a note of 8 August 1802 he apologized for not being able to do so, as he had not met Cottle. When Cottle began a correspondence on Saturday, 20 August, it was in the third person: since their meeting, he had received proof that the 'Asaphides' pieces in *Town and Country* were indeed by Chatterton, contrary to Haslewood's conjectures, and he would like Haslewood to call at Crane Court on the morning of Tuesday or Wednesday, as he himself 'walks at present rather worse than he usually does'. On 1 September, again obliquely, he begged a sight of the printed *Resignation*, to settle 'a couple of doubtful words'; another note, undated, asks for the 'other Edition of Love & Madness' and for some further material. But by Saturday, 26 November, they were on first-personal terms; Cottle enclosed all the books he had been lent, and asked for the only thing they now needed, 'the list of Books', by Monday if possible. Haslewood was on time, and on the Tuesday Cottle wrote explaining that he had struck out some parts of this list of publications, and hoping that his friend would not be hurt at these excisions. Haslewood replied the day after, with cordial agreement, and on the evening of Friday, 10 December, while confined to bed with a sore throat and a cold, wrote a friendly and jocose letter asking for a copy of the final publication. It had been timed for that week, but on the Saturday Cottle wrote that he would have loved to comply, but that the plates were not finished and that publication would be delayed until early in the next year; he was off to Bristol for a month, but he would leave directions with Longman and Rees to have one of the first copies ready for Haslewood. On 21 December, perhaps just before starting this Christmas holiday, he closed the extant correspondence by returning Haslewood's manuscript bibliography of Chatterton and a plate which he had borrowed, for reproduction, from one of Haslewood's books. Southey welcomed him back to Bristol in a letter of 19 December from 12 St James's Place, Kingsdown,[57] asking him to bring various Chattertoniana and the finished sheets of *Amadis*; his doomed baby Margaret was sprawling so like a frog that Southey thought she could swim.

1   Griggs, I.556-557, No.308.

2   Shaver, I.289-290, No.135.

3   Griggs, I.611-612, No.342.

4   See Chapter VI, note 1.

5   Curry, I.216.

6   MH.4, I.118n.

7   Bristol City Library MS.B 20857.

8   Bristol City Library MS.B 20856.

9   R.47, pp.220-221; and Berg Collection, New York Public Library.

10   R.47, pp.221-224; and *1795 Album*.

11   R.47, pp.224-225.

12   CCS, II.100.

13   Curry, I.223-227.

14   Orlo Williams, *Life and Letters of John Rickman* (London: Constable, 1911), pp.33, 36; a mistaken footnote on p.27 makes Amos the author of *Alfred*.

15 Coleridge, letter to Wedgwood, in British Museum MS.Add.35344 (Poole Correspondence), II, fol.2; Griggs, I.586-587, No.332.

16 *FFJ* for Saturday, 17 May 1800.

17 E. de Selincourt, *Journals of Dorothy Wordsworth* (London: Macmillan, 1952), 18 Aug.1820.

18 E.V. Lucas, *op.cit.*, I.209 ff.

19 British Museum MS.Add.30928, fol.7; this and similar comments to Danvers are published in Robert Southey, *Journals of a Residence in Portugal 1800-1801…*, ed. A. de O. Cabral (Oxford, 1960).

20 Curry, I.227-230.

21 E. de Selincourt, *Journals of Dorothy Wordsworth*, I.63.

22 *The Beauties of the Anti-Jacobin* (London: Plymsell, 1799), p.144.

23 E.V. Lucas, *op.cit.*, I.216-217.

24 Griggs, I.642-646, No.362.

25 *R.47*, pp.438-443.

26 Beaven's *Bristol Lists*, p.247, wrongly dates his death 25 March, but has the correct month on p.336.

27 Shaver, I.285-288, 290-293, 302-309, 311-312, Nos. 133, 134, 136, 137, 138, 139, 141, 142, 143, 144, 145, 147, 148, 149, 151.

28 Shaver, I.306, No.146.

29 Shaver, I.309-310, No.150.

30 *op.cit.*, p.494.

31 *MH.4*, I.viii; and *R.47*, p.291. By 25/26 Feb. 1801 John Wordsworth could write to Mary Hutchinson that 'Cottle had no *hand* in the correction of the press [—] it was entrusted to Mr Davy'; C.H. Ketcham, *The Letters of John Wordsworth* (Ithaca: Cornell U.P. 1969), p.95.

32 'Broadmead Baptist Church / Letters and Documents of Interest from 1650 on' (MS.volume of archives): fol.218 of *Broadmead Records*, 1779-1817.

33 Griggs, II.746, No.405.

34 CCS, II.153.

35 Griggs, II.749, No.407.

36 Curry, I.234-237.

37 Curry, I.237-242.

38 Curry, I.245-247.

39 Curry, I.254-257.

40 Curry, I.266-268.

41 Vol.LXX, 1800, ii.975-976.

42 Joseph Cottle's *Alfred*, 4th edn (London: Longman, Brown, Green and Longmans, 1850), p.xi; and *1795 Album*.

43 *R.47*, pp.146n-147n.

44 CCS, II.186.

45 W.W. Skeat ed., *The Poetical Works of Thomas Chatterton* (Aldine Edition) (London: Bell, 1890), I.271.

46 Meyerstein, *op.cit.*, p.495.

47 MH.4, II.412.

48 R.47, pp.225-227.

49 R.47, pp.227-228.

50 R.47, p.151.

51 E.V. Lucas, *op.cit.*, I.330-331.

52 British Museum MS.Add.30928, fol.29; Curry, I.272-275.

53 *Broadmead Records*, 1779-1817, fols.229-230.

54 *Broadmead Records*, 1779-1817, fol.223.

55 Broadmead MSS: 'Records of the Independent Church, 1757 to 1818', no foliation.

56 Collection of cuttings, MSS, and plates, relating to Chatterton, in the 1803 edn, British Museum Printed Books, c.39 h.20(1).

57 Berg Collection, New York Public Library.

Chapter 8

Chatterton: John Foster and George Cumberland

In January 1803 the Chatterton project was successfully completed, but with an unhappy aftermath;[1] for our story, the year is also signalized by the quiet entry of Thomas de Quincey. The definitive three-volume edition of Chatterton's verse and prose was printed by Biggs and Cottle at Crane Court for Longman and Rees. Mrs Newton was still complaining of being in want, so Cottle (now back in Bristol) wrote to Longman and Rees, and the firm sent him £30 – not having received a quarter of that themselves. He at once passed it on to her, and she receipted it on 12 March. But she seemed suspicious and, knowing nothing of the world, expected money on publication; she called on him several times, and had the idea that the publishers ought to give her a bond. Hurt as he was by this suggestion, he merely told her that it could not be given; in fact, he had to mortify himself by telling her that she could rely on his and Southey's honour. Or, worse, she sent people – a Mr Lewis, first of all, who felt he ought to say something of poetry and therefore remarked that Milton had cribbed almost all *Paradise Lost*. Lewis proved tractable enough, and two other persons, who came before the year was out, were anxious to know when all would be settled but admitted that her health, and not her money, had fallen low. Cottle promised that he would write to Longman and Rees at Christmas, and that if meanwhile she needed money he would send her some of his own. The whole business was so worrying that his mother advised him to drop it, but he was determined to go on and prove his integrity; in the event, he also proved his acumen. At the beginning of December he wrote to the firm, asking them to write to all subscribers who had not paid, and this they did.

At a quarter to five on the afternoon of Sunday, 15 May 1803, the seventeen-year-old Thomas de Quincey strolled into the shop of his grown-up friend James Wright, of Merritt and Wright, Booksellers at 60 Castle Street, Liverpool. His precocious conversation on this afternoon was punctuated by half a cup of coffee, and concerned *The Edinburgh Review*, Coleridge, Wordsworth, Southey, the Cottles, Longman and Rees, and Bree.[2] The Lake Poets were already objects of his admiration, and Cottle was

The Reverend John Foster: engraving (in the possession of Martin Crossley Evans) from a painting by an unknown artist

the means of his meeting Coleridge. Cottle, of course, was fast fading from the minds of the great men. Coleridge used a curious illustration in a letter to Southey on 1 August:[3] 'I was thought *vain*/ if there be no better word, to express what I was, so let it be/ but if Cottle be *vain*, Dyer be *vain*, J. Jennings be *vain*, the word is a vague one'. In a letter of 1802[4] he had thanked Southey for letting him know of an amusing 'Cottelism'. To him, in fact, Cottle was now one of the 'mere Scribblers', along with Pye and 'his Dative Case Plural' Pybus;[5] and the Reverend Richard Warner's praise of the two Cottles in his *Tour Through the Northern Counties*[6] — 'Arcades ambo', who had 'given, from their own press, works which would add to the fame of any poet of the day' – elicited from him the comment 'Ha! Ha! Ha!' when he wrote to Sara Hutchinson.[7]

Cottle had by now made the acquaintance of the Baptist minister and essayist, John Foster, who had been born in the same year as he, and who would eventually be one of his most persistent correspondents. They may have met between September 1791 and May 1792, when Foster was studying at the Bristol Baptist College, or after 1800, when Foster settled as pastor of a small congregation at Downend, on the fringe of Bristol. At any rate, he called on Cottle, wanting to publish; Cottle wrote on his behalf to Longman & Co., recommending them to publish the *Essays*, and they replied with their consent on 20 October 1803 – not having even seen the work.[8] They finally brought out the first of at least thirty-five English and American editions in 1805. Not all these *Essays in a Series of Letters to a Friend* (Foster's future wife) are interesting; but that *On the Application of the Epithet Romantic* is an exciting piece of pioneer criticism, and Cottle's fostering of it (if the phrase be permitted) gives him a new reflected importance in the Romantic movement, especially as he may well have introduced Foster to his poets or their poems. Paul Kaufman, in a paper read to the Modern Language Association meeting of 1917,[9] was the first to rescue from neglect Foster's perceptive study of 'the ascendancy of imagination over judgment', of romantic humanitarianism and its fallacies, of romantic egotism and reverie. Even if Kaufman went too far, in seeing an actual anticipation of Shelley and Byron in Foster's prophecies, yet there is little doubt that Foster was easily our first interpreter of Romanticism, and the most authoritative from 1805 until Hazlitt's discussion in *The Edinburgh Review* for February 1816.

At the beginning of January 1804 Cottle again wrote to Longman for an exact statement of the amount in their hands of the Chatterton money, and for permission to draw on them for the balance. He also told them of Mrs Newton's wish for a bond, which he thought an 'indelicacy, as we were the persons from whom she ought to expect every thing'. During the month, they informed him of the balance of £154.15s, and he then sent to her friend Mrs Cross, asking her to accompany him the following morning to the house in Cathay (an area in Redcliffe), to pay her the balance. Mrs Newton was abed, and they went to her room, where Cottle read her the publishers' statement. On receiving the draft, she joyfully said that she would put the money 'in the Stocks' at once; Cottle said she must do as she pleased, but should consult her friends. He told her that he and Southey had done all they could, and she replied that 'the conduct spoke for itself'. Holding the draft, she said ecstatically to her daughter, 'Well, Mary, I have often had valuable papers in my hands, but I never had such a valuable paper as this before'. He pointed out that they wished to comfort her last days; she must have good food, a nurse, and medical advice. This she promised to see to, and began to load him with thanks, but he said that he and his friend were merely instruments of a higher power. This interview may have taken place on 7 February 1804, the date of her receipt now in the Bristol Library. When he took his leave, he promised to write to her the next day, 'for the consideration of her & her friends'.

So, after composing a letter to her, he transcribed it for Southey's benefit, and explained to him his motives in writing it: he had written kindly because she was so ill and because she had been importunate on the advice of others, not by her own inclination. It is, indeed, a very courteous letter, reporting that he has now paid her £184.15s; if she still wants a bond, Longman and Rees are willing to give her one, and then he and Southey will resign their part with a statement of their stewardship; let her use her friends' advice – he and Southey are anxious only for her welfare. The account makes it clear that 'Profit to Mrs N' will amount to £502.7s.

She at once replied that she definitely wished them to carry on, contrary to the evil counsel of Mr Lewis. Cottle was by now mollified, but very glad that the work was nearly over. He advised Southey that, when various people had paid for their copies, they should publish an account in *The Monthly Magazine*, but Southey must decide.[10] Some time after the publication of the edition, Mrs Newton had gratefully given Cottle the only piece of Chattertoniana left to her after Croft's depredations, her brother's memorandum-book, with the melancholy credit and debit accounts of his stay in London;[11] it is now part of the Chatterton collection in the Bristol City Library. Southey, writing on 1 March[12] with news of his expected second child and with pleasure at Cottle's loss by marriage of his sister Sarah, praises him warmly for his patience with Mrs Newton and somewhat excuses her for her suspicions, in view of her status and the way she had already been cheated, but suggests that they publish statements in two magazines; he includes a long description of the genesis and fulfilment of his *Madoc*, delicately putting it parallel with *Alfred* – but four days later, writing to John King,[13] he called *Alfred* 'the great Half-read, which tho an uncommon poem, is of the common size' (quarto, that is). This formula for Southey's dealings with Cottle – undeviating kindness to his face, and behind his back contempt for his scribbling but tributes to his goodness – is reflected in a letter to Danvers on 11 October,[14] asking him to warn Cottle against his cadging ne'er-do-well brother Edward Southey, because 'to him he is likely first to apply, and would succeed there'.

Poor Mrs Newton survived her onset of good fortune by only sixteen days; but the £300 she left, and the £800 at which the will of her daughter Marianne was proved three years later, show that Cottle's voluntary effort had been worth while. Thus the Chatterton line glumly ended in 1807. The boy's suicide, as Meyerstein points out,[15] 'does not seem to have served his folk so badly, after all'. But how much of that £800 was earned by Cottle and Southey alone? In *The Gentleman's Magazine* for 1804[16] the two explain to 'Mr. Urban' how the work was financed. Since, after two years, they had not enough subscribers, they entered into an agreement with Longman's by which the firm undertook to print at their own expense, allowing Mrs Newton 350 copies *gratis* for her own subscribers, with a reversionary interest of fifty copies on the sale of every succeeding edition. The statement of accounts that follows shows the editors' expenses column with nothing against it! The dead woman and her daughter will have received about £500; and, since Mrs Newton appointed two other gentlemen as her executors, Cottle and Southey have handed affairs over to them. Their own work was honourably discharged.

Early in the year, the second edition of *Alfred* was ready, printed for Longman by J. Mills of Bristol in the case of the first volume, and by Fenley and Sheppard of Bristol in the case of the second. Again the trumpet-call of the *Arma virumque cano* first line rang out, 'Alfred victorious o'er the Danes, I sing'; again there was the preface, but this time there was an additional preface of forty-two pages, a fatuous compilation. Cottle is obviously answering objections, which he does in a fulsome style and with a spate of commas. Among other things, his 'style, by some persons, also, has been censured for not being sufficiently elevated'; this seems likely enough. To explain himself on the subject of Norse mythology, he brings in remembered bits of Amos's learning, but he is also at pains to state the aims of poetry; for instance, 'interest can only be attained by *moving the breast*'. He believes that blank verse should be read with a pause at the end of every line. Before beginning the work, he examined what others had done with like subjects, but the reader will find *here* no 'classical or scientific embellishments, ... learned references, ... metaphysical illustrations of abstract sentiments. It comes to him without sanction or patronage – with many disadvantages to encounter, and perhaps some prejudices to surmount'.

He at once sent Southey a copy, to await him at Longman's, and warned him of this in the big letter of 22 February, wherein he reported his dealings with Mrs Newton. When Southey was last in Bristol, Cottle showed him an outline of the preface, but now he had much enlarged it. He must have gone up to London at the time of publication, since he apologizes for leaving the two volumes there and not sending them from Bristol; this he did to save the expense of carriage and to be certain of Southey's receiving them. His sister Sarah is going to marry a 'respectable and worthy' Plymouth gentleman, Mr John Saunders, an attorney; they are very miserable at the thought of losing her. (We shall find that the Saunders dynasty will be gloomily linked with John Foster.) The Cottle sisters had called on Mrs Southey the day after she left Bristol, and were very sorry to miss her.

Southey's reply,[17] on 16 December, conveyed regards to Cottle's worthy friend Porter (who had visited Keswick in July), and news of his *Madoc*, the new baby Edith's inoculation, the Southey brothers (including the warning about Edward), and Scott's 'exceedingly civil' review of their Chatterton edition. But the letter is chiefly devoted to the excellent advice – which Cottle was too diffident, or too much of a poetaster, to follow – that he should write 'a book about Bristol': not a history, and certainly not another Barrett, but an *Anecdotes* of Bristol, illustrated with townscapes and portraits, drawing on the memories of old people like Mrs Cottle, recounting murders and mysteries, describing the city before the new Georgian Streets went up and St Leonard's Church came down, with Clifton and Kingsdown still villages. Cottle could include Henderson in the biographies, and the various navigators, sectaries, entertainers, and manufacturers, with a complete catalogue of books published in Bristol. Southey suggests this persuasively and even enthusiastically, and from what we know of Cottle's garrulous style and varied interests it was a very sensible idea, luring him away from his silly epics and planning for him a worthwhile book; but only with regard to Henderson did he follow its outlines, and his own memoirs, which were entirely literary, were disastrous when they erupted thirty-three years later.

Another new acquaintance and correspondent appears in 1804: the author, diarist, and Chattertonian scholar, George Cumberland, kinsman of the eminent seventeenth-century Bishop of Peterborough. His papers at the British Museum have many references to Cottle, though the topics are usually trivial enough. On 30 November Cottle wrote from Bristol to

Cumberland at Weston-super-Mare,[18] with his remarks on a poem, *Home*, that Cumberland had submitted to his criticism. Well, on the few occasions when friends have done this, he has always banished 'unmeaning compliments' and been frank; so he must say that *Home* 'is very far from being *a correct* poem'; though good in parts, its sentiments and characters are imperfectly drawn, and the poet will have to work hard at it – especially some words and lines that Cottle has marked with a dash. Of course, he may not always have understood what Cumberland was getting at, so why not bring in a third person? The thing probably has more 'Genius, than, accuracy or habit of writing'. He adds his respects to Mrs Cumberland and the ladies.

The rather formal friendship ripened in 1805. On Thursday, 21 March, Joseph and Mary and Ann Cottle 'rode out' into Clifton, where the Cumberlands were then staying. Mary was all for calling on them, but Ann felt 'too weak to bear the fatigue'. For nearly a month she had been unwell, and in bed almost all the time; and Joseph himself had been under Mr Baynton the surgeon for *over* a month (and had not yet dismissed him) on account of the inflammation and gathering from an ingrowing big-toe-nail, nearly all of which he had just had cut off by a nasty operation. Not long after this frustrating day, Cumberland returned a copy of the *Edda* without even a note, so on 25 March Cottle, assuming that he was hurt by their negligence, wrote with a full explanation, saying that he liked and admired Cumberland so much that he felt he must offer his explanatory excuses; he took the opportunity to congratulate them on the prospect of living at Weston in the coming summer. Cumberland, who thought the letter 'affectionate', replied the same day, since a Mr Jordan was coming into Bristol.[19]

Worse health followed for Cottle. From early in April until the end of May, he suffered frightful rheumatism, which confined him to bed in 'infantine weakness'. After that, he was for five weeks carried up and down stairs by two men, and even in August his hands were so swollen, and his fingers so rigid, that he could hardly write. He contracted all this through an exposure which would not have affected a healthy frame; but he, of course, could have little exercise and was always penned in one room, a sitting prey for all diseases. His lameness was worse; this summer he could hardly walk about the house, and since early in 1804 he had not stirred outside save to enter a coach or a sedan. In June, they suffered anxiety over Sarah, now Mrs Saunders, who had a stillborn child and recovered after over forty hours' touch-and-go.[20]

However, after a long intermission he was able to reach the Library on 15 August, and borrowed Grose's *Ancient Armour* and his *Military Antiquities*, Vol. I. And the weary months had not been entirely wasted. This year Cadell brought out Cottle's *Selection of Poems designed chiefly for schools and young persons*, which he compiled with his sister's school in mind; the poems were by various authors, including himself. Also, he had rewritten his translation of the Psalms, and the second edition, A *Version of the Psalms of David, attempted in Metre*, was published by Longman in this year. On page xii of the introduction he explains that this congenial task has been his day and night companion for a long time. 'It has cheered me in sickness and in solitude, and, at the same time, has tended, more than any external cause, to solace my mind under a permanent personal affliction'; it makes him hope that he will not have lived in vain.

In the pathos of these words, we might almost be listening to a different man from the patron of Wordsworth, the colleague of Davy, the expansive guide to Tintern. At thirty-five, he had reached a kind of hopeless middle age; and the poor Tate-and-Bradyish quatrains of his *Psalms* must be excused, in view of the comfort they afforded him. So it is hard to snigger at what Coleridge says of the *Psalms* in a remark to be found in the Notebooks: 'Diamond + x Oxygen = Charcoal N.B. Cottle's Psalms –'; the joke is that Cottle blew over King David's diamonds 'the oxygenous blast of his own inspiration', and turned them into charcoal. Incidently, the Notebooks have some other nasty references to Cottle. One of them sneers at his education: 'Advantage of public schools – content with school praise where others publish. Applied to Cottle & J. Jennings'. Another ridicules his Bristol dialect: 'The holy ghost left all the Solecisms, hebraisms, & low, Judaic prejudices as evidences of the credibility of the apostles/ so the Theopneusty left Cottle all his Bristolisms not to take away the credit from him & give it all to the Muses'. Even his 'moral character' is impugned: 'The ψευδο-poets, Campbell, Rogers, Cottle' (this is almost obliterated) 'etc., both by their writings & moral characters tend to bring poetry into disgrace'; and he is coupled with the 'oozy, hypocritical, praise-mad, canting, envious, concupiscent' Samuel Richardson. But *Alfred* is the principal butt: 'Your very humble men in company, if they produce any thing, are in that thing of the most exquisite irritability & vanity – Ex. gr. Cottle & his Alfred'.[21]

In a letter to Southey, posted on 20 August, Cottle poured out his accumulated troubles, partly to explain why he had not answered Southey's letter of the previous December. By this time, to add to his difficulties, his sedentary life and his long seclusion had induced lassitude of mind, and he could not feel interested in anything, or wish to meet a stranger, or extend his acquaintances; so that his old friends like Southey were all the more precious. He wanted to do good, but circumstances were preventing him from doing *anything*. 'The Theatre for great and good actions, to me, seems forever closed'; he had not done much when he could, and, if his harvest were nearly over, how small the produce!

Southey had sent him *Madoc*, and he felt he would like to review it, if only to save it from 'these dogmatizing Gentlemen' who cannot feel poetry. When it came, he was in bed, and for a month it had to lie by, since his dinners of bread and water, and his aperient draughts, left him no strength to sit up and read. Though he knew some of the first part, the second was largely new to him, and it has given him much pleasure; Southey deserves to be chaired by poets, and Cottle would give him his loudest 'Huzza! Southey forever!' He points out that, as a dabbler in heraldry, he notices that the title-page has a shield vert with three eagles unscientifically engraved; still, not many will spot that! He jokes of 'a Cross Pattee fitchen (?) at the mizzen mast'; after all, everyone turns to his professional interest, even as they look not at the Lord Mayor in his Show, but at some technicality that attracts them – the last Cottle saw 'was a sad ugly fellow Sir Wm Staines a Mason.' In his last letter, Southey suggested that Cottle write a history, or some such thing, of Bristol – but he would rather read one, and only Isaac James is qualified for the job; they seldom meet now, but Cottle recalls his wonderful memory. Southey *must* read Foster's *Essays*, marred only by long sentences; it has 'the vigor of Junius, with more than the imagery of Burke', and Foster's imagination dims that of almost everyone Cottle has known. If people thought it was by Milton, or Bacon, the country would be in tumult. 'The man who publishes a Book for the next twelve months ought to be hung for arrogance'; in any case, Foster has 'much private worth'.

As for his own endeavours, he has 'a large ship on the Stocks. The Ribs are up and lower deck laid' – Tom Southey could continue the image. It is on Edward I's conquest of Wales. (In other words, he was writing *The Fall of Cambria*.) It cheers him in his wearisome sitting; he has written six books and planned the whole, 'and if it were not for the Musick and the Dancing, which almost forever sounds' in his ear, would go further and better. There are to be lyrics; many will object to this, but praise or censure takes as long in reaching his retirement as the news of James II's flight did in reaching Skye. He hopes that Southey has had the book and letter left at Longman's house for him. He has also asked Longman to send him the new *Psalms*; though he enjoyed rendering them, he does not expect the book to pay its own expenses. Old Mrs Cottle, and Mary, Ann, and Robert, are all well, and desire to be remembered; likewise, he sends regards to Mrs Lovell, Mrs Coleridge, and the little Coleridges. He hopes Mrs Coleridge has not forgotten him, as they were always such good friends. He obtained Southey's new address from Miss Fricker (presumably this is Martha, she who was to have been Mrs Burnett); if only the Southeys could come and live in or near Bristol!

Southey, however, had not heard of the Book of the Year, or even heard Cottle mention Foster, its author. He wrote back quickly on 25 August,[22] in real concern over Cottle's misfortunes, and promised to try and get hold of it – 'but no new book ever reaches these mountains except such as come to me to be killed off'. He recommends Cottle to try the 'case-hardening' called by Franklin the air-bath, five minutes' rub with a coarse towel every morning on rising, such as Southey has practised for the past year: start gradually, for only half a minute, and remember how good is friction with coarse towel or flesh-brush; Cottle should change his chair a couple of times a day; and use the settee when he is simply in conversation. Southey kindly links his own Welsh *Madoc* with Cottle's *Fall of Cambria*; in fact, if only they lived nearer he could help, by turning over to him unused notes on the Welsh. It is interesting to see that he encourages Cottle to introduce lyrics, and that he wishes the poem could have been in the Spenserian stanza; the circle obviously realized that Cottle's worst equipment was blank verse.

For the remainder of 1805, while the war swept superbly by and left Romantics and their publishers aloof, Cottle must have regained a little of his mobility; on 23 August he revisited the Library, returned the two volumes of Grose, and borrowed as follows:

23 Aug. – 26 Aug.	Holinshed, *Chronicle*
23 Aug. – 26 Aug.	Dallaway, *Inquiries into the Origin and Progress of the Science of Heraldry in England*
26 Aug. – 11 Nov. (after letters of 15 Oct., 31 Oct., 7 Nov.)	Wm Jones, *Physiological Disquisitions*
26 Aug. – 9 Sept.	Henry's *England*, Vol. IV
4 Sept. – 9 Sept.	Froissart's *Chronicle*, Vol. III
11 Nov. – 4 Dec.	Pennant, *Tour of Wales*, Vols. I & II
4 Dec. – 19 Dec.	Rowland, *Mona Antiqua Restaurata*
4 Dec. – 10 Dec.	Froissart's *Chronicle*, Vol. II
19 Dec. – 6 Feb. 1806 (after letter of 30 Jan.)	Dallaway, *Anecdotes of the Arts in England*
19 Dec. – 6 Feb. 1806	Matthew's *Essay...*

Of Cottle's little day-to-day activities during 1806 we know more than of any other year of his life, since he pathetically related them, in all their pettiness and tedium, when he wrote to Southey in September. His few visits to the

Library reveal nothing of interest, save that his borrowing of Jones's *Brecknock* must have been in connection with *The Fall of Cambria*, now being completed with indecent haste:

28 March – 14 April	Junius's Letters, Vols. I & II
18 April – 1 May	Lewis, *Philosophical Commerce of Arts*
1 May – 8 May	T. Jones, *History of the County of Brecknock*
8 May – 5 June	W. Hayley, *Cowper's Life and Posthumous Writings*, Vol. II
5 June – 24 July	*ditto*, Vol. III (after letter of 17 June)
5 June – 24 July (after letter of 17 June)	G. Barry, *History of the Orkney Islands*
24 July – 10 Oct.	Bishop Horsley, *Tracts in Controversy with Dr. Priestly* ('Last leaf loose')
24 July – 10 Oct.	J. Dallaway, *Observations on English Architecture*
6 Nov.	Marquis Wellesley, *History of the transactions of the British Government in India* (consulted, but not taken out)
6 Nov. – 17 Dec.	S. Burder, *Oriental Customs*
17 Dec. – 22 Jan. 1807	Smellie, *Philosophy of Natural History*, Vol. I
17 Dec. – 22 Jan. 1807	Pennant, *Arctic Zoology*, Vol. I

The friendship with Foster, a rather bookish one, continued; he consulted Cottle on 4 April about parting with the copyright of his *Essays* to Longman, and in another letter on 8 April thanked him for a copy of Southey's *Madoc*.[23] On 10 August the twenty-five books of *The Fall of Cambria* were completed, with a preface which was, for some reason, held up and not printed until the second edition of 1811. His achievement in this huge poem, though very slight, is perhaps a little more solid than in *Alfred*; the same low level of jog trot is maintained, but there are fewer plunges into the mire. One might even enjoy the poem a little, simply for its story, if it were not for the pretentious claims set out in the *Preface*, from which we hear more of Cottle's poetic creed. Since writing *Alfred*, and eschewing therein accounts of battles, he has come to realize that poems like this must, unfortunately, show 'what *is*', not 'what *ought* to be'; so the reign of Edward I must be depicted with battles and tournaments 'and an extravagant respect for the Female Sex'. As for his blank verse, he is varying it to suit characters, but he has 'not aimed at the stately march of Milton', which would have been inconsistent with the theme; this is a *dramatic* poem, and the pauses and emphases fall where a speaker would apply them. He has so identified himself with each character in turn that he has gone from laughter to tears. If some passages 'have no poetic merit', let his readers remember that these are bound to occur if the writer is to be '*natural*'; the occasional lapses in *Paradise Lost* are caused by 'the inherent constitution of all narrative poems' and such lapses 'connect in their unattractive, though essential capacity, the more flowery walks of the garden'. What he enjoys is 'to display *feeling* and *passion*', but even an epic poem cannot be all heights, and there will be 'relaxing intervals'. The lyrics (or 'odes') are intended to diversify the narrative.

Readers will want to learn the origin of the poem: after finishing *Alfred*, he increasingly felt that he must put into one more poem his maturing taste and his chastised judgment, and so he began to look about for a subject. It was only after reading 'a regular History of Wales' that he felt he had found what he wanted – the 'final overthrow of the Aborigines of our Island'; and after a period of abstraction he experienced the pleasurable sensation of knowing he was on the right track. He planned the poem at that very hour, but a whole year of work did not perfect it … And so on for forty–three pages, chiefly devoted to the character of Edward, the relations between England and Wales, and the propriety of the poet's speaking in his own person. As for his motives in writing the poem, he has always tried to inculcate Christianity; and he is so apprehensive of the danger of misapplying one's talents that he quotes Chaucer's retraction at the close of the *Parson's Tale* – and that reminds him of some other Middle English, so he quotes *that* (not without understanding). But, whether engaged in amusement or utility, he has never concentrated on the former unless it would serve the latter.

1   The whole miserable story, up to the time of Mrs Newton's death, is contained in a letter of Cottle to Southey on 22 Feb. 1804, in Bristol City Library MS.B 20877.

2   H.A. Eaton, *A Diary of Thomas de Quincy*, 1803 (London: Noel Douglas, n.d.), p.171. Eaton prints 'Cottle', but the facsimile reproduction in the volume clearly says 'Cottles'; note 66, on p.231, also knocks eighteen years off the end of Cottle's life.

3   Griggs, II.959-960, No.509.

4   Griggs, II.846-848, No.452.

5   Griggs, II.828-834, No.449.

6   Printed by Cruttwell at Bath, and sold by G. & J. Robinson in London, 1802.

7   Griggs, II.825-828, No.448.

8   Their letter is listed by Cottle as No.1 of the Foster Correspondence in Bristol City Library MS.B 20878 (*olim* Bristol Museum and Art Gallery MS.G. 3676), but is missing.

9   P. Kaufman, 'John Foster's Pioneer Interpretation of the Romantic', *Modern Language Notes*, Vol.XXXVIII (Baltimore, 1923), pp.1-4, is a fuller statement of this.

10   The transactions will be found in Cottle's letter to Southey of 22 Feb. 1804 (see note 1 of this Chapter); see also Meyerstein, *op.cit.*, p.497.

11   *MH*.4, I.5n.

12   Berg Collection, New York Public Library.

13   Curry, I.353-355.

14   Curry, I.359-362.

15   *op.cit.*, p.498.

16   Vol.LXXIV, ii.722-723, letter dated 6 August.

17   Curry, I.366-369.

18   *Cumberland Papers*, British Museum MS.Add.36500, Vol.X (1804-1806), fol.64.

19   *Cumberland Papers*, Vol.X, fol.141.

20   Letter to Southey, franked 20 and 21 Aug. 1805, in Bristol City Library MS.B 20877.

21   Coburn, I.Text, items 477, 566, 1098, 1239, 2306, 2471, 2601.

22   Curry, I.394-396; scraps in *R*.47, p.228.

23   Numbered 2 and 3 in Cottle's list in the Foster Letter-Book, Bristol City Library MS.B 20878, but both missing.

Chapter 9

De Quincey: Accidie Sets In

The complacent Preface to *Cambria*, with its irritating account of how the germ of a poem burgeons in the mind of its maker, and with its silly surprise because 12,000 lines took more than a year to write, suggests to us that Cottle needed a shock. His huge letter to Southey of 7 September shows us the same picture of him – hemmed in by dull women, close and sickly and coddled, resignedly shuffling downhill – and his life of accidie. A return to the old life was imperative, and it came with rude violence in 1807, when Coleridge was back in Bristol. Meanwhile, he had only Southey to write to, and suggested to him that he write three epics, on the Conqueror, on Alaric, and on the expulsion of the Moors from Spain. Southey replied from Keswick on 11 August, 1806,[1] and pointed out that the heroes had unworthy motives; the expulsion, for instance, was carried out wickedly. He had bad news for Cottle of his own *Madoc*, but wanted to know how *Cambria* was getting on; this letter evoked from Cottle his long, animated, pluckily grumbling letter of 7 September.[2]

Delighted as he was with his friend's fidelity, he was worried over Southey's lack of true Christianity, which left him benevolence but deprived him of motive. In his 'many lonely moments' he often cries out, 'O that Southey might yet become a disciple of Jesus'; he himself depends utterly on the Bible, and in his 'solitary hours' it gives him more and more joy to read it. He realises his presumption in bringing the Bible to the notice of a genius like Southey, but he would be filled with remorse if Southey died without the mention of this new hope.

He is indignant at the mere £3 profit on *Madoc*, but sure that future generations will adjust matters; he will look forward to reading the reviews. He hears, by the way, that Godwin is the perpetrator of the attack on Southey in the *Monthly*. His informant is Thomas de Quincey, 'a Young Man of Fortune, and no common portion of Originality', who has often called during the last twelve months. Cottle had met him, it seems, through Hannah More: he had received 'a note from a lady, an old friend', saying she wanted to introduce a clever young man she knew. She even honoured him with the name of 'A little John Henderson' – about whom, in fact, the young man wished to enquire. Cottle invited them at once, and the lady introduced Thomas de Quincey; several more meetings followed, and Cottle was so impressed with the youth's talent that he felt he would 'shine in literature' or ('with steady perseverance') in one of the professions.[3] He gave him an introduction to Lamb at the beginning of the year; de Quincey was on his way to London, and asked for it. Lamb says that Godwin was out for revenge for a cutting review by Southey on *him*! Cottle cheers Southey by telling him that a 'blind horse has less radical aptitude to judge of Algebraic lines and tangents, than this driveller to feel Poetry'; this poor image would have been a little better if Cottle had written 'more' instead of 'less'.

By now his sisters, finding the house in Gloucester Street too small for their school, had taken a large house, formerly belonging to a Mr Cave, on the corner of Brunswick Square. Here there would be room for visitors like the Southeys. Cottle had been hearing much of Dr Henry Herbert Southey, the poet's brother, and would always be glad to know of his welfare. He thanks Southey for thinking about poor Amos, sends regards to Edith, hopes Tom will be a Rear-Admiral, and promises to order Southey's two new works as soon as they are published. Southey had asked about the unfortunate Brecon poetaster Walter Churchey, who had died at the end of 1805, and Cottle was daily awaiting a letter from Brecon on the subject. Cottle tells us in his *Reminiscences*[4] that this Churchey aspired to the name of poet, and advanced his claim with a monstrous great quarto of verses, 832 pages of them, which Cottle has seen only once for sale, at an old book-stall. He and Churchey, a much older man, were acquainted, since the latter had been a friend of Cottle's grandfather; Cottle exchanged a couple of letters with him a year before his death, and possessed an autograph letter from Wesley encouraging Churchey with news of subscriptions. When he published his *Essay on Man*, Cottle sent him a pound note for a couple of copies; and a few months before he died, he sent Cottle half-a-dozen copies of his pamphlet *An Apology for appearing before the Public as a Poet*.[5] Cottle heard that the widow was in poor circumstances, and sent her a guinea by a gentleman who was going to Brecon. A week later, she wrote to thank him, but said that the gentleman had pocketed the money in payment of a debt of her husband's. Cottle, bitterly disappointed in someone whom he had trusted, sent her another guinea; and the gentleman, for the remaining twenty years of his life, always avoided Cottle. This person had been wealthy at the time, with his own carriage; but thereafter he declined, and died in poverty. This may have been the narrative of eight lines scratched out from Cottle's letter of 7

September; after writing them, he repented of being censorious, especially about someone that Southey did not even know, and charity made him think 'placidly, if not approvingly', again.

His activities in this constricted year were five-fold: versifying, teaching, making varnish, practising as an amateur doctor, and carpentry. Last year's rheumatism, abetted by the natural weakness of his ankles, had forced both his legs into irons. Whatever be in store for him, he ventures to predict that he will never turn dancing-master, unless to teach Cousin Bruin; he can smile about it, but he often sighs, and feels the force of Shakespeare's lines about putting a shackle on the free-born spirit. Still, *Cambria* is done, though it will need years of correcting. (It was actually not published until 1809.) Since he has no inheritance and 'a low allotment', he must work for his living – or, at least, he helps his dear mother and sisters as best he can:

> I therefore, occasionally make huge bundles of Pens, write Copies in a large hand (that puts Copper-plate to the blush) for my Sisters' pupils to write from, keep the money accounts of the family, transcribe items from the School Book, and with "Permanent Ink", confer immortality on all the Table-cloths, Sheets and Bolster-cases of the house. Two mornings in the week I teach about 40 Young Ladies, the profound Science of Arithmetic (down in my Parlour) many of whom I am afraid will never reach fluxions. Some of the little ones have not yet solved the problem, and ceased to wonder, how it is that two & three can possibly make five; I however sit, like Patience, in my arm chair, and inculcate these abstruse truths, with mild and admirable perseverance. One morning in the week also, I teach Geography and the Use of the Globes to about 25, and talk till I am weary about Bays, Capes, Promontories, Seas, Gulfs, Oceans, Stars, Planets, and the fiery bearded Comet &c. &c. One afternoon I have two classes at spelling, and Saturday Morning, I have Grammar Classes, where they conjugate the Verbs, parse, and talk learnedly about Syntax. I think that I, and the Secretary for foreign affairs, are, at present, the two busiest men in the kingdom. Nevertheless I have two other irons in the fire. On my accommodating anvil, I manufacture, at one part of the day, an epic poem, and at another, "*Copal Varnish*".

Without printed or verbal assistance, he has discovered an incomparably better varnish than any known; artists have told him that he deserves the Gold Medal, and that he could make his fortune by it. 'As I am no shopkeeper, and do not consider this as my highest calling, I shall not give it my own name' – Sheppard has suggested *his*; it is an intricate process, and an unexpected result. 'When I am at the tip top of expectation, I begin to arrange the expenditure of my new-made Fortune, and to look with contempt on my old black thread-bare coat. Alass! I possess not the art of giving stability to my air-built Castles. I am too sanguine. A puff of wind comes and they are gone'. (We shall hear a lot more about this varnish; he even tried to enliven Wordsworth's closing days with the results of his researches.)

'I am also become a famous Chirurgeon. Cuts I smile at. In 3 dressings the other day, I cured one of our Servants' fingers, who, foolish girl, mistook it for a marrow-bone, and half chopped it off. I also make an improved Sticking plaster and Friar's Balsam, for the good of all my acquaintance.' He has made progress in the London and Edinburgh Practice of Physic: 'One of my out-dore Patients, lately *getting worse*, I sent for *an other* Doctor, & when he came, I had not courage, boldly to go into the room to him, & say "Medica sum. Let us consult". What a thing it is to want a Bag-wig and a Gold-headed Cain'. He finds the nomenclature puzzling, and he hopes that Dr Southey will not call him in for a consultation, but he knows enough for an Empiric; he has thought of putting out a 'Quack Medicine', but his conscience prevents him. And then he is carpentering – with gimlet, nail, hammer, and saw; if anything needs doing, short of building a house, the cry is 'Where is Brother Joe?' Southey was interested but pained by this humble, honourable record; he felt he wanted to hand it on to posterity. But Cottle must better himself; he must 'quack' his varnish by advertising it, and so obtain the luxuries that are, to *him*, necessities. Herbert is born, and Coleridge is returned.[6]

Cottle's fretful existence continued for years, until his health took a strange turn for the better after 1814. The year 1807 was a little more varied, with Coleridge in the city and causing anxiety. Cottle's few calls on the Library cannot reasonably be linked with this visit:

22 Jan. – 5 May	J. Berington, *History of the Lives of Abeillard and Heloisa*
(after letter of 30 April)	
14 May – 8 July	Sir W. Dugdale, *Baronage of England*, Vols. I & II
8 July – 16 July	F. Grose, *Antiquities of England and Wales, Supplement*, Vols. I & II
16 July – 20 Aug.	Smellie, *Philosophy of Natural History*, Vol. I
16 July – 17 July	G. Gregory, *Economy of Nature*, Vol. I
17 July – 20 Aug.	*Encyclopaedia Britannica*, Vol. III

20 Aug. – 5 Nov.	F. Grose, *Antiquities of England and Wales*, Vols. III & IV
5 Nov. – 7 Jan. 1808	Malkin, *Scenery, Antiquities and Biography, of South Wales*
5 Nov. – 7 Jan. 1808	Aristotle, *Treatise on Poetry*, ed. Twining

His family were well (so he told Southey on 10 May); at Broadmead, Ann Cottle and two others, having pleasingly described the work of God on their souls and been accepted on 7 April, were baptized by the Pastor on the 9th.[7] Mrs Churchey eventually replied, with a letter as 'bald as a tree in winter', and since old Mrs Cottle knew nothing more in particular, there was not much that Cottle could tell Southey about Walter Churchey when he wrote on 10 May. In his letter he apologizes for not writing before: he does not like letter-writing (as his brother, sisters, and cousins will witness), but as soon as he makes a start the spell is broken. He again urges Christianity on Southey, who had apparently rebuked him for obtruding his own opinions; oh, no! – he would persuade rather by life and example. He then launches into a defence of Calvinism, which Southey had opposed; there have been excellent Calvinists, and against the excusably murky figure of Calvin one can set Dr Philip Doddridge, 'Whose writings will perish only with the last Conflagration'. (This is not so wild as it sounds: one would hesitate to set a term on Doddridge's great hymns, *O God of Bethel*; *Ye servants of the Lord*; *My God, and is Thy Table spread*; and *Hark the glad sound!*) Southey should not have connected Calvinism with 'burning zeal'; and, though Southey objects to the doctrine of eternal hell-torments, Cottle must partly subscribe to it – they both have God's 'peculiar blessings' of birth in England in a civilized age, and of a taste for literature and refinement. And the Bible makes it quite clear that punishment is reserved for some, and reward for others. Still, he will 'now waive this subject', unless Southey wants to reopen it; Southey never did, and his letter of thanks on 18 June[8] concerns mainly the pleasure of writing history, the probable end of his own poetic career, and an invitation to the Cottles to come up to Keswick next midsummer.

It was Southey who told him that Coleridge was back in England: why must Cottle say in *Reminiscences*[9] that he heard it 'accidentally'? Southey's letter had been sanguine about the future of Coleridge's honourable employment, and now Cottle was musing over the pleasant prospect of meeting Coleridge as he had been in the early days. Last time they met, he was a changed man; and, at a harrowing time when Cottle could have borne the injustice of a stranger or an enemy, when he 'needed a soothing and not an austere voice', Coleridge had served him ill.

Knowing that Coleridge was at Poole's, and in poor health, Cottle wrote off to Stowey, hoping that his health would permit him soon to visit Bristol. Coleridge replied that, if ever he *did* come to Bristol, he would certainly give him 'the right hand of old friendship', but his pain, depression and regrets ('not remorseless') had left him a wreck of what he had been, 'rolling, rudderless'. Now what could all this mean? Cottle declares that he 'knew nothing of opium' at the time, but he worried until the day Coleridge arrived, when his appearance, his clear understanding, and his 'pious and orthodox' speech, were all a great relief – showing, in fact, an improvement. There is something of I-told-you-so in this report, since Coleridge had ceased to be a Socinian, and Cottle would attribute to this all kinds of rehabilitation. What with his projecting of new works, and a *New Review* that he would edit, the man of genius was, Cottle felt, at last going to justify his friends' trust; and he invited John Foster over from Frome to renew his acquaintance with this bigger and better Coleridge.

This was in June. Foster replied[10] fulsomely, as was his wont. Only a couple of weeks ago, he made an appointment in the depths of Somerset for the very time of Cottle's invitation! He realised what he would be missing, for he had had a huge admiration for Coleridge ever since he had been two or three times in his company. But he hoped that, next time a meeting was possible, he would be intellectually fitter to meet so great a man. Cottle must urge Coleridge to creative and instructive work. 'Tell me also, what is the state and progress of your *own* literary projects, — and I hope I may say, labours'. (Alas! This final innuendo is wasted: Cottle methodically executed everything he planned.)

'Some weeks after' Foster's letter (though Cottle's dates are all so much plausible padding), Coleridge called, and made himself 'unusually amiable', especially on the subject of his own character, confessing that he had always been arrogant … In other words, he apologized for his previous arrogance; there is no doubt that this is conveyed in Cottle's hint. On the other hand, Coleridge sent two letters to Southey in February 1808,[11] giving *his* version of the interviews, from which emerges a crushed and contrite Cottle upbraiding himself for his own smugness. Coleridge, considering how rarely he went out, saw a lot of Cottle, really, and found him 'quite himself again – nay, better than ever – He explained the past *satisfactorily* to me – for he did not deny or wish to conceal that he had wrapt up his Imagination in Delusions, that produced, while they lasted, an undesirable state of moral Feelings'. Coleridge felt so mollified that he even conceived a half-liking for *Cambria*, and wanted to review it whenever it came out; he liked the lyrical and dramatic parts best, and felt that better planning, and 'heroic Rhyme' instead of blank verse, would have made it popular. Yes, Coleridge 'was glad to be undeceived, and to find him returned to himself'; the epic was printing fast, and he would like to review Cottle's *Psalms* as well. The man certainly had 'an extraordinary happiness in rhyme versification'; witness the 'very fine' odes in the midst of the bad blank verse.

Between these two versions, and between these two incompatible creatures, truth swings out in the cold, where a Southey could easily discern her. According to Cottle, Coleridge went on to renounce the Unitarian heresy, and to affirm his belief in Revelation, the Fall, the Godhead of Christ, and Redemption through His blood alone. This made Cottle feel a new and closer bond between them, and a fine long theological conversation ensued. Coleridge, at his next calling on Cottle, told him of his Italian adventures, and especially of the kindly American sea-captain who had rescued him, from uncertainty at least, at Leghorn; but he had nothing to say of the buildings or the antiquities of the country. 'At this time' they were both invited to meet a Unitarian minister; soon after dinner, that religion became the topic of conversation, and the minister challengingly put his case. Coleridge, now very hostile to his old cause, told him that he gave up so much Christianity that the little he retained was not worth keeping; there was no reply to this, and the minister concentrated on the wine.

On 26 July de Quincey called at Brunswick Square and showed himself interested in meeting Coleridge. Cottle wrote him a letter of introduction to take to Poole,[12] calling him 'a Gentleman of Oxford, a Scholar and a man of Genius', who admired Coleridge and, knowing him to be with Poole or in that neighbourhood, wished 'to pay him a passing visit'. As usual in his *Reminiscences*, Cottle jumbles the dating of this friendship with de Quincey by cramming all their meetings into 1807, whereas we know that de Quincey had been calling for a twelvemonth before 7 September 1806. At first, they had talked mainly of John Henderson, of whom de Quincey had heard much; but now he was more interested in Coleridge, and asked if Cottle knew anything of his financial affairs. Cottle replied, 'I am afraid he is a legitimate son of genius'. De Quincey wondered whether Coleridge would accept a hundred or two hundred pounds, and Cottle, who would shortly be meeting him, promised to find out.

The occasion soon arose. Coleridge came to supper, and talked so long and so brilliantly that Cottle did his best, after his departure, to jot down what he had said and to make a digest of it in *Reminiscences*. If Coleridge really *did* write 'the next day', as Cottle says on page 341 of that book, and if this letter be one dated 9 August (No. 285 in Sotheby's 13-14 May 1904 sale of Sholto V. Hare's Library, 'chiefly on his health; mentions de Quincey'), then this eminent supper party took place on 8 August. Coleridge talked all ready for printing without correction, as Bolingbroke did in Pope's hearing: he discussed Unitarianism, the contrast of Newton with the wilfully blind, the Socinians as symbolized by Paul when he was Saul, and the atheists among the London *literati*. Cottle had a qualm – was Davy tainted in this way? Coleridge was utterly reassuring; and when Cottle asked how Davy compared with the clever men in London, he gave the jolly answer, 'Why, Davy could eat them all!' Then he went on to Holcroft the atheist, whose atheist wife was angry and tearful at Coleridge's tactless Christianity, whose 8-year-old boy came up uninvited and told Coleridge 'There is no God!', and whose elder son blew his brains out while running away to sea to escape his father's tyranny. He then spoke sublimely of the Saviour, of Doddridge's works, of Gilbert Burnet's narrative of Lord Rochester's conversion, of Jeremy Taylor, and of Archbishop Leighton. (His views were not without bias; Lamb had a high opinion of Holcroft; and the runaway son had just robbed his father of £40.)

As soon as this masterly oration was over, Cottle asked him about his finances; returning to earth (a process always made easier by Cottle's presence), Coleridge confessed that the money he had earned in Malta had been spent in Italy. Hearing immediately that 'a young man of fortune' was offering him a couple of hundred pounds in appreciation of his talents, he rose in agitation, was silent a moment, and then turned and said, 'Cottle, I will write to you. We will change the subject'.

His letter[13] arrived next day, so Cottle says – but it speaks of a dinner engagement with Danvers on the same day as the supper with Cottle, as well as of letter-writing and of dreadful pains through imprudently leaving off 'some medicines'. At any rate, on the day of writing, 13 October, he is calling on Dr Beddoes and John Colson in Clifton, mainly for the exercise, and hopes to spend the evening from seven o'clock with Cottle. As for the gift (which he will take as a loan), he accepts, providing the benefactor be not acting wrongly or recklessly. Only money is preventing him from the completion of works, though a tragedy of his may be staged this season; after a year, he will want to know the kindly stranger's name, and will give him proofs of how he has used his new gift of tranquillity.

'Soon after', Cottle invited de Quincey to call, and told him that Coleridge *was* financially embarrassed; the quickfire conversation that followed, as Cottle recalled or revised it, is best shown dramatically:

| de Q. | Then I will give him £500. |
| C. | Are you serious? |

de Q.   I am.

C.   Are you of age?

de Q.   I am.

C.   Can you afford it?

de Q.   I can. I shall not feel it. (A pause)

C.   Well, I can know nothing of your circumstances, but from your own statement, and not doubting its accuracy, I am willing to become an agent, in any way you prescribe.

de Q.   I authorize you to ask Mr. Coleridge if he will accept from a gentleman who admires his genius the sum of £500; but remember, I absolutely prohibit you from naming to him the source whence it was derived.

C.   To the latter part of your injunction, if you require it, I will accede; but although I am deeply interested in Mr. Coleridge's welfare, yet a spirit of equity compels me to recommend you, in the first instance, to present Mr. Coleridge with a smaller sum, and which, if you see it right, you can at any time augment.

de Q.   £300 I *will* give him, and you will oblige me by making this offer of mine to Mr. Coleridge.

C.   I will.

Cottle then gave him Coleridge's letter, asking him to pocket it and read it at his leisure. 'Soon after' (but really on 14 October), de Quincey sent a letter saying that he was writing for the £300, and would try to call in a day or two; he was very grateful for all Cottle's trouble in this matter. 'In a day or two' de Quincey enclosed the £300, and Cottle received from Coleridge (who had on 3 November asked him to deliver to the bearer, Morgan, the sum of 100 guineas – probably to repay Wordsworth[14]) a receipt dated 12 November 1807.[15] Cottle felt no doubt that Coleridge knew the identity of the giver, as he told de Quincey in a letter of 1808;[16] he himself had been bound to reveal it, indirectly, in discussing it with Coleridge. Years later, de Quincey found that Coleridge had known all the time, 'perhaps through some indiscretion of Mr. Cottle's'.[17] But Cottle had done his best in starting this friendship; he was not to blame for the shoals it encountered in 1821, when de Quincey himself expected financial help from Coleridge. Altogether, the poet and his patron had really meant something to one another in this crucial year of Coleridge's fortunes; and it was to a letter to Cottle,[18] written at the time, that Coleridge confided his famous words on Wordsworth: 'He is one whom, God knows, I love and honour as far beyond myself as both morally and intellectually he is above me'. At least one other serious, didactic letter,[19] on poetry, is assigned to 1807; and Cottle must have been surprised and hurt by the silence that closed between them when Coleridge left the district at the end of the year. For seven years Cottle saw nothing of him, and their reunion in 1814 brought only disaster.

But, of course, Coleridge's opinion of Cottle had not really changed for the better in 1807, and well Cottle knew it, having had a peep at a bright letter to Miss Cruikshank written in September;[20] in it, Coleridge says that his sonnet to Earl Stanhope, which he had wanted suppressed from his early *Poems*, was yet inserted 'by the fool of a Publisher' to give himself the opportunity of sending the volume, and a letter, to the Earl – who properly ignored them. Cottle, in *Early Recollections*, had his own masterly way of dealing with such a phrase: he altered it to 'by Biggs, the fool of a printer', accused Coleridge of 'obscured ... recollection' in his desire to please Lady Elizabeth Percival, and said that the book and letter had been sent by Coleridge himself.[21]

1808 was a year of new personal anxieties, relieved by the friendship of Cumberland and by a glowing letter from Southey. Cottle paid ten visits to the Library:

7 Jan. – 10 March	Gregory, *Economy of Nature*, Vols. I & II
10 Mar. – 16 March	Edward Williams, *Poems, Lyrical and Pastoral*, Vol. II
10 Mar. – 16 March	Pennant, *Arctic Zoology*, Vol. I
16 Mar. – 12 Apr.	Jones, *Bardic Museum*, Vol. II
12 Apr. – 20 Apr.	Grose, *Antiquities*, Vol. III
12 Apr. – 5 May	Adams, *Essays on the Microscope, & Plates*
20 Apr. – 5 May	Grose, *Antiquities*, Supplement I
5 May – 1 Dec.	Bp. Taylor, *Life of Christ*, folio
5 May – 28 Dec.	G. Heriot, *Travels through the Canadas*
6 July – 1 Dec.	Wm. Coxe, *History of the House of Austria*, Vol. I. Pt. I, Vol. II
11 Oct. – 9 Jan 1809	A. Parsons, *Travels in Asia and Africa*

Cambria was at last out, printed by Harris and Bryan, of 51 Corn Street, Bristol, for Longman. Cottle sent copies to his friends, of course; Foster returned thanks for his on 4 April;[22] and Southey used the occasion to send Cottle a moving letter,[23] of long-meditated gratitude, which ennobles both of them. Cottle, probably in sending the book, had casually mentioned his regret at not having returned Southey's copyrights when he closed his business – that is, those of *Joan*, the two volumes of *Poems*, and the *Letters*.

At Greta Hall, on the evening of Wednesday, 20 April 1808, Southey began his letter of thanks: he today opened a box that he had not examined since the winter of 1799, and *there* was Robert Hancock's best portrait, that of Cottle; he had been reading *Cambria*; now, before supper, he must answer Cottle's letter …

> What you say of my copy-rights affects me so much. Dear Cottle, set your heart at rest on that subject; it ought to be at rest. They were yours; — fairly bought and fairly sold; you bought them on the chance of their success, — which no London bookseller would have done; and had they not been bought, they could not have been published at all; — nay, if you had not published "Joan of Arc", the poem never would have existed, nor should I in all probability ever have obtained that reputation which is the capital on which I subsist, nor that power which enables me to support it. But this is not all. Do you suppose Cottle that I have forgotten those true and most essential acts of friendship which you showed me when I stood most in need of them? Your house was my house when I had no other; — the very money with which I bought my marriage-ring, and paid my marriage fees, was supplied by you; it was with your sisters that I left my Edith, during my six months' absence, — and for the six months after my return it was from you that I received week by week the little on which we lived, — till I was enabled to live by other means. It is not the settling of our cash-account that can cancel obligations like these. – You are in the habit of preserving your letters, and if you were not, *I would entreat you to preserve* this, *that it may be seen hereafter*. Sure am I that there never was a more generous, nor a kinder heart than yours, and you will believe me when I add that there does not live that man upon earth, whom I remember with more gratitude, and more affection.
>
> My heart throbs, and my eyes burn with these recollections. Good night my dear old friend and benefactor.

Next day, 21 April, the letter is resumed. Southey had now got through nineteen books of *Cambria*, so he cannot criticize the story until he finishes it tomorrow. But Cottle ought not to use blank verse, since it is so easy in this medium to 'dilate', a thing to which Cottle's facility of writing tempts him too often; why not use stanza, or Scott's irregular form, for long narratives? Further, Cottle's feelings keep carrying him away; from time to time he conceives 'strongly, but vaguely', and it is not always possible to see what he is getting at. So far, Southey is best pleased with Eleanor's 'exceedingly beautiful' Lament. The knight and squire who betray

Gloucester are inconsistently drawn, their characters altering violently. But Cottle has cleverly 'got rid of the main difficulty' by giving fair treatment to both Edward and Llewelyn, whereas Virgil and Tasso, and even Homer, fail through their partizanship! – and Southey's own *Madoc* is at fault in this. (Had Cottle but listened to some of this advice! He learned nothing of the technique of versifying from a man whom he claimed to revere; yet the advice to spin narratives readably by Scott's method might have made all the difference. He merely went on with *Messiah*.)

The Southeys were looking forward to welcoming Cottle and his sister Mary at Keswick in the summer of 1810; indeed, if Southey can put off some threatened visitors to the end of the summer of 1809, the Cottles can come now instead. Edith sends her regards to Cottle's mother and sister; this emphasis on Mary alone suggests that Ann was away, perhaps with the London half of the family, when Edith spent her solitary honeymoon under the Cottle roof. But holidays were out of the question for Cottle at the time; he could not come up to the Lake District in the summer of 1808, since his sisters would be off to Devon and his mother would otherwise be left alone. A 'stout hearted' man was needed, in so large a house, to frighten off malefactors and see to the locking-up; besides which, there was white-liming and painting for him to superintend – he was 'rising in the scale of importance'. Next summer, 1809, would be out of the question, too; not only had Southey his engagements but 'a whole Coachful of Relations' were descending on the Cottles. A holiday in 1810 seemed feasible; yet how could he know? – he had a frequent pain in his side, and spat blood on the morning of 27 May 1808.

His *Psalms*, which he had hoped would do so much good, were a grievous disappointment; the printing had cost him £50, and expenses £14, but only twenty-four copies were sold, for which Longman gave him £4.2s. He still believed that it was better than any other extant version, since it avoided 'bombast and false elevation', and he tried to hope that one day it would be like bread cast upon the waters. Only *The Critical Review* mentioned it, and that meanly; a bit which he had quoted in the preface to show the difficulty of the task was re-quoted as an example of his failure. Still, he had asked Longman to send Southey a copy.

When he wrote to Southey with all this news on 27 May,[24] he expressed himself as almost sorry that Southey had so directly acknowledged his little kindnesses; he always thanked God for such links, and would refer Southey to the same Being. Southey had praised Cottle for returning good for evil in Coleridge's case – a description which Cottle nimbly accepts; he wants to be remembered to Coleridge, but if only so talented a man would take the responsibility that goes with his endowments! Cottle knows the remedy (a spiritual one, of course). He sounds a little upset by what Southey said of *Cambria*; oh, he knows what's wrong with his blank verse – when unimpassioned and merely connecting, 'I am always too tame & prosaic. It is a difficult, but very necessary thing, to say even *a nothing* with dignity. I am always on a Canter or Full-Galop. I should use the Bit more, and imitate the slow pace of the Charger, in whom grace is substituted for speed'. He was quiet about the poem when he was writing it, and now he wants to forget all about it; his ideas on poetry and the poet's aim are advancing swiftly, and he appears to himself more and more insignificant.

George Cumberland's memorandum-books for this year have some fugitive glances at the Cottle household: some time between 4 and 12 January, 1808, 'Cottles Picture to Draw'; on 16 September, 'Sent Miss Cottle £1 – being what she had undercharged with her Bill', perhaps a reference to some little relative at Mary Cottle's school; and just before 4 December, 'Lent Mr Cottle 1 Vol. Stockdale'.[25]

No details – not even the coachload of kinsfolk – appear to survive of Cottle's life in 1809, save for his eleven visits to the Library:

9 Jan. – April 3	J. Steward, *Account of Prince Edward Island*
(after letters of 23 Feb., 23 March, 30 March)	
9 Jan. – 7 Feb.	Bp. Burnet, *History of his own Time*, Vol. I
7 Feb. – 3 April	Bp. Burnet, *History of his own Time*, Vol. II
7 Feb. – 3 April	Grose, *Antiquities*, Supplement, Vol. II
9 June – 5 July	Sir R. Kerr Porter, *Travelling Sketches in Russia and Sweden*
17 July – 28 Aug.	Bp. Taylor, *Ductor Dubitantium* (1660), Toms. I & II
28 Aug. – 5 Oct.	Bp. Taylor, *Holy Living*
28 Aug. – 5 Oct.	Bp. Taylor, *Holy Dying*
5 Oct. – 14 Nov.	Grose, *Antiquities*, Vol. II
5 Oct. – 14 Nov.	Malton, *Treatise on Perspective*
14 Nov. – 4 Dec.	*Memoirs of Carey, Earl of Monmouth*
14 Nov. – 4 Dec.	Mrs Montagu, *Letters*, Vol. II
27 Dec. – 10 Jan. 1810	Smellie, *Philosophy of Natural History*, Vol. I
27 Dec. – 4 Jan. 1810	White, *Natural History of Selbourne*

Otherwise, the year 1809 must have continued in the same dreary rhythm of teaching, of reading, of revising unwanted poems, and of safeguarding his precarious health. His current affliction was 'a long continued inflammation of the eyes, subdued ultimately, after bleeding, blistering, and cupping, by Singleton's eye ointment'; it was still causing him suffering on 16 March 1810, when Southey wrote,[26] commiserating, but assuring him that the complaint could be effectively treated. It did not prevent him from reading fairly hard in the early part of the year – or at least consulting, since some of these books are old favourites:

10 Jan. – 12 Jan.	Stow, *General Chronicle of England*
10 Jan. – 25 Jan.	Henry, *History of Great Britain*, Vol. IV
12 Jan. – 16 Jan.	*Archaeologia*, Vol. III
12 Jan. – 16 Jan.	Strutt, *Dresses, &c.*, Vol. II
16 Jan. – 22 Jan.	T. Fuller, *History of the Worthies of England*
16 Jan. – 22 Jan.	Duncomb, *History and Antiquities of the County of Hereford*
22 Jan. – 13 Feb.	Newcome, *History of the Abbey of St Alban*
22 Jan. – 13 Feb.	Henry, *Britain*, Vol. III
13 Feb. – 27 Feb.	Camden's *Britannia*, ed. Gough, Vol. I
13 Feb. – 27 Feb.	Sauer, *Account of an Expedition to the Northern Parts of Russia*
27 Feb. – 8 Mar.	Henry, *Britain*, Vol. II
27 Feb. – 8 Mar.	Gough's Camden, Vol. II
8 Mar. – 21 Mar.	Holinshed, *Chronicles*
8 Mar. – 21 Mar.	Pennant, *Wales*, Vol. I
21 Mar. – 29 Mar.	Gough's Camden, Vol. III
21 Mar. – 4 July	Bp. Newton, *Dissertations on the Prophecies*, Vol. I
19 June – 4 July	R. Robinson, *Ecclesiastical Researches*
4 July – 7 Aug.	Bacon, *Works*, Vol. I
4 July – 7 July	Rowland, *Mona Antiqua*
7 Aug. – 16 Aug.	Dugdale, *Baronage*, Vol. I
7 Aug. – 5 Sept.	T. Walsh, *Journal of the Expedition to Egypt*
16 Aug. – 22 Aug.	Josephus's *Works*, ed. T. Lodge
28 Aug. – 5 Sept.	J. Harrington, *Oceana*
4 Sept. – 5 Nov.	Pontoppidan, *Natural History of Norway*
18 Sept. – 5 Nov.	Sir J. Reynolds, *Works*, ed. Malone, Vol. I
5 Nov. – 4 Mar. 1811	Sir J. Reynolds, *Works*, ed. Malone, Vol. II
5 Nov. – 4 Dec.	Cave, *Lives of the Primitive Fathers*, Vol. I

For the time being, holidays were still out of the question, though on 9 February Southey wrote inviting him to Greta Hall;[27] there he would show him his books – *and* his children, he wanted to add, save that he was so fearful for them. He reminds his 'old friend that there is a covenant between' them to meet again, and recalls as in a dream the time when he met Joseph and Robert daily, and all the others who came to the shop. It is significant that he here tells Cottle that 'our blank verse is in my judgement the most dignified form of narrative and the best'; it was, as Cottle applied it, bad advice.

The financial affairs of the Cottle family were beginning to brighten. His sister Sarah Saunders's husband had an old uncle, who died at Christmas 1810, and left Saunders his house, nearly £1000 a year in land, and estates and personal property including 1,200 guineas.[28] (It would seem, from letters inserted in the 1795 *Album*, that young Saunders was a man of some influence: Lord Brougham, knowing his 'attachment to the cause of justice and humanity' in the case of the slave trade, asked him to investigate a flogging and a callous drowning on a naval vessel, and was highly impressed by his findings.) *Cambria* was very kindly noticed in the *Eclectic Review* of December 1810; and by 8 June 1811 Cottle could tell Southey that his own finances had been 'never so good', though he was afraid to reprint *Alfred*. We know that he was also one of the 569 subscribers to the posthumous *Poems and Letters* of William Isaac Roberts, who had died in Bristol of consumption at the age of nineteen, and for whose destitute family Southey made tireless and successful efforts.[29]

1811 was dominated by books, though he went on helping at the school. Cumberland lent him the two volumes of Bishop Cumberland's *Sanchoniatho*, and rolls of Egyptian tracings, in January; in November, he again sent him the two volumes, and 'Milton with Corrections'.[30] In the early part of the year, Southey sent his *Curse of Kehama* and Volume I of his *History of Brazil*; Cottle immediately realised that *Kehama* was 'beyond all doubt the greatest poetical effort which has appeared for the last hundred years', and what entertained him most in the *History* was the story of the old woman who didn't fancy her food except for a cut off 'a young Biped' – but she had no-one to go and kill him! The second edition of *Cambria* was out, too, and with his letter of 8 June he parcelled a big copy for Southey, another for de Quincey, and a small one each for Coleridge and Wordsworth; since they all lent each other their books, there was no point in his sending them all large ones. What a 'pleasure and privilege' it had been to know them all, and Davy, too – 'my superiors'!

His mere seven visits to the Library gave him some new reading:

4 Mar. – 16 Apr.[31]	Sir J. Hawkins, *Life of S. Johnson*, LL.D.
4 Mar. – 16 Apr.	Hon. D. Barrington, *Miscellanies*
16 Apr. – 10 Sep.	Sale, *Koran*, Vols. I & II
4 July – 6 Jan. 1812 (after letter of 12 Nov)	Gregory, *Economy of Nature*, Vol. I
4 July – 10 Sep.	Bp. Tomline, *Refutation of Calvinism* (He now had *four* books 'out')
8 Oct. – 21 Dec.	Bishop Hall, *Works*
23 Dec. – 7 Feb. 1812	Malkin, *South Wales* (?Vol. I)

During the first half of the year, he received 45 young ladies for Geography, Astronomy, the Globes, Drawing Maps, etc., and 60 for Cyphering. Different classes came down daily to his parlour, and, since his taking over Geography, numbers had increased from 12 to 45. In some respects, he may have been only the traditional chapter ahead: for the weekly Grammar classes, he taught conjugations, parsing, and syntax, and some grew '*very clever* (almost as clever as their Master, but mum!)' He kept a '*Bad Grammar Card*' with spaces for: Lady's name; inaccurate words; rule violated. This was exhibited publicly in the school-room, and the girls were very vigilant not to appear on 'Mr Cottle's Card'. Southey would smile to see him teaching Arithmetic to the little ones: 'Well, Miss W., how many are five and five?' 'Eight, Sir'… He also had to write out many lessons, and, altogether, he relished the calm that set in when the summer holidays began. In mid-June, his sisters celebrated their release by going off to Devon for six weeks; but old Mrs Cottle could not go, and she and Joseph would just 'wander about our large house in wearisome solitude'. Still, it was good to have respite from the 'noise' and 'bustle' and 'whirl' of the school, and he was content in a situation as humble and as honourable as any. But he regretted his exclusion from literary society; he was seeing hardly anyone outside his family, and even then they were people without his sympathies or his pursuits. 'The flower of Poesy blooms & withers in my own breast. Some of my Odes & best passages have never been seen or heard by human being, and that I have done no better may be ascribed to the unfavourable situation in which I am placed for developing the mind, or calling into light those qualities which shrink from the unceasing round of ordinary associations'.[32]

Eye trouble dogged him throughout 1812, but he paid a dozen visits to the Library:

6 Jan. – 7 Jan.	S. Turner, *Account of an Embassy to Thibet*
27 Feb. – 8 May	W. Robertson, *History of America*, Vols. I & II
8 May – 29 June	D. Williams, *History of Monmouthshire*
8 May – 9 June	W. Robertson, *History of the Reign of the Emperor Charles V*, Vol. I
9 June – 29 June	J. Fox, *Natural History of the Human Teeth and Treatment of their Diseases*
29 June – 31 July	R. Willan, *On Cutaneous Diseases* (Are these two connected with his own ailments?)
29 June – 31 July	D. Stewart, *Philosophical Essays*
31 July – 29 Sept.	J. Parkinson, *Organic Remains of a Former World*, Vols. I & II
(after letter of 17 Sept.)	
6 Oct. – 30 Dec.	*ditto* Vol. III
6 Oct. – 30 Dec.	*Calamities of Authors*, Vol. I
28 Dec. – 13 Apr. 1813	*ditto* Vol. II
28 Dec. – 1 Mar. 1813	Josephus

In 1813 the state of his eyes became so serious that during the summer he visited the oculist Adams in London, on Southey's recommendation; but the treatment did more harm than good. These inflammations occurred chiefly during the winter, and for the last three months of 1813 he had to wear a green shade; the green thought thereby engendered is in a wan letter to Southey written at the end of the year.[33] He had to delay writing because one eye, alone, bore the marks of seven leeches. Eventually he could see well only in the middle of the day, but could not read or write by candle-light. His lameness, too, was now far worse; he never went out, except by coach, and feared that he would soon be unable even to cross to the residents' garden in the square, then a pretty place of fruit and flowers.

His mother died on 18 December 1813, aged 74, and *The Bristol Mirror* recorded her as 'mother of the Misses Cottle of Brunswick Square', as if poor Joseph had ceased to have any identity. Southey wrote sympathetically on 23 December,[34] and Cottle replied with a catalogue of her angelic merits; Southey would have noticed her worth, but only her children could really understand. She had retained her faculties, and a calm countenance without one wrinkle; age made her lovely face even more soft and calm. Her death was caused ultimately by a cold, which affected her lungs, but she was not abed a single hour, and until her last day she was not prevented from writing or reading; in fact, on the two days previous, she wrote some grand letters about her approaching end – she was confident of ending up with Abraham, Isaac and Jacob. Cottle felt that the last hundred years had not shown a better example of the beneficial effects of Religion (or a better example for Southey to follow). By way of contrast, he cites the death of a neighbouring East India captain, whose failings were wine, women and cards, and who, having enough cash to secure his relatives' attention on his sick-bed, otherwise led a wretched life of anger, curses, and blasphemies; he had a 'pompous Funeral', but he will be alone in the grave.

Cottle's isolation was further increased by news of which we get the first rumours in this letter: his brother Robert 'is about to be respectably married'.

His Library borrowings were, on the whole, unfamiliar:

1 Mar. – 1 Apr.	Chateaubriand, *Travels in Greece, Palestine, Egypt and Barbary*, trans. from the French by F. Shoberl, Vol. II
1 Mar. – 1 Apr.	Viscount Valentia, *Voyages and Travels to India, Ceylon, the Red Sea, Abyssinia and Egypt*, Vol. I
1 Apr. – 30 Apr.	*ditto* Vol. II
30 Apr. – 11 June	*ditto* Vol. III
30 Apr. – 11 June	J. Parkinson, *Organic Remains of a Former World*, Vol. II
11 June – 6 Sept.	J. Galt, *Voyages & Travels in 1809-10-11*
25 June – 24 July	Bp. Lowth, *Translation of Isaiah*
25 June – 1 July	Statutes 52 Geo. III, Vol. 4, Pt. 3
6 Sept. – 1 Oct.	Junius, Woodfall's edn, Vol. I
6 Sept. – 8 Mar. 1814	G. Campbell, *Translation of the Four Gospels*, Vol. I
1 Oct. – 8 Dec.	A. Alison, *Essays on the Nature and Principles of Taste*, Vol. I
(after letter of 25 Nov.)	
1 Oct. – 8 Dec.	W. Robertson, *Charles V*, Vol. I
8 or 9 Dec. – 8 Mar. 1814	Alison, *Taste*, Vol. II

John Foster continued to call, and one Thursday evening he was lent a greatcoat, and then searched in the darkness, between eleven and midnight, for Councillor Smith's house, where he had been offered a bed; he thought it had a brass plate on the door facing the road, but, none appearing, he walked back to Downend through a night of lovely soft weather. On

Saturday he returned the coat to Cottle, with thanks and regards to the two sisters, by the postman; and at the same time he warned Cottle that he would be asking him for a line of introduction to the Assistant Librarian, for 'a few hours luxury there, — some day next week, if I am well — probably Friday'.[35]

Coleridge was in Bristol this year to start his lectures, and in a letter of October to the Morgans,[36] written at the White Hart, he mentions that he has met Danvers in the street, and Poole's brother-in-law King in the Commercial Rooms (still extant in Corn Street), but not Cottle or Estlin or King the Surgeon. Yet did he really want to meet these people? A letter to Mrs Morgan,[37] not a fortnight later, bewails his having to dine at Kiddle's, sup at Cottle's, dine at Stock's '& so on & so for the whole of next week – this is the worst evil'. Southey, as so often, was the consolation of Cottle's weary time: Cottle, in his December letter of mourning and sickness already noticed, could both congratulate Southey on new honours and mention his own *Messiah*, which he would like to show him; it is in the metre of *John the Baptist*, and has kept him interested: 'I like Rhyme better than Blank Verse, & it likes me better'.

There is evidence that his financial position was now more secure again. Some time in the winter of 1812-1813, Southey wrote to him on behalf of John Morgan, whom Cottle had met only twice. As soon as his eyes permitted, he drove out to Stapleton to visit Michael Castle, who had been one of the executors of Morgan's mother, and discussed the matter with him. There was no doubt that Morgan was in difficulties through his own extravagance, but Mrs Castle also spoke indignantly of Coleridge's share in his troubles. Castle had seen the Morgans two months before, near London. Castle, himself a sick man, handed over Southey's letter, and the charge that went with it, to his brother Thomas Castle, 'a man of weight' and benevolence. Cottle next called on *him* and found him 'hearty in the cause'. He had, in fact, prepared a list of people to call on, and they were much the same as Cottle had intended; so Cottle gave up his own intention of applying to people, and reckoned that Wade, the Castles, and others would make up an annuity of £50. In addition, he saw the Reverend Mr Porter, who once gave Morgan £50 but would still donate £5, and wrote to the Reverend Mr Rowe, since Morgan and his parents had been members of Lewin's Mead Meeting in Bristol. And what is Cottle giving? He

> cannot well do *any thing*. Since August last, I have given to one case ten pounds, & to an other five Guineas, besides many smaller sums. But notwithstanding this, I should have been *forward* to contribute on this occasion, but the fund from which alone I think myself justified to

draw, has lately been exhausted, by the *failure* of my Publishers *Button & Son*. Last month he sent me my annual account, with a letter. I first took up the *account*, & finding the *balance* due to me *one hundred & four* pounds, I began to revolve whether I should add it to my French, or my English Stock (for thro' the goodness of the Almighty I have a little in each, the fruit of my honest & arduous industry) when I opened the *letter* and found it to contain the information that they had just called their creditors together; had offered 7/6 in the pound, but were apprehensive of a Bankruptcy (which has since taken place). I first heaved a groan, & then smiled, & then again looked serious, I however took up my pen, & as I respected Old Mr Button, sent a kind letter in reply, telling them (Father & Son) that I was ready to accede to any terms of accommodation, & "the more favourable they were to themselves the better I should be pleased". The letter I received in reply was touchingly grateful; I suspect they had experienced harshness from other quarters. As I never have, so I never will take a Fellow Servant "by the throat". What I most regret in their conduct, was, that they received the *second part* of Messiah, & neither sent a copy to each of the Periodical Works, nor advertised it in a single Paper. This was not fair play, but it was doubtless occasioned by the confusion of their own affairs. My happiness is neither derived from, nor dependent upon, Fame, or Poetry.

But despite this reverse, his little benevolences had started once more. Apart from the unnamed charities from August 1812 onward, there was the case of the good Joseph Hughes, an acquaintance of Southey as of Cottle, and Secretary of the Bible Society. He was in low water, through putting his son into a moribund printing business, through deaths and moves in his congregation, and through not charging the Society for his great travelling expenses. His friends quietly got together £3,000! Robert Cottle mentioned it casually in a letter to Joseph, who, anxious to do something in Bristol, enlisted 'an active Friend' to join him in calling on people; a neighbouring gentleman headed the list with £25, and a week before writing to Southey Cottle remitted to London £250, with hopes of £150 more. 'God be praised'. This letter to Southey, written in mid-1813, is creditably devoted to these charities, and Cottle only just finds space for literature, when he thanks Southey for the third volume of the *Brazil*, which he is now reading with interest; but he sealed the letter with a fine king's head in red wax, with the proud legend 'AELFRED'.

1   CCS, III.51-53.
2   Bristol City Library MS.B 20877.
3   R.47, pp.340-341.
4   R.47, pp.230 ff.
5   Letter to Southey, 10 May 1807, in the Southey Letter-Book, Bristol City Library MS.B 20877.
6   *1795 Album*.
7   *Broadmead Records*, MS. volume, 1779-1817, fols.306-307.
8   *1795 Album* and (after a fashion) R.47, pp.229-230.
9   R.47, p.305. The account that follows, up to p.347, confused and highly-coloured as it is, is perhaps no more prejudiced than Coleridge's version contained in his two 1808 letters to Southey.
10 The original is in Bristol City Library MS.B 20878; Cottle wrongly lists it at the end as 'Jan.7'.
11 Griggs, III,56-59 and 68-72, Nos.675 and 679.
12 Poole Correspondence, British Museum MS.Add.35344, Vol.II, fol.204.
13 Griggs, III.33-34, No.658.
14 Griggs, III.34, No.659.
15 This, and de Quincey's letter of 14 October, are in the *1795 Album*.
16 Griggs, III. 34n-35n.
17 David Masson ed., *Collected Writings of Thomas de Quincey*, Vol.II (Edinburgh: A. and C. Black, 1889), p.163.
18 R.47, pp.143-144.
19 R.47, pp.345-346.
20 Griggs, III.26-28, No.655.
21 ER.37, I.202-204.
22 No.5 (missing) in Cottle's list in Bristol City Library MS.B 20878.
23 Bristol City Library MS.B 20864 (*olim* Bristol Museum and Art Gallery MS.G 3672). The deeply personal message is fairly well (by Cottle's standards) reproduced in R.47, pp.x-xi.
24 Bristol City Library MS.B 20877.
25 British Museum MS.Add.36519 H, fol.338r; H, fol.376v; I, fol.406r.
26 R.47, p.231; letter offered for sale by Bernard Quaritch, Catalogue No.817 of 1961, item 600.
27 Curry, I.526-529.
28 British Museum MS.Add.36520 A, fol.22r; B, fol.77v.
29 Curry, I.534n.
30 British Museum MS.Add.36520 A, fol.22r; B, fol.77v.

31 Here, and elsewhere in the Register, the last signature or two for a day bear the correct date of *borrowing*; but books *returned* at the same visit are dated on the day following.

32 All these details of his home life are in his letter to Southey of 8 June 1811.

33 Franked '2- Dec' (?), and headed by Cottle '1813' (in Bristol City Library MS.B 20877).

34 Berg Collection, New York Public Library.

35 Letter of Foster to Cottle, Bristol City Library MS.B 20878.

36 Griggs, III.444-446, No.895.

37 Griggs, III.450-452, No.900.

Chapter 10

Upheavals

The year that followed was anxious and painful: at 44, Cottle was brought to the lowest state of his physical health, and interwoven with this was the misery of an almost complete estrangement from Coleridge, and the beginning of a process which has brought Cottle nothing but discredit. On 8 March 1814, a day when Danvers, Dr Drummond, Admiral Sotheby and the Major were also in the Library, he borrowed Pennant's *Journey to the Isle of Wight*, Volumes I & II, but these were returned on the 18th of the same month; and, although Coleridge was in Bristol, there were no more borrowings until August.

Coleridge had arrived to give a course of lectures on Shakespeare, at the Great Room of the White Lion Inn.[1] Cottle sent him five pounds (or guineas) for his course ticket, and other subscribers were obtained by friends and by careful advertising. Coleridge had even sent Miss Cottle a 'complimentary' for herself and her brother – transferable, in case it might 'amuse' some of her 'younger friends'.[2] The first evening fell through, since Coleridge changed his mind in the coach at Bath and decided to escort a lady to North Wales, a fact of which George Cumberland was warned by his brother, who had been their fellow-traveller. This was a bad enough start. Coleridge turned up in a couple of days, agreed on another time, and was hauled from the bottle by his friends just in time to be an hour late for his audience. Cottle says that there were no further delays and 'the lectures gave great satisfaction'. Another course of six was well attended; a further one, of four, proved little attraction, and another on Homer was a failure. But, quite apart from the racy unpreparedness and informality of them, there was something odd in Coleridge's 'look and deportment'. After one lecture, Cottle met him at the inn door, and Coleridge, solemnly taking his hand, said he expected to be dead 'this day week'; Cottle, in alarm, told another friend, who said it would be merely one of Coleridge's fancies. After the lecture of Thursday, 7 April, Coleridge tried other tactics: he called Cottle outside and said 'Cottle, lend me ten pounds. A man, a dirty Fellow, has threaten'd to arrest me'. Cottle was shocked; he replied, 'Coleridge, you shall not go to gaol while I can help it', and at once *gave* him the ten pounds.

Meeting him during the next week, Cottle pointed out that a subscribed annuity was the only solution to his problems, and Coleridge offered no objection. Cottle drafted a letter to send round, and aimed at collecting £150 a year, to be administered by a committee of three, and not to be touched by Coleridge himself; he included references to Coleridge's family, genius, eloquence, and present depression of spirits. He sent the draft to Southey on 14 April, for suggestions, and asked him at the same time to be receiver or trustee; he himself was willing to give £20. By now the attendance at the lectures was declining; on one occasion, Coleridge had simply said he was too unwell, and dismissed the audience. Cottle still believed that he 'muddled' away his money somehow, and that he was penniless partly because of remittances to his family! Many others had given as much for their tickets as Cottle, who paid what sounds like £20 for the second course, yet Coleridge never seemed to have anything; it is possible that Cottle was quite ignorant of the opium and of its financial claims, and that (as he spells it) he just did not want his friend to be 'harrassed to death by Duns'.

So far, Cottle had tried to maintain the old life by little invitations, to which he prints Coleridge's replies, undated save for the year, in *Reminiscences*. Coleridge was not far away (at Wade's in 2 Queen Square), but the replies tend to be refusals. In one,[3] he seems to have returned from Cottle's unwell, and after a bad evening and night was somewhat relieved by magnesia and calomel; there was little chance of his stirring out that morning, but he might call later in the day. In another note,[4] after three mornings free from vomiting, he said that he had made only one call, and had been once to Meeting, but he hoped to be with Cottle at noon on the morrow – if he had no relapse. No doubt Cottle was a tedious companion: since Coleridge meant to attend Broadmead Meeting one Sunday, Cottle offered to call for him and take him there, and invited him to dinner; Coleridge swiftly sent back a note[5] that the maid had not risen and awakened anybody until nearly ten, that they were all in a hurry to get to Broadmead, that, as for dining, he had 'not five minutes to spare to the family below, at meals', and that Cottle should not call, as they will probably meet at the church.

Or, if physical suffering did not prevent him, some social engagement kept him from Cottle's quiet dinners and other earnest occasions. Cottle wished him to attend a meeting for the establishment of an Infant School, and sent him the local Dr Pole's pamphlet on the subject; but, although he had read two-thirds of it, and longed to express himself on the subject so near to his heart and so often in his prayers, he had been for three days engaged to dine with the Sheriff in Merchants' Hall at six o'clock on the very day of the meeting – though Cottle knows that he hates great public banquets, and that he would prefer 'a roast potatoe and Salt'. But, if the meeting can be postponed, and if Cottle will give him more notice, he will do his best to patronize it; he adds, as a sop, that he admires orthodox dissenters and their works.[6] There was further flattery: the second preface to *Alfred* is 'very well written'.[7]

Coleridge also followed up their long conversations with two letters,[8] of vast compass but more than usually suspect in the *Early Recollections* version, answering Cottle's query about his views on the Trinity, and incidentally giving great praise to Archbishop Leighton. As Cottle prints them, naughtily running the two together, they total twelve pages, and show something of the importance that Coleridge attached to him as an audience, a foil, and a sympathizer, even though a closer friendship was precluded. Another theological letter,[9] Cottle declares, is a 'Fragment'; it is still of two printed pages, but J.D. Campbell, having seen the manuscript, reported that Cottle had printed it 'very inaccurately'. This desultory correspondence, of spiritual monologues and defensive excuses, straddled the year 1814, both before and after the explosive incident that wrecked their relationship.

If we can trust Cottle's vague implications, it may have been between 14 April (when he knew nothing of a positive addiction to opium) and his receipt of Southey's sharp reply of 17 April (which opened his eyes) that he took Coleridge to visit Hannah More. At all events, one spring morning they went off in a chaise to Barley Wood, and he introduced Coleridge to the Mores. He had often praised Hannah, and Coleridge was delighted with her, thinking her 'the first Female he had ever conversed with', and outlining for her a great work which he was to undertake. All went well for two hours, until Lady Lifford arrived and claimed Hannah's good manners; 'the little folks' thereupon retired to the window to talk. But, though Coleridge had made so good an impression, Cottle was puzzled by the look in his eyes, and told a friend next day how worried he was to see Coleridge so paralytic, his hands shaking, and spilling a glass of wine, though he supported one hand with the other. The friend was unsympathetic: 'That arises from the immoderate quantity of OPIUM he takes'.

Cottle was 'astonished and afflicted' – partly, of course, by the thought that Coleridge had deceived and robbed him while speaking more frankly to others. Then came Southey's reply of 17 April,[10] and the horrible rumour was confirmed. Southey wrote gravely and unsparingly: no grounds existed for the annuity, and Coleridge did virtually nothing for his family; his disaster had been caused solely by opium, of which he took more than had ever been recorded of anyone before him, along with 'A frightful consumption of spirits'. True, the Morgans for a time broke him of the habit, but now he was deep in it again. Did Cottle realise how much the drug cost? The quantity Coleridge was taking would use up more than the proposed £150. Coleridge was neither disabled nor out of favour with publishers, and he had 'a footing in the theatre'; let him fulfil his promise to the eager reviews, and come up to Greta Hall, earning money on the way by lecturing at Birmingham and Liverpool, and then do his duty for even two hours a day. Cottle must do as he thought best, but Southey's name was not to be mentioned. 'Do not communicate this letter to Wade; he would report it to C. and make mischief'.

The next post brought Cottle a continuation of this letter,[11] written on the 18th and planning the relief of Coleridge's family. Southey had not relented; rather, he had hardened, and he pointed out that Cottle's hope of a prolific Coleridge with an adequate income was baseless, since he had had such an income for many years and had idled his time away. If Cottle was writing to Poole on the subject of Hartley and the others, let him tell Poole of Southey's plans for the lecture tour and the return to Keswick; if things went wrong thereafter, 'the humiliating solicitation' should be reserved for the upbringing and education of the Coleridge children.

On 24 April Coleridge, unaware of this well-meant intrigue, sent Cottle a grumbling letter in blotchy writing:[12]

April 24, 1814

My dear Cottle,

An erysipelatous complaint, of an alarming nature, has rendered me barely able to attend, & go thro' with, my Lectures – the Receipts of which have *almost* paid the expences of the Room, Advertisements, &c. – Whether this be to *my* Discredit, or that of the good Citizens of Bristol, it is not for me to judge. I have been persuaded to make another Trial, by advertising 3 Lectures, on the Rise, & Progress & Conclusion of the French revolution, with a critique on the proposed Constitution; but unless 50 names are procured, not a Lecture give I. –

Even so the two far, far more important Lectures, for which I have been long preparing myself and have given more thought to than to any other Subject, viz. those on female Education from infancy to Womanhood, practically systematized, I shall be (God permitting) ready to give, the latter end of the Week after next, but upon condition, that I am assured of 60 names – Why, as these are Lectures, that I must *write down*, I could *sell* them as a *recipe*, for twice the sum, at least. If therefore you or your Sisters are disposed to attend, be pleased to send your names. –

If I can walk out, I will be with you on Sunday. –

Has Mr Wade called on you? – Mr Le Breton, a near Neighbour of your's, in Portland Square, would (if you sent a note to him) converse with you on any subject relative to my Interests with congenial Sympathy – but indeed I think your Idea one of those Chimaeras, which kindness begets upon unacquaintance with Mankind – "Harry! Thy Wish was Father to that Thought". *Shakesp.*

God bless you & S.T.C.

J. Cottle, Esqre. Brunswick Square.

This letter, like the rest of the exchange, must have reached Cottle by hand the same day. Its slightly hectoring tone, combined with Southey's warnings, decided Cottle's immediate action, and on 25 April he despatched an enormous letter to Coleridge in 'indescribable sorrow', being resolved to save him from himself. He is 'influenced by the purest motives' in writing; he is Coleridge's oldest friend in Bristol, and was so when his friendship meant more to Coleridge than it now does. He does not want to hurt, but he 'must be *faithful*'. With that he launches into a terrific attack on Coleridge's depravity and its effects: his early promise blighted, his enthusiasm for religion compromised, a 'dirty fellow' chasing him for ten pounds; 'the wild eye! the sallow countenance! the tottering step! the trembling hand! the disordered frame!' If he is to be known by his fruits, he is giving arguments to the infidel and the blasphemer. As for the disastrous effects on his family, Cottle reminds him that he is still young enough to win for them and for himself 'honour, happiness, and independence'; if there were faults on either side, his Christianity must forgive them; if Cottle can mediate, he will do so, and will pay Coleridge's expenses to Keswick. If he *does* return, 'It will also look better in the eyes of the world'! For honour's sake, he should relieve Southey of the burden of supporting Sara and her three delightful children. How can Hartley enter the university – whatever the weight of his father's name – without money? (All this portion Southey struck through with a pen, when he was shown the letter.) The closing paragraphs employ the figure known as 'climax': he conjures Coleridge, by his duty to friendship, to his family, and to his God, that he renounce opium and spirits for ever; thus will he recover his genius, his good spirits, and the approbation of his Maker; even if he is at first offended by this letter, he may come to approve it, and later to thank Cottle and bless him … Cottle is weeping as he signs his name.

All this was very proper. True, the triton had been rather lordly in the past, and now the minnow could dart at him with an irresistible argument, but Cottle is little to blame for not knowing as much about Coleridge's sufferings as did the autopsy of 1834. The broken man, pouring what remained of his creative talent into self-pitying letters, sent Cottle a shocking reply the next day, 26 April: 'You have poured oil in the raw and festering Wound of an old friend's Conscience, Cottle! But it is oil of Vitriol!' The substance of the letter is not of the sort to appease Cottle, whose good advice is merely stigmatized as inopportune, 'a new visitor of affliction'. Moreover, Coleridge says he has been frank with his friends, and told them everything; the fact remains that he had told Cottle nothing, and had obtained money from him on the strength of it. Otherwise, the letter has a terrible pathos: his ignorant seduction into the habit after months of pain, his painful temporary 'cure' while with the Morgans, his longing to enter Dr Fox's madhouse – if only he could raise the money. In his infirmity, how can he rouse himself, as Cottle bids him? You might as well tell a paralytic to rub his arms briskly together. Even in this context, Coleridge found space for a flippant postscript. He had said many clever things to refute the Unitarians, and, at one of the lectures which Cottle was not well enough to attend, he had said publicly that Milton had meant Satan as a 'sceptical Socinian'. Now the battle was on, and 'Dr Estlin … is raising the city against me'. Cottle, in a wretched attempt to keep this matter tidy, to let us concentrate on the opium, and to keep his friend Estlin's name out of things, omits the postscript from his version of the letter, makes it into another letter printed under his 1807 narrative, and calls Estlin 'Mr —'.[13] (He might have shown more honesty, especially as the publication of this letter was the chief thing that involved him in the resentment of the Coleridges in and after 1837.)

The same day, Cottle's messenger returned to Queen Square with a note, which grieved that Satan was so busy with Coleridge: but had he not heard of salvation by Christ? And here the man of dull brain and easy soul thrusts in his sly dig at genius, with the purest of motives: 'Leave your idle speculations: forget your vain philosophy. Come as you are. Come and be healed.' Cottle is glad that Coleridge can confess: now he must pray. He is sorry if his former letter seemed unkind, but (a rebuke which he omitted when printing this note in *Reminiscences*) Coleridge had treated him deceitfully over the opium.

An hour later, back came a mournful note:[14] Coleridge, having in him so much to be forgiven, can forgive the cruellest enemy – and Cottle he has 'only to *thank*!' But Cottle must try to conceive the hell he is going through; and indeed, he *does* pray to be able to pray …

Next day, 27 April, distracted by this problem, and already unwell himself, Cottle collected up all these documents and sent them off for Southey's advice. First, there was his own huge upbraiding letter of 25 April, which he might have asked Southey to write if only the latter had not been the victim's brother-in-law; Southey need not return this, as one of the Misses Cottle has copied it. Cottle hopes he has not been '*too corrosive*' and has not done wrong in writing to Coleridge: his object was 'to touch on those strings which I thought could *alone* rouse from a state of lethargy; What a deplorable picture does he exhibit!' Coleridge has suggested going to Dr Cox or Dr Fox; so shall Cottle speak to one of them, or would it be better for Southey to write? Cottle is willing to pay for Coleridge's temporary residence, which 'may be the prelude to better days'. ('P.S. In my last, I spelt "*pennyless*" wrong, I smiled at the mistake & intended to alter it. I do sometimes make these careless mistakes'. Poor Cottle: it was very nearly his last little joke.)

We know now that Coleridge's cure began almost immediately. Many are to be thanked for this: the firm Dr Daniel, the generous Wade, the strong old 'valet' who kept a watch on the patient, the Bristol citizens Hood and Le Breton, perhaps even Cottle, whose excoriating letter may have finally frightened Coleridge into self-help, and who was in correspondence on the matter, as Coleridge admits,[15] with him and Hood. Up to the time when the process of cure began, Cottle had profitless dialogues with him: he would *not* visit Keswick, or go to Poole's, or lecture in the northern cities. He wrote, on or about 27 April, begging Cottle to call together at his home, any evening after seven, Wade and Hood and Le Breton, to see if money could be got together to put him in a private madhouse like Fox's ... 'I have to prepare my Lecture. O! with how *blank* a spirit!' Yet, meanwhile, on 3/4 May, he was advising Wade not to send a letter 'to a man who is unworthy even of a rebuke from you'[16] – and this is certainly Cottle. It is to the credit of Cottle and the other Bristol friends that they resisted the idea of dropping Coleridge, already so shaken in mind, into the surroundings of an asylum, although Cottle knew that his friend Fox would receive Coleridge *gratis*; and in Wade's kindly house, with Daniel calling daily, the long climb uphill began.

Southey, on the other hand, had just gone on being surly. He acknowledged the wad of correspondence in a letter[17] which Cottle dates 'April, 1814'; if this is accurate, he must have written in great haste at the very end of the month. And there is nothing new for him to say: the opium is being used as an indulgence, not a palliative; the Morgans' cure failed because it was followed by a chain first of laziness, then of shame at neglected duty, then self-accusation, and then again the relief of opium. Coleridge must restore his own self-respect by working for his family; he must lecture profitably in the cities, return to Keswick (where Southey would encourage him), and write articles for the reviews. First, he should have a holiday with Poole, and then aim at having a play performed, the profits going wholly to maintaining Hartley in College. As for the propriety of Cottle's great letter, 'A man with your feelings and principles my dear Cottle never does wrong'; *that* is a very silly thing to say to anyone, and Cottle took Southey's word for it, with grievous results when the *Recollections* were published. Southey adds that he has told poor Sara nothing of the contents of the letters, since she is in low spirits and health.

This was not a very helpful communication. It would have been hard for Southey, as Coleridge's breadwinner, to write cordially on the subject. And suddenly, on Wednesday, 4 May, Cottle, through the responsibilities he had taken on himself and through agitation of mind, was prostrated with the worst of his many illnesses; he himself certainly attributes it to worry over Coleridge.[18] His two sisters had taken their young ladies for a walk, and left him in his usual state; nor had he made any particular exertion. But when they returned, says Mary, they 'found him pale, & almost swooning from the loss of blood'. He had burst a blood vessel in the lung, and Mary at once sent for Mr Baynton, who bled him and continued to bleed and blister him, attending him daily for several weeks. Visits from friends were forbidden, and he was not allowed to speak; even by 17 May, when Mary wrote to Southey, he had to speak only in a whisper, receive no visitors, and use no exertion. The death of Danvers at this time further afflicted him. He wrote pluckily to Southey on 10 May, the Tuesday following his haemorrhage, while he was still losing blood and in great debility; he felt he would not survive, but he was happy – only, he could do no more for Coleridge. It is typical of the man that he uses this supposedly last opportunity to talk to Southey of his eternal state: let him read the Bible more often, and enjoy the blessings which Cottle knows: 'A *Crucified Saviour* is now *my only hope*'.

Coleridge called at Brunswick Square on Monday, 9 May,[19] to enquire after him, but suffered from the walk and swooned soon after he returned to Wade's, so that he was at once put to bed. He therefore sent a note on the Friday following, 13 May,[20] asking Mary for a verbal answer to the question 'How is your brother?' The note probably helped in Cottle's recovery: not just by reason of its kind enquiry, but because it contained the hint that Coleridge himself was slowly beginning to mend. He had asked for Mary's prayers, and called it 'an astonishing privilege, that a sinner should be permitted to cry, "Our Father!"' and that the Giver and Forgiver should actually encourage his petitioners to importunacy. These sentiments must have pleased the pious Mary enormously, and relieved her ailing brother.

On 13 May Southey, too, wrote,[21] reassuring him about haemorrhages: the younger Basil Montague bled for six weeks, and has just left Keswick, cured; and Southey knows of two other similar cases. Cottle must not die: if he did, with Danvers gone as well, Southey could never face visiting Bristol again. As for Cottle's 'exhortations', the two men are really very close in the substance of their beliefs, though the form may differ. These words, again, must have been a soothing balm to the invalid, who was by now recovering; Mary thanked Southey on 17 May, and said that with care, quiet, and attention for a month, her brother should be able to come with her and Ann into Devon at the mid-summer holidays.

Coleridge kept him in mind, and on 19 May wrote to Mary for news,[22] which his messenger Barnard would bring back orally; his own shaky knees would not permit him to walk to Brunswick Square, though he was otherwise recovering ... 'I hope, that finally this distressful accident may prove in some degree serviceable to him by removing or lessening the inflammatory ferment of his Blood and consequent turgescence and weakness of the Vessels. But I wish, he could sit in a more aery room: and still more, that he had a small riding chair, which a Lad might with ease push along thro' the open air'. In a letter to Cottle himself on 27 May,[23] he promises to call as soon as his own strength permits; he congratulates him on his convalescence and on the hope that 'has sustained and tranquillised' him in his peril. How different is Coleridge! He had always been attracted by annihilation, and 'when a *mere Boy*' wrote lines in praise of death. After a short disquisition on prayer, and an assurance that he *is* somewhat restored – though not as well as Mr Eden had told Cottle – he thanks Cottle for letting him meet Hannah More, and asks to be remembered to her when Cottle writes.

This kindness was almost effusive. But, although he was Mary's 'friend and servt' with 'unfeigned regard', and although he wished his 'affectionate respects' to be transmitted to Ann, he wrote to Morgan on 1 June[24] in quite another mood. He starts by saying that Lady Beaumont's sister, Miss Fermor, was 'doleful as a dull Tragedy, or as the Miss Cottles'; then he starts on Joseph.

> By the bye, Jo Cottle, who is *fizzling* and desperately disposed, spite of all poetric Decency, to *let* a third Epic, called Messiah (O such an Epic!!!) he gave me 10 pounds for reading thro', and correcting seven books out of TWENTY FOUR! & never galley-slave earned a penny so painfully and laboriously... Well, poor Jo. has burst a small blood Vessel in his Chest; but is convalescent — & instead of applying his Conscience to himself he has taken into his skull (heaven knows! there is *room* enough for any alien guest) to turn it all on me — & I have had some 4 or 5 letters, arm's length each, & (except the occasional bad spelling, very fairly *sentenced*) the object of all which is

to convince me, that it has not been Opium, quoad Opium, that has injured me; but – (what think you? –) the *DEVIL*. Yes, says he, the Devil, depend upon it, has got possession of you. It is the Devil, that is even now within you. – "A strong man armed (that is, this said *Devil*) has the mastery of you; but a stronger than he will not suffer him, I hope, to keep possession. – Do not deceive yourself about opium &c: it is the evil Spirit, it is the DEVIL, that is in you". Now is not Jo. a rare Comforter to a poor fellow in dreadful Low Spirits? – I verily believe that Wade would have gone & setting fire to all his Mss. have suffocated him in his own poetry, if I had not prevented it – & poor Jo. had not burst a Blood Vessel. – God bless him! He is a well-meaning Creature; but a great Fool.

This belittling paragraph is very jolly, of course, and shows that Coleridge was feeling better.

Better, but still able for his purposes to be a contrite wretch. On 26 June he wrote to Wade – that very Wade who had so little belief in the Devil – and called himself 'a spirit in hell'. This document, which Wade later gave to Cottle with a view to its publication, is of the utmost importance in our judgement of Cottle, since in it Coleridge plainly says: 'After my death, I earnestly entreat, that a full and unqualified narration of my wretchedness, and of its guilty cause, may be made public, that at least, some little good may be effected by the direful example'.

In the summer, Cottle and his sisters went down to Devon for a long and restorative holiday; this greatly improved his health, and after June he spat no blood, though he still had a pain in his side when he wrote to Southey in November. After his return, he paid three visits to the Library:

6 Aug. – 13 Oct.	J Beattie, *Essay on the Nature and Immutability of Truth*
6 Aug. – 13 Oct.	Hogarth, *Analysis of Beauty*
4 Oct. – 19 Jan. 1815	Eliz. Hamilton, *Series of Popular Essays*, Vol. I
4 Oct. – 19 Jan. 1815	General Dumourier, *Memoirs*

And he was now able to devote all his energies to finishing *Messiah* and getting it printed.

De Quincey had kept Southey informed of Cottle's health, but Southey wanted to hear from the patient himself, and wrote on 27 October begging for a letter:[25] once, hardly a day passed without their meeting, and nothing ever went wrong between them, but even the distance that now separated them would be a mere abstraction if they corresponded. Southey had, in fact, another motive in writing: he wanted precise news of Coleridge. He points out to Cottle that Coleridge is boarded and bedded for his conversation's sake, but leaves his family to chance. We must admit that Southey, however peevish he might be over Coleridge, was manfully doing all he could for the wayward father's neglected family, and was trying to get Hartley into College; here he solicits subscriptions, and informs Cottle of what others are giving. 'You will find among my Gothic names that of *Cottila*, doubtless the origin of yours'. (It isn't.) Cottle's 'attack' in the spring was of a type very alarming in appearance, but in reality far less perilous than many others; he must avoid frosty air this winter, and get a stove of the kind that heats and ventilates at the same time and so keep the room at an equable heat. Longman will be sending Cottle a new poem of Southey's when it comes out in November.

When Cottle replied on 1 November, his brother Robert was staying for a few days, and had brought his new wife, 'a most interesting and superior Young Woman, with whom we are all delighted'. (Poor Elizabeth became more interesting and less superior; after Robert had founded the Cottleite sect, and had died in 1858, she became a religious maniac, and got into two books of English eccentrics.) He was affected by Southey's reminder that there had never been any shyness between them, so he wrote at once instead of waiting until the next month, when *Messiah* would be available. His health was much improved, but he was still walking 'on the edge of a precipice ... without trepidation'. He congratulates Southey on the new poem, of which a friend has given him a glowing account; indeed, he is always glad to hear of Southey's triumphs, and proud of his fellow-townsman and their contiguous birth – so that he is all the more grateful that Southey, in his *Remains of Kirke White*, acknowledges him as his friend. He hears that Southey is engaged on *A Tale of Paraguay* and *Time and Eternity*; how wisely does he impress on his eldest daughter the issues of the latter subject!

Coleridge had called only once since Cottle had returned from his holiday; even then, he was in the house for only five minutes, promised to dine with them, recollected a prior engagement, said he would call again soon, and then moved to Morgan's straitened household at Calne. This is really all that Cottle can report of him at the moment, save that he claims to have something ready for the press; Gutch has bought the paper, and they have all promised to buy some copies. He will be glad to help Hartley, whom he often nursed, and whom he hopes God will raise 'to be a Father to his Family'; at first, he thought of ten guineas a year, but he has a big printer's bill to pay this Christmas, so it must be five, to be continued, as long as needed, if he dies. (At this point, in his 'elderly' hand, Cottle has later added that, on second thought, he 'will' subscribe £10 for four years. But Southey, writing to Bedford on 14 January 1815, and Wordsworth, in a letter to Poole of 13 March 1815,[26] confirms the sums as £40 from the Ottery uncles, £30 from Lady Beaumont, £10 from Poole, and £5 from Cottle.) After kind wishes to the Southeys and to Sara Coleridge, he accepts some little joke of Southey's which we have lost: 'You made me smile at Cottilon'.

John Foster was now at Bourton-on-the-Water in the Cotswolds,[27] and thither Cottle sent a manuscript of *Messiah* for comment, the printed version of it, a pencil-case as a gift (Coleridge would have called it a bribe), and another letter to follow. So slow were the wagons, and so carelessly were parcels left at inns, or at Stow-on-the-Wold, where no-one bothered to hand them to a postman, that the package had a long journey before reaching Bourton on the evening of 6 December, followed by the second letter on the 7th. Cottle, who throughout treated Foster generously, always paid the carriage or postage in advance; Foster replied on the 8th, urging him not to show such needless generosity, and advising him to send any further packets by the Oxford coach, the Bristol side of the route being so much tardier than Oxford-to-London. All this is by way of apology for having to keep the manuscript so long; Cottle must not expect a criticism, but he will read it carefully. He is glad to hear better news of Coleridge, and, of course, of Cottle's own health; Cottle must keep him informed of this, even if there is no literary matter to write about. He has grieved to read, in a Bristol paper, that old Mrs Cottle is dead; it seems so short a time ago that he was with her, and he well remembers 'her benign countenance and voice'.

By the time Foster returned *Messiah* on 27 December, he had read it 'several times over'. (Is this conceivable?) The man who would meet the coach was waiting for the parcel, so Foster dashed off a letter merely of observations on the poem; not that Cottle would find any detailed comments, which Foster felt diffident of making. The preface could hardly be shorter, as Cottle thought it might be; it all seemed relevant. As for the poem, there was much to praise, for its vigour and originality; but, when Cottle had read him a small portion, he doubted (and the feeling lasted) whether the whole had enough of a plan and was adequately connected. Lovers of the simple, tender, and pious, would enjoy it; but it was a pity that Cottle tackled the 'infernal economy' – Milton had left us a be-all and end-all account of it, 'as fixed as if it were actually a matter of geography' – and Foster preferred Cottle's 'patriarchal transactions'!

Messiah was published in 1815, printed for Button and Son, of Paternoster Row, by M. Bryan of Bristol. The earlier portion had been completed long ago, but now it ran to the vast size of twenty-eight books, with the usual preface, in which Cottle points out that he here treats the Old Testament, and hopes one day to treat the New also. In a hideous phrase, he flashes at us one facet of his creed: in view of his aims, his poem 'appeared not unconnected with utility'. But this is all, as it were, his Widow's Mite, and 'reflected light' is the most that he hopes for. He has interwoven two or three books 'descriptive of the Infernal Economy'. The poem is, in fact, as bad as his other epics, and although he escapes from 'blank' back to 'heroic', his couplets have lost whatever freshness they once had; from the first huge period-sentence, obviously based on the opening of *Paradise Lost*, the rhymed platitudes, copiously prolonged by bracketed triplets, galumph dully on, adding nothing to the combined powers of Holy Writ and John Milton. It is possible that the less impersonal, less Hebraic, figure of Jesus, in the projected work on the New Testament, would have inspired Cottle's best verse; but, as it stands, *Messiah* is an utter failure, having not even the newish stories of *Alfred* and *Cambria* to keep us awake.

1815 is not a well-documented year, especially in its latter half, apart from Cottle's ample use of the Library:

17 Jan. – 7 Feb.	L. von Buch, *Travels through Norway and Lapland*
17 Jan. – 7 Feb.	Sir R.K. Porter, *Narrative of the Campaign in Russia*
10 Mar. – 19 Apr.	ed. W. Cowper, *Homer's Iliad and Odyssey*, Vols. I & II
20 Apr. – 12 May	Clavigero, *History of Mexico*, Vols. I & II
12 May – 22 May	W. Henry, *Elements of Experimental Chemistry*, Vols. I & II
22 May – 29 May	S. Turner, *History of the Anglo-Saxons*, Vol. I
22 May – 4 July	*ditto*, Vol. II
23 May – 1 July	W. Robertson, *History of America*, Vol. I
1 July – 4 July	Carte, *General History of England*
1 July – 4 July	Rapin, *History of England*, Vol. I
4 July, returned same day	Camden, *Remaines concerning Britain*
4 July, returned same day	Strutt, *Chronicle of England*, Vol. I
4 July – 14 July	Barrington, *Miscellanies*
5 July, returned same day	J. Granger, *Biographical History of England*, Vol. I
5 July – 13 July	Tysilio, *Chronicle of the Kings of Britain*, ed. P. Roberts

5 July – 7 July	Richard of Cirencester, *Description of Britain, trans. from the Latin*
8 July – 13 July	Whitaker against Macpherson
11 July – 13 July	Robert of Gloucester, Vol. 1 (?and II)
11 July – 13 July	*Myvyrian Archaiology of Wales*, Vol. II
12 July – 29 July	Brady, *Introduction to the Old English History*
12 July – 29 July	Grafton, *Chronicle; or History of England*, Vol. I

(By this time, 12 July, he had seven books 'out', but some of these July dates must have slipped a day in the Register.)

29 July – 10 Aug.	W. Hutchinson, *History and Antiquities of Cumberland*, Vols. I & II
29 July – 10 Aug.	Strutt, *Chronicle*, Vol. II
10 Aug. – 15 Aug.	J. Nichols, *Illustrations of the Manners and Expences of Antient Times in England*
10 Aug. – 15 Aug.	Brand, *Observations on popular Antiquities*, Vols. I & II
15 Aug. – 25 Oct.	S. Turner, *History of the Anglo-Saxons*, Vol. I
15 Aug. – 13 Nov.	*ditto*, Vol. II
15 Aug. – 13 Nov.	Henry, *Britain*, Vol. II
25 Oct. – 16 Nov.	Lewis, *Commerce of Arts*
13 Nov. – 14 Nov.	Gibbon, *Decline and Fall*, Vols. II & III
14 Nov. – 15 Nov.	*ditto*, Vols. IV & V
15 Nov. – 16 Nov.	Busching, *Geography*, Vols. I & II
16 Nov. – 18 Nov.	Ducarel, *Anglo-Norman Antiquities*
16 Nov. – 18 Nov.	Hasted, *History of the County of Kent*, Vol. I
18 Nov. – 15 Dec.	*Modern Universal History*, Vol. 27
18 Nov. – 15 Dec.	Busching, *Geography*, Vol. III
15 Dec. – 20 Feb 1816	Peck, *Desiderata Curiosa*, Vol. I (2 in 1)
13 Dec. – 20 Feb 1816	S. Turner, *History of the Anglo-Saxons*, Vol. II
23 Dec. – 20 Feb 1816	Barrington, *Miscellanies*

Southey wrote on 2 March[28] – a letter which Cottle treated in his *Reminiscences* as part of the letter of the previous October – to thank him for his subscription to Hartley's education, for *Messiah*, for a brief monograph on old Mrs Cottle, and for a pencil. He then subjects *Messiah*, and its misleading title, to some mild criticism – including the encouragement to go on with two more parts of it! Cottle's 'ear is always good, and any one who studies the rhymed-couplet would do well to go to school to [him]'. Southey knows merely that Coleridge has left Wade's and is with the Morgans at Calne, but his family are left to 'chance and charity'; with all his innate virtues and talents, 'he is the slave of the vilest and most degrading sensuality, and sacrifices every thing to it. The case is equally deplorable and monstrous'. (Cottle and Southey, writing to each other from their own peculiar states of calm, about Coleridge's upheavals, make noises very like reciprocal congratulations.) Could Cottle and his sister possibly spend their summer holidays at Keswick? Sure-footed mountain ponies would be available, and a boat.

Coleridge was 'missing' until 7 March 1815, when he wrote from Calne in an ill-designed attempt to regain Cottle's patronage. Cottle, and others of the Bristol circle, had been worried about him, but the letter could hardly allay their fears. It begins politely, with a fairly frank criticism of *Messiah*, which Cottle coolly omitted when printing the letter in his memoirs;[29] someone – Hood, or Wade's son, Coleridge can't remember which – gave him the poem the other day. He seems to be attempting a criticism which will sound exalted, directed against the plan while praising the execution; but we feel that his tongue is firmly in his cheek. He says he must write to Cottle ' in *sincerity* – i.e. sine cerâ, without *wax*, entire, unrivetted'; but he hopes to give the poem a good review.

His object in writing, however, is obviously not to talk of *Messiah*: though his health has improved, he is in a poor way, but has collected manuscript poems enough for one volume, and will have enough for another. And he has such plans! – especially his schematizing of Christian Philosophy, but mean work for newspapers keeps detaining him; if only Cottle would buy his manuscripts for £30-£40! He is not going to submit 'as a slave to a Club of Subscribers to my Poverty'; it is not *his* fault that he is in debt, and he *could* live for less than £2.10s. a week, but only by cutting himself off from all social amenities; he wails that he never had '50£ before hand' for himself and his family; then, remembering that Cottle had procured him de Quincey's £300, he says of it that 'God knows ... *what went to myself*'. (Cottle's footnote sensibly supposes that it went on opium debts.) He has 'remained poor by always having been poor', and this lack of a competence has prevented his achieving any one great work. His kind regards to the dull sisters complete a pretty ill-rounded letter.

Cottle had expected matters to end just like this, and 'on the next day' (probably 10 March, the next day after receipt), convinced that even the £2.10s. a week was spent solely on opium, he won – or lost – a painful inner struggle and sent Coleridge as friendly a letter as he could, declining the request by enclosing a £5 note. But on the road his letter crossed another from Coleridge,[30] written at midnight on 10 March and more harrowing than the other. He has been waiting impatiently to get Cottle's offer, since his hospitable friends have done all they can; so now he has written to Hood, asking that the few gentlemen who seemed interested in him should raise the required sum for his manuscript poems, should Cottle 'not be able' (Cottle prints 'not find it convenient') to do so. Otherwise, he will have to sell them, 'fragments and all, for whatever I can get, from the first rapacious Bookseller', and then try to live where he is on day-pupils, children or adults; but he *must* first pay his hosts their expenses. *The Friend* is long out of print, and 'numbers' want it republished; it needs from eight to ten copies to complete it – would Cottle buy the copyright? … Coleridge has only to finish a paper on the Corn Laws; if only he had £20 for a week's peace of mind! But Cottle must write by return; he will not lose his money on the poems or on the prose essays. Coleridge will come to Bristol as soon as he can, get 'cheap Lodgings' near Cottle, and start his school, which is all planned for numbers, timetable, subjects, and fees; he is sure he can do it … But composition is harder, without 'a tolerable Competence': unlike the nightingale, he cannot sing with his breast against a thorn.

On this lyrical note Coleridge finished the last letter that he ever wrote to Cottle; apart from one brief meeting, he passes out of our hero's life-story, but his indignant shade, rustling in the Coleridge family cupboard, will be the villain of Cottle's later years. Cottle was poignantly grieved at this letter, but appalled by its contradictions and tergiversations, and disgusted at the thought of the University prizeman's sponging on the impoverished Morgans and hanging on the favour of assorted pupils at his cheap lodgings. Had he believed that the money would be spent lawfully, he would have given Coleridge all he asked '(without being an affluent man)', but he knew that it would be devoted to 'the Circean chalice', and 'COMPASSION STAYED MY HAND'. By return of post, therefore, he sent another £5 (surely a foolish piece of compromise) and a kind letter; Coleridge must come to Bristol, to be advised and assisted by Cottle and others. When Cottle left the business of bookseller sixteen years ago, he for ever quitted publishing, so he cannot take over these valuable manuscripts; but surely the London booksellers will treat Coleridge generously, now that his merits are so well established … Cottle even offered to write to a London publisher, who would pay twice as much as the £30-£40. No answer came; and Coleridge moved on, not to Bristol, but to London. Cottle remained in his mind as little more than one who disposed of the copyright of the 1796-1797 poems, as he says in a letter to Byron during Easter Week,[31] knowing 'that it was never considered by me or by himself, as a copy-right'.

Cottle and his sister had fully intended to accept Southey's invitation up to Greta Hall; but on 17 June he received a letter settling that their house in Bristol was that summer to receive all their 'distant Brothers & Sisters, some of whom are to meet for the first time'. This must include 'in-laws', since the only surviving Cottles were now Mary, Ann, Sarah, Joseph, and Robert; Mr Saunders, and Robert's wife, would complete the party. Though happy that his friendship with Southey could not be shaken by time or distance, Cottle was sickened by the thought of not seeing him, especially amid Lakeland scenery; but when he wrote apologizing on 19 June,[32] he had exciting schemes for the following summer, which came to nothing, but they suggest that he was starting a new life.

As far as he can plan, he hopes to put £50 'in a snug corner' of his pocket next summer, and come to Keswick, and thence go as far further as the money will last. Southey will smile at his speculation, but he wants to meet two like-minded friends who can put up with an invalid, and to proceed from Liverpool by chaise through North Wales to Holyhead, Dublin, Killarney, Northern Ireland, Drogheda, Glasgow (or rather, the nearest point of Scotland); then they could peep at the Highlands, or visit the principal towns, including Edinburgh. De Quincey would like to come: would Southey make a third, or suggest someone else instead of de Quincey? Even in a pecuniary way, it would be a good speculation for Southey, as a series of letters on his travels would have a good sale. Well, there is plenty of time, and, anyway, the mere thought of it makes him 'a great Traveller in an easy chair'.

He tells Southey what little he knows of Coleridge's movements; but thinking of Coleridge throws his mind into a fever. The rest of this cheerful letter is all books: he takes *The Quarterly Review*, and there he has detected Southey's hand in a criticism of Sylvester's Du Bartas (which he wants to procure) and of Flinders's Voyage, where Southey has expressed his regret that the territory to the west, over the Blue Mountains, has not been explored. Well, there *has* just been a successful expedition to this very part: one of the teachers at his sisters' school is a Miss Evans, and her brother, the Government Surveyor of Botany Bay, obtained permission from the Governor to take a party there. Ascending the Blue Mountains, he saw the luxuriant plain beneath, like 'a Gentleman's Park'; there were no dangerous beasts, and only two humans, terrified females. Evans has sent his sister a brief account, which Cottle will transcribe if Southey wants it. Cottle asks for news of the *Tale of Paraguay*; death and immortality are such interesting topics, and Southey knows how to grapple with them – witness Book XXI of

Don Roderick. He is glad that the *History of Portugal*, of which the research material so impressed him fifteen years ago, is on the way to completion; even if Southey does not get a fair remuneration for it, it will ensure his future reputation.

1816 was another quiet year, of which little but Cottle's reading survives. George Cumberland again lent him the Bishop's *Sanchoniatho*, in two volumes, and *Laws of Nature*, on 17 January, and puts a query in his memorandum book early in August whether *Messiah* had been delivered to his son Sydney Cumberland along with other books.[33] From the Library Cottle had:

8 March – 18 April (after letter of 13 April)	Eliz. Hamilton, *Essays*
15 April – 17 April	Imison, *Elements of Science and Art*, Vol. I
17 April – 18 April	*ditto,* Vol. II
17 April – 18 April	Albin, *Natural History of English Insects*
18 April – 19 April	Spallanzani, *Dissertations relative to the Natural History of Animals and Vegetables*, Vols. I and II
19 April – 14 May	Hooper, *Rational Recreations*, Vols. I and II
14 May – 7 June	Nichols, *Anecdotes of the XVIIIth century*, Vols. I & II
7 June – 17 June	*ditto*, Vols. III & V
17 June – 12 Aug.	*ditto*, Vols. IV & VI
12 Aug. – 14 Aug.	*Harleian Miscellany*, Vols. III & IV
15 Aug. – 16 Aug.	*ditto*, Vols. II & V
16 Aug. – 3 Sept.	*ditto*, Vol. I
16 Aug. – 10 Sept.	*ditto*, Vol. VI (a curious order in which to read them!)
28 Aug. – 4 Sept.	Sir G. Mackenzie, *Travels in the Island of Iceland*
3 Sept. – 7 Sept.	Locke, *Works*, Vol. 1
7 Sept. – 24 Sept.	*ditto*, Vol. II
24 Sept. – 26 Nov.	*ditto*, Vol. III
8 Oct. – 26 Nov.	J. Murphy, *Travels in Portugal in 1789 and 1790*
26 Nov. – 13 Dec.	Stedman, *Narrative of an Expedition to Surinam*, Vols. I & II
13 Dec. – 19 Dec.	J.C. Eustace, *Classical Tour through Italy*, Vol. I

13 Dec. – 19 Dec.	R. Cumberland, *Calvary, or the death of Christ*, Vol. I
20 Dec. – 3 Jan. 1817	E.D. Clarke, *Travels in Various Countries*, Vol. III
(after letter of 30 Dec.)	
20 Dec. – 3 Jan. 1817	A. Beatson, *Tracts relative to the Island of St Helena* (to be returned on 28 Dec.)

For thus exceeding the time-limit on the last item he was fined 3/- (a more savage fine than most others received).

On 17 April, Southey's adored only son Herbert died. (Cottle stupidly records this in *Reminiscences*[34] as the death of his 'youngest' boy; he was in fact an elder son, since Charles Cuthbert was born in 1819.) Since Cottle wrote him no letter on the subject, Southey sent him the news on 23 May,[35] asking if he had seen it in the papers; he and his wife were bearing it well, and it served to fix their hopes all the more earnestly on the after-life. Cottle would have read Southey's proem to *The Pilgrimage*: yet the child so delightedly mentioned in it was dead before it was published! At the same time, Southey invited him and one of his sisters to visit them in Keswick, entering the district the proper way by crossing the sands from Lancaster, calling at Furness Abbey, and proceeding from Ulverston by Coniston Water to Ambleside, or – better – to the not 'formidable' Windermere ferry and over to Bowness.

Cottle replied on 3 June,[36] with thanks for the invitation; but he cannot come; nor can his sister visit Mrs Southey, since she has to visit Sarah Saunders in Plymouth. Would that they could break natural laws, and pass the intermediate space! He himself is prevented by the expense; oh, he can *afford* it, but in these times of general distress and want and uncertainty he could not, with a clear conscience, take a £30 holiday – it would entail so many charities. (What kind of tortuous argument is this? – unless he means 'curtail'.) He says it is a 'sacrifice to principle'; having only a little time left on earth, he wants to pass it with eternal things in mind. (The little time proved to be thirty-seven years and four days.) He saw Herbert's death in the papers, and was about to reply, when Southey's letter arrived; he had felt that silence would be kinder for a while. He has the comforting thought of Herbert's present bliss; and, seeing how far Southey has risen above the views he once entertained, let him rise even higher, and become a great champion of divine truth. He must read his Bible more, especially 1 *Corinthians* 1 and 1 *Corinthians* 2, verse xiv. Cottle had received his copy of *The Pilgrimage to Waterloo*; the evening it arrived, Ann (than whom there is no better reader south of the Thames) read it aloud, and they were very interested and touched by the part about little Herbert. The passages about the toys, the children, and the showman, turned things into an April day of rain and shine by turns. If only Cottle could have been with him! But he adds of his own love of travel that it 'was perhaps wisely counteracted by *a clog on my heels*'. He has been within seven miles of Waterloo, 'but it is only like the next number to the prize in the Lottery'. This visit to Brussels (which is obviously what the 'seven miles' must mean) is an utter mystery: how war and business and lameness and poverty gave him the opportunity for it, is now impossible to say, and he nowhere else mentions any Continental visit.

To cheer Southey, he sent the third edition of *Alfred* for Edith (with a pointer to some consoling words in Book II), and the second edition of his school *Selection*, including a new piece of his own (*An Address to the Missionaries*) and an old anagram of Southey's. When he thought of sending this parcel, he wondered if there was anyone in the Southeys' native place from whom he could offer to enclose a letter – and there was no-one! So he feels that they are on a shifting scene, but luckily there is a 'stability beyond! Death to me is a delightful thought. I am almost too impatient to be gone'.

1817 was, again, quiet – save for an illness and a fairly quick recovery. The gap of the month of August in his visits to the Library suggests a summer holiday, and his health was certainly far better after this year:

13 Jan. – 11 March	E.D. Clarke, *Travels in Various Countries*, Vol. I
13 Jan. – 5 Feb.	B. Heyne, *Tracts, Historical and Statistical, on India* (to be returned on 28 Jan.)
(after a letter of 3 Feb.; fined 4/-!)	
11 Mar. – 19 Mar.	Neal, *History of the Puritans*, Vols. III & IV
19 Mar. – 1 June	D. Hume, *History of England*, Vol. VII8
Apr. –21 Apr.	*Quarrels of Authors* (due back on 16 April)
(after a letter of 19 April; fined 8d.)	
9 June – 7 July	T.D. Fosbrooke, *History of Gloucestershire*, Vols. I & II
10 June – 7 July	*Monthly Review* for March
7 July – 15 Dec.	Pascal's *Thoughts on Religion*, &c.
(renewed on 15 Sept. after letter of 11 Sept.; renewed again on 1 Nov.)	
9 July – 10 July	J. Bell, *Principles of Surgery*, Vol. II, Pts. 1 & 2
10 July – 11 July	*ditto*, Vol. III
11 July – 1 Aug.	*ditto*, Vol. II Pts. 1 & 2 (again)

26 July – 6 Sept.	Z. Grey's Examination of Neal's *History of the Puritans*, Vol. I
5 Sept. – 13 Oct.	Hayley, *Cowper's Life and Posthumous Writings*, Vol. I (2 in 1)
13 Oct. – 14 Nov.	Rudder, *History of Gloucestershire*
15 Dec. – 27 Dec. (?renewed) – 1 April, 1818	Smellie, *Natural History*, Vols. I & II

At the beginning of February, he had another haemorrhage, and spat much blood for a fortnight; Dr Stock attended him, and the medicines brought him low, but he was recovering by 22 March, when he wrote to Southey.[37] It was obvious to his advisers that his confined and sedentary life was telling on him, and in March he bought a horse and a low chair; the house already had a stable. He planned to ride out most days, and was overjoyed at the thought of looking at Nature again; but then he kept thinking of the straits of those around him, and hoped that he had not been selfish and self-indulgent. His purchase might lengthen his life a little, but he was ready to slip into eternity, and he hoped that Southey felt the same.

His chief purpose in writing on 22 March was to commiserate with Southey on the surreptitious publication of his pirated *Wat Tyler*. This little drama of Southey's republican youth was selling in tens of thousands, and he was furious with the dissenting minister, William Winterbotham, who had thus kept his gift and turned it against him.[38] The Radicals, Southey's political enemies, were jubilant at its appearance; and Cottle early realised how damaging it would be to his friend's reputation. As soon, therefore, as he saw a notice of it in a Bristol newspaper, he sent an explanation to another paper, and on 21 and 22 March sent this on to Southey, as well as a paper containing the discussion in the Court of Chancery. Knowing the circumstances of the play, he at first intended to send a news paragraph for insertion in the *Courier*, to counteract the wrong impression; but, on second thoughts, he preferred just to send for Southey's approval the card he had inserted in the Bristol papers, and he would then be willing to write, with any alterations that Southey thought fit, in a spirit unshrinking from any service to him. Or perhaps some London friend, on the spot, has anticipated Cottle; and why does not Southey prosecute? – There would be heavy damages. Ill-disposed persons can bring one unfair charge against the play, but only by assuming that the sentiments are Southey's own; by such an argument, an author could not delineate a miser or a murderer. (No, but then Southey *had* been a republican, even if he were now no more ashamed of having been one 'than of having been a boy'.)

There is a long P.S., a sorry tale of Coleridge, which Cottle is sure Southey will keep from the Coleridge family. Some time ago, Cottle was in the Bristol Library, when up came Mr Porter, the curate of St Paul's, Cottle's own parish; Southey would know him, since Cottle years before gave Porter a letter of introduction. He asked if Cottle knew anything of Coleridge, and, getting a negative answer, said that if he knew his whereabouts he would arrest him as a 'Swindler'. It appears that when Coleridge had first come back to Bristol to lecture he told Porter of his and the Morgans' straitened circumstances, and Porter gave him £50 between them; soon after, Coleridge called on him, mentioned a particular payment he had to make, and asked for the loan of £50 more – he was to get a considerable sum 'from one of the first Houses on the 20th of the next month', when it would be repaid with thanks. Though a mere curate, Porter had the money by him, and lent it. After the appointed time of payment, he met Coleridge and asked if it was convenient for the second £50 to be returned; Coleridge 'shuffled & said he had not borrowed the mony (sic), that he knew nothing at all about the matter', but Porter produced one of his Notes, and then he acknowledged receipt. If Southey wants further particulars, let him write to Porter.

This long letter 'crossed' one of Southey's[39] explaining *his* side of the *Wat Tyler* affair: his failure to obtain an injunction, his good health, his comparatively small annoyance at the whole affair, his smug consciousness of being sinless before men; and the scandal had given promise of good – Coleridge had rallied to his old friend in two articles for the *Courier* of 17 and 18 March. Cottle was delighted to hear this last bit; and, promising himself a peep at the articles, he wrote to Southey on 27 March[40] with the hope of one day seeing Coleridge 'bursting the Satanic trammels of Opium & … becoming a renovated character'. Is it not a strange thing about Coleridge and Porter? He is almost sorry to have told Southey what he has not even told his brother Robert, and there must be some qualification in the story, or Coleridge's memory was fuddled with opium. It is a shame that a man like Porter has the power to spread such a tale (what, we wonder, was wrong with Porter?); Cottle would like to refute it, and he would send to Coleridge for an explanation if only he knew his address.

Southey's letter had assumed that Winterbotham was dead, but now Cottle is not losing a minute to assure Southey that he is still alive; he once had a congregation at Plymouth, but now he is at Nailsworth in Gloucestershire. Cottle is sorry that Winterbotham is 'in this dirty and iniquitous business', and he does not want to know anything more about him. (In fact, Winterbotham was not directly to blame: two mysterious persons, at a house in Worcester, sat up all night secretly copying his copy, as revealed in a letter from John Foster to Cottle on 22 June 1843.[41]) Probably Southey has by now read Cottle's letter with the second paper, including his card to the printer about 'Uncle Wat'; he wrote it hastily, and even if it is not just what Southey would want, it was well meant, anyway. Though Cottle prints Southey's letter as stating that the writer is 'well in health' and pretty complacent, his reply expresses sorrow that Southey is in low spirits; he himself wants bracing, and hopes to improve in the coming warm weather. He has not yet received the second volume of Southey's *History of Brazil*.

Southey spent the summer of 1817 on a restorative tour of the Continent, and gave Cottle a rather potted account in a letter of 2 September from Keswick,[42] omitting (perhaps because Cottle was not in on the secret) his visit to Wordworth's French daughter, her husband, and her baby Dorothée. There is also some literary news and advice; and he says that a Cottle preface is written in prose of a 'natural ease which no study could acquire'.

Hartley Coleridge seemed to be rewarding the care of those who had made his education possible. He stayed for a while in Bristol during 1817, and also visited Thomas Poole; on 16 November, from Merton College, he wrote a letter of thanks for his hospitality,[43] adding that 'Several of my father's Bristol friends enquired particularly after you, among the rest the poet Cottle'.

1   Cottle's version of the events of the sorry years 1813-1814 is in R.47, pp.352 ff.; for special reasons, to which his excuses in pp.347 ff. lead us, the account is more than usually suspect, but some of his letters to Southey in Bristol City Library MS.B 20877 (14 April, 27 April, 10 May, 1 November 1814) help to correct it.

2   Griggs, III.448, No.898.

3   Griggs, III.488, No.925.

4   Griggs, III.487, No.924.

5   Griggs, III.472-473, No.916.

6   Griggs, III.473-474, No.917. Merchants' Hall (now in the Promenade, Clifton) was formerly (before being destroyed by bomb damage) at the junction of Marsh Street and King Street.

7   Griggs, III.488, No.925.

8   Griggs, III.478-480, 480-486, Nos.921, 922.

9   Griggs, III.467-469, No.913.

10 Curry, II.93-95.

11 Curry, II.95-96; Cottle misrepresented the real purpose of this extra letter by omitting all reference to the children.

12 In my own collection; printed, almost verbatim (though Cottle amazingly says that it has 'no date'), in R.47, pp.357-358; Griggs, III.474-475, No.918.

13　*R.*47, p.336; the full letter is printed in Griggs, III.476-478, No.919.

14　Griggs, III.478, No.920.

15　Griggs, III.489-491, No.927.

16　Griggs, III.486-487, No.923.

17　Curry, II.97-98.

18　*R.*47, p.379.

19　Griggs, III.487, No.924.

20　Griggs, III.488-489, No.926.

21　Berg Collection, New York Public Library.

22　Griggs, III.493, No.929. Even Griggs's hostile footnote to his edition of this in *Unpublished Letters*, II.114-115, No.248, ascribes Cottle's illness to his agitation in trying to 'pry loose the Devil which he was convinced was in possession of Coleridge'.

23　Griggs, III.498-500, No.933.

24　Griggs, III.502-503, No.935.

25　Part, grossly ill-treated, in *R.*47, p.386; and part in CCS, IV.81-83. CCS wrongly dates the letter 'Oct.17'. It is printed entire in Curry, II.106-108.

26　Moorman/Hill, p.209, No.352.

27　His two letters of December 1814 are in Bristol City Library MS.B 20878.

28　Curry, II.116-117.

29　*R.*47, pp.386 ff., which details the end of their correspondence; the whole letter is in Griggs, IV.545-547, No.956.

30　Griggs, IV.551-552, No.958.

31　Griggs, IV.559-563, No.963.

32　Bristol City Library MS.B 20877.

33　British Museum MS.Add.36520 E(Memo Book), fol. 242r, and F(Memo Book), fol. 269r.

34　*R.*47, p.233; Southey's letter of 23 May follows.

35　Berg Collection, New York Public Library.

36　Bristol City Library MS.B 20877.

37　Bristol City Library MS.B 20877.

38　*Dictionary of National Biography*, under 'William Winterbotham', renames the drama *William Tell*! For the whole story, and Southey's manly behaviour, see Simmons, pp.158-161.

39　*R.*47, pp.234-236.

40　Bristol City Library MS.B 20877.

41　*R.*47, p.235.

42　*R.*47, p.236-7, Berg Collection, New York Public Library.

43　Poole Correspondence, British Museum MS.Add.35344, II, fol.97.

Chapter 11

Reconstruction: Byron

What survives of Cottle's life in 1818 suggests a turning away from literature to religion, with Foster as his closest friend; however, his Library borrowings are not very revealing:

6 Jan. – 26 Jan.	*British Critic*, November
27 Jan. – 19 March	Fox, *On the Teeth*
19 March – 22 April	M. Graham, *Journal of a Residence in India*
19 March – 22 April	T. Gray, *Poems*
22 April – 11 May	Bp. Burnet, *History of his Own Time*, Vol. I
22 April – 11 May	Burnet, *Reformation*, Vol. I

(there is no gap, but there are no entries in the Register from 9 May to 25 May; so he may have borrowed things unrecorded)

5 June – 19 June	W. Jones, *Physiological Disquisitions*
30 July – 31 Aug.	Lodge, *Josephus*
28 Aug. – 28 Sept.	*Handmaid to the Arts*, Vol. I
28 Aug. – 30 Nov.	*ditto*, Vol. II
28 Nov. – 17 Dec.	Bp. Watson, *Anecdotes of his Life*, Vol. I

(after letter of 16 Dec.)

28 Nov. – 19 Dec.	W. Phillips, *Outlines of Mineral and Geology* (1818) or *Outlines of the Geology of England and Wales* (1818)
18 Dec. – 26 Dec.	T. Malthus, *On Population*, Vol. I
18 Dec. – 23 Dec.	*Edinburgh Review*, Vol. 29
23 Dec. – 26 Dec.	Malthus, *On Population*, Vol. II
28 Dec. – 30 Dec.	*ditto*, Vol. III
28 Dec. – 30 Dec.	Bp. Watson, *Apology for Christianity* (1777) or *Apology for the Bible* (1796)

On 16 April 1818, the full members of Broadmead Baptist Church, including Ann Cottle, signed the 'call' to the Reverend T.S. Crisp; on 19 April, Mary signed, along with eleven other members of the Independent Paedobaptist Church assembling therein; and thereafter Joseph signed, among a number of other 'Hearers & Subscribers'.[1] This status of the three continued thus for some years.

Robert Hall was preaching in Bristol this year; Cottle felt a truceless admiration for him, and never mentions that he sometimes took 120 grains of opium (with the same motive as Coleridge: the relief of terrible pain). John Foster came in from Downend and attended his sermon on the evening of Sunday, 3 May, and Cottle adopted a 'friendly expedient' for informing him that there would be another on Tuesday evening, 5 May. Foster had been impressed by the 'commanding' sermon on the Sunday, and fully intended to hear the next, if his health allowed him. Cottle wanted him to dine with him on the Tuesday, and he wrote thanking him but excusing himself, since he had a couple of little engagements.[2] Also, he wanted to look further at a manuscript of Cottle's before he returned it; so, as he would not be long in Bristol on the following day, he looked forward to seeing Cottle in Downend on Monday, 11 May. One Saturday morning early in this summer, Foster again wrote from Downend[3] asking Cottle to 'accept a small piece of literary manufacture'; he had been at it so many months that he had been unable to see Cottle and his other Bristol friends. (Cottle's hand has added the year '1818' to this letter, in the account-book wherein he mounted Foster's correspondence; if they really had *not* met for many months, we can only assume that they were together at neither of Hall's sermons.) The letter accompanied, with thanks, a book that one of the Misses Cottle had lent him before his last summer's excursion a year ago; he assumed that the Cottle family would be going south again towards the end of the month, and he promised to come and see them all before then. His wife was mending after an illness, but could sit up for only an hour or less every day. Foster wrote at least one other letter to Cottle on Hall's preaching, listed as No. 11 in Cottle's letter-book, but now missing.

Further proof of Cottle's more exclusively religious tastes lies in a letter, now in my possession, to a gentleman with whom he was still at the 'Dear Sir' stage. He had been at Cottle's in Brunswick Square on the evening of 26 May, and after his departure Cottle began writing an Address for the Tract Society; after dinner on the 27th, it was finished, and Cottle sent a note to the gentleman asking him to call in that evening, or any time he was passing, when Cottle would be happy to read it to him.

Cottle had his seaside holiday, and on 7 August wrote cordially to George Cumberland[4], enclosing the present of a book to which he had subscribed, 'in compliment to a friend' – but Cumberland will be able to judge 'the merit of the designs'; why does not Cumberland give him a chance to wish him well to his face? At the end of the month, Foster used Cottle's young manservant to send a verbal message that he would soon visit the Cottle family; but the promise was unfulfilled a fortnight later, when he wrote[5] with the apology that he seemed under some kind of spell with regard to getting out. By the same postman, he returned a number of the *Monthly Review*, Cottle's catalogue of the Library (with apologies for retaining it), and a manuscript of Cottle's, on the blank pages of which he had made some few slight remarks, there being no occasion for anything more 'assuming'. He is much obliged for the third edition of *Alfred* (this had come out in 1816); and, as for Cottle's note on Henderson, he only wishes that it could have been longer. He hopes the visit to the sea has done Cottle good and wishes to be remembered to his 'excellent sisters'. There had been some mix-up about invitations, and now Foster apologises for not having said, by the messenger, how glad he would be to see Cottle at Downend on the day Cottle suggested, or on any other; but then, he felt sure of seeing Cottle before that and would have told him personally. He feels that Cottle's kindness has gone too far in sending his man right out to Downend; the post will always do, since it comes every day.

Cottle was now nearly fifty. Middle age had brought less literature and more religion, less ambition and more content; his health was unexpectedly good, and his outlook sunny and interested. 1819 gave him another Devon holiday, shown by the gap of July in his many visits to the Library; and the books he read show him as a tireless arm-chair traveller:

4 Jan. – 26 Jan.	B. Hall, *Account of a Voyage of Discovery to the West Coast of Corea*
4 Jan. – 26 Jan.	Col. Wilks, *Historic Sketches of the South of India*, Vol. I
26 Jan. – 4 Feb.	Bp. Watson, *Anecdotes of his Life*, Vol. II
26 Jan. – 12 Feb.	J. Barrow, *Discoveries*
4 Feb. – 15 Feb.	Bp. Taylor, *Life of Christ*
13 Feb. – 19 Feb.	Lewis & Clarke, *Travels up the Missouri ...*, Vol. I
13 Feb. – 19 Feb.	Hawkesworth, *Account of Voyages for making Discoveries in the Southern Hemisphere*, Vol. I

19 Feb. – 3 Mar.	*ditto*, Vols. II & III
3 Mar. – 5 Mar.	Bougainville, *Voyage round the World*
5 Mar. – 9 Mar.	*Missionary Voyage to the Southern Pacific Ocean in 1796-7-8*
5 Mar. – 17 Mar.	J. Burney, *History of the Discoveries in the South Seas*, Vol. I
9 Mar. – 17 Mar.	S. Parkinson, *Journal of a Voyage to the South Seas*
17 Mar. – 22 (?23) Mar.	G. Vancouver, *Voyage to the North Pacific Ocean, and round the World*, Vols. I & II
22(?23) Mar. – 24 Mar.	*ditto*, Vol. III
22(?23) Mar. – 24 Mar.	G. Forster, *Voyage round the World with Captain Cook*, Vol. I
24 Mar. – 29 Mar.	*ditto*, Vol. II
24 Mar. – 29(?30) Mar.	G. Forster, *Observations during a Voyage round the World*
30 Mar. – 12 Apr.	J. Cook, *Voyage towards the South Pole, and Round the World*, Vols. I & II
12 Apr. – 14 Apr.	J. White, *Journal of a Voyage to New South Wales*
12 Apr. – 14 Apr.	*Voyage of Governor Phillip to Botany Bay*
14 Apr. – 19 Apr.	*Cook's Last Voyage*, Vols. I & II
19 Apr. – 27 Apr.	*ditto*, Vol. III
19 Apr. – 27 Apr.	J. Grant, *Voyage of Discovery*
13 May – 21 June	*Edinburgh Review*, Vol. 21
13 May – 9 June	Collins, *New South Wales*, Vol. II
9 June – 21 June	A. de Humboldt, *Personal Narrative of Travels to the Equinoctial Regions of the New Continent*, Vol. III
6 Aug. – 23 Nov.	*Life of Linnaeus*
6 Aug – 14 Aug.	Locke, *Works*, Vol. III
14 Aug. – 15/16 Oct.	Malkin, *South Wales*
15 Oct. – 30 Nov.	M. Elphinstone, *Account of the Kingdom of Caubul and its Dependencies*
(after letter of 23 Nov.)	
20 Nov. – 30 Nov.	J.C. Hobhouse, *Journey through Albania, and other Provinces of Turkey*

(Incidentally, most of his borrowings are by now in his own signature – more than are those of other members.)

Southey wrote pleasantly on 2 February,[6] thanking him for a *Messiah*, praising the preface except for its censure of the alexandrine, and advising him not to call attention in a preface to any novelties of composition. His own history of Brazil, printed by Cottle's 'old acquaintance Pople', is nearly ready, and his *Wesley* is forming; Cottle must not buy it, for Longman will be told to send him a copy. Hartley Coleridge has been awarded a 'second' at Oxford – which, considering his haphazard schooling, is as meritorious as another's 'first'; and Cottle will be pleased to know that Derwent may get to Cambridge, but when Southey thinks of the way Coleridge 'has left these boys to sink or swim', he 'cannot speak of him with patience'. Edith is having a wretched pregnancy (but the happy issue was their good son Cuthbert). If only Cottle would 'amuse' himself by writing his recollections of people! – and save his poor sight by using a device of tablets in a frame, in the manner of the Nocturnal Remembrancer. We should note that this persuasion, this hint that penned recollections could decently be trivial, involves Southey in the initial blame for Cottle's disastrous memoirs of 1837 and 1847.

Cottle's July holiday took him to Dartmoor, and this inspired his 598-line poem on that wild, fresh, suggestive region; his couplets here afford almost pleasure, since we can see in them the rejuvenated cripple escaping from disappointments and bereavements, and letting his body and mind wander over the grandeurs of nature and the platitudes of simple morality. He speaks of his 'weary steps' as he trudges up the slopes, but he did not journey entirely on foot; it was 'on driving up' to the pretty cottage, recently built by the Duke of Bedford, on a commanding site near Tavistock, that he discovered 'an odd coincidence': his Grace, who had not been there for two years, had arrived the evening before, and so visitors were not being allowed to enter.[7]

As he penetrates the moor, sterner feelings occur to him. He is leaving the fields of grain, the tracks, and (with inverted commas) 'the "hum" of human kind'; it reminds him, with a sudden line of real poetry, of the ship leaving its home port, losing more and more of the familiar landscape, until 'Each object fades that lingers near the soul'. Each of the succeeding wonders of the Moor allows Cottle to spin his couplets and then compose his chatty footnotes, which form the bulk of the poem: rock-idols; lichens; scattered crags. These last are blandly explained: whether they be crumbled primeval cliffs or volcanic remains like those within twenty miles of Exeter, or stones heaped there by mortals

> In times when men yoked lions to their car,
> Nothing is certain, but that – 'there they are'.

He was doing his best, consistently with his firm belief in the Deluge, to understand the geology of the region: hills like Haldon, which had been submerged in the sea and bore the sand and pebbles to prove it, and the stones he had assiduously collected near Bradninch, 'of an irregular brick-like size, heterogeneous, cavernous, vitrified, and in other respects presenting clear indications of having been operated upon by fire' – on these stones he had consulted 'several scientific friends' and the local inhabitants. Then on to the springs rising on the Moor, the incidence of plants like dwarf raspberry and digitalis (using Gray's phrase of 'desert air'), winter storms, wild goats, and the water supply of Plymouth and Devonport. When the pure Plymouth water, in its artificial channels presented by Sir Francis Drake, was ready to flow down into the town for the first time, Drake and the Corporation marched out in procession to meet it, and Cottle wisely comments that 'an incident more rationally joyous has rarely occurred'. The course of rivers like the Teign and the Dart seems to him an allegory of man's life, but then he strays away to the habits of moss, the laws of the Stannaries, Round Towers, the navy riding in the Hamoaze, and the matchlessness of England among the nations – her heaven-pointing spires and her 'princely institutions'. At line 209 he says that he has crossed Dartmoor *twice*, and we see later, at line 269, that this does not refer to a circular tour on this one expedition. A note to line 468 shows that he had also examined Exmoor for about fifteen miles, and another to line 484 speaks of his recent visit to the Stone Circles at Stanton Drew, just south of Bristol. He begins to feel lonely and awe-struck, until he sees a traveller proceeding below on the highway, which reminds him of turnpikes and leads on to a footnote against Sunday fairs and Monday markets. Little natural objects console him in the solitude (wherefore 'Welcome, ye ants!'), and we are given an admiring essay on Dartmoor ponies, with a digression on the enclosure of Exmoor. Then he comes to the white cottage in the marshes, where he had been entertained on his previous visit; the housewife had fed him and 'earnest press'd' him, and they had talked, and he had left what he called the 'splendid shilling'. Now he finds her again, in her serviceable kersey-coat and trim white bib, setting clothes from her basket to dry on the furze-bushes; she is a good woman, who reads her Bible and keeps it always on her table. Her hospitable husband is piling peat (long note on peat), and children with rosy cheeks and fair hair carry their little burdens; the family have a little corn-field, some hay, plenty of potatoes, and some scraggy cattle. They are not to be pitied: humble and pure, hardy and temperate, 'they know no contrast, and they fear no change'.

The longest passage in the poem attacks the Druids and their filthy rites; the thought then involves Brahmins, Hindus, Buddhists, and Moslems, and is closed only with a rather messy statement of Christianity. We hear of the refuge that the Britons found in Dartmoor, and of the Anglo-Saxon invasion as told by Gildas. The shifting of river beds reminds him of tree trunks found in the excavations for the 'New Cut' of the Bristol Avon; and so on to advocating something on the lines of the future Panama Canal – 'many an English Engineer' could do it, if only an enlightened government ruled Mexico. Here we catch a glimpse of the use he made of all his travel-books; he even quotes a Jesuit on the subject – but this Thomas Gage was a Jesuit after Cottle's own taste, who 'formally recanted, at St. Paul's Cross, the errors of the Romish Faith', so that Cottle deems his narrative credible. The long conclusion of the poem expresses the hope that one day the moor may be reclaimed for 'Ceres' reign', describes the prison and the attendant joys of the Devon town of Princetown, and winds up with a pretty incoherent apostrophe to Britain, Devon, and the moor which he is now leaving at sunset.

Dartmoor, apart perhaps from the wistful burgher's glance at the happy hind, is a healthy and lively document; furthermore, it reflects the recent advances in science and engineering, the recovery of Britain from an arduous war, and the onset of a new age. The invalid poet had awakened from a dream of self-pity, and in less than two decades he would be a typical Victorian; his 'great' period had been Napoleonic and valetudinarian, and it is unlikely that the presence of Wordsworth and Coleridge would have improved his bourgeois holiday in sunny Devon.

And what of Charles Lamb? He has by no means been the hero of any incident in this narrative, and now he pops up again with an action profoundly caddish; of course, it must have been difficult for him to make anything of Cottle, whose goodly temperament would provoke only the imp in him. In 1816, while he was staying with the Morgans at Calne, he had called on Cottle at Brunswick Square, but found him not at home; now, on 5 November 1819, he wrote asking a favour.[8] He is sorry to have missed Cottle three years ago; and he hopes that his request will not seem inconsistent with the long interruption in their acquaintance. Could Cottle lend any small portrait of himself? Lamb wants to have it copied, in order that it may join a selection of 'Likenesses of Living Bards' which a great friend of his is making; if Cottle will send it to 44 Russell Street, Covent Garden, he will make himself personally responsible for its safe and speedy return.

Nothing could be kinder or more flattering than this. Cottle at once replied to his 'Old Friend', and promised the picture within a fortnight; he would have welcomed Lamb when he called, and would like to see him in Bristol again. With Nathan Branwhite's miniature of himself (the glass broken in transit) he sent the second part of *Messiah*, so that when Lamb promised return of the one he also gave feigned thanks for the other. A 'daughter of Josephs, R.A.', had done the copying, and his friend would be sending back the original. *Messiah* had afforded Lamb much pleasure, since it had 'great sweetness and a New Testament plainness'. He had two precise criticisms to make: on page 63, lines 69 and 70,

> The willowy brook was there, but that sweet sound –
> *When* to be heard again on Earthly ground? –

('two very sweet lines and the sense perfect') should end the period; and on page 154, line 68, making Christ say that He comes '*ordained a world to save*' is not in accord with His modesty and too much anticipates the Baptist's lovely recognition of Him. Cottle 'will excuse the remarks of an old brother bard', who started his work when Cottle did but who has pretty well retired; he is sorry that their lives have been lived apart, and he will probably never be in Bristol again, but Cottle will always be welcome if he should visit London. Mary Lamb wishes to be remembered, and there is news of Morgan's improving health and finances. Will Cottle let him know if the portrait gets back safely, with the glass intact?

Yes, but who was the friend, and what was the book? Lamb's treachery is plain when we find that William Evans, of the *Pamphleteer*, was thus seeking to grangerize a copy of Byron's *English Bards and Scotch Reviewers*! In a P.S. to Evans, at about this time, Lamb sent 'a portrait of Joseph Cottle from memory'; it is a crude outline of a round face, staring eyes, little round mouth, and conventional straight nose, signed 'C.L. facit'. Lamb has added, facetiously, 'The lips should be a little thicker & perhaps the left eye has hardly justice done it but I should only spoil it by tampering with it'. Here we enter the murky regions of Cottle's fame; for, alas, his *monumentum aere perennius* is surely Bryron's excoriating attack on him in that sprightly poem. It may well astonish us that the little man could be so honoured as to come under the lash of the cosmopolitan peer. Cottle himself must have been horrified, especially as the superb structure was raised on a foundation of unchecked references and of unholy disrespect for the dead. The twenty-six lines are masterly: brutal, lordly, careless, and sparkling.

> Another Epic! Who inflicts again
> More books of blank upon the sons of men?
> Boeotian COTTLE, rich Bristowa's boast,
> Imports old stories from the Cambrian coast,

Charles Lamb's 'portrait of Joseph Cottle from memory' (from a photograph belonging to Basil Cottle)

And sends his goods to market – all alive!
Lines forty thousand, cantos twenty-five!
Fresh fish from Helicon! who'll buy? who'll buy?
The precious bargain's cheap – in faith, not I.
Your turtle-feeder's verse must needs be flat,
Though Bristol bloat him with the verdant fat;
If Commerce fills the purse, she clogs the brain,
And AMOS COTTLE strikes the Lyre in vain.
In him an author's luckless lot behold!
Condemned to make the books which once he sold.
Oh, AMOS COTTLE! – Phoebus! What a name
To fill the speaking-trump of future fame! –
Oh, AMOS COTTLE! for a moment think
What meagre profits spring from pen and ink!
When thus devoted to poetic dreams,
Who will peruse thy prostituted reams?
Oh! pen perverted! paper misapplied!
Had COTTLE still adorned the counter's side,
Bent o'er the desk, or, born to useful toils,
Been taught to make the paper which he soils,
Ploughed, delved, or plied the oar with lusty limb,
He had not sung of Wales, nor I of him.

(The subsequent changes in the couplet about turtles are merely more insulting to Bristolians in general:

Too much in Turtle Bristol's sons delight,
Too much in (or o'er) Bowls of Rack (or Sack) prolong the night.)

These lines were available in the first edition by 1809, and Cottle may have read them soon after; at any rate, he held his peace until 1819, when (possibly on looking into the project of Lamb's 'particular friend') he was moved to defend his poor brother's name and his own reputation which had become oddly attached to it. He tells us that he would have paid no attention to the attack; but, noticing that Byron's works were full of attacks on, and insinuations against, 'all that is *sacred*', he mused 'till the fire burned' and his own reply was ready.

Byron had inflicted one ugly wound on him, by using Amos's name just because it sounded funnier; the merry footnote makes no amends at all: 'Mr Cottle, Amos, Joseph, I don't know which, but one or both, once sellers of books they did not write, and now writers of books they do not sell, have published a pair of epics – *Alfred* (poor Alfred! Pye has been at him too!) –

Alfred and the *Fall of Cambria*'. Further, Byron partly recanted, and at Geneva, on 24 July 1816, wrote his afterthoughts in a copy of the fourth edition which was later preserved by Murray; he had come to despise his satire, and to regret and 'eat' some of the nasty things he had said of Jeffrey, Lamb, Wordsworth, Coleridge, Bowles, and others. But he stood by what he had said of Cottle, adding, 'All right. I saw some letters of this fellow (Jh. Cottle) to an unfortunate poetess, whose production, which the poor woman by no means thought vainly of, he attacked so roughly and bitterly, that I could hardly regret assailing him, even were it unjust, which is it not – for verily he is an ass'. (He also altered *Helicon* – a mountain, after all – to *Hippocrene*.)

Now what is all this about? E.H. Coleridge, in his 1918 edition of Byron's works,[9] makes the obvious suggestion that the poetess was Ann Yearsley, whom Wordsworth had discouraged; he points out, too, that Cottle did not number roughness and bitterness among his faults and foibles – and we know that, being no lover of Hannah More's snobbery, he had positively encouraged the milkwoman in her aspirations. Had Byron, therefore, seen letters of Cottle's, and muddled them with some of Wordsworth's? I think that proof of his gross unfairness lies in a recollection by the Reverend A. Dyce,[10] with corroboration from Samuel Rogers, of why Byron hated Wordsworth.

Wordsworth distinctly told Dyce the reasons for this hostility: a Bristol 'woman in distressed circumstances' wrote a volume of verse and sought to publish it, with a dedication to Wordsworth; she thought that she would make a fortune by her art. He advised her to try something else, saying that (despite the talent she showed) there was not much chance of impressing the public, since there were only two persons making money by their poetry. He did not mention their names, but he made it clear that they were Scott, whose poetic feeling was slight, and Byron, in whose poetry 'it was perverted'. Rogers told Wordsworth that, when he was travelling with Byron in Italy, Byron confessed that his hatred of Wordsworth came from this last remark, which the woman must have spread, and which someone had repeated to Byron.

Is not this a glorious mix-up? How could Wordsworth have said such a thing *before* the publication of *English Bards*, a poem which gives the first possible sign of the poet's perverted talents? Yet the poem is supposed to derive its venom from Wordsworth's remark. The woman cannot be Ann Yearsley, who died in 1806, far too early to have learned from Wordsworth's lips of Byron's satanism. And where does Cottle come in? I am not suggesting that the obloquy of *Alfred* is undeserved; but Byron's stated motive for the attack is as mistaken as his unchivalrous resurrection of Amos.

There was too much careless talk about the Cottle brothers. It was perhaps Tom Moore, in his seventeen-volume edition of Byron,[11] who started the rumour that George Canning had had a dig at Cottle in *The Anti-Jacobin*; admittedly, Canning lashed out wildly at Lamb and Lloyd, along with Southey and Coleridge, as if they were all revolutionaries, but there is no mention of the harmless Cottle. Still, the memorable couplet has been traditionally ascribed to Canning:

> And Cottle, not he that *Alfred* made famous,
> But Joseph of Bristol, the brother of Amos.

(Moore's version has the illiterate phrase 'he who that'.) Here is *more* confusion; the anonymous writer seems to believe that *Alfred* is not by Cottle's hand ... It all sounds like an epigram spoken and imperfectly remembered. By 1902 a correspondent in *Notes and Queries*[12] very properly demanded a real reference, but was unanswered. It is just feasible that Cottle occurs in lines 334-7 of the poem 'New Morality' in *The Anti-Jacobin*, where Frere and Canning distinctly refer to 'five wandering bards' (who are called on to praise Lepaux) and then list four only:

> C—dge and S-th-y, L—d. and L—be and Co.

(riming with Lepaux); 'Co.' surely stands for 'Company', but 'Cottle' is a possible explanation and would make up the correct number of bards.

At any rate, Victor Euphémon Philarète Chasles, the erudite French *comparatiste*, fell on these wavering references and worked them into a charming digression in his *L'Angleterre Littéraire*.[13] Chasles is not always at home with facts: he presses Yorkshire between two arms of the Irish Sea, and locates in it Manchester, Windermere, and Derwentwater; the Grampians are visible therefrom, and 'Bulwer' and 'sir Litlon' are two of Charlotte Brontë's supporters;[14] he, or his proof-reader, makes a bad mess of English words and quotations, turning 'son-in-law' into 'so-inn-low', and consistently giving Thackeray the second name of 'Makepence'! But his qualities, as an original critic in a wide field, and as an enthusiastic interpreter of English literature, make us regret all the more these unchecked *minutiae*. His remarks on Cottle are very bright and interesting, but his sources for them are in some doubt. In a work of which the preface is dated 1871, Cottle is said to be still alive (he would then have been 101), and Southey's Chatterton project would seem to be dated at about 1793.

Chasles tells us that Cottle had a brother 'mordu comme lui de la rage del'épopée'; these two were dear to Byron, Canning, Moore, and all the contemporary satirists. With this, he translates or devises the couplet

Ce couple siamois, ces Épiques-Libraires,
Et *cantare pares*, et dignes d'être frères!

Moore (says Chasles, in a translation or invention) wrote:

J'adore *Alfred-le-Grand*, par Cottle le cadet.
La *Cambrie* est aussi fort belle, s'il vous plaît;
Cottle l'aîné, l'auteur de ce dernier poëme,
Est encore sur mon âme, un poëte que j'aime.

Here is more confusion; the poems were both by Joseph, and 'l'aîné' would be Amos.

After a word of praise for Cottle's equation, in *Alfred*, of the Englishman with a boar and the Dane with a lion, Chasles passes on to one of the 'mille anecdotes littéraires piquantes' concerning the two Cottles, whom Southey always liked and defended. And this is a delicious story, true or not. An Italian poetaster from Ferrara, named Talassi, about as competent as the two brothers, passed through Bristol and, having met Southey in Portugal,[15] wished to pay his respects to Cottle. The latter was very rich (a fact which must date the incident somewhat later in his life), and when his 'valet de chambre' told him that an unknown Italian poet wanted to speak to him he suspected a premeditated encroachment on his purse and sent word that he was not at home. Talassi, who was bilingual in French and Italian, and a mediocre poet in both, asked for paper and pens, and wrote

Confrère en Apollon, je me fais un devoir
De me rendre chez vous par désir de vous voir.
Vous êtes occupé, je prendrai patience;
Je ne jouirai pas d'une aimable présence.
L'auteur d'*Alfred* se cache, et pourquoi, s'il vous plaît? ...
Je m'en vais désolé; mais, hélas! c'en est fait! ...

Then, dropping into his native tongue,

Signor Cottle riverito,
Men'andro come son ito,

E se voi, sublime vate,
Un poeta non curate,
Io del pari ve lo giuro,
Non vi cerco, e non vi curo.

(Which may be rendered:

Signor Cottle, o revered,
I'll depart as I appeared,
And if you, o bard sublime,
For a poet have no time,
Equally to you I swear
For you I neither seek nor care.)

And he signed, 'bravement', ANGE TALASSI DE FERRARE, poète 'au service actuel de la reine de Portugal'. Chasles holds that anecdotes of this sort, biographical scraps, and cullings from literary history, had a peculiar attraction for Southey; and that he made them up into his charming *Doctor*. The good Cottle would simply be one of the obscurer soldiers in the countless army of absurd epic poets, if Southey had not (out of gratitude, friendship and fellow-citizenship) taken it on himself to rehabilitate his memory; and Chasles quotes, in support of their real affection for one another, Southey's admirable letter of 20 April 1808.

But we are letting Byron go unpunished. Cottle set to work and produced the 229 heroic-couplet lines of *An Expostulatory Epistle to Lord Byron*,[16] so that they were ready for publication in the next year, 1820. He is in a very serious mood, and Byron figures as a kind of Comus attended by a subversive, godless and melancholy rabble. Endowed with talents, he has decided to desecrate them, and to reign proudly in hell like Lucifer. Among other vices, whims, and unnatural pastimes,

He, spurn'd of Nature, callous more than dull,
Can quaff libations from his *Father's Skull*!

From the start of the poem, no punches are pulled; Cottle was fighting back for Amos and himself. Byron's exile is sneered at, he is called pander, and (with a nice quotation from the 'Retraction' in Chaucer's *Parson's Tale*) his head is said to be stuffed with 'lecherous lays'; he has dared to attack his fellow-peers, and his slur on the gracious and unassailable Prince Regent puts him on a level with the 'bullying H***' and the 'base C******' (that is,

Leigh Hunt and Richard Carlile, the pirater of *Wat Tyler*). Milton and other bards are apostrophized, in contrast with *his* verse,

> Frothy, and vulgar, worthless as the weed.

Then Cottle turns to giving the fallen poet some good advice: he begs him to suffer from misgivings, to rise above the senses, to give his readers *some* useful lesson, and to profit by the example of the very bards whom he has attacked. Naturally, Southey is in the van of these, backed up by a footnote quoted from the Preface of his *Vision of Judgment*, and castigating the Satanic School. But again

> Which verse shall *Wordsworth* ever blush to own?
> Or *Coleridge*? spirit still of height unknown!
> What tongue of *Scotland's Regal Bard* shall say,
> Poison, with pleasure, mingles in his lay?
> When shall *Montgomery* baneful lines bewail?
> Or *Crabbe*? who haunts us, like the nursery tale: –
> *Bowles? Rogers? Barton?* rich in native store;
> Or *Campbell*? ('*Little?*' whelm'd in night,) or *Moore*?

This cacophonous catalogue is still an interesting document: these were on the side of the angels, and had emerged unscathed from Lucifer's machinations. Later, we grieve to say, *Moore* made such a compact with the fiend as even to edit his works, and Cottle therefore altered the line to 'Or Campbell? Would that I might add, or Moore'! '*Little*' (why the quotation marks?) thus lost what immortality Cottle could bestow. James Montgomery the hymnographer was certainly in Cottle's thought in 1819, and graciously declined by letter an offer of help and money.

Cottle further counsels Byron to think on eternity and to choose life therein with blest spirits like Howard, Thornton, Wilberforce, and More; he must repent of his own fall, which has involved 'erring thousands' who will curse him for their 'blasted peace'. Finally, let him avoid the fate of Shelley, who had said in *Queen Mab* that 'There is no God!' Thus, without a single reference to poor Amos, the poem ends:

> Redeem the *future*! Cleanse the Augean sty!
> Learn better how to live! and how to die!

It is doubtful whether Byron ever even saw the poem, and it would certainly not have had the desired effect on him; but Tom Moore, in the fifteenth volume of his edition of Byron, mockingly printed twenty-two lines of it under the heading 'Testimonies', and with the preface, 'Let us indulge our readers, before we return to the realms of prose, with another wreath from the myrtles of Parnassus'.

By the time the *Expostulatory Epistle* was bound up with the 1829 edition of *Malvern Hills*, Cottle had added a solemn prose preface explaining that his only motive was to counteract Byron's shocking influence, and justifying himself for republishing his strictures after Byron's death: the bad baron was '*still living in the spirit which pervades his works.*' Cottle had also found, on looking through his old papers, his own commentary on Byron's unfair lines; so he printed that as well. It attempts a pretty vein of cool contempt: 'Boeotian' is a hackneyed word, the loyal and industrious merchants of Bristol have something else to 'boast' about besides a mere bard like Cottle, Bristolians are *not* known for intemperance, they are altruistic enough to have built what the twentieth century calls Bridge Valley Road, and so forth. Byron's English comes in for some criticism, too: the last couplet is either illogical or a truism, and Cottle pretends not to understand the line 'Condemn'd to make the books which once he sold'. Byron is a liar in charging him with profiting by pen and ink – and, in any case, Johnson and Burke were not ashamed of such a profession; he is conceited in wondering who will peruse Cottle's reams – well, they will not *corrupt* anyone; he is a hypocrite in pretending to know anything about Cottle's works, since he obviously hasn't looked even at the author's name on the title-page; he is a snob in poking fun at a literary bookseller, when humbly-born people like Chatterton and Milton challenge the peerage's monopoly of these things; he is a fool to speak of Cottle's 'pen perverted' and 'paper misapplied', since he will have to face 'an ulterior *Tribunal*' that will decide to which of the two men these attributes better belong; and he is a knave to insult a good man like Amos, ten years dead. So he thinks 'Amos Cottle' is an amusing name? Doubtless he has never heard the name 'Amos' before (since it is neither in Horace, nor Ovid, nor the *Gradus*); '*Amas* would have been clear enough' – a venomous touch, indeed, coming from the mild Cottle. (He could have added, had he known, that *Byron* goes back to an Old English dative plural meaning 'at the cow-sheds'.) So, once again, let Byron think of repentance for his dissipated talents, bearing in mind the laudable *volte-face* of Rochester and Dryden, and the stirring prose 'Retraction,' which Cottle here quotes in full, at the end of the *Canterbury Tales*.

Lamb had also been writing to Southey, on behalf of John Morgan, the unlucky benefactor of Coleridge, ruined by his own generosity; and on 26 November 1819 Southey wrote to Cottle from Keswick, wondering if any annuity could be raised. Cottle prints the letter in his *Reminiscences*,[17] with a dark mention of '——, who has involved him in his own ruin'; in support of his momentary thesis, he suppresses a name which was obviously 'Coleridge'. Their charity would not be needed long, what with Morgan's liver and the palsy; but Lamb and Southey will give £10 each, Southey has written to Michael Castle, and Cottle would do well to get in touch with Morgan's friend Porter. Thus Morgan, the son of a rich Bristol spirit merchant, was rewarded for his devotion to Coleridge, who emerges from the affair with the discredit which Cottle and Southey always manage to give him.

In 1820 the Cottle family moved from Brunswick Square to Dighton Street – no great change for the better. Cottle's visits to the library suggest that he was absent from Bristol for a large part of the summer:

13 Jan. – 28 Jan.	Pennant, *Arctic Zoology*, Vol. II
13 Jan. – 9 Feb.	*ditto*, Vol. I
28 Jan. – 5 Feb.	*Quarterly review*, No. 42 (ie. part of 1819)
5 Feb. – 7 March	*British Review*, No. 27
9 Feb. – 17 Feb.	Johnson, *Works*, Vol. VIII
15 Feb. – 29 Feb.	A. de Humboldt, *Researches concerning the Institutions and Monuments of the Ancient Inhabitants of America*

(On the 16th the Library was closed, as the King was being buried.)

28 Feb. – 7 March	Brydone, *Tour through Sicily and Malta*, Vol. I
3 March – 8 May	E.D. Clarke, *Travels in Various Countries*, Vol. IV
8 May – 26 June	*Monthly Review*, Jan. 1820
8 May – 26 June	*Quarterly Review*, No. 43
11 Aug. – 21/22 Aug.	*Edinburgh Review*, No. 66
11 Aug. – 21/22 Aug.	*British Review*, No. 29
18 Aug. – 21 Aug.	J. Oxley, *New Holland*
18 Aug – 21 Aug.	J.S. Fry, *Essay on Wheel Carriages*
21 Aug. – 15 Sept.	Smellie, *Natural History*, Vol.I.
21 Aug. – 15 Sept.	Gregory, *Economy of Nature*, Vol. I
15 Sept. – 21 Oct.	R. Fenton, *Tour through Pembrokeshire*
15 Sept. – 21 Oct.	*Quarterly Review*, Vol. 22
23 Oct. – 25 Oct.	Hon. R. Boyle, *Works*

23 Oct. – 25 Oct.	*Edinburgh Review*, 1808
25 Oct. – 8 Dec.	*British Review*, No. 30
25 Oct. – 29 Nov.	W. Kirby & W. Spence, *Introduction to Entomology*, Vol. I
(after letter of 28 Nov.)	
29 Nov. – 24/25 Jan. 1821	*ditto*, Vol. II
5 Dec. – 24/25 Jan. 1821	*Edinburgh Review*, No. 67

The *Expostulatory Epistle* was given to its limited public in this year, and it was probably in connection with it that Cottle sent George Cumberland a note on 21 February,[18] thanking him for a polite letter and asking him to accept 'the Cancel, containing a substitution for the lines relating to *Murray*.' After the publication, Lamb wrote again,[19] in a flattering style, on 26 May; he has been kept from acknowledging Cottle's second gift by a mixture of something 'terribly like' forgetfulness, disrespect and incivility, and he is no longer the great letter-scribbler he used to be. Yet it is not surprising that Lamb had been slow in expressing any gratitude: the gift was merely the second *Messiah* and the *Cambria*. Lamb avers that he has read the poems 'with as much pleasure' as the first *Messiah*; though he had already seen bits of the second at a friend's house. He goes on, recklessly and naughtily, 'Your Cambrian poem is what I shall be tempted to repeat oftenest, as Human Poems take me in a mood more frequently congenial, than Divine. The Character of Llewellyn pleased me more than any thing else perhaps, & then some of the Lyrical Pieces, which are fine varieties –'. Cottle must have expressed a fear that Lamb would disapprove of his expostulation against Byron, for Lamb here takes pains to protest that he is thoroughly averse to Byron's character, that he admires his genius but moderately, that he has not read Cottle's poem (since he did not know it was out), and that he will procure it forthwith. Southey is in London, and they have met; Wordsworth he hopes to see there shortly; Michael Castle is up there, too, and will bring this letter back to his neighbour Cottle if Lamb does not get a frank. Lamb is writing in haste, in office hours, as 'two or three bothering Clerks & Brokers' are importuning him, 'as they always do when you seem to be doing something that is not business'. Lamb 'could exclaim a little profanely', but remembers that Cottle does not like swearing.

In Bristol, Cottle's closest friend was still Foster, and three of the latter's notes to Cottle survive from this year.[20] In one, Foster sends a newspaper with his note, by the postman, who will collect Byron's *English Bards*: can Foster have it for two or three days? When he and Cottle talked last Saturday, he did not say firmly enough that Cottle's just attack on Byron will be attributed to his resentment at Byron's spite, – and that will lessen the effect; in any case, nothing will change the public opinion of Byron. A second, written on a Wednesday evening, thanks Cottle for offering to come out to Downend instead of Foster's walking into Bristol – and he will accept, since he has had a (presumably) rheumatic affection about the hip for a few weeks, and walking is painful; Saturday will suit him better than tomorrow. On 21 July he sent a letter which reflects Cottle's growing opulence: Cottle keeps giving him valuable books, for which he has not returned a single thing. Not that he does not like being 'under unrequited obligations' to someone like Cottle – but these are so *wholly* unrequited. So here is Miss Batty's *Views in Italy*; her drawings have a great reputation, Mr Essex has played up with the binding, and the fact that the edges are uncut is merely the fault of the publishers. If Cottle or his sisters, whom Foster considers 'as all one', already have it, let them choose from his extravagant purchases another of equal value and beauty; he does not want to give them just a duplicate. He sends good wishes for the Cottles' new residence, and reports that his wife's health is improving.

Cottle's Library programme for 1821 shows no summer break, though we hear of a visit to London:

24 Jan. – 12 Feb.	J.R. Joliffe, *Letters from Palestine*
24 Jan. – 12 Feb.	Benger, *Memoirs of Mrs Elizabeth Hamilton*
12 Feb. – 13 Feb.	Borlase, *Antiquities of Cornwall*
12 Feb. – 2 Apr.	Polwhele, *History of Devonshire*. (Did he write *Dartmoor* in tranquillity?)
13 Feb. – 21 Mar.	*Life of Mrs (Elizabeth) Carter*, Vol. I
21 Mar. – 3 Apr.	Fosbrooke, *Gloucestershire*, Vol. II
1 May – 7 May	*Sketch Book of Geoffery Crayon, Gent.*, Vol. II
1 May – 7 May	R.L. Edgeworth, *Life*, Vol. I
10 May – 1 June	Lewis & Clarke, *Travels*, Vols. I & II
4 June – 2 July	W. Godwin, *On Population*
4 June – 2 July	W. Hutton, *Remarks upon North Wales*
2 July – 11 July	Strutt, *Dresses*, Vol. II
2 July – 11 July	J. Collinson, *History and Antiquities of Somersetshire*, Vol. II
9 July – 8 Aug.	J.B. Fraser, *Tour to the Himālā Mountains, &c.*
(after letter of 7 August)	
9 July – 4 Oct.	Mme de Stael, *Germany*, Vol. I (from the French)

9 Aug. – 20 Aug.	Earl of Liverpool, *Treatise on the Coins of the Realm*
9 Aug. (renewed 1 Oct.) – 16 Feb. 1822 (after letter of 15 Feb.)	Polwhele, *Devonshire*
17 Aug. – 24 Aug.	Camden, *Britannia*, Vol. I
23 Aug. – 30 Aug.	Prince, *Worthies of Devon*
23 Aug. – 30 Aug.	Henry, *England*, Vol. I
30 Aug. – 1 Oct.	*ditto*, Vol. II
30 Aug. – 1 Oct.	Collinson, *Somerset*, Vol. I (? or II)
1 Oct. – 16 Feb. 1822 (after letter of 15 Feb.)	Rapin, *History of England*, Vol. I
4 Dec. – 16 Feb. 1822	Carte, *General History of England*, Vol. I

The one traceable event of Cottle's year is his visit to London, perhaps to stay with Robert and his wife, perhaps to consult Cadell the publisher, with whom he was in correspondence soon after. The visit included one glum reunion: Coleridge was at Gillman's and Cottle visited him there, but got not a word out of him on the subject of the 'opium' letters, though he welcomed Cottle 'in his former kind and cordial manner'. Cottle was depressed to think that they would never meet again in this world; nor did they – but when Cottle left, Coleridge gave him his 'Statesman's Manual', and wrote on the title-page, 'Joseph Cottle, from his old and affectionate friend, S.T. Coleridge'.[21] Coleridge had another thirteen years to live, but this touching gesture marked the very end of their friendship.

1822, punctuated by a long Devon holiday, has fewer Library visits (some of them connected with his geologizing and archaeologizing at Plymouth):

16 Feb. – 1 Mar. (after letter of 28 Feb.)	*Sardanapalus*, &c.
7 Mar. – 12 Mar.	J.D. Fosbroke, *Berkeley MSS.*
7 Mar. – 12 Mar.	*Biblical Fragments*
28 Mar. – 20 June (after letter of 19 June)	*Edinburgh Review*, No. 71
28 Mar. – 26/27 Apr.	*Catalogue of Gough's Birds*
26 Apr. – 5 July	J. Parkinson, *Organic Remains of a Former World*, Vol. III
26 Apr. – 5 July	E.D. Clarke, *Travels*, Vol. III
19 Aug. – 14 Oct.	G. Belzoni, *Narrative of Discoveries in Egypt and Nubia*, 2nd edn
14 Oct. – 5 Nov.	*Pamphleteer*, No. 40

14 Oct. – 5 Nov.	W.D. Conybeare and W. Phillips, *Outlines of the Geology of England and Wales*
5 Nov. – 26 Dec.	*Philosophical Transactions*, Part I
5 Nov. – 26 Dec.	Parkinson, *Introduction to the Study of Fossil Organic Remains*
28 Dec. – 19 May 1823 (renewed 5 April 1823)	Parkinson, *Organic Remains*, Vol. III

In 1821, John Foster had given up his charge of the Baptist congregation at Downend and moved to nearby Stapleton. In 1822 he began to give fortnightly lectures at Broadmead Chapel in Bristol, to a large and miscellaneous audience. The Cottles attended keenly, and on 6 April 1822 Joseph wrote on behalf of all of them,[22] begging that he send them the adjunct to his 'last most excellent Lecture, by which the Antidote, in a natural order, will accompany the bane. The benefit is imperfect, when a stray traveller is informed of his wanderings, unless he is told at the same time of the way that is right.' Cottle hopes he will be excused if he expresses his appreciation of the lectures, especially for their being based on Foster's avowal of the three Pillars of Christianity – the Atonement, Justification by Faith, and the Holy Spirit – without which no preaching will convert. Is Foster's cold better? Foster's manuscripts also went back and fore between them, and one of his replies is a scrap[23] sent by means of Cottle's Messenger with regard to 'the ladies' and lending 'the last discourse – I am not quite certain … what was the subject of the lecture preceding that not returned by you.'

Dartmoor was finished by now, and Cottle offered it on 10 May 1822 to the publisher Thomas Cadell the Younger,[24] whose father had been a Bristolian born in Wine Street, and who was now flourishing in the Strand. Cottle merely calls it a descriptive poem, with notes; and he proposes that it be brought out in quarto. He wants Cadell to have the first offer of this first edition, and he will make good any loss that may arise; if the sale encourages Cadell to think of a second edition of 250-500, he is welcome to it. A year after publication, Cottle will include it in a fourth edition of his poems, which are long out of print. There is a 'remarkably neat Printer' in Bristol, whose charges are lower than London's; if Cadell accepts the proposal, let him send paper of really good quality – the poem will need six sheets. (As events turned out, *Dartmoor* was published in octavo in 1823, and the promised fourth edition, again by Cadell, was not ready until 1829.) Cottle has another work to offer: his *Selection of Poems, for Schools and Young Persons* is out of print and 'in uniform demand', so would Cadell like to print an edition, on the plan of dividing profits, Cottle to get nothing until Cadell be fully paid? Here, again, he wants to give Cadell the first offer; he has long been preparing for a third edition, to be 'more valuable than the last' printing of 1,500 copies, so he would welcome any hint from Cadell about it. Cadell was very obliging in this case also, and republished the *Selections* in 1823.

1   *Broadmead Baptist Church/Letters and Documents of Interest from 1650 on*, fol.144; *Broadmead Records*, Vol.III, 1818-1834, fol.11 and fols.14-15; *Records of the Independent Church, 1757 to 1818*, fol.53.

2   Bristol City Library MS.B 20878; date and year added in ?Cottle's hand.

3   Bristol City Library MS.B 20878, with '1818' added.

4   *Cumberland Papers*, British Museum MS.Add.36506, Vol.XVI (1817-1818), fol.310.

5   Bristol City Library MS.B 20878; Cottle adds the year.

6   Curry, II.195-197.

7   *MH*.4, I.85n.

8   Their interchange of letters during this year, and Lamb's relevant letter to Evans, are in E.V. Lucas, *op.cit.*, II.261 ff.

9   E.H. Coleridge, *The Works of Lord Byron* (London: John Murray, 1918), *Poetry*, Vol.I, pp.328-329.

10 Revd. A. Dyce, *Recollections of the Table-Talk of Samuel Rogers* (New Southgate: H.A. Rogers, 1887), p.238n.

11 T. Moore ed., *Works of Lord Byron* (London: John Murray, 1832-1833), VII.249n.

12 *Notes and Queries*, IX.x.208, 13 Sept. 1902.

13 P. Chasles, *L'Angleterre Littéraire* (Paris: G. Charpentier, 1876), pp.95-100.

14 P. Chasles, *L'Angleterre Littéraire*, on Charlotte Brontë, pp.341 ff.

15 A. de O. Cabral, *Southey e Portugal* (Lisbon: Fernandes, 1959), pp.168 ff.

16 *MH*.4, I. 221-239.

17 *R*.47, p.237.

18 *Cumberland Papers*, British Museum MS.Add.36507, Vol.XVII (1819-1920), fol.260.

19 E.V. Lucas, *op.cit.*, II.278-279.

20 Bristol City Library MS.B 20878.

21 *ER*.37, II.177n.

22 Bodleian MS.Eng.misc., c.36, fol.21.

23 Bristol City Library MS.B 20878; Cottle wrongly indexes it '1820'.

24 British Museum MS.Add.34486, A.5, fol.24.

Chapter 12

Fossils and Antinomians in Plymouth

Cottle spent two months of the summer of 1822 in Plymouth, with the Saunders family. In the recent blowing-up of the Oreston Rocks, as a quarry for the building of Plymouth Breakwater, a large number of prehistoric animal remains had been found in the caves, and he was enthusiastically interested.[1] He was one of the first amateur geologists to know of the discovery, and, in addition, he wanted to use the evidence as proof that the Deluge had really happened. On reaching Plymouth, he applied, in company with a friend, to one of the two government agents, who informed him that he had none of the finds, but that the workmen engaged at the quarry might be able to supply some. Cottle directed the men to bring him the remains, especially the jaws, just as they found them, embedded in clay; then, by carefully washing off the earth, he prevented many fractures and preserved the teeth of all the jaws. All this took time, trouble and expense; the honest quarrymen must have adored him. Virtually the whole find came into his hands, so that it was not scattered or lost; and he kept the collection long enough for geologists to examine it *en masse*, and then distributed it among various public bodies – the Bristol Philosophical Institution, especially, though Oxford begged and received one of his seventy lumps of osseous breccia. The fellows who brought him these seventy portions then took their hammers and, out of loyalty to him, destroyed all the remainder; we are not told, however, what the Cottle sisters thought of this addition to their furnishings, or of the eleven tigers' molars, fangs and incisors, the eighty-six wolves' jaws, the five bits of hyena, and the eight hundred horses' teeth. Since the whole complex of rocks was being destroyed, Cottle took a drawing of the cliff-face, and this was later lithographed; fifty objects from the collection were also engraved for Professor Buckland's new work. Altogether he seems to have worked earnestly at this enquiry. He was constantly on the spot, using alert agents and men who could scramble like cats in pursuit of his prizes, with candles in their hands and with a shrewd regard for what they were doing. We have an agreeable account of his talking to them and asking their opinions. His tour of the whole precinct involved him in a scramble of 'some miles'. The resulting essay is primarily scientific, and his dramatic hypothesis, that the mutually antagonistic beasts were thus crowded together by fear of the Deluge, will thrill or dismay according to one's religious beliefs; Davy, at any rate, accepted the observations, and gave permission for the essay to be dedicated to himself.

While in Plymouth, Cottle wrote (as 'Z') to the editor of *The Plymouth and Dock Journal*,[2] on 2 September, congratulating the magistracy on withdrawing half the hackney coaches from the stand on Sundays; this fine example is likely to be followed elsewhere. Now, what about shifting their Monday market to Tuesday? – since it at present involves desecration of the Sabbath by farmers, butchers, gardeners, drovers, 'and other subordinate agents'; these persons thus become estranged from religion, demoralized, and brutish. When he got back to Bristol he sent a note to George Cumberland on 12 October,[3] telling him of his new-found fossils and inviting him to see them at any time convenient to him; but I find no mention of them, among the plentiful *fossiliana*, in Cumberland's diaries and memoirs, and Eliza M. Cumberland re-used the note to write to her Papa about guitars.

1823 brought Southey and Davy back into Cottle's circle, and introduced the poet Thomas Campbell; there was another long summer holiday in Devon, shown by the July gap in his Library visits:

9 Jan. – 22 Jan.	Hon. J. Byron, *Narrative of his Distresses on the Coast of Patagonia*
22 Jan. – 29 Jan.	Scott, *Lay of the Last Minstrel*
22 Jan. – 29 Jan.	Lord Anson, *Voyage round the World*
27 Jan. – 14 Feb.	Brand, *Observations on Popular Antiquities*, Vol. I
18 Mar. – 29 Mar.	*Quarterly Review*, Vol. 27
18 Mar. – 29 Mar.	*Annals of Philosophy*, January (?1823)
22 Mar. – 29 Mar.	*Quarterly Review*, Vol. 24
27 Mar. – 7(?5) Apr.	G. Cuvier, *Lectures on Comparative Anatomy*, Vol. I
	(He now has five books 'out')
4 Apr. – 7(?5) Apr.	*ditto*, Vol. II
5 Apr. – 19 May	Rapin, *History of England*, Vol. I
16 May – 6 June	*Origin of Language*, Vol. I
16 May – 6 June	E. Davies, *Celtic Researches*
3 June (he 'does not take out,' as it does not circulate)	G. Penn, *Comparative Estimate of the Mineral and Mosaical Geologies*
4 June – 12 Aug.	*Philosophical Transactions*, 1822, Pt. 1

24 Nov. – 30 Dec. E.D. Clarke, *Travels*, Part VI
(after note of 29 Dec.)
24 Nov. – 12 Dec. J. Ray, *Collection of Curious Travels and Voyages* (1693)

The Reverend Dr Thomas Raffles, an eminent Congregational minister at Liverpool and a great collector of autographs, had written to him seeking one of Chatterton's, and on 29 May he replied with apologies for delay and for being as yet unable to obtain one.[4] But he will willingly 'filch' a bit from his own continuous manuscript to oblige someone whom he so respects. The John Rylands Library, Manchester, preserves with this letter a much-corrected digest of his life,[5] in his hand and perhaps included when he wrote. It adds almost nothing to our knowledge, though the emphasis is of some interest: no classical education, but voracious reading aided by the instruction and friendship of Henderson; business from 1791 to 1798, after which he was 'unconnected' with it save for a short time when he bought 'a share in a Printing Concern, where he was an inactive partner'; his bookselling girt with 'a Constellation of Geniuses' (seven listed, and Lovell and C.F. Williams carefully crossed out); his edition, with Southey, of Chatterton's poems, to the great pecuniary benefit of Mrs Newton; a catalogue of his own published works; and a text of his juvenile poem, *Ned and Will*. But he adds one exciting paragraph, affirming that Coleridge wrote on the flyleaf of the first edition of his Poems:

> Dear Cottle, on the blank leaf of my Poems, I can most appropriately write my acknowledgement to you for your *too disinterested* conduct in the purchase of them. Indeed if ever they should acquire a name and character, it may be truly said that the world owed them to you. Had it not been for you, none perhaps of them would have been published, and many not written. God bless you!
> Your obliged and affectionate friend
> April 15, 1796   S.T. Coleridge.

He was hard at work writing and revising – the *Oreston Caves*, the school *Selection*, *Dartmoor*, and an onslaught on the Plymouth Antinomians. This last tract he submitted to John Foster, and his messenger brought him Foster's reply,[6] which is not without criticism, though Foster seems to admire the substance. However, he warns Cottle that the Reverend Septimus Courtney, M.A., could easily 'take him up' on certain points. Let Cottle omit, as example, the names of Robert Hall (whose constructions are often incorrect), Foster himself, and Chalmers (whose diction is '*bad*, emphatically bad, – a perpetual and flagrant offence against good taste' and a defiance of the classical standards of English). The 'literary animadversion' on page 6 is a good piece of '*nettle-tickling*' for the learned gentlemen; but will not the general effect be to lower the subject into mere 'verbal cavil' and quibbling? If Cottle shows himself determined to be offensive, they will retaliate, and hardly anyone's writings are proof against this 'in dogged hands'. Yes, by all means let him add the supplementary pages, especially if he can compress them – a hard thing to do; but there must be less recital of what various religious institutions have done, and a cutting-down of 'the more splendid epithets'. Cottle is absolutely just in attacking, with 'pushes, kicks, and knocks', those who so wrongfully stay in the church; he must indeed insert the 'hideous piece of profane rant' which he has submitted on a separate sheet of paper, but omit the part about the child's remembering and repeating it. Foster cuts short this sensible letter because Cottle's messenger has been waiting long enough already. Another letter of Foster's in this year,[7] written on a Tuesday morning, is purely personal, putting off a dinner engagement at the last moment; Cottle will think it strange to have this letter a few hours before Foster is due there, but his wife has had two days of frightful headaches, with resultant languor; his sister Cox is away on a visit; he has passed hardly an evening with his wife; and there is no-one to keep her company except the children; so it would not be fair to her; instead of dining with Cottle today, may he take tea there towards the end of the week? – he hopes Cottle and his sisters will not mind; no more now, as the postman will be signalling any minute.

During the year, Cadell published Cottle's 111-page *Strictures on the Plymouth Antinomians*. These dissensions and mutual upbraidings in the ranks of honourable Protestants make sorry reading, and Cottle wrote far better when attempting to widen the gulf between himself and Rome. And, as Foster had warned him, the pamphlet did not go unanswered. Amiably reviewed in *The Christian Observer* (the organ of the 'Clapham Sect'), it was in 1824 attacked by James Babb with *The Reviewer reviewed; or an Examination of the remarks in the Christian Observer ... on Cottle's Strictures on the Plymouth Antinomians*; and Thomas Reed, also in 1824, published *A letter to Mr. Joseph Cottle, in which his 'Strictures' are examined*. Having thus made enemies enough in the town where he spent his summer holidays, Cottle stored up further rude remarks for a later occasion.

Dartmoor, and other Poems, printed for Cadell by T.J. Manchee of Bristol, is prefaced by an exceedingly curious 'Advertisement', forming no great recommendation of the volume to follow:

SIR,

Your Poem of 'Dartmoor' was duly presented at the Council Board of the Royal Society of Literature, and referred to the Committee of Examiners, who have adjudged the Prize to Mrs Heman, of Flintshire.

Sir,

Your most obedient,

Humble Servant,

THOS. YEATES.

PRO.SECRETARY.

To be 'pipped at the post' by Felicia Heman is disgrace enough, and Cottle's inclusion of the letter must be a little quirk of self-criticism. The volume contains a number of old favourites, and several poems on local scenes: the two written in the Tockington arbour; the Severn in a storm; and 'Sunset' (say the Contents and the title – but they probably mean 'sonnet') written at King's Weston Point; Mr Body and Mr Mind, intended as amusing, though it was 'written in winter' (says the title – the Contents says it was 'written in an Arbour'). All the poems, with many others, will be found again in the 1829 Malvern Hills.

On 3 June he sent a remarkably interesting letter to Cadell,[8] with glimpses of the author-publisher relationship and with a touching account of his own financial struggle. He tells Cadell that he has just completed the third edition of his Selection, and told the Bristol printer to send Cadell a thousand, packed carefully, last Saturday; he hopes that they have arrived, and herewith sends Cadell twelve copies for his immediate use. He wishes Cadell to have the work advertised on the covers of the Evangelical Magazine, Eclectic Review and Methodist Magazine (someone has ticked these three in red on his letter), and 'immediately' in the Courier, Times, Observer, Morning Post and Star (all save the Observer have been crossed out in black). Then let Cadell please subscribe the book to the trade, on the usual terms, and insert it in his trade catalogue; Cottle will gladly make the additional allowance and will be obliged if Cadell does all he can to further the sale. And after Cadell has subscribed the work, could his clerk write and tell Cottle how many were subscribed for? 'The delay of this edition has been a great disadvantage, but I hope not irretrievable'; he is sure that Cadell will comply, so he is anxious to get his letter. (On 10 June, the reply was forwarded that 105 copies had been subscribed for, that the advertisements had been sent out, and that a statement would be forthcoming at the end of June, when Cadell took stock.)

In the course of a long P.S., there are more instructions. In the list of books at the end of the Selection, Cadell will see that Cottle has reduced the price of his publications; so could Cadell's warehouseman now examine what copies Cadell has by him of each work, so that the new price will not interfere with the old? Cottle will put full reliance on the man's statement. He gave a hundred copies of the last edition of the *Selection* to Messrs Longman, Hurst and Rees, 'who sustained a loss by me'; Cottle cannot do all he would wish, but he will do what he can, so could Cadell let them have whatever they want of Cottle's publications at half the selling price in boards, e.g., *Selection*, 5/- bound, to Longman's 2/6 in sheets; *Alfred*, 10/- bound, to Longman's 5/3, etc. If Cadell finds that any booksellers have copies by them that they bought at the old price, let them not suffer, but let Cadell make up the amount of difference, in any of Cottle's publications; he will accede to anything that Cadell thinks 'equitable'.

But it is the substance of the postscript which must endear Cottle to us, for here he confides to Cadell the story of his failure twenty-four years before, and of his uphill fight to repay his creditors – a confession which we have already anticipated, under the year 1799. Now, thanks to the Almighty, he is in 'comfort & abundance, with the best of Sisters', who give him 'a small Independence, but this is not *alienable*'; thus he is all the more eager to get what he can out of the printing, so as to achieve an object so near his heart.

Davy wrote on 11 June,[9] with reference to the Oreston discoveries. He admitted that he held 'peculiar views' on the early history of the earth, but said that he was reserved about talking of it: 'all our knowledge on such matter is little more than ignorance'. He cannot have pleased Cottle by pointing out that recently-adduced facts merely proved the occurrence of the 'great catastrophe' of which records are found among the most barbarous nations; they did *not* prove the truth of Noah's Ark and the Mosaic Flood, which things were revelation. Sacred history and scientific investigation should be kept apart. Davy had met Coleridge that morning, after many years; he looked very well, and would dine with Davy on the next Monday.

A letter from Southey, on 25 June,[10] was very cordial as well as informative, pretending to rebuke Cottle for not sending by the faster mail coach the news of his restored eyesight. He was planning to finish *The Book of the Church*, and had other works in hand, which he wanted to show to Cottle, so he asked Cottle to bring his sister up for a summer. 'Our friendship', he goes on, 'is now of nine and twenty years standing and I will venture to say that for you and for us life cannot have many gratifications in store greater than this would prove.' There were ponies that could take Cottle safely to the top of Skiddaw, and he would be able to row Southey's own boat, *Royal Noah*, on the lake. There would be plenty to see: the children, from grown-up Edith May to toddling Cuthbert, and the books,

Sir Humphry Davy: engraving from a portrait by Sir Thomas Lawrence
(from the University of Bristol Library, Special Collections: Fry Portrait
Collection)

which meant as much to Southey as Cottle's bones meant to *him* (and Miss Cottle would agree with Southey 'that they are much prettier furniture, and much pleasanter companions,' even if they are not so old). He went on to assure Cottle that he had not written the *Quarterly* article on the presumed alteration in the plane of the ecliptic, since he never wrote on any subject of which, as of science, he was ignorant; and he promised to send Cottle a list of all the articles he had written for that journal, adding that Cottle would be in full agreement with him on nearly all of them. Their own several attacks on the 'miscreant' Byron would be bound to have their 'effect somewhere'; and he would like to show Cottle his correspondence with Shelley, and reveal 'his execrable history'. Cottle's proposed attack on the Antinomians is a 'worthy cause'.

During July, Cottle was at Plymouth again, clearing up the Oreston finds. When he was back, he wrote on 20 August to the poet Thomas Campbell,[11] c/o Messrs Taylor and Hessey of 93 Fleet Street, in Campbell's capacity as Editor of the *New Monthly Magazine*; he sealed the letter with his handsome black seal of a crowned head and the word 'AELFRED' – a nice piece of vanity. The two men must have been on good terms, since Cottle had put some of Campbell's poems in the *Selection*, a fact of which he here reminds him. The favour he now asks is that Campbell insert in his Notices the forthcoming *Oreston Caves*, dedicated to Davy and with engravings of the fossil remains of fourteen different animals; *Dartmoor, and other Poems*, out on 1 September at 5/-; and the *Strictures*, to be published on the same day. He points out that there is some new material on Chatterton in the third edition of the *Selection*, which Cadell has just published; if Campbell would like to insert it in his magazine, let him send to Cadell for a copy on Cottle's account.

For Christmas, 1823, Cottle compiled a verse Enigma[12] for his four Saunders nieces in Plymouth (Sarah, who was about sixteen, Mary Anne, Charlotte, then about eight, and Bess); he then had it written, in a beautiful hand, and signed it 'J.C.' Perhaps he sent a present as well; certainly the thing is of a desperate intricacy, and anyone who solves it has earned the pie promised in the last line:

> Dear Nieces, my Riddle, tho' not very prime,
> *For once* shall enliven your holiday time.
>   I am older than Tapestry, woven of yore,
> Yet (young as a Babe) I now stand at your door.
> Even Adam extoll'd me, Eve made me her theme
> When wandering at evening, by Gihon's fair stream,

Yet odd to declare, all befriendless, forlorn,
It is *long* since the reign of Queen Ann I was born.
Tho' endued with no flesh, and possessing no bones,
Like School-boys and Truants I too can throw stones.
I abominate noise, which most others delight
And like Beetles and Bats, chiefly roam in the night.
I am large (but how large is *your* business to show,)
Yet can creep thro' a hole where a Mouse cannot go.
Strange to say, at some seasons, (your wits to confound!)
Tho' you search the world over, I cannot be found.
I often am bloated, tho' not with disease,
But sometimes I am spare as the rind of a cheese.
Still your wonder to raise what strange thing I can be,
I rest on the land, and yet sleep in the sea.
In discharge of my duties, I ride, tho' no Rider;
I am fleet as a Race-horse, tho' fixed as a Spider;
With tumults the earth, I incessantly fill;
I am seen, and unseen, I advance, and am still.
In short, like a candle, burnt down to the wick,
I am old, I am young, I am thin, I am thick.
The proudest Land-owner, from hence to the Line,
Cannot boast a domain half so noble as mine;
Yet deem me no personage, lofty and great,
I am but a Servant, tho' used to much state;
My Mistress, whom others can tread under feet,
(So scorned!) I attend, with fidelity meet,
Yet while years roll along, oh ingratitude vile!
No praise have I heard, not received e'en a smile.
Tho' good-natured, I oft wear a lowering frown,
But my smiles cheer all hearts from the King to the Clown.
Great riches are min'd, tho' composed not of gold,
I have wealth which no eye but my own must behold,
And tho' *Ships* I possess not, with wet and dry Docks,
My fires, always burning, might roast a stout Ox.
Tho' a slave, I have Subjects, with many things more,
Which I want time and patience just now to explore.
    Now tell me my name, and my nature confess,
    Dear Sarah, and Mary-Anne, Charlotte, and Bess,
    And a *Pie*, at this Christmas, you all shall possess.

J.C.

The answer would appear to be 'the Moon'.

1   His three accounts of the Oreston Caves will be found in *MH*.4, I.112n; *MH*.4, II.478-503, in essay form; and in a full essay published as a pamphlet in 1830.
2   *MH*.4, I.92n-93n.
3   British Museum MS.Add.36509, Vol.XIX (1822-1823), fol.130.
4   John Rylands Library, Manchester, MS.351/49.
5   John Rylands Library, Manchester, MS.351/50.
6   Bristol City Library MS.B 20878.
7   Bristol City Library MS.B 20878.
8   British Museum MS.Add.34486, fol.26.
9   *R*.47, pp.292-293; letter offered for sale in Sotheby's Catalogue for 18-19 July 1960, 2nd day, item 464.
10 *R*.47, pp.238-240; Curry, II.247-250.
11 Bodleian MS.Montague d.4, fol.122.
12 Bodleian MS.Engl.misc., c.36, fol.23.

Chapter 13

Hannah More: 'Hold Every Thing with a Loose Hand'

Some time between 1814, when he took Coleridge to Barley Wood, and 1828, when Hannah More moved to Clifton, Cottle and the great bluestocking had become estranged. He never mentions this, for reasons which will soon be obvious; and our authority is de Quincey,[1] in an account which draws profitably on Cottle's own wit and on de Quincey's rancour against Mrs More. True, the date, and even the approximate period, are a matter of doubt, since de Quincey says he heard the story from Cottle 'pretty much about the same time' as certain happenings in 1809, and then proceeds to tell us how Cottle made, and has kept, an oath never to darken her doors again. Did Cottle relent, for Coleridge's sake, in 1814? Or has de Quincey simply transferred back a later incident for the convenience of his narrative? (It cannot have been later than 1818, since in 1836 Cottle told Southey that he had heard nothing of de Quincey for 18 years.[2]) Whatever the explanation, the story is delicious: de Quincey (who in the same narrative calls his own mother 'a lady with whose family I maintained a very intimate acquaintance') does not mention Cottle by name, but our hero comes to life at every turn of the ludicrous events, and Holy Hannah is effectively damned.

> Pretty much about the same time I learned another feature of Mrs. Hannah More's character, which was peculiarly revolting to my mind; or, rather, I ought to say, that I now learned a peculiarly revolting case, illustrating a weakness which I was already aware of. There was in Bristol an author, of very estimable private character, and, judging by the sale of his works, not altogether without claims to be considered as a favourite of the public. Indeed, I have heard the most original poet of modern times acknowledge that his works were rich in gleams of native genius, though he was disposed to pronounce them heavy as a whole. Some class, however, there must have been among the reading public to whom his writings were acceptable; for, without much favour amongst the professional critics, and with no private partisanship, assuredly, at work on his behalf, repeated impressions had been called

Thomas de Quincey: engraving from a daguerreotype by Howie, Junior (from the University of Bristol Library, Special Collections: Fry Portrait Collection), shown under scrap of a letter from de Quincey (formerly in the possession of Basil Cottle)

for of those amongst his works which were at all fitted for popularity by their subject. This author had originally been a bookseller and a publisher; and I have understood that, having been in some way or other unfortunate, he had retired – but with no loss of character – at an early period of life, from all his speculations as a tradesman. I called upon him, whenever I passed through Bristol, simply as a man of letters; and I thought him a very agreeable companion; for he wore upon the face of his manners an air of integrity; he was kind and courteous; and about his literary pursuits and plans he was communicative or not according to the interest, more or less, which his visitor manifested in such topics. This gentleman, and his sisters, with whom he lived, were uniformly in the habit of professing great esteem for Mrs. H. More, and admiration – more by a good deal than I could see any ground for – of her writings. In birth they were probably on a level with that lady; and, as to professional pursuits, there could be no difference of rank, seeing that the sisters presided over a large and brilliant establishment for educating young ladies, exactly as Mrs. Hannah More and *her* sisters had done many years before. Not understanding, therefore, what barrier it was which could divide people so united as they were in religious opinion, and with so much reverence on the one side towards the other, I said, one day, when paying my respects at this house, 'Pray, Mr.X.Z., what is the reason that, thinking as I know you think about Mrs. H. More, you do not cultivate her acquaintance? How is it that, amongst all the legions of gay people whom I meet at Barley Wood, never yet, by any accident, have I seen there either you or your sisters?'

– He smiled, and answered thus: 'My answer is partly anticipated in your question; it is precisely on account of those legions of gay people that I do not go to Barley Wood. I will own to you, very frankly, that I am not quite at home in such society. Some people of the very highest rank, in whose way I have sometimes fallen casually, have treated me with great affability; but, generally speaking, the fashionable mob whom one is liable to find at Barley Wood on a fine morning – those, I mean, who come over from Bath – look strangely upon me; and, doubtless, I suit them as little as they suit me. Meantime, you are to understand that in former times I *did* visit Mrs. Hannah More; and whether I gave up that practice on a sufficient reason, speaking in my own case, I will not take upon me to say: you shall judge. One day I was sitting alone with Mrs. Hannah More; and I believe that on that particular morning she did not expect any visitors. Suddenly I saw the heads of the leaders to a travelling carriage fairly looking in at the drawing-room windows before any noise of approach had reached us; and, in the next moment, a servant announced their Royal Highnesses the Princess A—, Prince W. of G—, and some lady of rank in attendance upon the Princess. Great was my perplexity as to what I ought to do. It appeared to me that Mrs. H. More, by a little decent exertion of firmness and self-respect, might have delivered both herself and me from all embarrassment. She, however, appeared flurried; not, as I fancied, from any trepidation about facing people of this distinguished rank, but at being here detected in a tête-à-tête with a man of my unfashionable air. She looked at me, then at the window, then at the fireplace, until, really, a strange fancy came over me that she wished me to jump out of the window, or to get up the chimney. Up the chimney, to say the truth, I would have been too happy to go, both for her sake and for my own. But the weather was cold; there was a hot fire, my dear Sir; and under those circumstances, …' 'Say no more, my friend: under no circumstances ought the most good-natured of men to go up a chimney, not though it were to oblige the Pope and the Dalai Lama. But did Mrs. H. More take it ill, then, that you blinked the question as to the chimney?' – 'Really it would be hard to say what she wished at that moment; but, doubtless, she wished fervently that Providence had called me on any other road that morning. Meantime, as Damien observed, no agony lasts for ever. I was attempting an exit by the door, when I saw the royal party advancing through the passage. To pass them was impossible without absolute rudeness. I waited until they had entered. The ladies advanced up to Mrs. H. More, and did not seem at all to observe me; but the Prince, who was in the rear, very courteously bowed to me as he advanced up the room. I made my acknowledgements by gestures; and, immediately after, making my way to the door, I opened it, and then, turning round, without speaking, I bowed once or twice with an air of reverence to the whole party, and made my exit. Afterwards, I called, as usual, on Mrs. H. More; but she received me with coldness; and, though I could well perceive this, I did not resent it, but paid her my usual respectful attentions; until at length I found myself a second time in the very same dilemma. A large party came in suddenly; this time it was not a royal party; but I heard the sounds of "Your Ladyship" and "My Lord" bandied about; and, from the number of out-riders, &c., doubtless they were some great people or other. I never staid to ask who; for, seeing, as before, a marked expression of vexation on Hannah More's countenance, I took my hat without saying a word, satisfied that nobody would miss me, and quitted her house, never again to enter it. That vow I made at the moment; that vow I have kept; and keep it I shall. I esteem, value, and highly admire Mrs. H. More; but I have also some respect for myself; and I will go no more to a house where I am tolerated only in a surreptitious way, and become a subject of scandal and offence if for one moment a collision occurs between myself and more privileged friends.'

Such was my friend's statement; which explained everything, and shocked me exceedingly. Never yet could I tolerate this double countenance and double tongue by which a man is welcomed as a friend in one situation, and frowned upon or disowned in another. And, doubtless, Mrs. H. More would have found secretly more respect from her great friends if she had protected her unassuming visitor, and had said firmly, 'This gentleman, or that gentleman' – for he would have absented himself, no doubt, immediately, – 'is a very respectable and old friend of mine.'

The few Library borrowings for 1824 show no summer break; and an undated letter of Foster's, with solicitude for Cottle's health, is probably to be assigned to this year.

3 Feb. – 22/23 May	G. Cuvier, *Lectures on Comparative Anatomy*, Vols. I & II
26 June – 1 Oct.	J. Evelyn, *Memoirs*, Vol. II
10 July – 9 Aug.	Collinson, *Somerset*, Vol. II
10 July – 19 July	E. Coplestone, *On the Doctrines of Necessity and Predestination*
19 July – 27 July	D.C. Wait, *Sermons* (?at Axbridge & Blagdon)
21 Aug. – 22/23 Nov.	*Remains of Henry Kirk White*, Vol. III
22 Nov. – 4 Jan. 1825	*Life of Evelyn*, Vol. I

A further cause of worry for Cottle was the declining health of his favourite niece, Sarah Saunders; during her last illness, Foster wrote her a series of decidedly bookish letters, which were published after her death in his *Life and Correspondence*. Cottle, tied to Bristol by his own health, relied more and more on Foster's visits, and spent a year of very little excitement. Foster is full of excuses, and I find it easy enough to distrust him. On 21 March, a Sunday, he writes that if it had not turned out wet, with a dark evening sure to follow, he was going to come into one of the evening services in the city, and would have called on Cottle with the latter's 'hand grenade against Satan's Plymouth garrison' slipped in his pocket. He is glad to hear that it is being recast at Fuller's – bigger, more explosive, and more missile; and he ventures to correct a fault of punctuation, already spotted by him and now pointed out by a friend. On 17 November he sent what Cottle indexed as 'A protest against destroying some melancholy M.S. Poems of Jno Henderson's'. This letter is now lost, along with many which Cottle recorded in the index of the letter-book now in the Bristol Library: an interchange on the Church of England, letters from Foster on Hannah More and on Byron's satire of George IV, and a note with a present of a book by 'Mr. Shepherd' given to Sarah Saunders. (The girls must have visited their uncle and aunts in Bristol, and there met with John Foster's approval.) On another occasion, in the winter of this year, his excuse was the slush: he would have called on Cottle yesterday, had the frost held, but the postman had reported the trying sequel of the thaw; he was thinking of it again today, when Cottle's man arrived, and, since Cottle would prefer tomorrow, he will call tomorrow, whatever the weather … 'I have not time now to inspect my friend Miss Saunders' sketch – It was too high a compliment to write so *much* of what was said. I have been sorry to hear of your uncomfortable state of health. I look forward toward the *spring* on your behalf.'

By now, Southey had sent *The Book of the Church*, and on 24 May Cottle returned thanks for it in a letter long owed.[3] He has been particularly interested in the martyrological part, and has never felt so intensely interested in our reformers. But – he must be forgiven for saying so – Southey is hard on the Puritans, without whom 1688 could not have been; what would have happened if they had given in to Laud and the High Church party? If called on to *act*, Cottle would do what appeared right; had he lived under the Charleses, he would have been a Puritan and perhaps sent a plea (not vain) to Southey 'to remember the poor incarcerated writer.' Southey has clearly refuted the lie of Milner, Bishop of Castabala, that Elizabeth killed more Papists than Mary Protestants on account of their *faith*; and Cottle reminds him that the revocation of the Edict of Nantes saved England from Popery, when the 50,000 fleeing families opened our eyes to the horrors that James II had ready for us.

Cottle then turns to the Antinomians; he is enclosing the second edition of his *Strictures* – the first prose, save for prefaces, that he has attempted. (We do not need Cottle to tell us that he found verse too easy.) Southey, of course, will find defects. Cottle, though hostile, has tried to avoid 'personal language', since '*contention* is a stranger' to him; he is told that his life will be in danger from the Antinomians if he goes to Plymouth again, but he will go, if duty calls, and 'once more appear amongst the Crowds at the "New Church"'. He encloses Babb's outrageous article, which does not try to deny Cottle's charges; no clergyman has been so anti-Christian while remaining in the church, and the Bible, to which Babb appeals, condemns him endlessly. If only Southey could see Babb's revolting '*Phiz*'! – it becomes an Antinomian, and one can hardly glance at it before looking, for relief, at a flower or a green field; Cottle has observed his devilish smile.

He goes on to talk of the twenty-nine years since Lovell introduced them; he remembers being struck by the fiery eye, the intelligent features, and the fine head of hair, shown in its glory in the Vandyke portrait, made soon after, which he still owns. So time has turned it grey! And the same has happened to Cottle's: valuable indeed are these warnings that we should 'hold every thing with a loose hand'. But Southey has delighted him by saying that he now takes more thought for the morrow; in Cottle's own case, his faith, and the thought of eternity, have brought him peace for twenty or thirty years. Not so Lord Byron, who has just died, and who would now gladly change his state for that of some poor, persecuted Puritan; well, 'Here our enmities, (or rather displeasures,) cease. "Lions prey not upon Carcasses, and we war not with the dust!"' He is pleased by Southey's remarks on Shelley, and would like to hear more: 'The discord of Error increases the harmony of truth'. Also, he is grateful for the promise of a list of Southey's *Quarterly* articles; he will be able to re-read them with all the more pleasure. He concludes with more domestic matters, regretting that he cannot come and row in *Royal Noah*, and see the Southeys and the books, Skiddaw and the Lakes; his travelling days are over – he is less and less able to walk – and fancy going to a picturesque district like Keswick & then sitting 'demurely' in an armchair! Further, his sister must decline Mrs Southey's invitation; if only Southey had visited Bristol last summer, when he came south!

Whatever Cottle's own opinion of his *Strictures*, Robert Hall was dissatisfied, especially with 'the perpetual deference paid to the Church of England'. He suspected that this habit of 'bowing' was contracted at Barley Wood.[4]

1825 brought a new bereavement; and the Library visits again suggest that there was no summer holiday among the Antinomians:

4 Jan. – 13/14 Jan.	*Edinburgh Review*, No. 80
4 Jan. – 21 March	Collier, *Essay on the Law of Patents for New Inventions* (was he perfecting the varnish of which we shall hear so much?)
13 Jan. – 4 Feb.	*Philosophical Transactions*, 1823, Pt. II
13 Jan. – 4 Feb.	Wittman, *Travels in Turkey, Syria, and Egypt, in 1799, 1800, and 1801*
4 Feb. – 21 March	Henry, *England*, Vol. III
21 March – 18 May (after note of 8 May)	Debrett, *Baronetage*, Vol. I
1 June – 11 July	Lord Somers, *Collection of Scarce and Valuable Tracts*, Vol. I
7 June – 8/9 July (after note of 5 July)	*Scenes in Egypt*

8 July – 26 July	Lord Somers, *Tracts*, Vols. III & IV
29 Aug. – 27 Sept.	Fenn, *Collection of Original Letters by Persons of Rank during the Reigns of Henry VI, Edward IV and Richard III*, Vol. 1
29 Aug. – 27 Sept.	Lucan, Vol. I
21 Sept. – 1 Nov.	*Harleian Miscellany*, Vols. I & II
28 Oct. – 11 Nov.	Southey, *Tale of Paraguay*
28 Oct. – 4 Nov.	Fosbrooke, *Essay* (?*British Monachism*)
4 Nov. – 11 Nov.	*Quarterly Review*, No. 54 (?64)
11 Nov. – 29 Aug. 1826	*Rowley's Poems*; *Tracts on Rowley*; Bryant & Sherwin, *on Rowley* (A scribble on the last flyleaf of Register 47 says 'Cottle/Bryant & Sherwin on Rowley Nov. 11', so it must have been a special privilege.)

The year was overshadowed by the death, in February, of his eldest niece Sarah Saunders. She was only eighteen, but she was already full of promise, virtuous, intellectual, witty, of 'mellifluous' voice, and extraordinarily pious, and it says something for her attainments that Foster had been moved to cheer her decline with a wad of publishable letters. On the 15th of the month, Cottle wrote to Robert's wife Elizabeth[5] expressing his grief at the loss of their niece, and his own consequent disinclination to write; but he has written some verses in Sarah's memory, and these have in some measure comforted him. This first draft has thirteen quatrains of memorial jargon, but a tidier version, printed in the 1829 *Malvern Hills*, re-uses only seven and adds one by way of introduction; this is quite the best of the quatrains, and smacks of Tennyson and Fitzgerald:

> We yield our treasure to the dust!
> A lovely blossom, torn away!
> Lord, we would own thee kind and just,
> Thou art the potter! we are clay!

Foster wrote him four notes during the month, on Sarah's death and the sermon for her funeral; but, though Cottle indexes them in his Foster letter-book, they are now apparently lost. On 7 April, Southey wrote sympathetically:[6] 'You have indeed had a sore life'; he himself feels the end is near, but if Cottle were under his roof, as Southey hopes he *will* be one day, he would recognize as much as he wished of the original Southey, 'tho the body is somewhat the worse for the wear.' Cottle must have asked him if he had received the *Strictures* safely, because Southey here says that he thought he had thanked him for them; they were well deserved and well delivered. At present, he is attacking the papists, and Cottle will be able to read his exposing of their systematic imposture; and he dislikes Calvinism as much as Cottle does. He is going on a continental tour soon, to get rid of catarrh, and he hopes to send himself some books from Belgium; but he cannot really afford the loss of time and income. Cottle would enjoy seeing his huge library at Keswick, and recognizing his own gifts of nearly thirty years ago; the 6,000 books range from the spruce denizens of 'Peacock Place' to the ragged mob of 'Duck Row'. Southey encloses the long-promised list of his *Quarterly* papers, and concludes, after thanks for Cottle's help towards a Tom Southey subscription, 'Write to me oftener: – your letters will always have a reply, let whose may go unanswered.'

The three Cottles, enjoying a time of prosperity so great that Mary had even refused a gentleman worth £100,000, now kept two establishments: the Dighton Street house and a rural, Severn-side retreat at 'the Passage', presumably the Old Passage at Aust rather than the New, which is a little nearer to Bristol. Here they must have spent much of the summer of 1825, and John Foster did not manage to visit them there. He met Robert Cottle at a committee meeting on the evening of Wednesday, 7 September, and understood that Joseph had returned to Dighton Street, so he walked into Bristol again on the next day in hopes of seeing him and his brother and sister-in-law. But the person in the house said that Cottle's had been only a transient visit, and that he had returned to the Passage for some time longer. Cottle, in fact, had enjoyed beautiful weather there, and Foster, writing on 10 September,[7] warned him that he must return to the city, and in winter! Foster is sorry not to have seen him for so long, 'excepting one short evening', and now he is himself going home to Lyme for three weeks on Monday next, so he must send Cottle a couple of lines to keep continuity; he is sorry, too, not to be seeing the two London Cottles making up 'family society', and he sends regards to them, to Mary and Ann, and to his 'three young friends' (the surviving Saunders girls). His letter is really an excuse for not calling: he has all the time been busy on a literary task, a preliminary essay for a reprint of Doddridge's *Rise and Progress of Religion*. He started it over two years ago, officially; and the reprint itself has all the time been waiting for him. He did not write a line until the end of last year, and then, after a few pages, broke off to write his series to Cottle's niece, which by 'its lively interest' disinclined him further from the task; but he resumed 'soon after her removal' (a vile phrase). The article is long, but represents a waste of time, in its author's opinion; it is correct and clear, but of only moderate merit. 'I shall have a little parcel of copies, and shall presume to request the acceptance of one in Dighton Street'. A lost letter of this year, indexed 33 in the Foster letter-book, is another apology – for not having come to dine.

During this year, Cottle became more familiar with another great Baptist minister – a far better preacher than Foster, and one whose physical sufferings gave Cottle some kind of ill-favoured inspiration: the Reverend Robert Hall. Cottle's eight-page digression on him, in the 1847 Reminiscences,[8] asserts so many coruscations of his eye, and such nectar from his lips, that one is almost astonished when he slips in that 'It is not meant to imply that Mr. Hall was perfect'. Cottle was privileged to hear the famous Sermon on 'Infidelity', and knew the good opinion of Hall entertained by Foster (who called him 'Jupiter'), Hannah More (who found his talents incomparable), Dugald Steward, and clergy of all sects. Hall became his friend, and often discoursed to him on style, claiming that Cicero had been his principal model. On his last preaching visit, before he finally settled in Bristol, Cottle took him to see the natural beauties of the district. Hitherto, an expanse of water had wrung from him the remark that 'We have no water in Cambridgeshire,' and on another occasion the foliage inspired a similar disparagement of Leicestershire; now, faced with the Avon, St Vincent's Rocks, Leigh Woods, the silver line of the Severn, and the blue foot-hills of Wales, he burst out in ecstasy: 'Oh, if these outskirts of the Almighty's dominion can, with one glance, so oppress the heart with gladness, what will be the disclosures of eternity, when the full revelation shall be made of the things not seen, and the river of the city of God!' In 1825, one hundred and eighty members of Broadmead signed his 'call', including Ann Cottle; Mary signed among the eleven paedobaptists, and Joseph with the 'hearers', as before.[9]

Southey did not write during his 1825 tour abroad, but on 26 February 1826, having sent his vindication of his Book of the Church, he followed it up[10] with violent words against popery, especially the fraudulent revelations of Sister Nativity. He had been disastrously bitten by a bug in France, with the happy sequel of a recuperation in the home of the Dutch poet Bilderdijk; erysipelas had followed, but at least his annual catarrh had been checked. When is Cottle coming to see him and his hair, greying but still curly? He looks at Cottle's portrait every day, and thus sees him accurately as he was thirty years ago. (With the letter thus far, Cottle perversely prints, showing no break, Southey's thanks for the fourth edition of Malvern Hills – not published until 1829 – and for help with a Bunyan problem which did not arise until 1828.)

Foster was planning a memoir of Sarah Saunders. A year after her death, he sent Cottle some books: one for Hannah More, though it is 'almost too late', and duplicate copies of Pascal and Bruyère to help the remaining Saunders girls with their French.[11]

Cottle made little use of the Library in 1826; his first visit was as late as 29 August, when he returned books which he had borrowed nine months before. Thereafter, during 1827, his few visits show no very long break:

1 Sept. – 9 Oct.	Wm. Godwin, *History of the Commonwealth of England*, Vol. II
6 Oct. – 24 Oct.	Bp. Burnet, *History of the Reformation*, Vols. I & II
24 Oct. – 11 Nov.	Debrett, *Peerage*, Vols. I & II
9 Nov. – 11 Dec.	*Journal of Science*, No. 43
9 Nov. – 11 Dec.	Bp. Burnet, *History of the Reformation*, Vol. III
8 Dec. – 17 Jan. 1827	Pegge, *Curialia*, Pts. I & III
13 Jan. 1827 – 26/27 Feb.	Gray's Examination of Neal's *History of the Puritans*, Vol. I
13 Jan. 1827 – 26/27 Feb.	E. Lodge, *Illustrations of British History*, Vol. I
26 Feb. – 16/17 July	Foxe, *Martyrs*, Vols. I & II
16 July – 4 Aug.	Smith, *Theory (?of Moral Sentiments)*
16 July – 16 Oct.	Smith, *Essays (?On Philosophical Subjects)*
4 Aug. – 23 Oct.	J. Clarke and J. McArthur, *Life of Admiral Lord Viscount Nelson*
(after note on the same day)	
4 Aug. – 22 Aug.	G.F. Lyon, *Travels in Northern Africa in 1818-20*
6 Sept. – 25 Oct. (after note of 23 Oct.)	Gilby, *Narrative* ...
25 Oct. – 28/29 March 1828 (after note of 14 March)	Fox, *On the Teeth*
31 Oct. – 28/29 March 1828 (after note of 14 March)	*Diversions of Poetry*, Vol. I

On 7 February 1827 he wrote to his banker[12] in terms that suggest how far away were the days of financial anxiety: 'I should be very much obliged if you would favour me with a statement of my Account, to the end of last year. It is now *two* years since I received any account, and, whatever the balance

may be, I should thank you to allow me to draw on you at *three months*, from the 1st of this month.' They replied on 12 March, and on the 19th accepted his draft for £76.13s.

By 15 September, Southey's friend John May had moved to a house and bank in Bristol, and Southey was anxious to come and show him his old haunts. Further, he wanted May to meet his old friend Cottle, 'the best-hearted of men, with whom my biographical letters will one day have much to do.' Cottle will welcome anyone to talk with about Southey, and May must tell him and his sisters that he is Southey's friend. 'You will see a notable portrait of me before my mane (Cuthbert Southey prints *name*) was shorn, and become acquainted with one who has a larger portion of original *goodness* than falls to the lot of most men'. Cottle and King the surgeon are Southey's only friends left in Bristol, 'both warmly attached' to him.[13] May duly made Cottle's acquaintance, and will figure later in our narrative.

On 2 November, Cottle wrote three fussy foolscap pages, surviving only as his own late copy in the Foster letter-book, to the Reverend Thomas Roberts. His subject is not a promising one: the word 'but'. Apparently he had asked Roberts to get Foster's opinion on what part of speech 'but' was; here he thanks Roberts for the information, but must cross swords with Foster, and goes on to prove it conjunction, adverb, or preposition. He quotes (and misquotes) 'Saxon', and says that Dr Chalmers once told him that 'the Teutonic dialect is still partially retained' in Scotland; he has read Horne Tooke and Baily and Todd and Smith and Crombie and Tyrwhitt on the matter, and thinks it's all very well for Tooke to say that all your parts of speech emanated from nouns & verbs … He apologizes for using a sacred sentence by way of illustration.

The year 1828 brought prosperity and the renewal of the old friendships with Wordsworth and Hannah More. Ann Cottle burgeoned with a none-too-early romance, and Joseph got his teeth into a Bunyan problem and a weighty controversy over the Serampore missionaries. A volume of devotional verse came out, called *Hymns and Sacred Lyrics* : 'the production, and, it may be added, the solace of my latter years'; at first it was 'by Constantius', but most of the edition bore his name on the title page. Starting late at the Library, he borrowed mostly topography, perhaps in connection with the notes for the new edition of *Malvern Hills* and its attendant pieces:

28 March – 31 March/1 April	*Archaeologia*, Vol. 21, 2 pts
1 April – 8 May	E.D. Clarke, *Travels in Various Countries*, Vol. I

1 April – 8 May	Newton, *on the Prophecies*
8 May – 21 May	Hutchins, *History and Antiquities of Dorset*, Vols. I & II
19 May – 14 June	Peck, *Desiderata Curiosa*
11 June – 31 July	Malkin, *South Wales*
11 June – 31 July	Nash, *Collections for the History of Worcestershire*, Vol. I
31 July – 31 Aug. (says the register; but the Library was closed)	Keate, *Pelew Islands* (of which he never tires!)
2 Oct. – 15 Nov.	J. O'Driscol, *Views of Ireland, Moral, Political and Religious*, Vols. I & II
15 Nov. – 22 Nov.	Lord Somers, *Tracts*, Vol. II
15 Nov. – 6 Jan. 1829	E.D. Clarke, *Travels in Various Countries*, Vol. II
22 Nov. – 25 Nov.	T. Warton, *Poetry*, 8vo, Vol. I
28 Nov – 6 Jan. 1829	T. Warton, *English Poetry*, Vol. I
28 Nov. – 6 Jan. 1829	*Extinct Peerage of England* (which he used in his Chatterton essays)
31 Dec. – 1 Jan. 1829	Duc de Sully, *Memoirs*, Vols. I & II

The Serampore row involved the eminent missionaries and translators William Carey and Joshua Marshman, supported by many admirers like Cottle and Southey, against the Committee that backed the young insubordinates at the mission; Robert Hall was of the latter party. While Dr. Marshman was on a visit to England, Cottle invited him and Foster to dine on the evening of 30 January 1828, and tried to patch up the quarrel by proposing to have Hall there also. But, when Foster replied on the 29th, he started jovially by thanking the Cottles for the present of a ham, and then went on to make difficulties: Dr Marshman, Mr Roberts (apparently Cottle's correspondent the Reverend Thomas Roberts), and Mr Angus, from London, are with him reading papers, and he will ask Marshman to come to the dinner, but he is sure of a refusal. Marshman just cannot meet Hall, who behaved as his inveterate enemy in the Serampore affair; not that he bears resentment (he isn't that kind of man), but he would feel ungracious in Hall's presence. As for Foster himself, he will try to come; but the Cottles, who are always prompt, need not wait for him – he will be on time, if he comes at all. (By the end of the letter, he had changed his mind: he would not even ask Marshman, but would tell him about the dinner when it was all over.)

Hannah More: engraving (in the possession of Martin Crossley Evans)
from a painting by William Pickersgill, 1822

Cottle had long been interested in the Serampore mission, and about a year after a disaster had overtaken it he wrote to Hannah More and 'casually mentioned' the fact. She sent him £5, regretting that she could not send more; but in addition she had left some money for the mission in the hands of Dr Ryland. He died in 1825 (Cottle, in fact, who had worshipped in his church, wrote a memorial poem to him), and soon she wrote asking if she should now transfer it. Cottle, feeling that he had misinformed her about the immediacy of the need, since during the year that had elapsed an adequate subscription had been raised, returned the £5 with an explanation; and in her receipt she told him that she had sent it by the same post to another applicant.[14]

Meanwhile, whatever had excluded Cottle from Barley Wood was forgotten, and when Hannah More came to live in Bristol she received him as an old friend. The circumstances of her quitting Barley Wood, the perfidy of the servants, and her resounding *coup d'état*, are all merrily recorded in Cottle's 1837 *Recollections*,[15] with a scattering of sundry menials' Christian names – whence a trail of disaster for him (but we must not anticipate the bizarre story). On 18 April 1828, at the age of eighty-three, she moved into No. 4 Windsor Terrace, that elegant yet dramatic cliff of houses perched daringly on the Avon Gorge. Soon after, Cottle took Robert Hall to call on her, and she seemed quite contented with her move. Certainly, the view was immeasurably finer than any she had enjoyed down in Somerset: she took the two men to her drawing-room windows, and showed them the new docks, the shipping, and the arresting green hill of Dundry; and from her back room they could see Leigh Woods, St. Vincent's Rocks, Clifton Down, and the ribbon of the Avon. The parlour at Barley Wood had been lined with paintings, drawings, and prints; she parted with the whole collection when she moved, and gave them all to her friend Sir T.D. Acland, Bart., with the sole exception of William Palmer's *John Henderson*, which she presented to Cottle.

Ann Cottle, now 48, at length flouted the family tradition and married; her choice was John Hare of Firfield, a rich floor-cloth manufacturer, and in retirement since 1820, aged 76, and a widower. Firfield was an important mansion on the west of Knowle Hill, just outside Bristol on the Wells Road. It, and its drive and trees and grounds, including what was reputed the most majestic oak in Bristol, have all been swept away by later building, and the present Belluton Road occupies the site; but at some distance the great house was commemorated by Firfield Street and even by the Firfield Tennis Club. By his first wife he was the father of Sir John Hare; the grandfather of Eliza Leonard (the second wife of poor Charlotte Saunders's husband David

Thomas); and likewise the ancestor of George Hare Leonard, the first Professor of Modern History in the University of Bristol.

The whole story of John Hare's settlement and prosperity in the city is decidedly romantic.[16] The younger son of a gentleman of Crowcombe near Taunton, he determined to come and make his fortune in Bristol, and in May 1773, at the age of twenty-one, came up from the country by wagon with a few guineas. He arrived at the foot of Redcliffe Hill before daybreak, 'clambered over a dwarf wall, and [lay] down to rest upon a bank with a stone for a pillow, like Jacob of old.' He had a beautiful dream, and his waking seemed only to continue it, since he found himself in a perfect May morning – the orchard-trees in blossom, the birds singing, and the sky cloudless; already a pious young man, he vowed that, if God spared his life and prospered the business, he would build a church on that very spot. After several attempts to buy the ground, he at length secured it from the Corporation in 1827, took down the tumbled buildings, and prepared to erect a church for 'Protestant Dissenters of the Independent denomination', at his sole cost of £4,000, to which he later added an endowment. Henceforth, his story is bound up with Cottle's, especially as the latter lived only on the fringe of the Baptists and would soon be an Independent. But some idea of Hare's forceful character can be gained from the fact that, soon after removing to a larger factory at Temple Gate, he chased his absconding cashier to America in a faster vessel than the man had caught, waited for him, and recovered his £500 as soon as the man arrived. He was also a keen Liberal, and had his factory pillaged by a pro-slavery mob in 1830. He is said to have been tall, handsome, and of fine presence. He was certainly pious and honest, and able enough to amass a huge fortune in 47 years.

On 25 July 1828, Cottle suddenly wrote to Wordsworth,[17] after 'a mutual epistolary intermission of thirty years', which he puts down to their distance apart (no very cogent reason for a lapsed correspondence). He feels that this is a pity, since *now* circumstances would not be financially clouded, whereas he realises that they both must occasionally direct their 'retrospective thoughts' to the 'pecuniary affairs' of the former period. He has watched Wordworth's rise with interest and approval, and he sees no sign of abatement. At the moment, since the third edition of *Malvern Hills* is long out of print, he is 'laboriously' preparing a fourth, which involves hacking nearly 400 lines out of the principal poem and inserting 700 *en revanche*; and he trots out, to impress Wordsworth, the lines on Chatterton, which tell how he went off 'unprepared, in audit dread, To meet his Judge!' All this is but preliminary: Cottle is begging a favour. He feels it would improve the edition, and suggest his *'high value'*, if he prefixed the unsolicited poems which Coleridge and Southey addressed to him.

> It was a combination of very remarkable events which threw you, and other Men of Genius in my way, in the early years of my life, and I derive pleasure from the recollection that I never, I trust, omitted any opportunity of showing them every act of kindness in my power, as they well know, and their letters sufficiently testify. My only concern then arose (as it does at present), from the recollection that imperative and uncontrollable circumstances restrained me from doing one half of that which was in my heart.
>
> It was indeed a very remarkable coincidence that in the few years in which I was a Bookseller in Bristol, (for I quitted the profession at the age of twenty eight), I should have been the means of introducing to the world, by publishing their First Volume of Poems, three such men as *Wordsworth*, *Coleridge* and *Southey*, and that with a liberality towards them which almost exceeded my ability. On this head I can have no self-accusation.

(This is not only smug but untrue, since all three had previously used other publishers.) So, could Wordsworth write him a few lines – 'a *Sonnet*, or any thing else, by *October next*'? He fumbles on with a dark reference to this as some kind of reimbursement to himself, but assures Wordsworth that he will not be offended if no lines are forthcoming; he will preserve a happy memory of Wordsworth, and is confident that he would be even happier to know him after the changes of thirty years. (Wordsworth's muse, alas, was not stirred, either instantly or eventually; he was abroad at the time, and it took him six months even to refuse.) He wishes to be remembered to Mrs and Miss Wordsworth, whose visit to Bristol had impressed everyone; and here is some gossip for their next tea-table: since they left the city, Ann has married a 'valuable' gentleman called John Hare, etc … He is 'unconnected with business,' 'keeps his carriage', has thousands a year, and lives in a house 'of his own building, which may be termed a Little Paradise'. Mary, the eldest sister, will not go so soon, as she long ago refused someone worth £100,000; 'but this latter Swain has been more fortunate, and so the world goes round.' Poor Cottle, making the best of the senile romance, does not add that the world goes round in no very giddy turns for a swain of seventy-six, but merely says that Ann 'is a lovely character, who will adorn any station', and that her husband seems to realise this; poets may talk of higher things, but a good dinner is worth having. Finally, he wishes to be remembered to Dorothy, 'Who was always a great favourite of' his; and he is sure that, if his sisters and nieces knew he was writing, they would wish to send their regards to Wordsworth's wife and daughter. (What does this imply? Ann was now at Firfield, but was not Mary still housekeeping for her brother in Dighton Street? Perhaps she was out when the letter was written and posted; but it is possible that, for the time being, she accompanied her sister to the mansion after the wedding.) Wordsworth, who may well have detested the letter, has used the outside of it to practise writing 'My Lord', 'My de', 'My', and four more capital 'M's; but Dorothy, empowered to open his mail, had already answered it graciously on 31 July, recalling the 'many happy days' of her youth spent in Cottle's company, and saying how much Mrs and Miss Wordsworth had enjoyed their holiday. She was sure that her brother would fulfil the request, and sent news of the Southeys and Coleridges; Mrs Lovell was unwell, and Cottle (or someone of like mind) has scored out five non-committal lines in which Asra wanted to be remembered from Sockburn days. Cottle had paid postage on his letter; he mustn't, and Dorothy has a good mind to do so in revenge (but she didn't).[18]

Southey, wanting help in a small research, wrote on 4 November,[19] with apologies for his long delay. He had promised to write a life of Bunyan as an introduction to an edition of *Pilgrim's Progress* by Major, of Fleet Street, but Major could not find a first edition in any public or private library, so could Cottle find whether there was one in the Bristol Baptist Library and, if so, how it differed from the folio edition? If Isaac James is alive, Southey would 'like to know whether his dream of the Pilgrims Voyage has ever been realized'. He is better after his operation, but of course it prevented their meeting in the summer. He sends regards to the Misses Cottle, and to Robert when Cottle writes: 'When I think of you all, old times return, with the freshness of a dream'. Cottle advertised and enquired, but heard nothing of a first edition 'in these parts'. (In fact, he finally tracked it down in 1847, when Southey was long past requiring it.)

He replied, in a letter franked 12 December, explaining his delay and his failure, and attempting a bibliography, with references to Bunyan material in Sion College and the Bristol Baptist College Library;[20] two or three days ago, he rode over to Brislington, where a very old man was reported to have the required edition, but it all proved to be a false alarm. As for Isaac James, of whom Southey had enquired, he is still alive and cheerful, but blind; Cottle sees him occasionally, and he was grateful for Southey's interest. The Cottles were sorry not to see Southey in the previous summer; Bristol lovers of literature are proud of their Laureate son. Tom Southey has told Cottle in a letter that Robert has had an operation; it is good to know that he has recovered, but, of course, they are now at a time of life when hill succeeds hill. Tom sent no address, so would Southey clear up a misunderstanding next time he writes to his brother: tell him that Cottle, on receipt of his letter, wrote to Longman's with proof of having paid for all the copies of Tom's *West Indies* which were sent to Bristol. They had forgotten that Cottle had paid for a single copy before paying for the rest; so it is *their* mistake, due to 'the multiplicity of their concerns'. He hopes Tom gets an appointment.

He is glad that Southey is soon going to send some prose and verse; he will wait patiently to know what it is – he reads everything of Southey's with interest. As for his own pursuits, the fourth *Malvern Hills* is in the press, and he will prefix Southey's and Coleridge's complimentary lines, and the former's lines to Amos; if either needs alteration, let Southey inform him of the changes by 1 January. He *had* hoped for half-a-dozen lines from Wordsworth (it would have served him right if Wordsworth had made him the hero of a limerick), all the more necessary because of the harsh things Byron had said. To *Malvern Hills* itself he is adding some of his best poems, published and unpublished, and (though prose is not his element) a few essays. Since *John the Baptist* is his 'best specimen of versification', he 'thought it worthwhile to re-write' it. His two or three essays on Chatterton he has enlarged, under persuasion, into a paper to be delivered by the Reverend J. Eden on the following Thursday evening (18 December) at the Institution in Park Street, so that the 'good people here will be bored with it'. The boy poet was certainly in his thoughts again, and on Monday the 29th George Cumberland 'Left Chatterton's Life with Mr. Cottle'.[21]

Southey was grateful for his efforts, and wrote thanking him (perhaps in the next year, 1829) for the trouble he had taken; they still could not find a first edition, or even the date of it. Anyway, *Pilgrim's Progress*, which Southey valued so highly, was certainly not a translation from the Dutch, as some impudent fellow had claimed; when he and Cottle met in the next world, they would go and see Bunyan on the matter, and tell him how Southey had 'tinkered' the man who had dared to make the charge of plagiarism. P.S. He keeps dreaming that he is at Westminster again, without any books, and that he has been long at Bristol but has not been to find Cottle in Brunswick Square, which upsets his conscience.[22] Southey, after this, wrote to George Offer, asking for a loan of his *Pilgrim's Progress* 'original' and returning it with thanks, in two letters of 16 and 25 April 1829, which Offer transmitted to Cottle in a letter of 6 March 1847. For 1829, the library register shows borrowing up to the end of April, and then nothing save a patch in August:

1 Jan. – 3 Jan.	Duc de Sully, *Memoirs*, Vols. III & VI
2 Jan. – 5 Jan.	Johnson, *Works*, Vol. XII

5 Jan. – 19 Feb.	*Psalmanazar's Life*
5 Jan. – 18 March	*Ancient Universal History*, Vol. III
(and he was returning books on 6 Jan.)	
19 Jan. – 20 Feb.	Collinson, *Somerset*, Vol. I
19 Feb. – 2 March	*Philosophical Transactions*, Vols. I & VI
2 March – 9 March	I. Newton, *Opera quae extant omnia*, Vols. I & II
4 March – 18 April	I. Newton, Vols. IV & V
(after note of 13 April)	
15 April – 22 April	*Paris Life*, Vol. I (surely not !)
15 April – 22 April	T.T. Biddulph, *Remarks …*
24 April – 4 Aug.	Daubeny, *On Volcanoes*
24 April – 4 Aug.	Wm. Godwin, *Commonwealth*, Vol. III
4 Aug. – 14 Aug.	Gibbon, Vols. XI & XII
4 Aug. – 14 Aug.	Henry, *England*, Vol. VI
11 Aug. – 26 Jan. 1830	Johnson, *Works*, Vol. VIII
11 Aug. – 26 Jan. 1830	Henry, *England*, Vol V
(after note of 22 Jan.)	

The life of Chatterton which Cumberland had left with him was Cumberland's own memoir. Cottle was grateful, especially for the testimony of old Mrs Edkins that the Redcliffe 'muniments' had been removed thither from Canynges' house in Redcliffe Street, and he worked Cumberland's information into a note on page 422 of the new *Malvern Hills*. But, in case Cumberland wanted the note suppressed in his own interest, Cottle wrote to him on 16 January 1829,[23] pointing out that the footnote would really be advantageous to any account that Cumberland might write; the late Mr Birtill had already told Cottle that the parchments had not long left the house (which he occupied) when Chatterton found them in the muniment room, but Mrs Edkin's evidence put the matter beyond all doubt.

Wordsworth's reply,[24] written eventually on 27 January 1829, was unsatisfactory. He is sorry to have been so tardy in answering Cottle's 'very kind letter', with its suggestion of dedicatory verses; well, he cannot manage anything – 'subjects either proposed, or imposed' always defeat him. In this case, he feels quite poetic about the times and places that Cottle mentions; but it was just the same once before, when he spent a year trying to carry out such a commission for one of his 'most valued friends'. Having got this ungraciousness off his chest (for surely the writer of a sonnet to swell the funds of a bazaar for building an ugly 'Norman' church in Bute Street, Cardiff, could have spun a few lines for his old subsidizer), he begins to sound more cordial. He is glad to hear that *Malvern Hills* will soon be out again; he often looks at the poem, from which Cottle gave him 'a valuable extract' ... 'It was always a favourite of mine. Some passages – and especially one, closing

> To him who slept at noon and wakes at eve –

I thought super-excellent'. His wife and daughter, who send their kind regards, have brought back an agreeable account of the Cottle family, which is confirmed by Cottle's letter. Wordsworth often thinks of his Bristol days, 'not setting the least value on those passed under the roof of your good father.' He spent the previous week at Keswick, and can thus give news of the health of the Southeys, the Coleridges, and Mrs Lovell; Coleridge's trip to the continent with the two Wordsworths has done him good; Hartley lives nearby, and is soon publishing a volume of poems, but he is not very 'steady'.

Cottle's *Advertisement*, dated 2 March 1829, opens the new two-volume *Malvern Hills*, and is altogether self-flattering, with its quoted praise from Coleridge, Southey, and Davy; on the other hand, he admits that there will be no more editions of *The Fall of Cambria*, so he has put the lyrical portions into the present volumes. He had, in fact, some reason to be proud of this edition; it contains much of interest – pictures, diffuse notes, the Chatterton research, the memorials of Amos and of John Henderson, the Byron affair, and all Cottle's more endurable verse. Nor was it unfavourably reviewed: the *Gentleman's Magazine*[25] said that the items, especially the descriptions of Henderson and Chatterton, 'justly merit much praise'; they agree with him in 'the folly of insuring and underwriting the souls of murderers and atrocious malefactors, as to the *certainty* of their receiving Heaven in return for their being hanged on Earth'. It is further evidence of the worth of the book that, solely among Cottle's books at the Library, it was not presented by him: he gave them the 1796 *Poems, Messiah*, the *Expostulatory Epistle, Alfred, Cambria*, the *Psalms*, the *Strictures*, but it looks as if they laid in the fourth *Malvern Hills* themselves. He was prodigal in sending copies to his friends, and, in the case of those whose good will had not been prepared, he could slip the book in with something more certainly acceptable. Thus on 14 March he wrote to Dr Cox,[26] Librarian of the University of London (which had opened under that title on 1 October 1828): 'Will the Council of the London University condescend to accept from one who cordially desires the welfare of their Institution, "Rolt's Lives of the Reformers"? I have accompanied it with a copy of the 4th Edition of my Poems and Essays.' In this instance, the Library escaped with the bribe only; 'Jos: Hughes' has added a footnote to the effect that the edition could not be obtained from the binders in time.

On 12 May,[27] Ann Hare laid the foundation stone of Zion Chapel, the church of her husband's vow, at the junction of the turnpike roads to Long Ashton and to Bedminster. Nearby, the New Cut of the Avon swirled with increasing murk under Bedminster Bridge, and soon the chapel rose, four-square and rather grim in local stone from Conham, with four burly pillars on its façade, and a little graveyard lying round. A primitive oil painting of 1832 shows people flocking to the church in poke-bonnets, while Hare's towering carriage, with its top-hatted coachman, moves magnificently from the portal; Zion's younger neighbour, the tower of St Paul's, peeps over the houses of Coronation Road, and a boat sails along the Cut past the gaol.

Cottle had sent to Wordsworth, through Southey, the two volumes of his new miscellany, which Wordsworth thought 'a very agreeable mark' of his regard, finding *Malvern Hills* much improved; his favourites were still the title poem itself, and the *Monody on Henderson*, and he had always admired the notes on Chatterton, which seemed to him 'conclusive on the subject of the forgery'. His letter of thanks,[28] on 2 August, must have mollified Cottle in his sonnetless state.

The 1830-1853 Records of the Independent Church meeting at Broadmead begin, for the first eight folios, in Cottle's hand, and this secretaryship was one of the many voluntary employments of his long years of quiet. These brethren met on 20 January 1830, elected deacons, and laid down eight points of doctrine (though 6 and 7 are disciplinary, and 8 concerns only the Annual Meeting and the finances). Under this new order, a list of members was drawn up on 1 March: a mere ten men, including Cottle, and twenty-three women, including his sister Mary, who is one of the four women to have their Christian names filled in. They both live in Dighton Street, and he is a 'Gent.' by profession.[29] The opening of Zion Chapel on 15 June must have detached Ann from Broadmead, but her brother and sister remained faithful for the time being.

Little suggestion remains of literary pursuits in 1830; apart from returning two overdue books on 26 January, Cottle visited the Library only twice, on 10 and 16 December, to borrow and take back the *Annual Register* for 1819. The University of Bristol Library copy of his *Oreston Caves* monograph contains a note by him, dated from Dighton Street on 27 September, presenting the four plates to Mr Richard Smith; other sets had been given to the geologist, Professor Buckland (who supported Moses), and to various friends.

The year 1831 was the last in which Cottle used the Library. He started by misusing it: he borrowed Vol. 38 of the *Quarterly Review* on 14 February, and was sent notes on the subject on 5 August and 5 October, and again on 9 February 1832; it was at length 'replaced Dec. 1842'. Perhaps he denied responsibility for it, and this led to altercation, or his move to Bedminster made the Library inaccessible; at all events, his very last borrowing was on 9 August 1831.

6 April – 13 April	Racine, Tome I
6 April – 2 May	Sadler, *On Population*, Vol. I
15 April – 2 May	Southey, *Life of Nelson*
3 May – 4 June	Sadler, *On Population*, Vol. II
3 May – 9 Aug. (after note of 5 Aug.)	Smellie, *Philosophy of Natural History*, Vol. I
3 June – 9 Aug.	*Life of Davy*
9 Aug. – 15 Feb. 1832 (after note of 9 Feb.)	Lewis, *On the Arts*
9 Aug. – 15 Feb. 1832 (after note of 9 Feb.)	*Handmaid to the Arts* (1764), Vol. I

The year was early clouded by the death of Robert Hall; but Southey's valuable friendship was at hand. On Monday, 17 January 1831, after a journey from London via Chichester, Tichfield, Southampton, Buckland (Miss Bowles's), Dorchester, Exeter, Crediton (Nicholas Lightfoot's), and Taunton (his aunt's), he reached John May's at Clifton, made nostalgic excursions to his father's shop and his grandfather Hill's house, and dined on Friday the 21st with Cottle, 'the simplest and kindest hearted of men'.[30]

Cottle was earning the esteem of local scientists. At the eighth annual meeting of the Bristol Institution, on 10 February, it was announced that he had presented to the Geological Department the whole of his collection of antediluvian animal remains from Oreston. The collection of Müller (the late curator), which had been offered to them for £730, had also been secured; and thus the Department 'will excel in variety any other provincial establishment'.[31]

Gifts to Southey followed. On 3 March, Cottle sent him a writing-desk for Miss Southey, and Mary added pens and paper, with her own good wishes. It was a very special desk, with secret drawers: you took out the right-hand ink-bottle and pressed hard against the point where Cottle had put a cross, when the front would fly out and reveal the drawers; the spring would work better with use. He also sent Speed's *Chronicle*, Guillim's *Heraldry*, Luther's

Table Talk, and Walpole's *British Traveller*; and, after much labour of amassing, a complete set of pamphlets on the unhappy Serampore missionary squabble. In this affair, Cottle was firmly on the side of Carey and Marshman; they had always been friends of Southey, who, Cottle hoped, would be their advocate. Marshman had told Cottle of the place, including the fact that servants who brought in the dinner would not remove it. The Committee backed the young insubordinates against these two great men, and a Committee member, grossly misinformed, told Cottle that the two had made themselves as much as £16,000 a year – when all the time they were doing without the necessities of life so as to continue their translations and their other work! Cottle's letter of 3 March,[32] accompanying the presents, marches on for three pages of this praise and invective. He would have written earlier, but Cadell had been late in sending some Anthologies, and had addressed them to Downend; but now they had come, and Cottle would enclose them. His letter shows, too, that he had made the acquaintance of Estlin's son-in-law Dr James Cowles Prichard, the ethnologist and Egyptologist, who long lived at the Red Lodge in Park Row, Bristol. On Southey's behalf, Cottle sent him a book, and asked him for two impressions of his Egyptian seals. In a day or two, Prichard called on him with the seals, and with information on their motifs; he also left for Southey 'one of his printed accounts of the Abraxean Gems, in our Institution'. Finally, this bulky letter enclosed a paper about Robert Hall's death; a letter from Mary which should have gone with the parcel – so that Cottle deserves the penalty of double postage; and a sentiment, so near both *theirs*, extolling Humility and Charity, quoted from Archbishop Leighton, his '2nd Bible', which he had been reading that morning. He sealed it in red with what looks like a leopard sejant, the crest of the Cottles. The package arrived safely at Keswick on the afternoon of 21 March, and next day Southey returned thanks:[33] the books would be 'furbished up', and Cottle's name, as the donor, would be inscribed in each – 'a pleasant memorandum' often found on Southey's shelves. Since Cottle has known him from the beginning of his 'authorial life', he ought to come and see the library in which the owner takes so much blameless delight and pride. He promises to peruse the Serampore pamphlets, and to write to Cottle's satisfaction in the *Quarterly* on behalf of the wronged men. Since his return from Bristol, through Shrewsbury and some fearful winter weather, he has been hard at work at his desk, and will soon be sending more prose and verse. Cottle was planning a move to Bedminster, where Southey hopes one day to stay with him, in easy reach of his old haunts: Ashton, Bishopsworth (he still spells it 'Bishford'), Dundry, and Chew Magna. And Cottle, once he is settled, must get on with those recollections to which Southey has urged him; the resulting book could be as delightful as Izaak Walton's, bring him in a fortune, and stand in prose side by side with Southey's verse on Bristol Library shelves, until the Corporation commemorates them by ordering 'statues of us to be the Gog and Magog of their Guildhall.'

1 David Masson ed., *Collected Writings of Thomas de Quincey*, Vol.XIV (Edinburgh: A. and C. Black, 1890), pp.118-121.

2 Letter of Cottle to Southey, 9 April 1836, in Bristol City Library MS.B 20877.

3 Bristol City Library MS.B 20877.

4 *1795 Album*, letter to Cottle on 11 June 1824.

5 Bodleian MS.Engl.misc., c.36, fol.29.

6 *R.47*, pp.240-243; Berg Collection, New York Public Library.

7 Bristol City Library MS.B 20878; badly mauled in *R.47*, pp.333n-335n.

8 pp.56-63.

9 *Broadmead Records*, Vol.III (1817-1834), fols.155 ff.

10 *R.47*, pp.243-246.

11 *1795 Album*.

12 This letter is now in my collection.

13 CCS, V.310.

14 ER.37, I.78.

15 I.83 ff.

16 It will be found in H.B. Cozens, *The Church of the Vow* (Bristol: St Stephen's Press, 1930), *passim*.

17 University of Bristol Library MS.3/1.

18 *1795 Album*.

19 *R.47*, pp.248-253; Berg Collection, New York Public Library.

20 Bristol City Library MS.B 20877. On Sion College (in Cripplegate, London), which had strong links with and outposts in Bristol, see the biography of its founder by Walter Adam Sampson, *The Life of Reverend Thomas White DD* (Bristol: Arrowsmith, 1912). The Baptist Academy in North Street, Bristol, had changed its name to the Baptist College when, in 1812, it moved half a mile north; it remained in its new location in Stokes Croft until 1916.

21 *Cumberland Papers*, British Museum MS.Add.36521 C (Diary for 1828), fol.214v.

22 Cottle, in *R.47*, p.245, foolishly prints the Bunyaniana along with a letter of 1826.

23 *Cumberland Papers*, British Museum MS.Add.36512, Vol.XXII (1827-1830), fol.160.

24   de S, No.853.

25   Vol.XCIX, 1829, i.619.

26   This letter is now in my collection.

27   H.B. Cozens, *op.cit.*, p.3.

28   de S, No.874. L.N. Broughton, *Some Letters of the Wordsworth Family, Now First Published* (Ithaca, N.Y.: Cornell U.P., 1942), pp.66-67, Letter No.53, at this point suggests Cottle as the recipient of a Wordsworth letter of 7 August, on the back of which are the words 'Penrith Aug 7th 1829 Joseph Cottle Esq Bristol Marshall'. But there are at least four arguments against this ascription: (1) Wordsworth ends by calling his correspondent 'Mr. D-'. (2) He asks him to thank his father for a kind invitation (Cottle *père* had died in 1800). (3) He had, we know, written to Cottle only five days before. (4) The letter is mainly of politics, Lord Lowther, tithes, and other things far from Cottle's sphere.

29   *Broadmead Records, Records of the Independent Church* ..., fols.5, 7.

30   Letter to Grosvenor Bedford; Curry, II.361.

31   *Gentleman's Magazine*, Vol.CI, 1831, i.251.

32   Bristol City Library MS.B 20877. Cottle wrongly heads this, in pencil, '1834', because he misreads the blurred franking.

33   *R*.47, p.253; Curry, II.362-364.

Chapter 14

Bedminster: Quarrel with Poole

On 14 November 1831, Joseph and Mary Cottle signed, among the Independent Paedobaptists of Broadmead, a call to the Reverend Samuel Nicholson; by this time, Joseph had moved up from the Hearers, but sister Ann had left the congregation altogether. It was clear that Joseph would not stay much longer, and 1832 saw him settled in a new church and a new dwelling nearer Ann's. On 15 January 1832 he wrote to George Cumberland,[1] since he remembered Cumberland's saying that he had a fine remedy for rheumatism; and now his old servant, the bearer of the note, was afflicted, and Cottle well knew Cumberland's 'readiness to assist in the cause of humanity'. He concludes by demanding if he will *never* see Cumberland at Bedminster. So now the school and business were things of the past, and he and his sister had taken the freehold of No. 1 Carlton Place, Bedminster, a fine house with rather meaner neighbours; it has long vanished, and Carlton Place is simply part of the present North Street, a busy thoroughfare of shops, inns, cinema, works, and churches, all very Victorian and twentieth-century; but Cottle's residence is strangely commemorated by a damaged stone head of Wordsworth set in ugly brick at the first road junction, with the words 'Poets' Corner'. No-one would now seek Bedminster as a rural retreat, and it is hard to imagine it as a village outside Bristol with a tiny church not yet rebuilt or bombed; but it must have been a pretty spot, and even in 1834 Cottle was writing to Southey enthusiastically about his 'cottage',[2] as if he had made a real escape from the trials of the city. The house had every convenience. 'There is an ornamental flower garden in the front of the house, larger I can assure you than your Pocket-hankerchief, with *Dundry* before us, and another flower Garden behind the house, in which stands my Library. Directly behind this garden, separated by iron rails, a Paddock, & large Kitching Garden. But what crowns the whole, as I sit by my fire, with nothing to interrupt, I have a full & delightful view of Tyndle's Park, Brandon Hill, Clifton, & Leigh Woods.' Within a mile of Bristol, he could be 'as retired as a Hermit, alike above the *little* world & eke the *great*.'

So, either through dispute or distance, he ceased to use the Library, and his last borrowings were returned on 15 February 1832. Next, he transferred his religious allegiance to his brother-in-law's new church; the Reverend J.H Good, of Salisbury, was 'called' in the signatures of John and Ann Hare, Joseph and Mary Cottle, twenty-four trustees, and 333 members of the congregation – these members including W. D. Wills the tobacco merchant. (Alas, Mr Good's stay was short, and he had 'a difference of opinion' with Mr Hare, who was even refused by the trustees a pew in perpetuity; the founder ceased to attend there for a while, since the preacher used him on three Sundays as an apt illustration: 'the congregation were pointed to the least amiable of the two characters in the parable of Dives and Lazarus'.[3]) Cottle left Broadmead with its blessing: on 7 December, having desired to be dismissed to Zion, this 'respected Member' of the Independent Paedobaptists was granted a letter of dismission, and Mary was likewise sped on the same day.[4] Their address is given as 'Dighton Street', which suggests that Carlton Place was at first meant as a country home; but it is certain that they were soon clear of the city altogether. Thus by 1833 Cottle was somewhat isolated from the calls even of hardy pedestrians like Foster, and little record survives of what must have been a very quiet year. He visited Foster, with what the latter gratefully calls 'accompaniments', and these called forth a gift in return: in the course of their interminable correspondence on Serampore, Foster mentioned a book that Cottle was to accept, and insisted that he had a duplicate, so that there was no excuse for Cottle's refusing it. He had bought the first copy at one of old Wise's auctions and had recently got the second, as a bargain, so as to give it in acknowledgment to a friend; Cottle seemed to fit the picture best. The book was on botany, and attractive not so much for its subject or its letterpress as for its eminent plates by Redouté; and Cottle must look at the showy sale binding, which might be *called* morocco, though it was probably inferior.[5] In this year, too, Cottle subscribed to an annuity for the educationist Joseph Lancaster. George Cumberland had organized the collection among a few friends, and on 17 December paid the official Bristol collector, Richard Ball of Redland, the sum of £6.10. Cottle is apparently the lowest on the list, with a mere five shillings, but it is a muddled account, certainly not totalling £6.10, and Cottle perhaps gave five *pounds*. (Next year, Cumberland was able to hand on £18.13.6.[6])

By 1834, Cottle, at the age of 64, might well have supposed himself on the threshold of complete retirement in the undisturbed sanctuary of Bedminster. But on 25 July occurred that event, which, in its consequences, would bring him notoriety and the penalties of the law: Samuel Taylor

Coleridge died at Highgate. Cottle joined his 'own inobtrusive sympathies' with those of other old friends, but he felt disturbed by mis-statements circulating in the press and elsewhere;[7] already, it seems, he was being gnawed by a desire to reveal the whole truth as he thought he knew it.

The year brought a family bereavement also, when on 5 August Sarah Saunders died peacefully at her brother's home after six months of illness.[8] (This left only Ann, Mary, Joseph and Robert, who was certainly living in London in 1832.[9]) Cumberland was still calling, and on one occasion missed him through his not being at home. On 26 July Cottle wrote expressing regret, and saying that he was always glad to see Cumberland and to hear of his welfare – and could he again borrow Bishop Cumberland's works (in two volumes, octavo) to refer to? Receiving this note on the same day, Cumberland sent off the two volumes of *Sanchoniatho* immediately. Cottle called on him on 9 September and read the family two or three of Coleridge's letters admitting his opium addiction, wishing to be put under Dr Fox, and blaming Southey for cajoling him into his marriage.[10]

In the autumn, probably early in October, Wade came to see Cottle. He brought a copy of Coleridge's will, and a letter to Wade from 'a Mr Green', an expression which suggests that this was Cottle's first acquaintance with Green – he would live to wish that he had never heard of him. Green was asking for the loan of any Coleridge letters that Wade might have, or that he might obtain from his friends in Bristol. Cottle, of course, had many, especially from the poet's early life, and (perhaps remembering what Croft had done with the Chattertoniana) he would *never* let the originals go, but Green would be welcome to copies, on two conditions: that the Coleridge family approved of him as editor, and that Southey had no such project himself. Cottle had discussed an edition of this sort with others, and all had agreed that Southey was the only person qualified 'to superintend Coleridge's Remains'; further, the work could then bring profit to the unhappy widow and her family (instead, presumably, of benefitting the Highgate end of Coleridge's folk). So Cottle wrote on 9 October and told Southey of the visit,[11] and urged him to the task: after all, biography is 'too uniformly encomiastic. It wants faithfulness.' He was confident that Southey would not put his hero in another world and make him perfect, but would erect a biography both interesting and of '*a very beneficial tendency*', neither omitting his faults nor letting them overshadow his genius; Southey would certainly mention his life as a soldier, and things of that sort, but the edifying part of the narrative would be an analysis of the causes of Coleridge's failure – why he 'tossed about his diamonds, instead of setting them in array.' Cottle realises that Coleridge may have left posthumous works; but it looks as if he preferred the present to the future, and wasted his strength in 'evanescent *conversation*. *Poetry*, not *Philosophy*, was his *natural province*,' but his talents were misdirected. (These words are mildly eloquent of the ability of the Romantic publisher to judge of S.T.C.)

John May had called on Cottle the previous day, 8 October, bringing him Southey's letter about poor Edith's madness. Cottle trusts that 'the mysterious providence ... may prove a blessing'; the affliction may be only temporary, as were Robert Hall's two bouts. Mary Cottle is very sorry, since she is so fond of Edith. Of course, they, too, have had their grief, in the death of Sarah Saunders, and it is a relief to turn to other things – at this point, he begins to disinter Coleridge. In his letter to May, Southey had mentioned bringing his son to Bristol, and Cottle longs to welcome them at Carlton Place, where he has such comforts and so inspiring a view. The journey would do Southey good, and he should come 'in this fine autumnal month. There is no man living whom I should so heartily welcome'. As for himself, his growing infirmities, especially in his '*under*-standing', make him look forward to the Christian change-for-the-better.

Early in 1835 he published a volume *On the Predictions and Miracles of Jesus Christ, with Reference to Sceptics, Infidels, and Socinians, by a Layman*; and the *Congregational Magazine* for August transcribed from it his 'valuable' note on Coleridge. It is clear that he was gathering materials for a life, and on 13 July Cumberland notes in his diary that he 'Sent Mr Cottle Coleridge's letter to Bonucci'.[12] In other ways, too, he was active. In August, his youngest Saunders niece came of age, whereupon they auctioned the family estates of her dead father to very great advantage, getting £4,000 more than the estimated value. A Devon baronet had a sharp engagement in the auction room with one of his own tenants, over the Newland estate; and the tenant won, with £4,510 for what had been valued at £2,700. Cottle was there, and felt so far from a peacemaker that he half wished their strife to continue. As acting executor, he had received and paid everything for the last fifteen years – a further proof of his disinterested charity and of the many claims on his time of retirement. Thus on 1 September all four executors met to audit his numerous accounts and documents, and finished it all in two days. They found neither error in casting nor item amiss, and on 2 September the account was signed in his cash-book by William Prance, Henry Bowden, and Robert and Joseph Cottle.[13] The business of these trustee accounts interrupted a renewed and baleful correspondence with Poole,[14] who kindly received Cottle's nephew and niece on a little tour of North Devon, whence they made for Plymouth and so back to Bristol. As early as September 1834, Poole urged H.N. Coleridge, and *vice versa*, to write a *Life* or something like it. Poole & Green were similarly urging each other in June 1835. Cottle, when applied to, was clearly a last resort.

However much he was bursting to write his account of Coleridge, he affects a coy attitude to the task. The first thing that happened – if we are to believe what he writes to Southey on 22 February 1836 – was that Gillman wrote 'some months before' that date, and asked Cottle to furnish the editor of Coleridge's life and posthumous works with an account of his stay in Bristol. Cottle learnt that this part of the life was a 'chasm', since Coleridge had hardly mentioned it in *Biographia Literaria*; but he felt that he could not give the labour to it, though he had already thought of preparing 'a compendious outline ... of my literary life.' (This is almost an admission that it was vanity which chiefly impelled him.) So he refused Gillman; but he must have refused in such terms, and with such censure of Coleridge, that on 2 November Gillman, induced by 'some expressions' in Cottle's letter, sent to him from Highgate the harrowing report of the autopsy.[15] And, as its sombre words sounded in his compassionate old ears, how could he not forgive *everything* that Coleridge had inflicted on himself and on his friends? Yet, to his shame, he lived to forget, or to underrate, the poignant fact that 'The left side of his chest was nearly occupied by the heart, which was immensely enlarged, and the sides of which were so thin as not to be able to sustain it's [*sic*] weight when raised. The right side of the chest was filled with a fluid enclosed in a membrane having the appearance of a cyst, amounting in quantity to upwards of three quarts, so that the lungs on each side were completely compressed'. Gillman went on to state plainly that this condition, which had begun more than thirty years before, was enough to account for Coleridge's horrible suffering and for his recourse to narcotics; the *Lancet*, on 15 June 1895, added that his 'indolence' had a physical basis, too.[16]

Meanwhile, although Cottle had thought that the matter was over, Poole had written urging him to change his mind, saying that the period must be recorded and that no-one could do it better than he; further, it was to be published for the benefit of Mrs Coleridge. This transaction (diligently revealed to Southey) appears in the 1837 *Recollections*[17] in an elliptical form: 'an influential friend', aware of how well he had known Coleridge, begged him to write a memoir of the Bristol days, but the idea was repugnant to him on account of his years and his health, and of having to borrow letters and pry on others' relations with Coleridge; he therefore declined, but when the same gentleman wrote more insistently, he slowly came round, and the project began to swell. His letter to Southey, however, frankly admits his show of reluctance; his determination shaken, he wrote and told Poole that he would accede if he received a second application, whereupon Poole returned his own answer and two more enclosures, from Gillman and from Green.

On 7 August Cottle wrote to Poole of his plans for a life of Coleridge, and asked for help with the Stowey episode. Some ladies called Cruikshanks had come to live near Firfield House, the residence of the Hares, and had given Cottle's sister, for him, some letters that Coleridge had written to one of their number. Cottle wants to know who they are, since his sister 'hardly knows how to receive them' (and he printed two of the letters in his memoir – one, a *jeu d'esprit*, with the drawing of a metaphysical port-bottle). He has heard from Gillman, but will not be helping him with the loan of letters, despite an earlier promise. He himself will write very fairly and kindly – and, as if by way of self-recommendation, he adds that this month's *Congregational Magazine* has borrowed his note on Coleridge. One thoroughly unpleasant feature of the letter is his request to Poole to show him a copy of a 'faithful' letter that Poole had sent to Coleridge, and Coleridge's 'rather testy' reply; now, on the other hand, Cottle had written to him 'in the *same feeling*, and received from him a long and interesting reply'. That Poole's answer to this, and to other letters, is lost may perhaps be ascribed to an outburst of temper on Cottle's part, since he was normally an assiduous collector of other people's letters. At any rate, Cottle wrote again on 8 September, saying that he had not helped Gillman, out of 'delicacy' towards living persons; but Poole's last letter had rather changed his plans. He had intended simply to link Coleridge's letters to him with a connecting narrative, as in Mason's life of Gray, to be published after his own death, 'when all personal feelings should cease to be violated'. He now felt, however, that the portions of Coleridge's life on which he could speak authoritively might well be illustrated from the letters; but, after having refused Gillman, he did not want to 'manifest such versatility as voluntarily to propose a change' in his resolution, so could Poole ask Gillman to send Cottle 'one line' asking for such a communication? Then Poole would be indirectly responsible for conveying this portion of Coleridge's life to the public. He has some portraits available in his collection – Coleridge, Wordsworth, Southey, Lamb – and he can get Nathan Branwhite (at four guineas) to engrave the Coleridge for a Green-Gillman volume; as it turned out, he used all four for his own volume.

Poole, in growing alarm at what Cottle might do, sent both these letters to H.N. Coleridge, who must already have been afflicted with the same doubts about Cottle's discretion. As nephew, son-in-law and literary executor of the poet, he must have been the chief enemy of all Cottle's schemes, and he replied on 21 September, with a smilingly grim attack on him, and with thanks from all to Poole for 'extinguishing' the publication.

Cottle must let Green have the letters, or copies of them; and he must be told that Coleridge, in his will, entrusted the task of collecting letters to Green. He has one use for Cottle: could Poole ask him for a copy of his best Coleridge portrait, and see to paying him? H. N. Coleridge finally returned the two Cottle letters to Poole on 3 November.

After Gillman's letter of 2 November, concerning the autopsy, Cottle – far from 'extinguished' – replied to him on 1 December, saying that his manuscript was completed and that he would 'now have it copied out fair' (for Green, so Gillman supposed). By the following June it had still not arrived, for the good reason that it had found its way to the press of Cottle's own publisher! The real anguish of the more sensitive Coleridges was heightened at this season by Moxon's publication of Allsop's unworthy book on the poet; the sea must have seemed full of roguish pirates, but, whereas nothing could now be done against Allsop, they felt that they still had time to take measures against Cottle. They had not reckoned with his pious obstinacy; and he was being backed by people like Foster, to whom he sent the manuscript, and who simply *had* to go on with it, although it hurt his eyes. One reason why Foster was grateful for a sight of it was that there was 'no prospect of seeing any large proportion of it in print'. To him, the Coleridge story seemed divinely intended 'to abase the pride of human intellect and genius'. But, of course, the compiler will not admit the very portions – opium letters and awful warnings – which ought to be printed entire, because the compiler can hardly be bent, as is Cottle, 'on doing faithful homage to truth, virtue and religion'. Foster despises biography, 'as the business is commonly managed' (he is here simply expressing the justifiable preference for the Boswell over the encomiast). Foster's encouraging letter of 19 December and Southey's advice combined to make Cottle insist on the verbatim printing of the letters; and it was when this was refused that he decided to throw his 'materials into a separate work'.[18]

On 23 December he wrote to Poole again, in a tone so bland and innocent that he can have known nothing of the worry he was causing. Since receiving Poole's last letter, he has had others from Green and Gillman, 'expressing a somewhat earnest wish' for a Bristol narrative from Cottle's pen; so, for two months, he has been 'throwing' all his old papers into shape – a pretty revelation of his literary method. But, of course, the passage of forty years and the fact that Coleridge rarely dated his letters are hindering him; for the sake of accuracy, he is referring to the very few people who knew Coleridge, and the principal of these is Poole. There follows a list of eight questions referring to Stowey and coming to a climax in the eighth: had Coleridge 'begun the practice of opium, during his residence at Stowey?'

He points out that Poole, in answering these, will be expediting an object which he himself urged Cottle to pursue. In another way, it seems, Cottle had been unhelpful: he had not yet sent H. N. Coleridge a copy of the portrait, since he hoped to submit it through Poole when the latter fulfilled a promised visit to Bedminster. Well, he has two portraits available (Hancock's 1795 profile and Vandyke's 1796 three-quarter face), and Wade is also willing for an engraving to be made of Washington Allston's full-size portrait of 1814; 'good likenesses of so intellectual a countenance taken, respectively, at early and middle life' will greatly improve the intended volume, and Cottle means to write to Green on the matter, but meanwhile Poole must come and judge. – There is a huge postscript – even Cottle, with a slight mis-spelling, exclaims 'What a Postcript!' – about Captain Southey's book on the West Indies. Some years before, Poole had sent Cottle £5 for a copy, and Cottle had decided to give £5 for *his*, also. So, after paying £2.10s. for each of their copies, he held back £5 as a present for the Captain, and wondered how to send it. As it happened, the author came to Clifton with a sick child, and his first call was to ask Cottle to discount a draft for £30, drawn on his London agent; this Cottle did, as Poole would have done, *'without the Jew's discount'*, but it occurred to him that he had 'better defer a little' the £5 gift. The child died, and Captain Southey dropped Cottle a line of the news, whereat he at once sent the £5 without incongruous explanations, meaning to explain next time the Captain called; instead, the Captain acknowledged it by letter and said that he had set off for home that morning. Thus Poole gets no honours, and Cottle seems to have taken all the credit; he has been worried about it, and he promises to do Poole justice when the opportunity arises.

By 22 February he was able to send Southey his MS. draft, along with one letter each from Green and Gillman,[19] all to be returned as soon as possible, after Southey has pencilled out any portions to which he objects, and has also corrected the style of composition – because he is 'a *Veteran* in Prose', whereas Cottle is 'a somewhat Raw Recruit'. Cottle stresses that he did not volunteer for this task, and that Southey has necessarily to be included, 'but, unless the effect be in direct opposition to my intention, you will appear, wherever I have found it necessary to introduce you, in a light highly creditable, without any one shade, from which your maturer views & experience would revolt'. Further, Gillman cannot have the MS. unless he promises not to curtail it. This admission of partiality and this arrogance prejudice us against the work; and there is no doubt that submitting the MS. to Southey conditions what he has to say of Southey. The ostensible motive for Cottle's letter is to enquire about poor Edith, in hopes of some improvement; he and Southey do not correspond often, but their friendship depends on other factors.

He follows these opening sentiments with various trifles, and further encloses three copies (one for Wordsworth and one for de Quincey) of his little work against the Socinians, who have been rampant in Bristol; distinctions between Church and Dissent mean nothing to him, but in the case of the Socinians he respects their humanity and abhors their sentiments – so Southey must tell him whether he has been 'a little too warm'. A reminder of the old days had turned up in Bristol, in the person of a clergyman named Scott, who had been invited to preach in St Werburgh's on behalf of the Serampore translations; he had no friends in Bristol, so Cottle (who had known his father, Scott the Commentator) invited him and his wife to stay for a few days. They were nice people, and Mrs Scott proved to be the niece of William 'Hurricane' Gilbert; she told Cottle of his death and how he had almost raved against Southey for calling him 'mad' in one of his works … Cottle has just finished reading a life of Sir J. Mackintosh, who was with Robert Hall in a Scots university, and whom Hall once praised to Cottle; Mackintosh refers respectfully to Foster, Coleridge, Wordsworth, and Southey, though he actually says that Southey modelled his style on Horace Walpole – a 'Recluse' imitating 'a witty worldling' … Then there is news of the profitable selling-up of the Saunders estate, and a message intended for Tom Southey to explain Poole's share of the £5. And there are some pieces of scandal: the last time Cottle saw Wade, Wade told him that Coleridge had spoken very slightingly of John Morgan and his wife for 'their pride & ignorance'; Cottle concluded that they must have fallen out. Wade has a copy of a 'long & acrimonious' letter from Coleridge to Southey, written at the time of their quarrel; knowing its errors, Cottle has urged Wade to destroy it … The Socinian Dr Carpenter has been violent against the doctrines of the Church: he preached a scandalous funeral sermon on a girl who had turned from his doctrines at her end, and he made a wicked remark from the pulpit against the Atonement. Michael Castle left one child, a daughter, to whom Carpenter was very attentive in her last illness; she died a year ago, and wronged her relatives by leaving him £300 a year … How is Southey's health? Though they are both 'getting on, or rather, *got on* in life', and though he has not yet heard anyone say 'The venerable Mr Cottle', it won't be long if his hair gets much whiter. This leads him to a favourite thesis – the transitoriness of life, its toys, of which they tire, and eternity where all is real. His sight has been better during the last twelve months than for twenty years, a fact which he ascribes to warm camomile tea. His general health is good, though he has so little exercise. Water is his only beverage, and (weather permitting) he takes short rides, so that his face looks healthy and he has survived to 65 after thrice rupturing a blood vessel and being brought nigh to the grave.

Southey acknowledged this letter on 26 February,[20] and said that he now went out of doors only for regular exercise, and kept going by being busy, a daily walk, his 'constitutional buoyancy', the comfort of his children, the feeling that everything possible was being done for poor Edith, and his trust in God's mercy. If Edith had not gone crazy, he would have come to see Cottle in October 1834, with Cuthbert; and, if he is ever able to make a long journey from home, he still hopes to see him. 'If you are not then in a better place than Bedminster' (a present-day visitor might not realise that this is his inept way of saying 'Heaven'), 'I am selfish enough to wish you may stay there till we meet ... I would give a great deal to pass a week with you in this world.' He had called on Robert Cottle, in London, five years before – and Robert did not recognize him, though Southey was the less changed. He asked his brother Henry to call on Cottle some four months ago in Bristol, but Henry, to his regret, could not find him. This letter, with its many literary and other references to Gilbert, James Mackintosh, Wade, John Morgan, Coleridge, Lamb, Cowper, and Wesley, was ridiculously padded out by Cottle in his *Reminiscences* with a bit from a letter of thirteen years before, where Southey would like to show him his correspondence with that bad man Shelley; Cottle, in reporting this, is obviously delighted at the way in which Southey had rebuked the wayward fellow.

By 5 March, Southey had read the draft, and returned it with several passages erased in ink; and Cottle had sufficient awe of him not to publish them. Between receiving and returning the MS., Southey had acquired Allsop's book, and Moxon's letter upon it and upon his motives for publishing it; Southey found it all so hateful, and so unfriendly to Coleridge, that Cottle's account had an unfair advantage, and the arrival of the Allsop perhaps saved the *Recollections* from Southey's pruning and from being a far worthier book. In his covering letter,[21] Southey, along with a wise diffidence about appearing in any monograph on Coleridge, and with a fierce attack on Allsop, supplied a summary of his Pantisocratic days, especially of those before his introduction to Cottle. It is interesting that he puts the long-dead Joseph Hucks and Robert Allen at the very origin of the scheme; and since he expressly mentions that Coleridge had published *The Fall of Robespierre*, and that Lovell and Southey had been slimly published at Bath, before their Cottle period began, it was very wrong of Cottle afterwards to claim to be their first publisher. He wrote to Poole on 12 March, saying that his recollections were finished and that he had had them expurgated by Southey; they were now ready for perusal, so could Poole write and tell him when he is calling?

While the other party prepared their counter-attack, he fumbled on with his inventive research. At the beginning of April, he had a letter from Dr Parry of Bath, who had been with Coleridge at Göttingen; it was to tell him that Dr Carlyon of Truro, who had also been with them, had just come to Bath on his way to London, and had a large and interesting manuscript ready for printing, all about Coleridge in Germany. This Cottle reported to Southey in a letter of 9 April,[22] promising to obliterate the passages scored through in his draft, and asking whether he should insert certain lovely stanzas of Southey's which, as they stand, could be misinterpreted, and which look as if they were Coleridge's.

When a man is famous, he goes on, all his life is bound to come out sooner or later. He would have liked to omit the racy account of the poets' quarrel, but thought it best to mention it, so as to give Southey his own added testimony as an observer. He feels he had good cause for this bias, since he once nearly quarrelled with Coleridge over Southey, and a Coleridge letter of 1795 contained 'some very unwarrantable expressions' which Cottle knew to be unfounded; his opposition quelled repetition of them – to Cottle at any rate, though Coleridge doubtless talked to others. Well, some damaging letter like that may one day appear, so Cottle has 'applied an *antidote*, in anticipation of the *bane*', but he will cut it all out if Southey so wishes.

Having thus charmed Southey's ear, he goes on to undermine Coleridge's status even more toughly: the man had always longed for applause, from *any* source, and thence arose his neglect of old friends, his seeking after new, and his fickleness. Not only had he treated Southey badly, but in 1800 he attacked Cottle (sunk in deep family affliction) 'with downright ferocity', even charging him with the design of 'cheating' Wordsworth out of his *Ballads*. To others he no doubt said the same, and so Cottle has thrown all the Coleridge and Wordsworth correspondence into his memoir, for the whole transaction to be revealed. Again, despite all Poole's kindnesses, Coleridge speaks scathingly of Poole in a letter that Cottle has by him; it remarks that Mrs Coleridge has had a 'paltry' subscription from Poole for Hartley, and hot coals are on her husband's skin until he can send it back without injuring Hartley. After Coleridge's heartlessness of 1800, Cottle 'had determined to give him up', and Amos supported the idea, being disgusted with Coleridge's vanity (though Amos had always liked Southey!); but when Cottle heard that Coleridge was back from Malta, and ill at Poole's, his 'old kind feelings revived', and he invited him to Bristol, 'determined to forget and forgive'.

He has been hesitating about telling Southey the following melancholy story of Coleridge (a fine piece of perfidy, for he had told him all of it in a letter of nineteen years before): herewith he repeats the financial misadventure of the Reverend Mr Porter, with certain changes. In 1814, Porter had subscribed to the lectures, and talked several times to Coleridge, who called on him before leaving for Calne and asked for the loan of £100 for six months, on his promissory note; Porter, anxious to help genius, lent it and took the note. Cottle says that Coleridge knew he could not repay, and that he obviously did not intend to do so. After the six months, Porter applied for the money, but was told to wait six months longer; then he was put off again, and yet again, until he wrote it off as a dead loss. One day the Philosophical Institution wanted Coleridge to give a course of lectures, and as the committee knew that Porter knew Coleridge, they asked him to write the invitation; Porter (by then Rector of St John's) knew that the promissory note might be an impediment, so he sent it back and said he would for ever relinquish his claim. Coleridge wrote back declining the lectures, and said nothing of the cancelled note! So, to the day of his death, Porter thought Coleridge 'little better than a swindler!!' With this £100 Coleridge went on buying opium until 7 March 1815, when he wrote to Cottle begging £30-£40.

Cottle remembers having given Coleridge money and, some time after, a manuscript poem of his own to read over; he promised to give him £10 for doing this, and made no reference to the previous sum. Coleridge gladly accepted the offer, and began reading next morning; but next day he sent Cottle a note 'saying he had a particular call for money', asking for the £10 at once, and promising to finish the MS. without delay. Cottle sent the £10, but no more was read; even for *this*, Cottle forgave him. Indeed, Cottle never refused him money save on the last grim application, when he knew it would go on opium; and he knows that Coleridge always remembered it against him, despite so many past favours, and for his last twenty years neither wrote to Cottle nor sent a remembrance by common friends. 'Never before did I utter a half sentence on this subject, and for *this* perhaps, tomorrow, I shall feel regret.' He has not yet seen the Allsop, but he is grieved that Coleridge should have spoken so disrespectfully of Southey, to whom he was uniquely indebted. A friend of Cottle's talked for two hours with Gillman a few months before Coleridge's death, and Gillman detailed the nasty things that Coleridge was then saying about *Wordsworth*! Cottle, who here appears as the low comedian of the Romantic Comedy, affects to find all this quite beyond him, since he is 'Too humble for Envy, & too retired for notice.' There are only a dozen people in the world who have heard of him, so he is four-fifths dead already – 'This is what I like'. (He little knew that the resurrection-men were lurking for him.) Oh, how opium excluded Coleridge from literary and moral heights! Cottle wants to see Coleridge's posthumous works, but expects little from them: 'C rarely took a *lucid* view of any complex subject, or steadily & *exclusively* pursued it. Opium! Opium! Opium!'

The rest of the letter is more personal. He often wishes he had followed Southey's old advice and written the annals of Bristol, since the city and suburbs teem with interest; 'but all the old oral Chroniclers are dead', his own time for such a task is over, and he is getting his mind ready for eternal things. 'There is *one* subject to which I cannot *again* advert!' (and we may be sure that it is Southey's religious views). P.S. There is a story connected with the verse he sent to Southey, but it will be better suited to conversation – if only they could meet at Carlton Place! How does Southey like Cottle's *Predictions*? How is de Quincey, after eighteen years during which Cottle has heard nothing? Finally comes the assurance that if Southey goes to wars, or is warred on, Cottle will be his 'doughty champion'.

Southey replied promptly on 14 April,[23] in a letter beginning:

> If you were drawing up your recollections of Coleridge for separate publication, you should be most welcome to insert any thing of mine which you thought proper. But in the present case it is my wish that nothing of mine may go into the hands of any persons who are concerned in bringing forward his papers, or repeating what they may have heard from him.

Now hear Curry's absolutely convincing note on Cottle's perfidy in printing this:

> Cottle's shocking treatment of the manuscript, for what appear to be deceptive purposes, is illustrated by his published version of these two sentences: "If you are drawing up your 'Recollections of Coleridge', for separate publication, you are most welcome to insert anything of mine which you might think proper; but it is my wish that nothing of mine may go into the hands of any person concerned in bringing forward Coleridge's MSS."...

Southey's letter to Cottle is very carefully and tactfully worded; he was trying to extricate himself from a difficult situation and, at the same time, to avoid hurting Cottle's feelings. As he wrote it, Southey's first sentence amounted to a polite refusal; and, indeed, Cottle did not use Southey's material on Coleridge in 1837. Cottle tried to make this letter reinforce his statement in the preface to the *Reminiscences* that Southey had encouraged and approved the 1837 *Early Recollections*: 'Mr. Southey, on previous occasions had advised me to write my "Recollections of Persons and Things", and it having been understood that I was about to prepare a memoir of Mr. Coleridge (1836), Mr S. renewed his solicitation, as will appear by the following extracts.' Cottle then printed paragraph 5 out of its context, and its garbled text with the garbling of the first two sentences of the letter of April 14 helped him make his point. At the very time of this letter Cottle had already written his book and submitted the manuscript to Southey. What Southey had encouraged Cottle to write (and still suggested) was an account of his memories of Bristol, anecdotal and topographical. Southey's idea of the sort of book that Cottle might write was elaborately detailed in his letter of December 16, 1804. On March 22, 1831, he again urged Cottle to write about Bristol. Cottle – for his own purposes – has taken a clause from this letter and inserted it into his composite paragraph on p.xi; but if the fifth paragraph is carefully read, it is clear that Southey, by saying 'there is I hope time enough for you to make a very interesting book of your own recollections', is implying that the manuscript of *Early Recollections* is not that work, nor that work by which Cottle might most valuably be employed. Southey may be further suggesting that Cottle still has time to revise his present work into something more in keeping with his talents. Cottle by his mishandling of the manuscripts makes it appear that Southey was encouraging him to write a book which he had already written.

Employed on the Bristol book, says Southey, Cottle will be 'keeping up that habitual preparation "for the Enduring Inheritance" in which the greater part' of his life has been spent; such men as Cottle and Southey, writing sincerely and trying to make others think and feel sincerely, are working as hard in their vocation as if they were composing and delivering sermons. Southey realises 'that Coleridge at different times of his life never let pass an opportunity of speaking ill' of him; latterly too, he had slandered Wordsworth. Both of them had done Coleridge great services; but, whereas Wordsworth was unaware of the duplicity, Southey went on being kind to Coleridge's family long after he had forfeited Southey's friendship. They would both lament the exposure of his treachery, which must ensue if the letters are published.

By this time Poole must have seen the draft, since a letter from him to Southey had arrived by the same post as Cottle's last. Cottle's staggering footnote in his *Reminiscences* glosses him as 'Mr. Poole, who requested it as a favour, came all the way from Stowey to peruse my MS. "Recollections of Coleridge", and who I have good reason to believe, without any unkind intention, communicated a report to *C's relations'*. But (unless Southey is tempering Poole's ire) all Poole said in his letter was that the revelations of opium would less deter others than flatter them into indulging in it, as perhaps in the case of de Quincey. So Southey thinks that the biographer will not use the material that Cottle sends, but will only find excuses for the drug-taking, just as Allsop put it down to the state of Coleridge's chest, whereas 'the much more likely inference is that the excess brought on the disease.' (Cottle, of course, quotes all this advice in his *Reminiscences*, as an excuse for his vain biography, to show that it was Southey's estimable influence that dipped him in ink.) Southey has enjoyed Cottle's *Predictions*, but he cannot forward Cottle's work against the Socinians to the reprobate de Quincey, now lost to him somewhere in Edinburgh. Whenever he can travel, he will come to Cottle in Bedminster, a village which he remembers with deep feeling.

Even if Poole had seen the draft, he must have written rather evasively of it to Green; or else he had not seen it (but had merely discussed Cottle's general plans) by the time that his letter to Green had been passed on to H.N. Coleridge, who wrote again to Poole on 16 April. Poole, he says, must write his own recollections of Coleridge, since he can write more and better on the subject than any other man. H.N. Coleridge has read what Poole wrote to Green, and he and Green entirely agree with Poole and Wade on the 'naked statements and disclosures'. The life must be written whole, and by one man, who will put the story together from the statements of many; Cottle's memoirs will be valuable in any form, and Poole must thank him for them (as Green also intends to do), but surely Cottle will trust 'the honour, zeal and discretion' of Green, to whom Coleridge's will committed this charge.

Cumberland, of course, had to be given a peep at the precious draft, and in his diary on 3 May a list of books 'owed' includes 'Mr Cottle Recols., of Coleridge'.[24] As for Poole, his reaction to its perusal in Cottle's presence was flattering enough: having 'come all the way from Stowey', he read it approvingly, kept commending the writing, and said at the end, 'This is the only long MS. I ever read, or heard read, without yawning'. He did, however, object to one part – curiously, the letter in which Coleridge asked for the opium story to be published. This is Cottle's version of the interview, in his letter to Poole of 15 June. Poole, writing back on 19 June, merely says that he 'did not for a moment disguise' his sentiments about (it seems) the whole course of the drug-addiction and the letters written under its influence. Still, he admits that one other big doubt rose in his mind afterwards: on leaving Cottle's, he rushed round to Wade's, and urged Wade to join him in persuading Cottle to suppress the letter, and 'on very little consideration' it also occurred to him that de Quincey's gift ought not to be revealed either, unless with the consent of Coleridge's representatives and of de Quincey himself. After all, would a sensitive genius ever accept a gift from anyone, without making sure that it was not to be publicized?

Cottle, after this amiable interview, sent Poole on 18 May an innocuous-looking letter asking for advice: he just wanted Poole and Green to decide what could best be done with his narrative. Should it be given to Green, on condition that he published it entire? Or should it be published by Cottle with no mention of any communication between them, and ultimately quoted by Green in his own volume? Cottle thought that no upright mind would find these proposals unreasonable. But the next few weeks showed him that one party, at least, was out of the perpendicular. Poole was very busy when this letter arrived, and had not time to copy it; perhaps by reading the post mark instead of the dating, he calls it Cottle's letter of 20 May,[25] which was presumably also the date when he 'at once enclosed it' to H.N. Coleridge 'in a short letter stating the substance verbatim as nearly as I could recollect of what I had said to you [Cottle] in reply to that letter of the 20th May.' Whatever can this mean? If he *at once* sent it to H.N. Coleridge, how could there be any difficulty in his recollecting his own reply to it? Whatever he sent, its effect on H.N. Coleridge was emphatic. He saw Green on the subject, and they agreed to wait until Monday or Tuesday, 6–7 June, when Derwent Coleridge, one of the principal sufferers, would be in town. Meanwhile, the two of them felt it best to ask Poole, in H.N. Coleridge's hurried letter of 31 May, to write to Cottle and tell him two facts: that he had informed Green and the Coleridges pretty precisely of the nature of Cottle's narrative, and that 'their sentiments upon the matter in question would be communicated to him' early in the following week. H.N. Coleridge was inexpressibly afflicted 'at Cottle's unthinking and ruthless vanity', and, having no hope of crushing the whole work, would at lest try to have the 'wretched details' excised. Poor Poole complied with the request by writing to Cottle on 4 June, warning him that not only Coleridge's reputation, but that of his family, was held to be affected, and that they would be writing to him. Cottle, for the first time, may have been seriously alarmed: 'This conjoint Family Letter, I rather anxiously awaited, imagining what its contents would probably be, and determining, as far as possible, to make every sacrifice to the feeling of Coleridge's Family, not incompatible with *Truth*'. It is just possible that he was ready to repent, for the sake of Sara, whose misalliance he had helped to precipitate, and of Hartley, whose infant form he had dandled; and a pleading letter might have stifled him. But what *did* arrive turned his head and heart for ever, bringing out the worst in his obstinacy and self-righteousness. It was a letter neither from the Coleridges nor from Green, but from Gillman, writing in stern anger at Highgate on 8 June. Cottle found it 'rude, and ungentlemanly', but it was sadly deserved. Gillman reminded him of his wavering resolution, his prejudice about the opium, the real knowledge available to him (from Gillman's own report) of the true state of Coleridge's body, and his broken promise to send his narrative to Green. In planning to publish the letters, Cottle is showing himself ignorant of the law: 'In the case of Murray versus Dallas, it was ruled by the Lord Chancellor, that property in Letters is not the property of the possessor, but where there is a Will that of the Executor'; and, as soon as Cottle publishes, able lawyers have advised that there can be an injunction against him. His 'conduct admits of no *delicacy*, and in such a case, Executors and Trustees have no choice'; so he had better hand over the letters, or copies of them.

We know, from Poole's letter to H.N. Coleridge on 1 September, that Gillman wrote this on a personal impulse, and that neither Green nor H.N. Coleridge was aware of his writing it. In fact, both Green and Derwent Coleridge wrote letters to Cottle, which must have been more carefully composed, and from which he should have gathered that they were not so deeply in the plot as Gillman. But he did not answer them, and he did not even tell Wade, who occasionally saw him, that he had received them. It is probable that he mistrusted Wade, who, on hearing the manuscript read, warned him that he would be ridiculed for all his egotism in it, by which he meant the record of 'every little kindness' to the needy. The mistrust was reciprocated: E.L. Griggs reminds us that Wade's letter to H.N. Coleridge of 26 September 'shows that Cottle misrepresented the facts in order to obtain possession of Coleridge's letters to Wade'.[26] Nor did he answer Gillman. Instead, he gathered all his fury and vented it on Poole, in a huge letter of 15 June. It begins 'Sir', ends with a mere signature, and is rich in exclamation marks and underlinings. He is in a towering rage at the unfairness of Poole, who, he argues, must have misrepresented to the Coleridges the contents of the manuscript and the reasonable proposals contained in his letter of 18 May: for how else could they have gleaned their material for Gillman's 'vulgar and bullying' letter? So Poole must have moved away 'from Coleridge's old and steady friends, who have proved their friendship by something more substantial than words', and has compacted with the newer group who are planning a literary lie, 'to cheat the *Public* with a *Life* of Coleridge, which is no *Life*'. Cottle will not thus temporize; he has done justice to Coleridge, and has 'set an example of what Biography *ought to be* –

a faithful exhibition of *the man*, not a stream of undeviating Eulogy'. Those who are now clamouring to hide the facts are unwilling to admit that Coleridge in his agony was ever helped by strangers, sometimes at great hardship to themselves, when his relatives deserted him (so much for H.N.'s father!). Cottle, faced by Gillman's *volte-face* from obsequiousness to insolence and impotent threats, will *not* conceal the opium-taking, or the gift from the now fallen de Quincey, or that '*redeeming*' letter in which Coleridge asks for his addiction to be made public – 'a letter which propitiates the Reader, and converts *condemnation* into *compassion*'. When Poole argues that publication will inspire perverse imitation, he is as good as suggesting that no felon should be punished for fear 'others should be stimulated to taste the sweet luxury of getting *hanged*' (Cottle's wit at its feeblest). The new group remind him, in their attitude, of what Robert Lovell said of Chatterton, 'When living starved, and when dead adored'. He will have no more communication with Green or Gillman or any Coleridge; as for Poole, it is obvious – from his running with hare and holding with hounds, from his courteous words to Cottle and his inflammatory promptings to the rest – that he has 'deteriorated' since their last meeting 38 years ago, and Cottle neither expects nor wants to hear from him again, though his 'good wishes will continue'! The harm that Gillman's letter had done is then admitted in the first postscript: 'Mildness might have produced some effect, but I have been attacked on a side where I am invulnerable'. The second postscript admits that Green sounds a worthy editor of what will, after all, be Coleridge's real monument; but Cottle goes on to develop again a kind of proof that Coleridge meant to have his 'confessional letters' published. Gillman, in claiming that Coleridge '*abhorred* Opium', and that his physical suffering preceded it, speaks as justly as if he said 'that the Sun's rays are *dark*'; he should imitate the sensible attitude of Crabbe's son to his father's addiction … 'I am fighting the Battle of the Public.'

Poole, who had not heard from the Coleridge circle, was genuinely astonished at receiving this token of rage. He had known nothing of Gillman's letter, and now he must have perceived that it had turned Cottle from a vain author, hoping to gain some money from a unique little book, into a self-elected prophet. He put a note on it – 'a curious letter... No man can be more wrong' – and answered it very temperately on 19 June. He gave Cottle no salutation at all, and made it plain that Cottle's argument from Gillman's letter was quite fallacious. He then outlined his treatment of Cottle's letter of 18 May, and honestly reiterated his grave objections to the disclosure of the opium and of the de Quincey gift. He added that he was as surprised as the others when Cottle did not transmit the promised draft, and still held that Cottle should cast his work into two parts – one relating to Coleridge, and the other to other matter. Obviously, Poole was not the man to wish to continue this quarrel: he trusted that Cottle would now feel milder towards him, and even excused himself for writing contrary to Cottle's *'expectation or desire'*. Indeed, he would have written more fully, but he had arranged to come to Bristol on Wednesday next, 22 June, to be godfather to the son of his nephew Richard King on the following day; so, unless he found a note from Cottle at 2 Redcliff Parade, declining to receive him, he would call on Wednesday evening or soon after 9 on Thursday morning, in the hope of convincing Cottle that their twenty-three (?) years' friendship 'ought not to be given up for the groundless suspicion of an hour'. They could start calling each other 'my dear Sir' again.

But the note was waiting for him. Cottle timed it nicely, on the 21st, and while he apologized for his unfounded 'surmizes', and begged Poole's pardon for the hasty affront, he remained quite uncompromising about the two crucial points. They differ on these, they have written to this effect, and they are not given to changing their minds, so verbal discussion will achieve nothing but pain. Cottle will not be at home at the time proposed, and Poole can save himself the trouble of calling. And then, weakly, Cottle adds, 'On your *next* visit to Bristol, it will give me much pleasure to see you. My respect for you is undiminished'.

There the matter had to rest, and Poole postponed any further action until he could see Cottle personally. But meanwhile others were becoming involved: Foster (on the side of Truth), and a newcomer into Cottle's literary life, the peripatetic bibliophile, Henry Crabb Robinson. He came into Cottle's orbit through a chance meeting with Charlotte, one of the Saunders nieces, who in July of this year married the Reverend David Thomas, minister of Zion. Her sister Sarah was the celebrated correspondent, in her last illness, of John Foster, whose letters to her were so like essays that they were published; and Charlotte herself was dead of consumption within a year. But when Crabb Robinson had the young couple as travelling-companions on 10 August, they seemed 'very sensible & interesting',[27] being familiar both with Coleridge and with books about him. Thomas told Robinson the story of Cottle's conditional offer to Gillman, and Gillman's threatening reply; and, since Robinson was trying to help Talfourd with his similar work on Lamb, Thomas added that Cottle had some of Lamb's letters and would be willing to hand them over. Robinson seems to have introduced himself by letter, and was soon calling.

About this time, Foster wrote to Cottle with encouragement and a warning.[28] He knows that Cottle will not have been surprised when they rejected the essential part of his biography, or at their change of tone; and Cottle has apparently steeled himself to incurring their rancour, knowing that his work will do good and be honest. On the other hand, Cottle must make sure, by professional advice, that they cannot sue him, because that could be a costly business; there are a Judge Coleridge and a Bishop Coleridge, who might prove big and indignant enemies. Foster knows nothing, save for the judgment in the case of Pope v. Curll, relevant to the legal decision which Gillman mentions. He would have suggested an expurgation, but now realises that the contents of a letter cannot be altered in that way (*O si sic Cottle!* – no letter was sacrosanct to *him*); but if the book is published locally, that will at least somewhat shield him from malice and the law. Charlotte Saunders must have domesticated with Cottle, for Foster here hopes that her adventure may prove happy, though it is a pity for Cottle and his sisters; Foster was pleased to see their young friends in London 'well and happy'.[29]

The late summer brought Cottle further friendship. On 16 August Southey wrote from Keswick,[30] promising to come to Cottle's whenever he could, with 'unabated friendship' and bringing Cuthbert, so as to show the boy the scenes of his own boyhood and youth. At the same time he told Cottle of his publishing plans, but had no good news of poor Edith. The promise of a visit was fulfilled by November, and the hope of Southey's presence no doubt confirmed Cottle in his resolve.

Poole made a last attempt to speak reason with him. At the end of August there was a meeting of the British Association at Bristol, which Poole was attending, so he postponed his visit until then; and, by now not trusting correspondence in dealing 'with such a publishing gentleman', he wrote nothing to H.N. Coleridge until 1 September, when his stay was over and he could report in full what little there *was* to report. The morning after he arrived at Bristol, he called at Carlton Place, and had to wait a little until Mary Cottle returned home and said that Joseph was too unwell to see him, being abed 'with a blister on for the relief of his eyes'. Poole told her he was sorry about this; he would be in Bristol for the week, and a note to King's, where he was staying, would bring him to Cottle at any hour of any day. During the week, he called at his friend Jack Pritchard's, and there met the elderly widow of the Reverend J.P. Estlin. She told him 'in a large party' the rumour that Coleridge's friends were going to prosecute Cottle if he published, and Poole admitted that the 'differences of opinion' were some basis for the report. But he had no note from Cottle, and on the day before he left the city he called on their 'simple hearted very different friend Wade', and begged him to see Cottle with a view to exculpating Poole and Green and H.N. and Derwent. Wade promised to see Cottle at once, and to report all the explanation that Poole had given him, and Poole resolved that, if he did not hear from Cottle soon, he would write to him. We do not know whether either applied to the other again. The aggrieved Cottle may have done some tearing-up, or perhaps Poole finally repudiated him. At all events, Cottle went on reminiscing in his own way.

1   *Cumberland Papers*, British Museum MS.Add.36513, Vol.XXIII (1831-1835), fol.180.

2   Letter of 9 Oct. 1834, in Bristol City Library MS.B 20877.

3   H.B. Cozens, *op.cit.*, pp.21-29.

4   *Broadmead Records, Records of the Independent Church ...*, 1830-1853, fols.12-13, 14-15, 22.

5   Bristol City Library MS.B 20878, n.d., unsigned.

6   *Cumberland Papers*, British Museum MS.Add.36521 H (Diary for 1833), fol.545v, and I (Diary for 1833), fol.582v.

7   *R*.47, pp.viii-ix.

8   Letter from Cottle to Southey, 9 Oct. 1834, in Bristol City Library MS.B 20877.

9   Letter from Southey to Cottle, 26 Feb. 1836, in *R*.47, pp.401-402.

10 British Museum MS.Add.36513, Vol.XXIII, fol.280; 36521 I, fols.598r and 604v.

11 Bristol City Library MS.B 20877.

12 British Museum MS.Add.36521 J (1835), fol.661v.

13 Bristol City Library MS.B 20877; letter from Cottle to Southey, 22 Feb. 1836 (which also gives Cottle's account of his early dealings with Poole and Gillman).

14 Much of this vast interchange of letters survives in the Poole Correspondence of British Museum MS.Add.35344, Vol.II.2.p., fols.122-131 and 204-218. Warren E. Gibbs, in *Publications of the Modern Language Association of America*, XLIX (1934), pp.208-228, prints it in part, with a commentary, though he sometimes gives Vol.II as Vol.I.

15 Lucy E. Watson (née Gillman), *Coleridge at Highgate* (London: Longmans, 1925), pp.27 ff.

16 The various reports are well presented in Griggs, VI.992n-993n.

17 pp.ix ff.

18 *R*.47, pp.481-482.

19 Bristol City Library MS.B 20877.

20 Curry, II.441-444; utterly mangled in *R*.47, pp.401-402.

21 Curry, II.444-448, and (incorrectly) *R*.47, pp.402-407 (which even alters the date to 6 March). Curry's excellent note (II.444n-445n) is needed as a

corrective to Cottle's statements, and perhaps even to some of Southey's nonplussed remarks in such a letter as this.

22 Bristol City Library MS.B 20877.

23 Curry, II.449-452. Here Cottle's editing (R.47, pp.407-409) rises to a terrible crescendo, as detailed in Curry's note.

24 British Museum MS.Add.36521 K (1836), fol.708v; the wording of the entry is doubtful.

25 The letter is lost; I have accepted the date quoted in a letter of 15 June by Cottle, who, after all, wrote it – but even *he* mentions it in the same letter twice as '18th' and once as '10th'.

26 Griggs, III.511n.

27 Edith J. Morley, *Henry Crabb Robinson on Books and their Writers*, 3 Vols (London: Dent, 1938), II.499.

28 Bristol City Library MS.B 20878.

29 Robert's family, or Sarah's? The rest of the letter is mutilated.

30 R.47, pp.409-410.

Chapter 15

Crabb Robinson: Landor: Recollections

However ill Cottle was in this last week of August 1836, he and Mary received Crabb Robinson when he called on the morning of the 29th.[1] They were expecting him, and were ready to show him every attention, but he resisted their invitation to dine. He found the house comfortable, albeit 'in a low neighbourhood'. As for Cottle himself, Robinson already knew that his nickname, even among his own friends, was 'The Regicide', on account of his treatment of King Alfred; but he formed a good opinion of him. He was an older man than Robinson, club-footed and otherwise lame, so that he had to walk with crutches; his face was good and 'by no means … sanctimonious'; his speech had a not unpleasing simplicity; everything about him had 'an air of neatness, not gentility'. Robinson thoroughly enjoyed the morning, and after 'several hours' was eager to see more of him. But in one respect Cottle proved a little difficult. He soon showed Robinson his collection of little portraits – all, he assured him, excellent likenesses – and that of Lamb was so attractive that Robinson asked for the loan of it on behalf of Talfourd. At first Cottle seemed to consent, but then retracted and said that the Bristol painter Branwhite would make a fine copy of it for two guineas. (Robinson was less impressed by the larger portraits of Wordsworth, Coleridge, and Southey.) Again, Cottle said he was willing to give Talfourd any of his letters from Lamb, but it then appeared that he had mislaid his papers, and could find none of them. Most of their conversation, however, concerned the *Recollections*, and Robinson gave both advice and backing: he read Cottle's preface, with its account of the behaviour of Coleridge's executors, and recommended him not to print it; but in the matter of the two points he was firmly on Cottle's side, and furthermore doubted whether Gillman's threats had any real basis. As he saw it, 'the supposed property of executors in their testators' letters has been much too broadly stated'; also, it was absolutely certain that Coleridge had meant the principal letter to be published as a warning, and Cottle had not merely a right, but a duty, to announce de Quincey's youthful generosity. Cottle must have been gratified by the attitude of Robinson, who wanted the opposition to be treated with silent

Henry Crabb Robinson at the age of 86: engraving (from a photograph) by William Holl (in the possession of Martin Crossley Evans)

contempt, and who found nothing of merit in their actions save that Green 'wrote civilly'. Afterwards, Cottle's 'very valuable collection of autographs' was brought out, and the morning passed pleasantly. Robinson returned to spend the evening with them, and 'had an agreeable chat'. He felt that he had done Cottle a service by strengthening his resolve against the Coleridge faction.

On 5 September he visited Cottle again, and had another interesting talk. Cottle showed him a long theological letter from Coleridge attacking 'the idea of an eternity of suffering', and a much weaker letter to a lady in which he tried to tell her that his sonnet to Lord Stanhope was just ironical, just exaggerated Jacobinism; and Cottle remarked that Coleridge's 'anxiety to stand well with the lady disturbed his memory!' Cottle also read him the letter from Coleridge praising Wordsworth's 'absolutely wonderful' tragedy. Yet he appeared to Robinson 'an uncertain man': Robinson had decided on getting Branwhite to engrave the Lamb portrait, when Cottle again changed his mind and said he would be using it himself.

On 10 September, Robinson noted in his diary that he was 'first writing a short letter introducing Moxon to Cottle': Moxon was off to Bristol, and Robinson left this note with him in the hope that he would be luckier in getting material out of Cottle. Two days later, he wrote to Wordsworth also,[2] with an account of his visit to Bristol to introduce himself 'to that most worthy of regicides' (a joke which Wordsworth and Coleridge also shared). Though Cottle had produced nothing for Robinson, he had at least promised to send some material to Talfourd. Robinson here supports Cottle in his plans, and gives Wordsworth an outline of Cottle's fearless honesty, his generous offer to the conspirators, Gillman's insolence, and the four portraits intended as illustrations – including one of Wordsworth, if he consents. Robinson feels sure that Wordsworth will find little to disapprove of in the finished volume.

In addition to such advocacy, and despite Cottle's close clutching of his treasures, Robinson quietly did him another favour: he induced Talfourd to suppress that brilliant letter in which Lamb ridiculed Joseph on the occasion of the mourning for Amos. This was indeed kind of Robinson, who was certainly not above being amused by Cottle's muse: in 1808, he and Amyot had laughed together at the lines from *Malvern Hills* about 'the evidence of close deduction'. Moxon had called on Cottle before 1 October, when Robinson noted the fact in his diary. Apparently the *Recollections* was to be published by Cadell (though it was finally undertaken by Longman). Cottle had made it clear to Moxon that he had been delighted with Robinson's visit, and he also said that his book had Southey's approval. But a letter from

Southey to Cottle on 30 September[3] sounds suddenly cautious. The Coleridge family, says Southey, are uneasy at the intended publication, and yesterday one of their distinguished members, the Judge, told him the two specific and oft-reiterated objections. (Cottle quite wickedly prints this letter as if it were the first intimation of the family upheaval: 'It appears, from the following letter, that the family of Mr Coleridge felt uneasy'.) Southey seems to join them in their 'most uncomfortable position', since he does not deny that there are many things which anyone with 'any regard for [Coleridge's] memory would wish to be buried with him'; he will discuss it all with Cottle when they met, and meanwhile he has assured the influential Judge Coleridge that Cottle's feelings about his imperfect hero are, as always, 'friendly in the highest degree'. Southey and Cuthbert will come and stay in Bedminster some time after 17 October. He ends with an expression of his anguish at Edith's present hopeless state and of his urgent need for a period of refreshment to equip him for a renewal of his ordeal. The long and varied holiday in the South-West which he soon gave himself sounds well suited to his purpose.

His letter reached Bedminster on the morning of 2 October, and the delighted Cottle at once wrote welcoming him and his son Cuthbert,[4] who would have so much to see, and insisting that they stay a fortnight at least, not a week. He has found some more Coleridge letters, but otherwise the memoir is the same as when Southey saw it, and it ought to be out by Christmas. Tediously, he again reiterates the half-truths of his motives – how he offered the manuscript to the executors as a free gift, how they did not accept, and how Gillman laughably threatened legal action: 'This at once decided me. Mine is a faithful, & at the same time, a favourable account of S.T.C.'. They must talk more of this when they meet; but those who have read the work find it very interesting. He goes on to ask permission to print two letters from Spain and Portugal, and to include an engraving of Southey. He also sends regards from Mary, and regards to Wordsworth, with the hope that he, too, will allow his portrait to appear. As soon as the Cottles know by what coach the Southeys are coming, their 'Car' will be waiting to bring the visitors out to Bedminster.

Cottle must have been very happy and excited, but the succeeding days brought trouble. Southey wrote far more gravely on 10 October,[5] after an interview with the Head of the Family: John Taylor Coleridge, the elder brother of H.N. Southey not only found him 'thoroughly good ... mild, unassuming, amiable, and judicious', but also realised that there was something to be said for respecting the family feelings, not roused by the 'gross and wanton insult' of Allsop, but now deeply moved. This he said to

Cottle pretty plainly, urging that the book would suffer little from the omission of what would give so much pain; he added the wicked whisper that Cottle was 'not like a witness who is required to tell all which he knows'. Southey obviously wanted the opium letters to go, and lamely offered to read over the memoir when they met, and then perhaps many other things might 'come to mind' instead. He is sure that Cottle will understand his motives in pressing this upon him.

Cottle claims that his first reaction to this was 'wholly to *withdraw the work*'; and then he decided to wait until he could discuss it with Southey. It is difficult to believe this: the publisher in him must have realised that he was 'on to something good', that the opium would sell the book. We shall soon see how little Southey's gravity affected him. 'We shall soon see', indeed, wrote Robinson to Mary Wordsworth on 27 October,[6] 'what Cottle will make of C's youth'. Moxon, on his visit, had been given to understand that Southey had read and approved of the account: 'If so nothing wrong will come from that quarter'. Hartley Coleridge was not so sanguine, and wrote to his mother from 'Rotha Some place', on 28 October,[7] with his views on the subject of his father's biography. In his indolent, grinning way he utters real venom: 'I am provoked that you should be tormented by this evocation of evil spirits by D.Q., Cottle, Allsop and Co. – though I cannot say I feel much anger at any but the first – the rest may plead idiocy and dotage in their defence.' (She was lucky; Cottle might have put out the story of her inadequacy, or – if he knew it – of the other Sara.) Hartley seems here to forget that Cottle helped him into University.

Mary Wordsworth, though less involved, sounds more worried, in her reply to Robinson on 1 November.[8] She says that the Wordsworths are always delighted to follow him on his excursions and that his Bristol visit was especially interesting. She and Dora felt they were really with him in 'Cottle's Sanctum', where, seven or eight years before, they had been shown the precious collection of portraits. As for that 'benevolent Regicide's' forthcoming book, she emphasizes that he *has* been disingenuous: 'If Southey saw all the M.S. he could not & does not approve'. The story is too long and intricate for her, but William will tell him all about it. Judge Coleridge showed William letters proving that Cottle was determined to publish 'the objectionable matter' *before* getting Gillman's letter, which *he* afterwards said had motivated him. Well, Southey will be seeing Cottle soon, on his tour. She hopes that Robinson will succeed in detaching Lamb's letters from Bristol: she had rather see them in Talfourd's hands 'than left to the mercy of C'.

The promised visit drew near, and on Tuesday, 1 November, Southey wrote from Pipe Hayes, north of Birmingham.[9] They had booked seats in the coach leaving the Hen and Chickens, Birmingham, on Thursday morning, but Southey had not enquired at what Bristol inn it arrived in the evening; so if they did not find Cottle's vehicle when they reached Bristol, they would at once pack themselves and their luggage into a hackney-coach and come out to Carlton Villa. He had obtained Wordsworth's permission for the portrait, save that Southey was to decide whether it was a good enough likeness. Thus they arrived on the evening of 3 November, and gratified Cottle's wish by staying until Saturday the 12th. There must have been plenty to talk about, but they first of all got down to business, and Southey re-read the manuscript. If we are to believe Cottle's report,[10] Southey 'objected alone to a few trifles, which were expunged', interdicted no part of the opium letters, and distinctly said that the 'testamentary' letter to Wade must be printed as Cottle's authority for what he had done. In fact, he so enlarged on the merits of this course that his approval determined Cottle 'to publish the whole of the opium letters'. So it sounds as if Southey's closing counsel did more harm than good. But where, alas, is the real truth of this sorry story to be found? Within nine months Southey was writing of the book with scorn and censure.

Throughout the visit, Southey was as kind and cordial as ever, and cheerfully upbraided Cottle for not having visited Greta Hall, where he could have explored the district, sailed on the lake in *Royal Noah*, and seen the Southey library of 14,000 volumes, which needed only 500 more to make it complete in its master's eyes.[11] Cottle showed him 'Old Holly', the stick which Southey had borrowed in 1795, and which had perhaps saved his life.[12] Cottle's infirmity probably denied him the pleasure of Southey's company when the latter walked out. For instance, Southey went alone to the old manor-house of Bedminster, where his grandmother had lived and where he himself had spent so many happy young hours, and the new tenants readily allowed him to 'renew his acquaintance with the old trees' which he had once climbed.[13] He and his son likewise went alone to Bedminster Church on Sunday, 6 November '(for the Cottles are dissenters)'. The sextoness placed him in the churchwardens' pew, and he remembered its atmosphere, despite repairing and re-seating, from 55 years before.[14] All that he recalled has long since been rebuilt, and even its successor has been destroyed by bombs. During his stay, he accepted no invitations save to breakfast, since he was a mile and a half from Bristol and needed his evenings for work;[15] and throughout his holiday, although he was well and in good spirits, he was looking forward to returning home, since he was sleeping no better and was missing his after-dinner nap, which was now his soundest sleep.[16]

One of his callers was the local admirer of genius, John Dix (father of Chatterton Dix the hymnographer), who one evening lifted Cottle's knocker, in some trepidation at the thought of Southey's rumoured 'coldness'. Cottle had invited him to meet the great man, and he was shown into the little parlour, where a couple of other people – and, of course, young Cuthbert – were also visiting. Tea was soon announced, and was presided over by the host's beloved sister Mary, who poured out 'the well manufactured infusion of Congou' and addressed Southey as 'Doctor'; he begged her to call him 'Mr Southey' or 'Robert', as she had done *lang syne*, for he disliked his new title among old friends. There was a pleasant hour of talk: on Byron ('a ticklish subject' for Southey and Cottle, Dix points out); on Cowper (Southey called his edition of the poems a task of 'Coopering', proved that the name was not pronounced *Cowper*, and read them a Cowper letter he had just discovered); and on a forthcoming meeting of the British Association (which Southey was going to shun, since he egotistically avoided crowds). His characteristic attitude was to lie back in his chair, keep his elbows on the arms, and stroke the insides of his eyebrows with his forefingers, his eyes shut save when he was speaking. For Dix, the visit led to a friendship with him: they called on the Bishop together, and corresponded after Southey's return.[17]

One of the most promising features of Southey's holiday was that he saw much of Walter Savage Landor, who was then living at Penrose Cottage (in Harley Place, by Christ Church, Clifton), and with whom Cottle must also have become acquainted at this time, since by 28 April 1837 he was forwarding a parcel from Landor to Southey. On 12 November Southey left Bristol for ever, and made his way to Bremhill (in Wiltshire) to see Bowles.

At last, early in 1837, Longman, Rees & Co. and Hamilton Adams & Co. published, in London, in two volumes, the *Early Recollections, Chiefly Relating to the Late Samuel Taylor Coleridge, During his Long Residence in Bristol*, and the storm was ready to break. The book had been held up while its illustrations were prepared, but they were worth waiting for; the engraver, R. Woodman, did his work well, though he had not always kept his promises to Cottle. As soon as they were ready, Cottle began distributing copies to his friends: two to Southey on 28 April, one to Wordsworth on the 29th. His covering letter to Southey[18] says that the extra copy is for Cuthbert; or let them give it to a friend, and he will then send Cuthbert another. Conscious though he is of the risk of offending as well as pleasing, he understands that there may be a second edition, which he will improve with Branwhite's Southey and with a portrait of Landor (the latter must have come into Cottle's life too late to be incorporated, but Cottle now knew him well enough to boast of him, and he would presumably have been given a digression in any new edition). Southey must correct the work frankly, and judge whether the bits about Byron and Amos should stay. Cottle is anxious over the sale, since the engraving has been costly; Peace, the City Librarian, says that he will eat any remainders, so Cottle has wished him a good appetite and digestion. He encloses all the books (Bristol purchases, possibly) which Southey left in his care, others that Southey had sent on to him *en route*, a parcel from Landor, and an engraving of the Southey portrait worked off on large French paper. He did his best for Southey's November holiday, and he will do better next time – but let it be in the summer, in fairness to this unequalled neighbourhood; Ann Hare will welcome Southey and his daughters at Firfield. He had hoped for a letter during Southey's excursion, but realises that Southey was busy with reading and other things. He keeps laughing over Southey's story of George Dyer's mistaking New River for a green field, and walking into it; and at the even funnier one of George's feeling at the point of death and summoning his two daughters, who found him tucking into beefsteak and porter, an anecdote which had reached Cottle from Lamb *via* Coleridge, and which he recorded as far as mirth would let him. The Bishop of Bristol told Peace that he was sorry to have been engaged when Southey called on him, and he had meant to call on the day that Southey left Bristol (can this mean that the Bishop would really come out to Cottle's modest villa?). The family are very afflicted by the health of their dear niece Mrs Thomas, who is now gravely ill: she caught a cold in the autumn, developed a pain in her side, and was then leeched, bled and blistered until she was in 'infantine weakness'. Cottle, as one of the uninitiated, is suspicious of the eight dozen leeches in three months, applied to a delicate young woman; he prays to be delivered from 'Fire, Famine, Pestilence, Slaughter, and *Doctors*'. In a P.S., he asks for approval of his omitting a Southey poem whose sentiments are Southey's no longer, thanks him for his *Lives* of Essex and Raleigh, and refers him to a note in *Malvern Hills*. Mary sends her kind regards.

In his letter to Wordsworth on 29 April,[19] Cottle begs him to accept a copy of the book, and to send him any hints for its improvement, in case there be a second edition. Wordsworth will see that *he* has been mentioned uniformly with respect. But how have the mentions of Amos and Byron 'operated' on his mind? And does he think Cottle has gone too far in his disclosures of Coleridge? Much has been withheld, in deference to the family. 'I have understood from one source and another', he goes on, that, in the latter periods of Coleridge's life, he occasionally spoke and wrote of you, in a way, not exactly conformable with what might have been expected from his previous declarations. This information gave me *great pain*, and marked the want of stability in C's mind, which was, in him, I am afraid, rather a prominent peculiarity; so often is interwoven, the good and the defective, in the human mind! This circumstance occasioned me to be the more particular in transferring into my pages every reference in Coleridge's letters of an *opposite tendency*.

Wordsworth's mind, as he reads, will perhaps be moved by the recollection of these distant happenings, by which Cottle's own mind is even more sharply affected. Isn't life odd? It seems to him a kind of 'tumultuous dream', and few alive are really awake enough to direct their thoughts, as befits, wholly to the eternity ahead, when nothing matters save whether they are Christians, and where he hopes for no bliss in which his friends cannot participate; Wordsworth must pardon this 'salutary' hint. Cottle and his sister Mary wish to be remembered to Mrs Wordsworth and Dora, with hopes that the latter has now fully recovered. Should they or Wordsworth ever be in Bristol again, Cottle's villa is waiting for them, and his heart would 'bound' to see his old friend. But Cottle has heard the sombre news of Dorothy's madness; 'she was a great favourite' of his, and if she still remembers him, he sends her his love, and 'May God bless her!'

Southey wrote one of his last letters to Cottle on 9 May[20] (though it got 'buried' in his desk, and was not posted until the 15th), saying that he thought of him every day and that, of course, his last correction of *Joan* had brought Cottle more and more to mind. His journey, after leaving Cottle's 'comfortable house', was quite fortunate, and he and his son had much enjoyed their holiday, though only Cuthbert's pleasure had been unmixed with pain. His 'poor Edith manifested no emotion of any kind' at his return. Southey's mention at this point of his 'friend Miss Bowles' marks the beginning of Cottle's long acquaintance with her, during which he was on her side in the distressing family quarrel which burst out on her marriage to Southey.

Cottle's public life, soon to be glaring, was interrupted on 17 June by the death, at the age of 22, of his niece Charlotte Thomas. She was buried in a vault at Zion Chapel. Her widower, the minister of the Chapel, went to live with Cottle,[21] and was under his roof for two years, thus meeting 'men of genius and literary attainment'.[22] Charlotte's body was later reinterred at Arno's Vale, along with Thomas's four young children by his second marriage, in the Hare vault. Thomas survived until 1875.

Those periodicals which mentioned the *Recollections* did so with distaste or venom. In June, a reviewer in *Tait's Edinburgh Magazine*[23] said that Scott's life could be recorded in the same manner as this treatment of Coleridge, but doubted the justifiability. But it was left to *The Quarterly Review*[24] to fall on the book with all its notorious fury, and their July notice is well worth reading as a piece of masterly invective. They prejudice his case at the outset by reviewing him straight after a pleasant notice of H.N. Coleridge's edition of his uncle's literary remains, and then they fire the first broadside: only pity for Cottle's 'age and self-exposure' will temper the frontal attack which he has earned. He says that he is showing 'what biography *ought to be*': do we need any pattern other than that of Walton, Hackett, Johnson, Southey? Anyway, let us hope that his model will not be taken. His book is nothing but 'the refuse of advertisments and handbills, the sweepings of a shop, the shreds of a ledger, the rank residuum of a life of gossip, – this forty-years' deposit of Bristol garbage, smeared in the very idiocy of anecdote-mongering on a shapeless fragment, and a false name scratched in the filth'. He has made himself familiar with Coleridge's *name*, but knows as much of his 'heart, mind, principles, or works' as a fly does of an elephant's proboscis when alighting on it. They quote, for Cottle's consideration, a long passage from *The Friend*, on biography, and then return to the attack: they could easily rout him by quotations from his own 'injurious fooleries', but they will not so sully their pages. Admittedly, he was the publisher of Coleridge's first volume of poems, and helped him with 'small sums of money, and by other friendly services'; but the trouble is that he records them all, guinea and shilling, as if from an account book. In his preface he pretends that false shame might withold mention of *one* piece of liberality, de Quincey's £300. They do not agree: surely no friend of Coleridge would want to conceal his poverty, its origins, and the way it was mitigated. (This attitude to the gift shows that *The Quarterly* was not 'in' with the Coleridges in launching this onslaught.) But 'to take up receipts, and to schedule every guinea for the wretched guinea's sake! ...' Cottle, on re-reading his work, will admit that he has paid himself the balance with interest. They quote from Cottle Coleridge's *Admonition* on judging others for what they have produced; significantly, Cottle breaks it off just where it accuses *him*, when it says that a man's evil is now in his grave: 'FOLLOW IT NOT THITHER'.

Much of Volume II, they go on, is devoted to opium and to the wrongly-used word 'passion' for it. Cottle is resolved not to be partial about it, and is happy that his course was concurred in by many of Coleridge's best friends. The reviewer doubts this, and when Cottle anxiously mentions Wade, why does he not cite some of the 'many' others? And what of Wade even? Cottle says that Wade told him that '*all* his friends' agreed; they do not believe it, because since the publication they have 'heard the direct reverse stated in society'. So wrong-headed is Cottle morally, and so 'conscience-bound', that he records sickening details more likely to corrupt than to dissuade, and does not distinguish between vice and weakness. Who gave him the authority to deal so with Coleridge's memory? He says that Coleridge is the kind of man who 'ceases to be private property, but is transferred, with all his appendages, to the treasury of the public'. 'Gracious Heaven!' they exclaim. 'Is it poetasters and foolish gossips only that may be loved? Does a great man cease to be a man?' What of his family's feelings, which Cottle is so 'barbarous' in violating? Now, of course, Coleridge in his depths wrote Wade a letter, and Cottle speaks of Coleridge's 'injunctions' to publish it, as if they were contained in the letter itself: they are *not* – and, in any case, Cottle had determined on his course before he even heard of the letter! But Coleridge recovered, became a great Christian teacher, owned his former weakness, deprecated de Quincey's self-exposure, and in his will bade his executor publish what letters he thought expedient; Cottle has published much else, against that 'accredited representative's' respectful but earnest entreaties. Finally, Cottle will observe that they are motivated 'more in sorrow than in anger'; had they been hostile, they could have gratified themselves in full, making him a fool by *one* page of selections, more damning than Byron's satire. They refrain. 'The mistake of a strong desire for the actual possession of literary ability, is not peculiar to Mr Cottle'; and their remarks come to him only in a moral tone. Had his style been ruffianly, as was that of the recent anonymous publication (that is, Allsop's), they could have passed it by; but *here* 'conscience' and 'duty' and 'religion' are given as motives, and dreadful harm may be done. They do not remember 'a more pernicious example' of this kind of thing.

This was the official verdict; and private opinion was just as hostile (though James Montgomery found nothing in the book dishonourable or derogatory[25]). Southey was very unhappy about it all. He wrote to Moxon on 19 July, saying how saddened he was by reading so many reminders of the past: Scott's *Memoirs*, Lamb's *Letters*, and now Cottle's 'Recollections of so many things which had better have been forgotten'.[26] Caroline Bowles hated it, too, and Southey wrote to her on 23 July:[27]

> That you should like Cottle's book, dear Caroline, is as impossible as it would be for you to dislike Cottle himself, if you knew him as I know him; but unless you knew him thus thoroughly, you could not believe that such simple-heartedness and such inordinate vanity were to be found in the same person. One thing he has made me fully sensible of,

and that is, how liable the most cautious biographer is to be misled by what should seem to be the most trustworthy documents. Such a confusion of times and circumstances as he has made in his *Recollections* I never met with in any other book ...

He, Southey, and Wordsworth always 'dreaded the indiscretion of Coleridge's admirers'. Cottle has actually withheld a lot, through 'his own sense of propriety, little scrupulous as he may seem to have been', and he expunged some more at Southey's request. But 'the impression which his book leaves is just what you describe upon all those who feel that intellectual strength affords no excuse for the disregard of moral obligation'.

Wordsworth, replying on 19 August to a letter four months old, says that he often remembers Cottle's company in Bristol; he will not be able to see the book until he has visited the Hutchinsons in Herefordshire – but he here utters both a warning against writing a book on Coleridge, and his own feeling that the public should not be let into friends' secrets. He and his 'dear and good old Friend' are unlikely to meet again – and Dorothy is a 'wreck'.[28]

Crabb Robinson adds his own testimony, in his diary.[29] On 13 August he 'went early to bed reading Cottle's book on Coleridge'; the later part of 14 August he 'spent lounging', and 'skimmed' the book, which he found not quite as bad as *The Quarterly* made out, 'but bad enough. It is a poor thing; vulgar cant and in a mean style, but still in the main points, the publication of Coleridge's letter on opium-taking and making known de Quincey's present of £300, Cottle is in the right, and Coleridge's family and the *Quarterly Review*, proceeding at least indirectly from the family, are in the wrong'. (Robinson seems also to have 'skimmed' the review in one patch.) 'The review is most ungenerous, and the author of the book deserved milder treatment, poor as it is.'

Lesser men liked it no better. Hudson Gurney (1775-1864), the archaeologist and versifier, who claimed to have dipped into all his library of nearly 15,000 books, decked his copy (now in the University of Bristol Library) with angry scribbles. Against Cottle's remarks on the six portraits he writes, '*Boys* with the Double Coxcombs of puppyism & Philosophy but a very interesting *Set* of Portraits of the *Boys* which the *Men* rose from'. Lovell he admires little: 'I remember this Lovell in 1793. His Mother was a Quaker Preacher who was drowned in a Voyage to Ireland – He Himself Had no outward appearance of a Quaker – but much such a powdered youth as I was – '. Coleridge writes asking Cottle to send his servant for bacon and beans, so he adds:

Himself alone – He *not* His friend Convenes

To A *Pound* of Bacon & Two Quarts of Beans!

Nor does Gurney altogether like Mrs. Yearsley, calling her 'a woman of Strong Masculine understanding ... But in Politics she was a Democrat – in Religion a Freethinker – in Mind an Independent ... in 1793 I was a Daily Lounger in Her Shop — & Heard her Discuss all things ... I have no doubt she was very violent'. He has no sympathy with Hannah More against her faithless servants:

> Of these Family Prayers the success was but middling
> So the Servants in Pairs all went forth to the Fiddling ...

When Cottle says that George Burnett the Pantisocrat died in 1807, aged 32, Gurney adds: 'I have Somewhere read in Mary le Bone Workhouse – after being an Unitarian Minister – '. From page 253 of the first volume, Cottle had much to say of the tricky Sir Herbert Croft; Gurney, knowing the man, amplifies these notes, especially about Croft's term in Exeter Gaol (Cottle prints 'Goal'):

> He was in great Embarrassment & the Prince of Wales sent Him £150 by Lord Moira which He employed in the purchase of 3 coach Horses which He named Prince[,] Peer, & Piper because He said the prince through the peer paid the Piper ... Sir Herbert Croft shewed me a New Edition of his Love & Madness about Half printed – when He was at Yarmouth – with some admirable things added in it ...

Upon Cottle's calling him 'Herbert Croft, Esq., an opulent man', he adds: 'Croft was *then* a Baronet & Had not a Shilling – His Daughters by His first Wife Had something from a property in London'; and he altogether weakens Cottle's case against Croft. He does not believe that Sara Coleridge wrote her lines (about the thimble) to Cottle: 'This was Evidently written by Coleridge or Tinkered between them –'. Cottle himself becomes the subject of an epigram at the end of the first book; he is boastfully hoping that Bristol will never be without a bookseller ready to give a friendly hand to genius, and Gurney comments:

> Like me, who foster'd the *Desarving*,
> And kept *three Poet Lads* from Starving!

Gurney's remarks on the second volume start with sneers against the

Pantisocrats, and he mentions that Southey's Uncle 'did not know that He was married – & ... to prevent His Marrying was His reason for Getting Him to Lisbon'. Then Wordsworth receives some just censure, for thinking that *The Ancient Mariner* had ruined *Lyrical Ballads*: '!!! Well done Wordsworth – The only *magnificent* thing in it – To Sink *His* fooleries!!!' To Coleridge, Gurney is uniformly more charitable, refusing to believe that he sent no money to his wife; but Coleridge's phrase in a letter, saying how 'thoughts on thoughts, feelings on feelings', crowded in on him when reading a certain pamphlet, moves Gurney to doggerel again:

> 'Feelings on Feelings!'
> Make precious Dealings ...

He has no faith in the Henderson saga; the margins are enlivened with question marks, and he once exclaims: 'Being merely a Talker I suspect *Many* of His acquirements were but Superficial'.

Posterity will endorse most of these verdicts on a book which ought to have been interesting, moving, and indispensable. In compiling this biography, I myself have found Cottle's directions thoroughly benighting: a tattered tapestry of inventions, transpositions, exaggerations, truth suppressed, wrong dates, misplaced wit, and sheer bad English. Yet we need the book, and it has been part of my task to wrench its statements nearer to the truth. On the moral issues of opium and £300, I have nothing against it, if only he had not perpetually thrust into the foreground his own figure, muttering minor prophecies.

Though we know that Cottle had, by this point, been threatened with legal action, we have probably been lulled, as he, into thinking that it could never happen, that the threat was a mere gesture. So we shall be astounded to know that he *was* sued quite disastrously – but we must still not anticipate this most ludicrous and expensive of all his adventures. In the intervening period, the day declined. Southey became an object of mourning, and no longer of inspiration. On 16 November he wrote to Cottle his last news of the mad Edith, who had died that very day.[30] His daughters, he said, were now suffering from the strain they had undergone. He signed himself 'My dear old friend,/Yours affectionately, in weal or in woe,/Robert Southey'; yet it was the end of Cottle's greatest friendship, and the letter is endorsed, 'The last letter which Joseph Cottle received from his old friend Robert Southey'. Southey, on his Continental tour in 1838, went on evincing signs that his own mind was failing, a process further aided by the death of his brother Tom, and even his second marriage did not save him from the vacancy in which he spent his last four years, neither opening his loved books nor writing to his faithful friends.

Cottle replied as soon as he received the letter on the morning of 19 November 1837. He has not seen Edith for 35 years, so that he sees her image as it was. Southey, he feels, will be consoled by the thought of his own fidelity to her, and heaven will bless the piety of his dutiful daughters; Mary is grieved at the loss of her old friend, Ann would be if she were present, and Joseph wants to send his special sympathy to young Cuthbert. We know, too, that he had just afforded some pleasure to Mary Wordsworth: writing to Dora in September,[31] she says, 'Cottle's present to me of the *Youthful Poets* was a grand treat.'

1   His three visits are recorded in Edith J. Morley, *op.cit.*, II.500 ff.

2   Edith J. Morley, *The Correspondence of Henry Crabb Robinson with the Wordsworth Circle*, 2 Vols (Oxford, 1927), I.315-316.

3   Curry, II.455-457; and (piecemeal) *R.47*, pp.410-411.

4   Bristol City Library MS.B 20877.

5   *R.47*, pp.411-413.

6   Edith J. Morley, *The Correspondence*, I.321.

7   G.E. and E.L. Griggs, *Letters of Hartley Coleridge* (London: Oxford University Press, 1936), p.201.

8   Edith J. Morley, *The Correspondence*, I.322-323.

9   *R.47*, p.413; Cottle prints 'Friday'.

10   *R.47*, p.414.

11   *R.47*, pp.423-424.

12   *R.47*, p.190n.

13   *R.47*, p.409n.

14   E. Dowden, *The Correspondence of Robert Southey with Caroline Bowles* (Dublin: University Press Series, 1881), p.344.

15   E. Dowden, *op.cit.*, p.345.

16   CCS, VI.311-314.

17   [J. Dix], *Pen and Ink Sketches of Poets, Preachers, and Politicians*, 2nd edn (London: D. Bogue, 1847), pp.159-168.

18   Bristol City Library MS.B 20877.

19   University of Bristol Library MS.3/2.

20   Curry, II.467-468; and (piecemeal) *R.47*, pp.414-415.

21   At Firfield House, says Cozens (*op.cit.*, pp.18-19); but Cottle did not move in until John Hare's death in 1839.

22   H.A. Thomas, *Memorials of the Rev. David Thomas, B.A., of Bristol* (London: Hodder and Stoughton, 1876), p.19.

23   IV.341-348.

24 Vol.LIX, No.CXVII, pp.25-32.

25 S.C. Hall, *A Book of Memories of Great Men and Women of this Age* (London: Virtue, 1871), p.30.

26 CCS, VI.335.

27 E. Dowden, *op.cit.*, p.351.

28 *1795 Album*. Mary Wordsworth had on 29 July urged William to answer Cottle's letter 'briefly ... from town ... before you need give any opinion of his books' (Mary E. Burton, *The Letters of Mary Wordsworth 1800-1853* (Oxford, 1958), p.161, No.78).

29 Edith J. Morley, *Henry Crabb Robinson ...*, II.533-534.

30 CCS, VI.347.

31 Mary E. Burton, *op.cit.*, p.182, No.84.

Chapter 16
Wealth: Somerset Assizes

After the excitement of the previous years, 1838 was so featureless as to leave no record of Cottle's activities. 1839, on the other hand, was a tragic and harassing year, clouded by the virtual death of Southey and by losses in the little family circle. On 11 January Cottle's brother-in-law, John Hare, died at Firfield House at the age of 87; on 18 January he was buried at Zion Chapel, though the body was removed to Arno's Vale on 13 January 1848. Though he had children by his first wife, Ann must have been given the use of the mansion: she was now left alone there – a problem lugubriously solved on 31 March, when Mary died at Carlton Place 'greatly respected',[1] leaving Cottle without a housekeeper. He forthwith moved into Firfield, and was from then on a citizen of substance, with a carriage and an estate. One of his first callers was Wordsworth, who came with Peace the Librarian on 26 April; unfortunately, Cottle and his sole remaining sister were out, and Wordsworth had no time to wait, since he had to catch an early coach to Bath, so he merely left a note with best wishes from 'your old and true Friend' and with regards to Ann Hare.[2]

Meanwhile the storm was gathering. The feelings of the Coleridges had settled into contempt, and Hartley could write to his sister Sara on 23 February[3] that Gillman's first volume had a good spirit, in that he had 'shewn no inclination to set himself in the foreground, or to blazon the extent to which ὁ μακαρίτης was indebted to him'. Then, from quite another quarter, the fury of the law marshalled and struck Cottle when he least expected it.

At the end of his *Essays in Reference to Socinianism* (1842) there is an advertisement for books written by him, including *Early Recollections* reduced to 10/6d. He wants to explain why, and must therefore refer to a law-suit: he had been 'pressed from various quarters' to publish a memoir of Coleridge, not excluding his eccentricities and especially his opium addition (as *he*, too, had stipulated 'verbally and by letter'). So 'after due consideration', he decided to comply, because it would be beneficial and would not subtract from Coleridge's 'high moral and intellectual character'. He added notices of the other two great ones (after all, he was their '*Encourager* and *Publisher*') and of Amos, Chatterton, Henderson, Hannah More, etc. It was 'impossible' not to mention why Hannah More left Barley Wood: her servants' conduct was 'notorious to the whole kingdom' – as published lives of her, her own statements, and those of a relative, made clear. But soon afterwards the coachman, Charles Tidy, called and complained 'civilly' that Cottle's publication had made it difficult for him to get a place as a jobbing gardener. Cottle knew this was untrue, since Hannah More had sacked him eight or ten years before, but although his mind 'experienced a revolt at coming into contact' with someone who had behaved so badly, he was touched by the real or feigned distress, and said he had not meant any harm and was sure he had not caused any, but he would alter the passage if there were a second edition. Tidy thanked him, appeared satisfied, and asked for an old coat; not having one 'disposable', Cottle sent him down half a sovereign, with his best wishes, for which he returned thanks and '*dutiful respects*'.

Soon after, however, the fellow thought, or had it suggested to him, that a prosecution for libel might be '*a good speculation*', with a claim for heavy damages. An attorney was found to undertake it, and damages were laid at £500. Cottle simply *had* to defend the action, at Bridgwater in the autumn of 1839, before Mr Justice Erskine; *Felix Farley's Bristol Journal* on Saturday, 17 August 1839, locates the case at Somerset Assizes in *Wells*. Cottle's account merely adds that his own counsel, 'from a knowledge of the witnesses, put in a Plea which, while it *justified* what was written, required the Plaintiff to prove' that Cottle was the writer. As he failed to do so, 'a Nonsuit followed'; so Cottle had won, and all he had to do was to get his costs, nearly £300, out of the jobbing gardener! *Felix Farley* goes into much greater detail: Tidy had been both coachman and bailiff, and was now a gardener at Weston-super-Mare, and Cottle's words 'had proved very injurious' to him. His counsel, Mr Erle, outlined the garrulous story in the *Recollections*. Tidy – 'Timothy, the coachman', in Cottle's version – claimed that there was not a word of truth in it, but that it was all gossip and exaggeration and fiction: so openly, and with such official approval, did the servants entertain their friends, that Mrs More and her visitors left the communicating doors open, the better to hear their innocent songs. So Mr Erle, assisted by Mr Barstow, called a string of witnesses to fix the book on Cottle: John Wright who printed it (a matter on which he proved evasive); Joseph Edgar, the plaintiff's attorney, who bought it at Wright's before that establishment became James Ackland's; James Ackland, who succeeded Wright in the shop (and didn't remember Edgar's purchase); the Reverend David Thomas, who had read it in manuscript, and had no doubt that the printed work was by Cottle (on the previous

Wednesday or Thursday, he and Cottle, thinking about the coming trial, compared the passage in the book with corroborating bits in other books and in the *Bristol Gazette*); and Josiah Wade, who also rather 'tied up' the manuscript and the book (and perhaps hoped that Cottle would now get what he deserved). But Mr Crowder, defending, submitted that there was nothing to go to a jury; the Judge astonishingly said that the book produced was not admissible as evidence, and that there was no legal proof of Cottle's authorship; and the plaintiff was therefore nonsuited. Round one to Cottle, who brought out the second 500 *Recollections* in this very year. Apparently this defiant step was not taken until the result of the case was known: one copy of the *Recollections* has a note signed by John Silver of Leamington, stating that 'The publication of this book was discontinued for a time in consequence of a threat of action for libel on the part of Hannah More's servants'.[4] Cottle's attorney told him that as the next assizes were six months away, there was plenty of time to proceed against the plaintiff for costs; if he concealed himself, then they could proceed to outlawry and thus restrain him from 'doing further mischief'.

In 1839 Robert Cottle founded a sect of 120 members, called the *Cottleites*; they met in an upper school-room at Putney, under a pastor, the Reverent Robert Ashton. Since the widowed Elizabeth Cottle afterwards claimed to have been 'sacrificed from April 8, 1839' for the redemption of 'the black gentlemen', we may take that as the date of founding. Little is known of Robert's doctrines, save that they were anti-Roman, and he may well have acted in good faith, little realising that his addled widow would blasphemously erect him into Messiah.[5]

In December, the Reverend David Thomas, who had been living at Cottle's since the death of his young wife, attached himself further to Cottle's kin (while detaching himself from Cottle's roof) by marrying Eliza Leonard, the grand-daughter of John Hare by his first marriage. The son of this union was the Reverend H. Arnold Thomas, who was his father's biographer. Amid all these disappearing friends, Cottle still had the services of John Foster; and even the old literary life flickered again in 1840, when subscriptions were desired for the Chatterton memorial in Redcliffe churchyard. He, and other generous citizens, are not to be blamed for the puppetry of the statue (demolished in 1967) or for its gross Gothick base; the mere existence of a suicide's memorial – albeit on unconsecrated ground – was a concession. (When Cottle, 'a year or two' before 1829, had wanted to start a subscription for a monument in the Cathedral, the Dean informed him through a friend that the suicide made this quite impossible.) Bowles produced £5, and George Cumberland only half a guinea; Cottle, who had

The Reverend David Thomas: engraving (from a photograph) by J. Cochran (from University of Bristol Library, Special Collections: from Priscilla Fry's extra-illustrated copy of John Latimer, *Annals of Bristol in the Nineteenth Century*)

done as much as anyone for Chatterton's memory and family, even to concealing the poet's precocious turpitude, gave one guinea. But the time was coming when he must husband his resources: Tidy brought an action against the printer.

Cottle could not hesitate to protect John Wright. So he promised that he would not be put to a penny's expense – nor was he. Further, 'unexpected impediments' prevented Tidy's being made an outlaw in time to stop the action; and, worse, Hannah More's companion – who knew the facts, had communicated them to one of the biographers, had come forward in the first action, and had said to another lady in court, 'I should have been glad not to be here, but being here, I will *tell all*' – could not be found, and no subpoena could be served on her. As she was the chief witness, they had to move the court to put the trial off to the next assizes. There followed six months 'of intense and wearing anxiety … moderated, it is hoped, by the remembrance of Him, who rules, and over-rules'. He was advised not to incur the expense of outlawry. The lady was traced and subpoenaed, but just before the trial was due to start she said she would refuse to attend and would rather incur the penalty of £100. Since Cottle did not feel vindictive, he directed his attorney not to proceed against her for the sum, and his plea of justification not being supported, 'the best preparation was made for the Trial which the case admitted'.

Now until July 1840, the libel law let unprincipled lawyers bring libel cases for penniless clients if there was a chance of getting a farthing damages, and then collected the costs: *they* gained, the plaintiff gained nothing, the defendant was plundered. Lord Denman's bill provided that damages of under 40/- should not entitle to costs unless the judge certified that the grievance was 'wilful and malicious' – when even a farthing would carry costs. And the trial was the first under the new act.

On Saturday, 8 August 1840,[6] the Somerset Assizes opened at Wells before Mr Justice Coleridge and Mr Baron Maule, the former presiding at the Crown Court and the latter at the Civil Court. A narrow escape! If their rôles had been reversed, the result might have been very different. According to *Felix Farley*, Maule heard a new version of the case of the libels agains Hannah More's servants, again presented by Mr Erle. This time, Charles Tedy (not Tidy) brought an action against Wright the printer, and it was quite clear that this choice of victim was a second best, *faute de* Cottle. Wright's canny attitude at the previous hearing was summarized, and the jury were treated to another idyllic picture of Mrs More's happy and trusted household. Once more it was Mr Crowder who came to the rescue, and surely spoke the truth when he said there was no

JOSEPH COTTLE AND THE ROMANTICS

sign of an intention by the writer to injure any particular person; and he was severe against the course of suing people one by one in the hope of eventually winning your case. Witnesses were called to show how badly the servants had behaved. But Mr Tedy or Tidy *did* win this time. The jury awarded him damages of one farthing, 'which, under the Frivolous Suits Bill, passed in the Session of Parliament just over, does not carry costs'. Round two to Tidy/Tedy, by a narrow margin – or so *Felix Farley* too hastily assumed.

But Cottle has a sadder tale to tell. Everything seemed to be going against the plaintiff: his cause was obviously 'destitute of the shadow of foundation', and just for gain; no damage was proved, and his only character-witness was a 'Pot-Companion'. John Scandrett Harford, Esq., of Blaize Castle, came forward voluntarily without being subpoenaed, and said that his friend Hannah More had consulted him 'in her perplexity' and had sent for him; and having examined the state of affairs, he advised her to dismiss all eight servants. The Reverend H. Thompson of Wrington, her biographer, said that Tidy had called on him after his dismissal to say that she had left owing him a lot of money, which he could not recover; he asked Thompson to intercede, so he wrote to her and received in return an '*elegant and pathetic*' letter disclaiming the debt and expressing her astonishment. When the letter was read aloud in court, all were 'deeply affected at the recapitulation of *such* delinquences and in-gratitude'. One of her executors also proved that she had settled every account before leaving Barley Wood; and another witness, who knew the establishment, spoke of its disorganization and of Tidy's 'frequent intoxication'.

Maule addressed the special jury. One of his remarks was that, although Tidy had been proved drunken, he had not been proved more so than 'many *other Gentleman* frequently were'. All the same, the jury, 'with scarcely a moment's hesitation', brought in the minimum damages, a farthing. Cottle adds that if the lady companion had given her evidence 'the Justification would have been established', and a nonsuit would have followed. Maule was now asked to certify – and acceded! So by this first trial under an act intended by Lord Denman to discourage mischievous suits of this kind, all the costs of both sides 'were thrown on' Cottle. He had been unspeakably worried for two years, and now he had had nearly £1,000 'wrested from a small Independence, and that, at the decline of life' (but, of course, he adds, of all the less consequence accordingly). Sales had been increasing fast, but the actions had naturally checked the circulation (I should have thought that they would increase it), so there would be no second edition, and the price was reduced from a guinea to half a guinea.

Cottle's friends were growing indignant at this 'persecution', as Foster called it when he wrote on 12 October (adding that Providence would bring good out of evil). Cottle and Mrs Hare had enquired of him that very day, and had called the week before, when his 'awkward plight' had prevented his seeing them: he had an odd complaint – a heaviness in the head, without pain yet responding to no medical treatment, probably brought on by clearing his books out from a damp and dusty room in the hottest weather. On 6 February 1841, on returning some manuscript Essays on Socinianism, he began his huge series of letters to Cottle on Eternal Punishment and Fatalism. The letter of this date is indexed '1' in Cottle's letter-book,[7] but it and all the other nineteen, some of mighty proportions, seem to be lost. Cottle must have been keeping them with a view to some kind of edition, and they were long enough to be exhaustive even of this unfathomable topic. Letter 1 had about four pages; 2, 3, and 4 (which had ten pages) followed thick and fast on 11, 12, and 16 February.

The spring brought two reunions. On 28 April, Crabb Robinson, who was staying at the 'White Lion', dined with his consumptive nephew at Clifton, and then left at 5 so as to call on Cottle, 'one of the worst of poets' but 'one of the kindest of men'. He made his way out to Knowle Hill, and thought the house 'a charming place on a height'. They made him stay to tea, he was there until 8.30, and 'really enjoyed' his visit. Mrs Hare seemed 'sensible', and Cottle was 'a very worthy man' despite his bad poetry. Above all, Robinson was the means of getting Wordsworth to accept an invitation. The great man was in the vicinity, and we do not know if he had to make heavy weather of visiting his old benefactor, but he promised to take his ladies to Firfield on the morrow.[8] So on 29 April they dined with Cottle, who was thus given the latest glum news of Southey's madness.[9]

Cottle was in correspondence with the second Mrs Southey on this subject, and he sent one of her letters for Foster to see. Foster's reply[10] expressed some sympathy, and admitted that Southey was a great and talented man, deserving of Cottle's praise. But Southey had done harm, by advocating often what was 'injurious to the community' and by attacking those who were trying to reform corrupt institutions. Foster cannot forget that Southey 'could laud, as a pattern of royalty to be imitated, that most fetid offal of humanity, – George the 4th!' Foster sounds far more sorry about the legal proceedings, and feels that it is an indictment of our social system when Cottle's little piece of 'retributive justice' is called a crime; he hopes that Cottle's belief in Divine justice will see him through, and that he will get away with the least possible injury. On 28 December, Foster sent the fifth of the Eternal Punishment letters, which occupied so much of his time in the ensuing year; in fact, Cottle was now at the mercy of his principal admirer, who would go on cheerfully justifying the *Recollections* on all grounds. However, Stapleton and Bedminster, though suburban to the same city, were far enough away to keep this mainly as an epistolary friendship.

As if not caring how many more people he offended *en masse*, Cottle in 1842 brought out (with Longman and Cadell) the first part, running to 243 pages, of his *Essays with reference to Socinianism*, but the second part did not appear. On 31 January 1842 Foster sent him a letter[11] which I find it hard to admire. It is on the recent deaths of their 'coevals'. First, there is Mr Stokes at Worcester (though Cottle decided not to include his name when he copied Foster's original). Well, Foster was just back from the funeral in time for that of John Hare. Then there was Cottle's 'excellent sister Mary'; Mr Coles of Bourton, known for forty years; Mr Addington; Mr Dove, recently, in Scotland; last and unexpectedly, Mr Roberts, with whom Foster had dined at Wade's not ten days before – he was one, alas, who had held 'strange dispositions' towards Messrs Cottle, Hare, and Goode, whereat Foster had repeatedly rebuked him. The 'I remain', at the close, gives a jolly touch of the macabre. Apart from this catalogue, the only business of the letter is to thank Cottle for a 'plaister' to relieve his chest and (along with Mrs Hare) for so many kindnesses, such as luxury foods; and he is sorry that he could not attend David Thomas's lecture. But Cottle was eager to hear more of Eternal Punishment, and wrote asking for a renewal of the series. On 10 February Foster replied in a gratified mood, and expressed his interest in Cottle's pious remarks on the next world. He is aware that their end is approaching, since they are both in their seventy-second year, but they must be thankful for their good health, seeing that Cottle is so well and that he himself is nearly as he was before. With that, he again explores eternity, and lost letters come with a rush on 11 February, 24 March, 20 April, 10 and 24 May (surely the latter did not cover pages 91-127 of Cottle's letter-book, as the index suggests!), 28 May, 2 and 21 June. This last letter, indeed, survives and has little enough on the score of eternity, but it thanks Cottle for the present of a salmon, a fish rarely seen in the Foster household. He is grateful, too, for Cottle's transcription of all the letters, in his own hand: since the time of Adam, or at least of Noah, no-one has been so tolerant – so enamoured, even – of labour. Cottle has said something about Foster's forgiving him for anything other than friendly in their correspondence; but there is nothing to forgive. (Now what can *this* have been? Perhaps a defence of Southey, made more palatable with a salmon?) Foster is very sorry to hear of the set-back in Cottle's health through 'an aggravation of another complaint', and he tactlessly chooses this moment to add to his catalogue of coevals called away: for Wade was dead by now, and that meant that eleven (three-quarters, in fact) of his old friends had died in three-and-a-half years, leaving Cottle as the oldest but one. Their own day is not far off, and he trusts that they will be ready to welcome it. On 25 June, eternity is again the theme.

But Cottle dodged this issue in an enormous letter of 6 July,[12] when he rallied to the defence of Southey, now 'worse than dead'. Only Wordsworth and Foster survive of his old friends. He tries to overwhelm Foster with pages and pages of proof of his hero's blameless character, his love of Bristol and of books, and even, by a pretty anecdote, Queen Victoria's admiration of him (which would hardly impress the republican Foster). It is a truly moving letter, and we may believe in the tear, which, says Cottle, is dimming his eye. He mentions Southey's magnanimity when Cottle could not return the copyrights of *Joan* and of the two volumes of poems, and, of course, he speaks with authority, since few can have known Southey better. Their correspondence lasted from 1795 to 1837, and he is just about to transcribe for Ann all the wonderful Southey letters. When they are complete, perhaps Foster would like to peruse them? We do not know how Foster countered this defence, but he rounded off the Eternal Punishment collection with two final letters on 18 and 20 July.

In August, Cottle and his sister invited him and his daughter to visit them. He replied on the 10th, with the apology that his old friend Dr Murch, with whom he once domesticated at Frome, was expected, and so was Mrs Cox. When Christmas came, Firfield again extended its liberality, in the form of a ham (which kept beautiful company with a turkey sent by a friend of Foster's in Pembrokeshire), a stone hot-water-bottle, and, for the Foster daughters, some envelopes and many elegant wafers – how fine art, Foster observes in his letter of 30 December,[13] is now finding its way into everyday things! (And, indeed, they were now perilously near the Great Exhibition.) He has read Archbishop Whately's volume; it is good and liberal, coming from a prelate of the Establishment, though naturally a Churchman cannot treat his subject with '*perfect* freedom and independence'. It is a pity that Whately insists so much on the necessity for a man's belonging to an organised church; but Foster is glad that he attacks Puseyism, which will eventually be exposed for what it is. He knows, too, that Cottle will be pleased by the success of the Anti-Corn-Law League and the shending of the worst knaves in England. Another year over! Will they know yet another? Cottle and his sisters are very well, and Foster is glad of it; but he himself has not recovered from his illness of the previous winter (and, had he but known, the answer to his question was, in his own case, 'No').

1   *FFJ* for Saturday, 6 April 1839, Vol.XCV, No.4914.

2   de S, No.1295.

3   G.E. and E.L. Griggs, *op.cit.*, p.230.

4   I am very grateful to the owner, Miss Martha Cottle, of Audley House, Buckland, Faringdon, for notice of this copy.

5   On the Cottleites, see A. de Morgan, *Budget of Paradoxes* (London: Longmans, Green, 1872), pp.313-316; and J. Timbs, *English Eccentrics*, new edn (London: Chatto and Windus, 1875).

6   *FFJ* for Saturday, 15 Aug. 1840, Vol.XCVI, No.4985.

7   Bristol City Library MS.B 20878.

8   Edith J. Morley, *Henry Crabb Robinson*, II.594.

9   Cottle to Foster, 6 July 1842, in Bristol City Library MS.B 20878.

10   In Bristol City Library MS.B 20878, with no date save '1841'.

11   Bristol City Library MS.B 20878, and (maimed) *R.47*, pp.417-418.

12   Bristol City Library MS.B 20878, and (abbreviated) *R.47*, pp.418-425.

13   Bristol City Library MS.B 20878.

Chapter 17

Miss Mitford: A Southey Memorial

1843 brought more grief and loneliness, by the deaths of both Southey and the hardy Foster: but it also brought Mary Russell Mitford on a June afternoon. On 24 March, Cottle heard with a pang that Southey was dead at last, and on the following day he wrote to Mrs Southey,[1] the former Caroline Bowles, trying to express the 'feeling almost of desolation' which had struck him, and his hope that those who weep and those who are wept for are not long separated. She is to be congratulated on having tended Southey in his terrible state, and when she is more composed she must write Cottle a few lines about him. He has often meant to send her a second letter, and to thank her for her 'obliging communication', but he knew all the time that enquiries were hopeless. Over many years, he has written to Southey on many private and family matters, so could the executors please return such letters? (We may well ask where they are now. Perhaps Southey destroyed them as he answered them. But Cottle was taking no chances: he was in a position to know what could be done with confidential letters.) He and Mrs Hare would welcome her at Firfield if she is ever in the neighbourhood. This letter he sealed with a black device of a bust, and sent it off by the new penny post on 4 April, allowing these few days to elapse lest it should arrive 'at an unsuitable time'. With unusual tact, he suppressed another letter which he had written on 25 March, until it should be more suitable. Mrs Southey's reply gave Cottle a 'melancholy pleasure', and he wrote back on 10 April, though, he claimed, 'far from being well', and averse to writing. His chief purpose, it seems, is to enclose his second letter of 25 March, to which he now sees no objection. It is a vast thing of four foolscap pages, with an introduction much like that already sent, but with the addition of Southey's recent visit, when Cottle got him to have his portrait made by Branwhite, and of Cottle's joy that Southey spoke so nicely of him in his last work, the supplementary volume of his *Cowper*. A couple more such losses, and Cottle will be 'in a land of strangers'. But the letter has one unsuitable feature, which should still have supressed it at this time of mourning: it includes his letter of 6 July 1842 to Foster, itself including

Southey's to *him* of 20 April 1808 (which, of course, is all in praise of Cottle).

In June, Miss Mitford was staying at Bath, and came over to Bristol on a visit.[2] There she found the remnants of a society that had made Clifton illustrious fifty years before – bits of the Edgeworth, Beddoes, and Porter families; Mrs Schimmelpenninck and Mrs Harriet Lee; and 'the Sketcher of Blackwood' (the Reverend John Eagles), a fine amateur artist, writer, scholar, wit, whose one picture was there (the *St Catherine* of Domenichino from which Reynolds borrowed the attitude of his Tragic Muse). It was Eagles who drove her out to take tea, by invitation, with 'the most interesting resident of the neighbourhood', now firmly settled at Firfield, which Miss Mitford knew had once been big enough to house French prisoners. Cottle was, as she expected, 'a mild and venerable man, distinguished for courtesy and intelligence'. She records, perhaps from his own words, how in his seven years of bookselling he had been lucky enough – and, of course, she adds, liberal and enlightened enough – to be the first publisher of Southey, Coleridge, and Wordsworth. (Irritatingly, no-one ever mentions Lamb, the only writer to whom Cottle could make exactly this claim.) She knew him as 'the author of many works of excellent feeling and tendency, and of one … of the very highest merit' (the *Recollections!*), and he received his visitors in a room piled with books and portfolios, the latter having carefully inserted in them the correspondence of an enviable array of friends: Wordsworth, Coleridge, Southey, Landor, Lamb, Davy, Lloyd, Foster, Hall, Hannah More, and, of course, Henderson – who, said Cottle, might have excelled them all, had he not 'evaporated in talk'. But Dr Valpy had given Miss Mitford other information of Henderson, and she doubted in herself whether he would really have achieved anything by living. (Among these bulky portfolios were some collections from men whose names escaped her.) In addition, the walls were hung with portraits of these friends – engravings, drawings, oils – many repeated twice or thrice at different ages. Cottle was actually engaged on transcribing Southey's letters for the life then projected, and afterwards executed, by Cuthbert, and Cottle thought them the most amusing he had received, even above Lamb's. But she noted that Cuthbert used very few of them – through *embarras de richesses*, she supposed. Still, she felt that a selection from all the portfolios 'would be a very welcome gift to the literary world', which can hardly know too much of these poets or of prose-writers like Lamb, Foster, and Hall.

We hear a lot more about this task of transcription from a series of letters,[3] three out of the five undated, which Foster sent to Cottle at this time. Here, at the very end of his life, Foster gave Cottle a pile of new prose for the Foster folio, and unkindly devoted much of it to an attack on Southey. In what seems to be the first note, he excuses its shortness by saying that he had not expected Cottle's messenger so early. He is grateful for his peep at the Southey letters, and he senses the same 'serious *desideratum*' in them that Cottle senses. But Southey's goodness, integrity, purity, etc., *without* 'the humbling sense of a sinful nature' made him take on 'a settled satisfied self-righteousness!' Again, he is grateful for Cottle's showing him Southey's ten volumes. Yet he keeps feeling that it is 'all *shop-work*': Southey turned out poetry as a man produces cabinet-work or weaving, calculating 'by the yard against time ... It gives a rather low idea of literature.'

In another note, Foster says that he must not let Cottle's messenger return without a line of thanks for kindnesses, including his daughters' thanks for a valuable present – they will certainly get the continuation of the *Museum*. Yes, the Southey letters were interesting, and he has always respected Southey (though less than Cottle does). But then there *was* his tergiversation, 'his somewhat *insolent* manner of exhibiting his later opinions – his scornful way of noticing reformers and dissenters'. (Cottle, a dissenter himself, had admittedly turned a blind eye to all this.) And observe how *The Edinburgh Review* flagellated his 'magisterial' letter to W. Smith! Oh, the editor will mutilate the most characteristic of the letters: 'How worthless, in general, is Biography!' He will return Cottle's theological letters of the previous year whenever he wants them, and he does not want copies, since he does not feel like reverting to the subject in his own reading; nor has he re-read his own letters, save to put them in sequence. He is somewhat better, with no return of last winter's haemorrhage.

Two days later, Foster realised that he had made a bad *faux pas* in saying that he did not want copies of Cottle's letters: of course, what he meant was that he would not give Cottle the trouble of transcribing them! Why, he himself would have undertaken it willingly! But the point is that he does not want them, as he has no intention of writing on the subject. (Perhaps he realised that his researches into eternity were about to take a more practical turn.) He has read half through Southey's letters; but the raciest, he fears, will not be admitted to the edition. Southey's friends, like Wordsworth, are Tories, and they will suppress his early politics, despite the testimony of his later bigoted Church-and-Tory outlook. In fact, their view of his early works will be like his own view of *Wat Tyler*, and the biography may well be a 'tiresome' affair. Oh, how amusing (or something tarter) it is to see Southey's fury of writing, as if readers were in the last pangs of a literary famine! His cart-load of compositions has *some* excuse, as being his means of support, but it was produced too rapidly for due thought and polishing; and, not being a soldier, he should never have penned his *Peninsular War*, which is already discredited. So his library is to be auctioned in London? Well, his extravagance on books will now bring some good to his family, for he could never have read the lot!

This letter must surely have ruffled Cottle, who at 73 was entitled to his dreams; and Foster's next letter, on 17 June, does not renew the subject. Foster is enclosing a packet which was ready tied up on the previous Tuesday morning, when he expected it to be sent for (Cottle's messenger seems to have seen a lot of the Stapleton Road). Foster would like to read the rest of the Southey letters, but Cottle need not bother to send them: let them be taken to Strong's, where Foster will have to call in a couple of days. Cottle, it appears, had taken the hint about Foster's daughters, and had promised to send them the subsequent numbers of the *Museum*; so now Foster is uneasy about taxing Cottle's kindness just to gratify 'these girls' – but, if Cottle feels he *must*, let him leave these also at Strong's. He doubts whether Cottle will like what he finds contained in a sheet in the parcel (and this may well be some further slight on Southey).

Finally, on 22 June, after an absence from Bristol of seven or eight weeks, Foster wrote that he had gone in by cart a few days before and had found Cottle's roll of transcriptions waiting for him at Strong's. What a labour it is for Cottle! – And the biographers will probably make only a meagre selection. It seems that people just do not want to let Southey and Coleridge have Cottle as 'so intimate and valuable a friend'. At this point, Foster starts to criticise Southey again – for his pride (especially in the *Wat Tyler* affair, the truth of which Foster here reports from an eye-witness) and for his unjustified behaviour over Jeffery's review. Foster is afraid of teasing Cottle by urging him to correct many lapses in writing, but surely Southey mentioned the *meritorious* or *marvellous* exertions of the Jesuits in Paraguay – not *monstrous*! He wants news of the Reverend David Thomas, and is sorry to hear that he is disabled from services which he performs so well … On Sunday, 15 October, Foster was found dead in bed, and Bristol must suddenly have seemed to Cottle a very dreary place. All the more gratifying, therefore, was a note from Wordsworth on 24 November[4] with affirmations of friendship and with thanks for the *Essays* on Socinianism, a subject which Cottle had treated 'in a masterly manner, which is entirely and absolutely convincing'.

But now, astonishingly, Cottle took on a new life of planning and contention, centred on the cold marble of a memorial to Southey.[5] Ever since the death of Southey, he had assumed that Bristol would honour her great citizen by some tangible and permanent mark of respect, and he waited anxiously for some leading man to inaugurate a project in which he could 'become a hearty auxiliary'. But no-one did anything except praise Southey's memory, and at length Cottle, 'as the oldest of Southey's friends', felt it his duty (a pretty show of unwillingness) to emerge from his elected privacy and to try to rescue the city from the disgrace of neglecting her greatest genius save Chatterton. It was obvious to him 'that the most lasting memorial would be a handsome Monument' in the Cathedral. Having now determined to lead, since he could not follow, he recalled that when he had projected a similar monument to Chatterton in the same setting the then Dean of Bristol had replied to his letter with a firm refusal based on the 'circumstances of C's death'. But, feeling that a Dean would look well at the head of the list, he wrote to him asking for a subscription and for permission to erect the monument; and, though Dr Lamb declined the former invitation, he gave the permission requested and even suggested that he would propose the waiving of the usual Cathedral fees. Cottle next tried the Bishop of Gloucester and Bristol, whose name would look even better, and thereafter aimed even higher. In each case he sent a covering letter, with personal touches varied according to the nobleman or gentleman solicited; and he asked them to state how much they would be willing to contribute, so that he could budget for the particular type of statue. With each letter, too, went his own *Recollections* – simply to show what right he had to interfere; and, worst of all, he enclosed a copy of Southey's letter of 28 April, 1808, which would prove to his correspondents how Southey's heart and eyes had throbbed and burned for him.

After the fair start with the Dean, the Bishop sent both good wishes and £5. Cottle jubilantly packed it off to the Bristol Branch of the Bank of England, asking for an account to be opened in the names of 'The Committee for Southey's Monument'. He 'had not yet nominated the Committee, but this could be done when the business was a little more advanced'. Next, although the Archbishop of Canterbury sent nothing, Cottle was not to be deterred, happy to make any sacrifice for the memory of his friend of forty years, who had always been so kind to him and had continued so even from the topmost height of the literary world. Peel, the Prime Minister (his letter to whom, on 29 December 1843, survives in British Museum Additional MS. 40537), thought the project local, but might subscribe thereafter. Cottle had been grossly tactless in this case, making Peel read the heart-throb letter and asking him to mention the project to the Queen when he had the chance. The rest of his list provides us with some interesting figures:

Robert Cottle, £5

Lord Brougham – civil and promissory, but no sum mentioned

Longmans, *nil*, as they had given £5 to a tablet in the north (which Cottle would have supported but for his own project)

Lord Jeffery, £10, with a letter of generous praise of Southey (and this munificence should be better known, in view of their official feelings against one another)

J.S. Harford of Blaise Castle, £5

Sir T.D. Acland – no notice taken

Duke of Wellington – likewise ignored

Queen Victoria – but she had too many applications

Rt.Hon. C.W.W. Wynn, Southey's old friend – he and some friends would support the Bristol scheme if they failed to place a bust in Westminster Abbey

Rt.Hon. J.W. Croker[6] — 'much of the same reply'

Sir R.H. Inglis, Bart., £2

Mr Gutch,[7] 2 guineas

Mr C.B. Fripp, £5

Dr Pritchard, £5

W.L. Bowles the poet (who was now 81) – no notice taken

James Montgomery – no notice

Samuel Rogers, £5

W.S. Landor, £20

"Our member", H. Berkeley – no notice; but

"our other member", Mr Miles, £5

E.H. Bailey, £20

Sir W. Milman, Bart. – no time for an answer, and likewise

C.H. Standert

Reverend J. Eagles, 1 guinea

Sir C.A. Elton, Bart., £5

This, quite apart from promises, made over £95, but Cottle realised that the chief effort must be in Bristol. And, since the machine was now in motion, he felt that he must call in a couple of 'respectable friends' to form with him a sub-committee and thus to expedite the scheme. Bailey's contribution of £20 was a curious affair, since he was to be the sculptor. Cottle applied to him both as an eminent artist and as Bristol-born, and asked him to send a drawing of a suitable monument. In March 1844 a case arrived containing the design. Cottle had suggested a bas-relief bust taken from the likeness in the *Recollections*, and when he saw this carried out, with Southey's name upon it, he burst into tears, remembering the joys and trials of that half-century when they had been at one.

Some weeks before, he had sent a volume (presumably in MS.) of Southey's letters to Dr Henry Southey, the poet's brother, who returned it the day after the drawing arrived, and said that he would like to borrow it again when the editor was decided on. He was pleased to hear of the monument. But he also had bad news – of the rift in Southey's family. Cottle, writing to Wordsworth the day after, exclaimed that but for his infirmity he 'would go up to the North, on a mission of peace, to see whether they could not be brought to a right mind'. He asked Wordsworth to give him fuller information on the quarrel, and urged him to use his 'powerful influence' to resolve the discord. But Cottle cannot yet have know that, for instance, Henry Southey and Wordsworth were already on opposite sides, the former siding with Mrs Southey II and backed by Landor, and Wordsworth supporting Kate and Cuthbert, the poet's children; and Cottle, as it worked out, was not going to be of Wordsworth's party.

As soon as this letter to Wordsworth was finished, he would, he wrote, start on the Bristol campaign, by writing to ask the Mayor to head the city subscription list. We now know that he was going to be disappointed by the citizens' response, but it was through no lack of energy on his part, and the frank explanation may be that he was personally held in slight regard, and that another promoter would have done far better. That he was by now hale and energetic is shown in the postscript of this March letter to Wordsworth:

Sunday last I was *overturned* in my Sister's carriage. I wanted to let out, on Totter-down hill, two Gentlemen who were riding with me, when the Coachman gave the reins to another Servant, who was riding with him on the box, and jumped down, quite unnecessarily, to open & close the door. The Gentlemen had but just stepped out, when, from some cause, which "I could not well make out", the wheels got locked, & I was over in a moment. – I found myself (thro the goodness of the Almighty) unhurt, & lying *comfortably* on my side & there I determined to lie, till things were righted: except that the glass being *up*, I quietly raised my hand, & put it *down*. (The Lamp & the handle of the door, prevented it from being broken). I heard bustle enough *without*, but I was very *snug* in my corner. While musing on my odd, & unexpected position, a posse of able-bodies men without, gradually raised the Carriage, & I soon found myself in my *first position*. Plenty of anxious enquiries, & not a few congratulations. – No harm, of consequence, to person, place, or thing, and I soon reached Firfield, I hope, with a thankful heart. The Coachman, poor fellow, from not

hearing me move, or call out, thought I was killed! – It was the worse
for being Night!

'Sunday last' must have been Sunday 21 March, since by the following
Sunday, the 28th, his big letter to Wordsworth was written but not posted,
and he then adopted a curious method of sending it: he wrote to Mrs
Southey at Buckland, near Lymington, explaining that he could not write
fully at present, as he had several letters to attend to, so would she mind
having this letter to Wordsworth instead, perusing it, and forwarding it by
post? (Wordsworth, no doubt, thus detected that Cottle was in treasonable
communication with the other party.) Apparently she made and kept a copy,
omitting the Totterdown affair.

Wordsworth was secretly perturbed on Cottle's behalf by the publication
in 1843 of J.W. Robberd's two-volume *Memoir* of William Taylor, in that it
included several things from Southey's letters which Southey should never
have passed for printing, or perhaps had no time to deal with: in particular,
a sneer at Cottle's *Alfred* 'which will cut the poor old man to the heart. He
was so proud of Southey's notice', and on Wordsworth's last visit he had
brought out 'several memorials of Southey with the greatest Delight. Besides
C. really was, by publishing S's juvenile works, his patron when he stood in
need of one'. (Wordsworth by now believed Cottle to be *his* first publisher
also, forgetting James Johnson's edition of *An Evening Walk* and *Descriptive
Sketches*; then came Longman, then Moxon, and no others – so he tells R.
Shelton Mackenzie, for the latter's *Dictionary of Living Authors*, in a letter of
1 June.[8]) And, anyway, Taylor shows 'a licentious opinion in morals'! Thus
Wordsworth wrote to Moxon on 11 March.[9] But in a letter to John Peace,
the City Librarian, on 8 April,[10] he showed little sympathy for Cottle's new
scheme: he wonders whether Peace has been applied to; there is going to be
a monument in Keswick parish church, too, but Wordsworth does not care
for monuments in churches, 'at least in modern times', and in Southey's case
he would prefer 'a bronze bust, in some accessible and not likely to be
disturbed part of St Vincent's Rocks'. St Vincent's Rocks were soon disturbed
for the erection of the Clifton Suspension Bridge, but Wordsworth's idea is
anyway unattractive; and Southey's bust is not inappropriate to a cathedral
which visibly commemorates Richard Hakluyt, Bishop Butler, Sydney
Smith, Catherine Winkworth the Hymnographer, and 'Hugh Conway' the
novelist.

Wordsworth answered Cottle's letter on 4 April, with praise for the Bristol
project: but he could not subscribe or get people at Keswick to do so. The
parent of a grown-up family should take care over marrying a second time;

but such was Southey's state of mind that now nothing could be done, save by time.[11] Cottle told Mrs Southey that this letter was very moderately written, without any accusations, as if Wordsworth were abstaining from interference 'from the caution which seems natural to him', and because he had no hope of doing any good. On 15 April, the Dean of Bristol wrote remitting the usual Cathedral fees of £35. Mrs Southey had replied by 22 April, when Cottle again wrote to her. She had offered to send a copy of Cuthbert Southey's letter, which sounded intemperate, so that Cottle begged her not to take the trouble of copying it: 'I do not wish to interfere in Family differences, unless it were with the prospect of reconciling the unhappy interruption of harmony'. He was sorry that she had lost the social and literary advantages which were her right; she must look above ... All Southey's friends must grieve at the quarrel of his loved ones, and no-one does so more than Cottle himself. So he reverts to the pleasant subject of the monument: he has chosen the Committee of Management – her cousin Charles Bowles Fripp, J.H. Swayne the medico, and the Reverend John Eagles – and in the names of the four trustees he has opened an account in the Bristol branch of the Bank of England, where the monies are deposited. The proposed monument will be very striking, with its raised bust in the centre and its emblematical figures of Poetry and History. Baily is charging 500 guineas, so they will have to work hard, and Cottle will enjoy that. He wrote to the Mayor a few days ago, and got £5 and the promise to preside at a public meeting on 10 May. Subscription books would be left at the Banks and at the Commercial Rooms. All this information he asked Mrs Southey to pass on to her stepson-in-law Warter, who luckily was on the right side, but whose address he had mislaid.

He wrote to her again on 3 July, but the envelope is now empty save for her rough draft of a letter of 30 January 1841 to someone else (which she may have lent to Cottle and which he is here returning). We do not hear anything of the public meeting on 10 May, but on 13 July a meeting was held in the Bristol Institution, with the Mayor (W.L. Clarke) in the chair, and a Committee of seventeen was elected: the Mayor, the Dean, the Canon in Residence, Sir Charles A. Elton, Landor, John Scandrett Harford of Blaise, the Reverend John Eagles, Dr Pritchard, C.L. Walker, Cottle, the Reverend T. Grinfield, Dr Symonds (the father of John Addington Symonds), P.F. Aikan, S.S. Wayte, J.C. Swayne, J. Hill, C. Bowles Fripp. This was, in fact, the end of Cottle's leadership, but his and Robert Cottle's two subscriptions of £5 were bracketed fourth highest out of forty-six; his connexion Charles B. Hare gave two guineas. The resolutions of this meeting were published on 18 July, and Cottle sent copies off to Mrs Southey; on 6 September, having written a further letter to Baily, he packed it off to her for her to read, seal, and post to Baily's office.

But the grandiose project was doomed. Before the public meeting, when his sole part ended, he had himself collected or secured £127 plus promises. Then came the meeting, with the Mayor's advocacy and an impressive committee, followed up with advertisements, circulars, and the hospitality of the Bristol press: and it all produced £19 – 'less than one distant Gentleman', Landor (and less, by an ugly twist, than the expectant sculptor). They needed £500 (so Cottle now quotes it) for an object by their fellow-townsman which would adorn their Cathedral and would be a credit to their city; yet the gentlemen at the meeting, with a few exceptions, gave 'their *solitary guineas!*' After three more months, during which the banks collected from the public, the total included not one third ascribable to the meeting or the public appeal. Cottle was very cross and scornful. Although a member of the committee, he could not attend its meetings 'from physical incapacity', so on 4 November he put his remarks on paper in a letter to the honorary secretary, J.C. Swayne,[12] upbraiding him for the tardiness of the 'Friends of Literature' – as they *must* be, by their terms of reference. It is an impolite letter, and a boastful one; and, for the sake of a memorial that sounds pretty tasteless, it suggests a series of desperate expedients just to prove Bristol's 'respect for her illustrious dead': weekly meetings of the committee; advertisements in University papers at Oxford and Cambridge, and in the press of Liverpool, Manchester, and Edinburgh; more importantly, '*a liberal Addition to the meagre Subscriptions now on the List*'. He is sorry that they will have to think of '*foreign subscriptions*', an idea degrading to Bristol; had not even Southey's friend Peel said that the object was '*local*'? So the committee must make new efforts, and at the next meeting a vote must be carried to send each committee-member a little book for him to collect among his friends; Cottle would welcome one himself.

The letter received something of the answer it deserved. Swayne – who, like most of the committee, was a busier man than Cottle – wrote firmly on 10 November: the Committee did not accept the suggestion for members' canvassing their friends; they would close the public subscription (and let 'private zeal' do the rest); and they would not advertise in provincial papers. In fact, their three resolutions were (1) that Baily be asked to send a design for a bust; (2) that subscription-books be put in the Institution and the Commercial Rooms; and (3) that the subscription be closed on 30 November.

Initially chafed at this, with thoughts of his hard-won £127, Cottle read it a second time and suddenly noticed 'one little ill-written word, without a

Capital, to my great surprise; the word "bust"!' While Swayne was writing an eloquent letter to the editor of *The Bristol Mercury* on 14 November, appealing to the public for funds, Cottle was bringing his feelings to the boil, and on the 16th wrote to Swayne, more in anger than in sorrow, ordering him to change his plans. His attitude was not altogether unjust: apparently only four of the committee had been at the meeting, so that the change had been rather hustled through. Swayne had not mentioned the number in his letter, but Cottle had somehow obtained the information, and thus led off by expressing himself shocked at the decision of a mere four members. At the risk of being over-ruled, nothing 'on earth' will persuade him to agree to a bust *vice* a monument, for six reasons:

1. All the money which he himself had collected was expressly subscribed for a *monument*.
2. The Dean's letter gave permission to erect a *monument*.
3 The monies subscribed at and since the public meetings were for a *monument*.
4. He is sure that the Dean and Chapter would reject any proposal for turning the Cathedral into a '*Pantheon*, a receptacle for Busts'; Westminster Abbey has none, save in the little vestibule leading into it.
5. A bust belongs properly to a public room – the Bristol Library or the Institution, or the Commercial Rooms – not in 'a Sacred Edifice'.
6. He is sorry to have to say that four out of so large a committee had no right, without appealing to the rest, and without due notice, to change what had been the object of the endeavour. It *must* be a monument now, however humble it may be if they stay too proud to seek outside aid, which would certainly be granted in such a cause.

So he has another plan: that they call a meeting of the whole committee to decide for a monument or a bust. As Cottle cannot attend, perhaps Swayne would have the goodness to read out his letter and, if proxy voting is allowed, accept Cottle's vote for a moment, to contain a bas-relief of 'one of the finest, & most Intellectual of Countenances'.

Two days later, on 18 November, he wrote to Mrs Southey at Buckland, wishing that his letter could be 'the harbinger of good news'; but it could not be; he enclosed copies of his letters to and from Swayne, and promised to tell her the outcome. And he was moved to say to her, 'Do not judge too harshly of Bristol. I love the Place, & I love the People, but I am very angry with them! At least with those who have not subscribed'.

Memorial bust of Robert Southey, in the north choir of Bristol Cathedral
(reproduced by kind permission of the Dean and Chapter)

Thus his darling plan was jettisoned, and in 1845 Baily executed a bust of Southey on a base as Gothick as Chatterton had been given. The proportions are heroic (though the nose and lips, and the rest, are all rather too flabby, and the height and glare of the thing still have something of the coxcomb about them). In its soapy-looking white marble, it may even be said to add brightness and interest to the north choir aisle of the Cathedral, where the proposed monument could have been overpowering.

1   His nine letters (1843-1847) to Mrs Southey are in the collection presented to the Bristol City Library by Mrs Eleanor Boult, Southey's great-grand-daughter.

2   Mary Russell Mitford, *Recollections of a Literary Life: or, Books, Places, and People* (London: Bentley, 1852), III.6 ff.

3   Bristol City Library MS.B 20878.

4   de S, No.1503.

5   His account of the preliminary stages is in his letter to Wordsworth, March 1844 (University of Bristol Library MS.3/3).

6   Secretary to the Admiralty and *Quarterly* reviewer. Cottle's letter to him (9. Feb. 1844) was advertised by Winifred A. Myers Ltd on 11 Oct. 1963.

7   The friend of Coleridge and Lamb at Christ's Hospital; Cottle's letter to him (6 Feb. 1844) was advertised by Winifred A. Myers Ltd on 1 Jan. 1958.

8   de S, No.1531.

9   de S, No.1520.

10 de S, No.1525.

11 *1795 Album.*

12 Cottle had a tenuous connexion with Swayne (one of the original staff of the Bristol Medical School), who lived in the corner house of St James's Barton, near St James's Square, the house once inhabited by the Cottles. See A. Prichard, *Bristol Medical School* (Bristol: Arrowsmith, 1894), p.9.

Chapter 18
Varnish: Gloucestershire Assizes

Otherwise, life must have been quiet out at Firfield. Cottle went on with the preparation of a little tract called *The Heresiarch Church of Rome*, which was soon selling at twopence; and Ann Hare had rebound, on 13 August 1845, that Bible which had survived Eliza and Amos and their mother. John Dix, computing Cottle's age as about 75, gives us a description of him at this time.[1] His 'carriage, drawn by an old white horse', stands before Zion Chapel, and he lamely alights and enters, tottering to his place in the pew farthest from the pulpit. His shapely head is rather flat-topped, and has a thick covering of grey hair; his 'benevolent' grey eyes are almost hidden by spectacles. His face is kindly, yet not lacking in decision, and his lips are firmly compressed. He seems 'a gentleman in easy circumstances', without 'any peculiarities telling of striking genius'. To Dix it is astonishing that this mild figure can have caused Byron's, or any man's, resentment.

Wordsworth was keeping Cottle in mind, and had mentioned him in a letter[2] to Basil Montagu on 1 October 1844 as his only friend, save John Pinney, still alive from the early days in Bristol and Somerset; he had lost trace of Pinney – but he and Cottle 'are only in our 75th year'. On 6 December 1845, Wordsworth wrote[3] to him as 'My dear old Friend', with praises for the anti-popish tract; Wordsworth would go further, since he has spent quite three years in Romanist countries, but it is well-timed, and he hopes that it will affect readers' minds in the way intended. 'And now let me bid you affectionately good-bye, with assurance that I do and shall retain to the last a remembrance of your kindness and of the many pleasant and happy hours which at one of the most interesting periods of my life, I passed in your neighbourhood and in your company'.

This sounds regretfully firm and final, but their active friendship was not yet over; they were held together by some rather clever varnish that Cottle had invented – the only known result of his researches with Davy. On 15 January 1846, Wordsworth wrote to Moxon,[4] asking him not to send some required books until he had procured, for forwarding in the parcel, a 'bottle of lustre varnish which Mr Cottle of Bristol gave orders should wait for my call at Mr R. Green's 36 King Wm. Street, London Bridge'. His son John had sent him three pictures from Italy, and they were going to be cleaned by a painter staying in Ambleside; Cottle had given so flattering an account of the varnish that Wordsworth wanted to have it tried. Its inventor felt that he had brought it to perfection 'by a series of experiments carried on at different periods through his long life'.

On his 76th birthday, 9 March 1846, Cottle wrote a poem of thirty-five quatrains called *The Weary Pilgrim* and sent it to Wordsworth. The manuscript, in the University of Bristol Library,[5] is in a good style of penmanship but signed very shakily by Cottle. It has once been in a little folder, and the stitch-holes remain; we shall see that he sent another 'bound' poem to Wordsworth in 1848. The theme had been the theme of many Cottle letters: the transience of earthly pleasures, the immutability of what lies beyond, the ineffable weariness of an old and difficult life, the Christian's sure hope. By the time that he published it, at the very end of his 1847 *Reminiscences*, he had expanded it to thirty-eight stanzas and tinkered with it mightily, so that a collation (which I do not offer here) would reveal some sad facts about his poetic method. At any rate, his elderly muse was no better at showing mysteries in seven-syllabled trochaics than she had been in blank verse during her prime.

Wordsworth must have acknowledged this tribute and also asked for some papers to be sent, and Cottle, on receipt of his note, despatched them on 2 April. The rest of his covering letter gives a dull picture of the closing stages of a literary partnership: it is a highly technical piece of unvarnished truth about how to varnish oil-paintings. Cottle is sorry that Wordsworth has bought three more bottles of porcelain varnish from Mr R. Green in King William Street. This is a disaster, and to prevent a recurrence Cottle will send Green, at the beginning of the next week, a pint of the same varnish in a tin, so that there will be nothing to break – and if Wordsworth will tell Cottle of some bookseller in the Lakes who has a London correspondent, then Green can enclose the tin in the latter's next parcel. The three-and-a-half bottles of varnish which Wordsworth has applied to his three nice big pictures would have been enough for fifty or even a hundred, and if Cottle had been present he would have saved him the trouble and the possible risk. The varnish may have penetrated any cracks and may thus have flooded the canvas behind, whereas this could have been prevented by giving the canvas two good coats of isinglass solution; the varnish would not then have soaked through, and could have been used far more economically, but Cottle hopes that Wordsworth's satisfaction is securely based. As for making the solution, you put an ounce of isinglass in a pint jug, and add half a pint of spring water;

let it soak all night, or for a few hours, and then put the jug in a saucepan containing water; boil, to dissolve the isinglass; when it is warm, strain it through muslin, and when it is nearly cold add an ounce of spirits of wine to prevent the animal substance from decomposing and to make the solution white; it will then harden, so that when needed for use it might be put by the fire or dipped in warm water. And you must have a brush exclusively for use with it, which must be washed immediately after.

Cottle, jealous for the reputation of his varnish, next has to deal with the fate of some little paintings by Sir George Beaumont, which Wordsworth fears are now injured by having too much gloss; yes, but one or two R.As. have approved this very property, since the gloss brings out the finer parts. It is only from one angle that the gloss can appear excessive; shift your position, and the beneficial effect can be seen. However, if the Beaumonts still seem ruined, here is a useful tip for removing the varnish instead of rubbing it off with pumice-stone powder or cuttle-fish: take a piece of sponge, the size of a nutmeg, dip it in turpentine, and rub, squeezing and refilling it with turpentine whenever it clogs; you thus get right down to the original painting, and with paintings so long executed there can be no risk of damage, but you should try it first on one corner … Cottle has 'had some little experience in these things', so, if anything goes wrong, Wordsworth must drop him a line and ask for advice; for the desired surface without too much shine, one coat of thin varnish will be best, but Cottle will have to prepare it specially, so he will defer sending the promised pint until Wordsworth gives his orders. In a touching postscript, Cottle promises to give a message to Peace the Librarian, and joins with Ann in respects to Mary Wordsworth; Ann disapproves of his work on varnish (and, indeed, if this *was* the sum of his researches, then Davy inspired in vain), but the pursuit has kept him occupied and even turned his thoughts to other subjects: 'I generally go down to Bedminster, where my apparatus is, for two or three hours, once a week. Do you think I do wrong?'

We do not know if Wordsworth even cared, since all his last letters to Cottle seem to have disappeared. Meanwhile, two new literary problems were engaging Cottle's attention. The first was the reshaping of the *Recollections* as one volume of *Reminiscences*, with more emphasis on Southey and – needless to say – the suppression of Hannah More's unruly servants: still a bad and confusing book, but neater and much improved. Secondly, there was the old query of Southey's about a first edition of *Pilgrim's Progress*. Cottle had done his best to find one, by inquiring and by advertising, but without result until 1847, long after Southey's death, when he suddenly learned that one had been discovered and that a gentleman called Edward B.

Underhill, of Newmarket House, near Nailsworth in Gloucestershire, could give particulars. Cottle wrote at once, and Mr Underhill replied pleasantly on 27 February 1847, naming Mr J.S. Holford as the owner and Mr George Offer as the accredited editor. So Cottle wrote to Offer, who gratifyingly replied from Hackney on 6 March, enclosing a copy of his voluminous correspondence with Southey on the subject. Here Southey satisfactorily proves that Bunyan had *not* plagiarised from a book published at Antwerp in 1627 – a decision reflecting credit on Southey's scholarship and giving great pleasure to Cottle, who was naturally an upholder of Bunyan. And Cottle, in fact, had helped in this little research by referring Southey to a similar German book mentioned in Dunlop's *History of Fiction*.[6]

While the *Reminiscences* were being polished, their elder brother suddenly struck his final blow. Gloucestershire Assizes opened at Gloucester on Monday, 5 April 1847, and Tidy was back in the fray. Mr Justice Maule was in a filthy temper, and stayed at Cheltenham, since, as he publicly announced, the Gloucester magistrates, in their 'liberality, good taste, and gentlemanly consideration', had provided as lodgings for Her Majesty's Judges of Assize an 'unventilated, undrained, foetid doghole'.[7] In the Nisi Prius court things went against Cottle, and when he wrote to Wordsworth on the 24th he said wanly that his three trials arising out of the *Recollections* had cost him nearly £1,000; 'Judge Maule was exceedingly and unusually hostile, but it has furnished me with an opportunity of forgiveness'[8] – a hideous development of the sour grapes theme. Cottle's feeling that the judge was 'unusually' hard on him is perhaps justified, for Sir William Henry Maule had an excellent reputation for courtesy and sense and humour; the Gloucester magistrates may have been chiefly to blame, but, on the other hand, Maule had been known to mislead juries by the exercise of a pretty irony. So we have heard of three trials – under Erskine in 1839, Maule in 1840, and again Maule in 1847; but when was that under Baron James Parke, Lord Wensleydale, which Crabb Robinson mentions with disapproval?[9]

> Baron James Parke most unwarrantably charged the jury against him in an action for libel brought by the drunken and worthless servant of Hannah Moore, who was accused of what everybody knew to be true, but could not be legally proved, that he had plundered his mistress. And years after her death Cottle having thoughtlessly printed this, an attorney, for costs only, in all probability, brought an action, on which damages for £1,000 were given. The baron had a contempt for all saints, and made no allowance for the simplicity of well-intentioned Methodists or Evangelicals. It nearly ruined the poor old man.

There is a further mystery: we have seen that by 1840 the case had cost Cottle nearly £1,000; yet even after the 1847 action his loss is stated as just this amount for the three trials.

It says something for Cottle's spirit that he went ahead with the *Reminiscences*. The introduction, dated 20 April, justifies his task and his method by quoting Coleridge and Southey in support. How many are dead! Lovell, Burnett, Lloyd, Catcott, Beddoes, Danvers, Amos Cottle, Gilbert, John Morgan, Ann Yearsley, Davy, Hannah More, Hall, Coleridge, Lamb, Poole (forgiven, no doubt), Wade, Southey, Foster! It all confirms 'What shadows we are and what shadows we pursue!' In his letter to Wordsworth on 24 April he announces that the printing will be finished in a fortnight, and that he has no interest in the venture, since a publisher has unsolicited taken it off his hands. Cottle has expunged and added freely; the enlargements include the Coleridge-Wedgwood correspondence and some Southey letters, and he hopes that Wordsworth will approve of the new features. If Wordsworth will send him the name of his nearest bookseller's London agent, he will tell the publishers to send Wordsworth an early copy, and Wordsworth *fils* or *fille* can have one, if they wish. He is sorry that Wordsworth's friend, Taylor, of whom Wordsworth wrote to him some years ago, did not undertake Southey's biography: 'but *health* frustrates many a laudable plan'. Cottle must have written this letter in some disappointment: Firfield was remote from Bristol, and when Wordsworth had come over from Bath a few days before, he had not found time to visit his old friend before catching a train back; Peace passed this apology on to Cottle; but it was the second time that Wordsworth had evaded him.

On the same day, 24 April, he wrote to Mrs Southey, offering to send her the new book in the same way, through her bookseller's London agent. Thus in May, Houlston and Stoneman, of 65 Paternoster Row, published *Reminiscences of Samuel Taylor Coleridge and Robert Southey*; but it could well pass almost unnoticed, since what was new in it was by no means startling. Wordsworth did not send the required address, and had to be prodded; Mrs Southey, who had a cold, gave the obliging information that her own publisher was at 37 Paternoster Row, so that would be easy. Cottle and his sister went to Weston-super-Mare for the sake of 'breathing the sea air', and when they returned to Firfield they found her 'elegant volume' awaiting them on the table. It would be all the more interesting, he said, from being a joint affair. (So this must be Robert and Caroline Southey's *Robin Hood: a Fragment* (1847).) And they hoped her cold was better.

Wordsworth's sloth in beseeching his copy had adequate excuses: Dora was dying, and when Cottle again wrote asking for names and addresses, he had not heart to reply. On 17 July, Cottle read with interest her Portuguese narrative, and felt a hope that she was recovering after that warm climate, but next day he read in the Bristol paper that she was dead! His shock was soon merged in his pity for her parents, and he wrote to Wordsworth on the 19th,[10] with appropriate sentiments gently phrased, the spelling lapsing with the rising emotion. He says that he 'can but imperfectly conceive' the affliction of losing an only daughter of such worth, but exhorts Wordsworth to be sustained by the Christian hope and by the thought of Him Who is the Resurrection and the Life; they are both nearing those four-score years which are 'the boundary of man's hope', but they believe that mansions are prepared for them. Cottle has some cause to be thankful to Providence, and Wordsworth has been showered with 'many of Earth's choicest blessings', but 'the hope that extends beyond the Grave is worth it all. It is the setting sun with us, and night is hastening, but the morning of a brighter day is hastening also, which will have neither cloud nor termination'; and the death of a loved one is only a promise of final reunion.

To change the subject, could Wordsworth send that address? Cottle realises that his last letter must have found Wordsworth in great anxiety, but he much wants to send this token of respect to a friend 'who is now the solitary remainder of those who were prized in early life!' He owes Wordsworth an explanation for having printed some of Southey's letters, bearing in mind that four years previously Wordsworth had asked him to help Taylor with the loan of material for *his* memoir; Cottle had instantly promised Taylor his help, but Taylor subsequently wrote saying that he was giving up the undertaking on grounds of health; Cottle went on hoping to help someone else, but when a publisher actually applied to him to reprint his book, he inserted a few of Southey's letters with no stirrings of conscience. Does Wordsworth think that he has done wrong? He had no-one to advise him, and he wishes that Wordsworth could have been nearer. He is full of admiration for the Laureate's Cambridge Ode, and among more conventional qualities he picks out its brave avowal of '*Protestant principles*'; the poem is all the more meritorious in view of the tragic time at which it was written, and the agonized father must have shown 'stern resolution'. Cottle and Ann commend Wordsworth and Mary to the comfort of the Almighty; what has happened will be blessed, if it urges them 'to look beyond the low horizon of this world'. And then there is a touching little postscript: 'will you convey my kind remembrance to your good Sister Dorothy. – It is now about fifty years since you read me your Lyrical Ballad's in M.S. at Allfoxden!'

It was indeed fifty years since their Annus Mirabilis, but when Cottle came to repeat his preface, on 1 January 1848, for a second edition of *Reminiscences*, he was not so struck by the jubilee date that he made any special mention of it. He and Ann were making preparations for their final dissolution, and on 13 January John Hare's body was removed from Zion to Brick Grave, Square O, No. 22, at Arno's Vale, the necropolis on the Bath Road. This was done, not on account of any ill-feeling, but solely at the insistence of his widow, who wanted to be buried with him, and to whose request the trustees reluctantly consented[11]. But Cottle still had some verse in him, and on 25 March he wrote Wordsworth a really jocose letter[12] reminding him that *Malvern Hills*, 'my first poem' (which is quite untrue), had been published fifty years before; likewise, here is his last, which he has recently written: 'another stanza will never proceed from my pen'. And he enclosed *The Wizard*, or *Wishing Cured*, written in his small, shaky hand on pale-blue-tinted, lined paper, sewn into a simple card folder;[13] its twenty-two stanzas are trivial enough, but may be judged 'not bad for seventy-eight', especially when (as here) the punctuation has been tidied:

Is it a noon-day random dream,
   Or else a vision of the night?
Whatever jarring Casuists deem,
   It must be wrong, or must be right.
For once, let *Reason* yield her sway,
And *Fancy* hold her holyday.

In Albion's matchless Isle was born
   (No matter where) a lovely Mary:
Her cheek was like the blush of morn,
   Lightsome and gay as fawn or fairy.
Yet still she was not free from ailing:
She had one small, but common failing.

To *Wish*, and *wish* was her delight, –
   More changeful than the Shepherd's Fold.
The weather never suited quite:
   It was too hot, or else too cold;
And then, some *distant* object pleased her,
But what was *present* always teased her.

A *Wizard Sage*, with stately stride,
   Once cross'd her path, and saw her sad.
"What ails thee, Gentle Maid?" he cried;
   "I like the Damsel blithe and glad".
"O, Sir!" she said, "I *wish* in vain,
"And when I'm weary, *Wish* again.

"I see the *hoar*-frost deck the sprays,
　　But Winter has no charms for me;
I love the long and joyous days,
　　When Nature smiles in exstasy."
"'Tis done!" the Wizard cried; when, lo!
The heavens with Cancer's radiance glow!

Pleased with the change the Sun she hails,
　　But soon his scorching beams opprest her.
"I like", she cried, "bleak *Winter's* gales,
　　His ice-bound streams, and rugged vesture.
"I *Wish* 'twas *Winter*", slow she said,
"When Parties meet, and Books are read".

The Wizard hear'd, when, instant, round,
　　Old Frost's teeth-chattering empire spread, –
The leafless tree, the iron ground,
　　With darkening clouds, portentous, dread!
The Snows now mantle Vale and Hill,
And th'*Wintry* winds are loud and chill!

The Maiden, shrinking, shivering cried,
　　"I wish sweet *Summer's* balm were near!"
The *Wizard* heard, and thus replied,
　　"Haste, *Summer*!" – when the prospect drear
Vanish'd! and, at the potent sound,
All forms luxuriant reign around!

When thus the Wizard: "From this hour,
　　Summers and *Winters* thee obey!
Call either! Well improve thy power!"
　　Exulting in imperial sway,
With views, like Ocean, unconfined,
All rapturous visions fill her mind.

She first on *Winter* calls, and then
　　The *Summer* pleased her taste the best;
Then surly *Winter* comes again,
　　And then the *Hours* in garlands drest.
Each follows each, as Fancy reasons,
And thus successive pass the *Seasons*.

Alas! In her tumultuous dream,
    She thought not of the *March of Years*!
She heeds not Time's retreating Stream,
    That never in its *flood* appears!
And now, on her once lovely face,
The eye the stamp of *Age* might trace!

It chanced that, on a Summer's morn,
    She, musing, stray'd o'er neighbouring mountains,
And as she sped through brake and thorn,
    She look'd into a *Glassy Fountain*.
She starts! She shrieks! The frantic cry
Proclaims the Sufferer's agony!

In loneliness, she breathes her pain:
    "How shall my heart its anguish hide!
I never shall be young again!
    The bud has drooped! The flower has died!
Wishes have been my broken reed,
And my days have pass'd with lightning speed!"

While in the depths of sorrow drown'd
    (Where Hope no transient gleam might borrow),
The *Wizard* Mary weeping found,
    When thus she faltering told her sorrow:
"For *Wishes* I my life have sold!
I once was *Young*, but now am *Old*!

"I scarce have breathed th'inspiring air,
    Before my earthly periods close!
The slow-declining years prepare
    The weary Spirit for repose;
And reverend is the Mouldring Tree;
But *Youth* and *Age* are one to me!"

The *Wizard* thus: "I *read* thy fate!
    In vain thou mourn'st thy days misspent!
Knowledge with thee hath come too late.
    So, steep'd in thankless discontent,
Mourn *on* thy wasted hours and years,
And shed thine unavailing tears!"

Bereft, disconsolate, opprest,
  The Mourner stands with down-cast head!
Commotion revels in her breast,
  But utterance from her lips has fled.
The Tear (to Magic Power allied!)
Now softens *him*, who came to chide.

"Thou hast been first in Folly's Train,
  But *if*" (he utter'd) "at this time,
I raise my *Wand*, and once again
  Restore thee to thy pristine prime,
Wilt thou renounce thy *Wishing Chains*,
And deem that best which Heaven ordains?"

She cried, Joy flashing from her eyes:
  "Let others grasp at phantoms vain!
Wishes! Your treacheries I despise!
  I spurn my *fetters* with disdain!
Give me my *Youth*, and I will strive
To keep Contentment's spark alive!"

He touch'd her! – When she stands array'd,
  All lovely, as the Roseate spring !
The graceful Mien! The blooming Maid!
  Brief honours, ever on the wing!
When thus the Sage, impressive, spake:
"To loftier aspirations wake!

* "With *thee*, all excellence is *Youth*,
*   Unmindful of thy *nobler part*!
* Prize, rather, Wisdom, Virtue, Truth,
*   The graces of the Mind and Heart;
** These shall survive and lustre shed,
** When *Beauty* fades, and *Youth* is fled.

* "The days of Mortal Man are few!
*   There is a *Heritage* in sight:
* *That Object*, steadfast, keep in view,
*   And plume thy Pinions for the flight!
* Man's Life is emblem'd by the Grass.
* Improve the moments as they pass!"

(Cottle has wrestled with the last twelve lines: those marked * have a piece of paper stuck over their original, and those marked ** have yet another piece.)

He is full of excuses for this flight of fancy; he knows that he is not being his age when venturing into the realm of fable, but at least there is a moral. Did not Cowper admit that he lay awake half the night laughing as he planned *John Gilpin*? It was even so with Cottle in the composition of this swansong, and the night waned as his mind ran on 'earnest, though somewhat amusing thought'. Wordsworth may find the theme foolish, and Cottle rather agrees; but 'in some moods, lively nonsense is more acceptable than dull sense'. Besides, *some* may find an occult meaning; and at least the Wizard is a white one, not a black, and for his sober speech one may compare Balaam. Actually, Cottle 'prompted the fellow', but the two or three readers are not to know this; and the wizard's 'rather extra mundane qualities' were honestly come by ... So he rambles on with this sleepy nonsense, and then pulls himself up sharply, to give an interesting picture of his state of body and mind:

I hope you continue in your usual good state of health, the comfortable possession of which, possessed by myself, demands from me gratitude to the Almighty; especially as I am disabled from using *exercise*, not having been able, for some years past, even to walk out on my Sister's lawn. This has arisen, as you know, out of a Gig accident in early life, when my ancles were dislocated, the effects of which, (as is usual) increases with age. At present, I never put any foot to the ground without feeling pain, more or less; sometimes acute; but, from evil, in some form, few are exempt, and, while possessing so many alleviations it is profitable to consider, how much more severely many are exercised: – and it ill becomes those to complain who have nearly passed over the bridge, or a hilly and rough road, and who see *something better*, in a fine campaign country *before*.

The disaster alluded to, throws me largely on my own resources, and deprives me of many social and other advantages, but an Old Man has no right to repine, who can eat, drink, and sleep well; whose sight and hearing are good; and who is a stranger to Gout, Indigestion, or any known malady. To complain therefore of one providential evil, out of Humanity's dark catalogue, would be monstrous. I cannot doubt but that the bodily evils, to which some are subject, arise, often at least, less from the inflictions of Nature, than their own indiscretion. This inference is reasonably entertained by one, who (as secondary causes) ascribes his own *present* state of health, to tolerable equanimity of mind, temperance, early rising, and the luxury of *cold water*. I say *'present'*, for it would be delusion not to know that I am standing on the verge of life, yet the hope of the Christian converts, in one sense, the most gloomy of prospects into a source of Joy! I trust this feeling is entertained by you, with more justice than by myself, and in a higher degree.

There is a strength here, and buoyancy; and, though the years had brought ill health and lameness, constant bereavement, deadly hostility, strange loneliness, and a life second-hand and second-rate, there is no repining. It is all the more unfortunate, therefore, that we have lost Wordsworth's last letters to him, so that we can only guess the effect which these faithful, cheerful letters had on the old poet.

Crabb Robinson did not call again, but the existence of Cottle's books and Cottle's acquaintances kept Cottle in his mind and in his diary. On 18 March 1847 Robinson had visited Dr Brabant at Devizes, and the Doctor repeated Coleridge's pun against *Amos* Cottle: 'He wrote a poem that bore a lie on the title page, for he called it *Alfred*, and it was never *halfread* by any human being';[14] so even Robinson can muddle Joseph and his brother. On 18 October 1848 he visited young Sara Coleridge; she was 'justly incensed against Cottle' for bringing out another book on her father, and found it hard to parry the reproaches cast on her father's memory. Still, she was more nearly impartial than might have been expected. Robinson had not yet seen the *Reminiscences*, but agreed with her that Cottle should not have printed 'a very offensive letter by Southey against Coleridge'. She held that the opium letters should not have been published either: 'from which,' says Robinson, 'I altogether dissent'.[15] In fact, he read the book, when he at last picked it up, in a very desultory way: on 20 August 1850, at Rydal (Wordsworth's home in Cumbria), he found that it contained much about Coleridge that should not have been printed, along with much that was interesting; in the forenoon of 21 August 1851, he finished 'the unpleasant but interesting book of Cottle, containing too true an exposure of Coleridge's infirmities, by which only mediocrity has been comforted & malignity gratified'; but he returned to it as late as August 1855, when he 'lounged over the enlarged work of Cottle ... partly new, partly a repetition of the first which he sent me, and which gave offence as betraying the bad opinion Southey entertained of Coleridge needlessly...'[16]

Up to 1850, Cottle was a regular communicant at Zion,[17] and his interest in the history of religion clearly sprang from more than the mere writing of polemical tracts. On 7 January 1848, C.J. Whittuck sent him some sermon notes by the Reverend Philip Henry (1631-1696) and these he incorporated in his 1795 *Album*. 1850 brought that inevitable woe which would have killed a man of less equanimity than he. On St George's Day died William Wordsworth, his last link with the promising and disappointing past, his equal in age, the Laureate and the shedder of lustre on his life. When he read the news in the paper, he was stilled, and could only utter with a sigh, 'Now the *last* of my early friends is gone!' Mrs Wordsworth wrote to him on the subject, and on 11 June he replied in deep sympathy,[18] though he delayed until some Remarks on the Papacy left the press, and sent them to cheer her up! He did this with no feeling of incongruity, since he and Wordsworth had been perfectly agreed on the subject of popery; and, had the fourth edition of *Alfred* been ready, he would have sent that as well, even as he had hoped to give Wordsworth a copy. In his grief, he recalls how hale and active and temperate Wordsworth had seemed, so that Cottle had never expected to be the survivor; but he hopes to follow him soon. He ends by associating Ann in his condolences, and assures Mrs Wordsworth that she and her sons, although the latter are unknown to him, will always be welcome at Firfield.

1   [J.Dix], *op.cit.*, pp. 163-164.
2   de S, No. 1546.
3   de S, No. 1588.
4   de S, No. 1597.
5   MS. 3/9.
6   All this correspondence is in *R.47*, pp. 249-252.
7   *FFJ* for Saturday, 10 April 1847, Vol. CIII, No. 5341.
8   University of Bristol Library MS. 3/5.
9   In the later version of his visits to Cottle, in Edith J. Morley, *Henry Crabb Robinson*, II.502 ff.
10   University of Bristol Library MS. 3/6.
11   Cozens, *op.cit.*, p. 19.
12   University of Bristol Library MS. 3/7.
13   University of Bristol Library MS. 3/10.
14   Edith J. Morley, *Henry Crabb Robinson*, II.663.
15   Edith J. Morley, *Henry Crabb Robinson*, II.680-681.
16   Edith J. Morley, *Henry Crabb Robinson*, II.703, 754.
17   Information supplied by the Revd T.C. Lewis.
18   University of Bristol Library MS. 3/8.

Chapter 19

'It Is The Setting Sun With Us'

Other literary endeavours occupied Cottle in 1850; a note to Pearce, a bookbinder in Baldwin Street, Bristol, dated 2 March and now in my collection, asks him to let the bearer have Cottle's 'Books, with any waste sheets which may be over. Also Mr P's note'. During the year, the fourth *Alfred* came out, prefaced by the anti-papal pamphlet and by a prologue which Cottle styles an 'excrescence' retained as 'the sport of a youthful fancy'. The poem itself, he points out, is virtually an *Alfred II*, since he had re-read his original and made a reconstruction out of the old materials, he being still 'all song and sentiment' despite his advancing years. Longman was again his publisher, and he was on good terms with Houlston and Stoneman, who had called for a second edition of the *Reminiscences*. This flattering invitation he put down to the puff of the first edition in the *Times* of 3 November 1847, but the notice is not so uniformly favourable as he seemed to think. The review, not signed, on the whole praises 'the venerable and chatty Joseph', but compares him with 'Bozzy' and says that he 'reminds us at every step of those very good-natured friends who are always saying unkind things with a view to one's piece (*sic*) of mind and eventual improvement'. It blames him for revealing the '*tête-à-tête* conferences', etc., but 'the reader must love Cottle'. So on 1 November he wrote a persuasive little letter to the reviewer.[1] It is clear that he had been at poetry again, but since the poem seems to have disappeared we may never know what a 'Banorial Hall' is (baronial, manorial, banal, or a bit of all three?).

Firfield House, near Bristol.
Nov[r] 1. 1850

Dear Sir

I hold myself greatly indebted to you, as a stranger, for your generous advocacy, in the *Times*, of my 'Reminiscences of Coleridge and Southey'. You will not be displeased to learn, that I may fairly ascribe it to *your* notice, that soon after its appearance, the Publishers contracted for a Second Edition.

You are aware of my having recently published 'Alfred', an expensive Work, concerning the sale of which I am naturally anxious. Since then I have written a small Poem, called the *Banorial Hall*, (a copy of which I enclose.) It has occurred to me, that, by being brought before the Public, especially in the *Times*, it might assist the sale of Alfred. With this thought your name was immediately associated. If on the perusal you should approve of the Poem, would it be too great a liberty, if I were to ask for your influence with the Editor of the *Times* to obtain its insertion? – If I have, in past years been of any little service to the cause of Literature, the consideration might, with your recommendation, induce the Editor of the Times to deviate from his usual custom of inserting Poetry.

The *Banorial Hall* is perhaps rather singular, in having been written (certainly his last Poem) by a man nearer Eighty one than Eighty, and all of whose early Friends (Wordsworth the last) are now dead, whilst he himself, at so advanced an age, awaits a speedy entrance into the New Economy! – As secondary causes, the exemption of many of the usual infirmities of age, I may name, early rising, temperance, and cold water.

If you think my request inadmissible, will you add to my sense of obligation, by favouring me with one line expressive of the same, and believe me still to remain,

Dear Sir
Your ever obliged Hum^e Sert
Joseph Cottle.

P.S. Had the 'Banorial Hall' been written a little earlier, I should have given it to Montalto, in the 11th Book of Alfred.

Meanwhile, he was helping Wordsworth's nephew Christopher, the future Bishop of Lincoln, to write a memoir of his uncle. For this purpose he sent him manuscript copies, made in the first place to please Ann Hare, of all Wordsworth's letters to him, and these the Canon returned by the morning of 8 October 1850, along with his own sermon *On the Prophecy of St Paul on the Man of Sin*. Cottle at once read the sermon 'with much satisfaction', and replied encomiastically the same day. Delighted that so eminent a churchman should 'condescend' to ask his opinion on the expediency of publishing separately Lectures XI and XII of his *Lectures on the Apocalypse*, but regretting that he has not yet read the series, he nevertheless recommends the idea, from his conjecture that the two bear particularly on Romanism. Whereat the letter develops into a warning that we live in perilous times …, when Popery issues from her secret coverts, and is now, more than ever, making a formidable effort to subvert Protestantism, and to 'deceive the nations'. In times of extreme danger to Christianity, the Almighty has always raised up Champions for the Truth, before whom the Enemy has been discomfited. This is one of those perilous periods, when it may be again asked, 'Who is on the Lord's side?' Being in my 81st year, I shall not live to see the result of the present spiritual movement, but, I am assured, the Spirit from on high will descend on some honoured Instrument, who will arrest the Enemy in his triumphs, and 'stay the plague'. May you be one, and the chief.

In this ominous crisis, I reflect on *you* with great pleasure. In my humble, but *hearty*, endeavour, I have attempted to explore the pernicious qualities of Popery, but to do it effectively required something more than a rapid advertence to its chief enormities. It demanded, to produce any determinate effect, that Learning which I admire in others, more happily circumstanced, and deplore in myself.

This regret is moderated when he thinks of Canon Wordsworth, his talents and his zeal. In any letter to Rydal Mount, would he please remember Cottle to Mrs Wordsworth, 'of whose health and welfare I shall always rejoice to hear. – Your good *Uncle* was the very last survivor of my Early Friends!'

When Cottle next wrote, on 25 April, 1851, he had a few days before received a copy of the *Memoirs*, whether from the Canon or from Moxon he did not know. His thanks are movingly expressed, with their reasonable claim that the *Memoirs* can interest no one more than him, since they had recalled scenes and happenings of which he is the only remaining partaker, 'the *last* of the whole generation of acquaintance'. One reason for his admiring the Canon's editorial work is that it so resembles Mason's treatment of the life of Gray, 'which I have always regarded as a model of Biography for one recently deceased. In the completion of your work, you possessed fine materials, and in the use of them, it is the highest praise to say, – You have done them justice. Mr Wordsworth's *strong good sense* was as conspicuous as his Genius.' In a postscript, he strangely requested the return of his copies of Wordsworth's letters, which he had receipted on 8 October 1850; so a hasty apology for his forgetfulness followed on 3 May 1851 – 'Such an occurrence never happened to me before'.[2]

The Quarterly Review had no scruples about Cottle's white hairs; in its issue of March 1852 it pounced delightedly on poor *Alfred* and six other epics, and worried them to shreds.[3] It contrasts with them Coleridge's plans for an epic, and his modest realisation that it would be a huge task: ten years

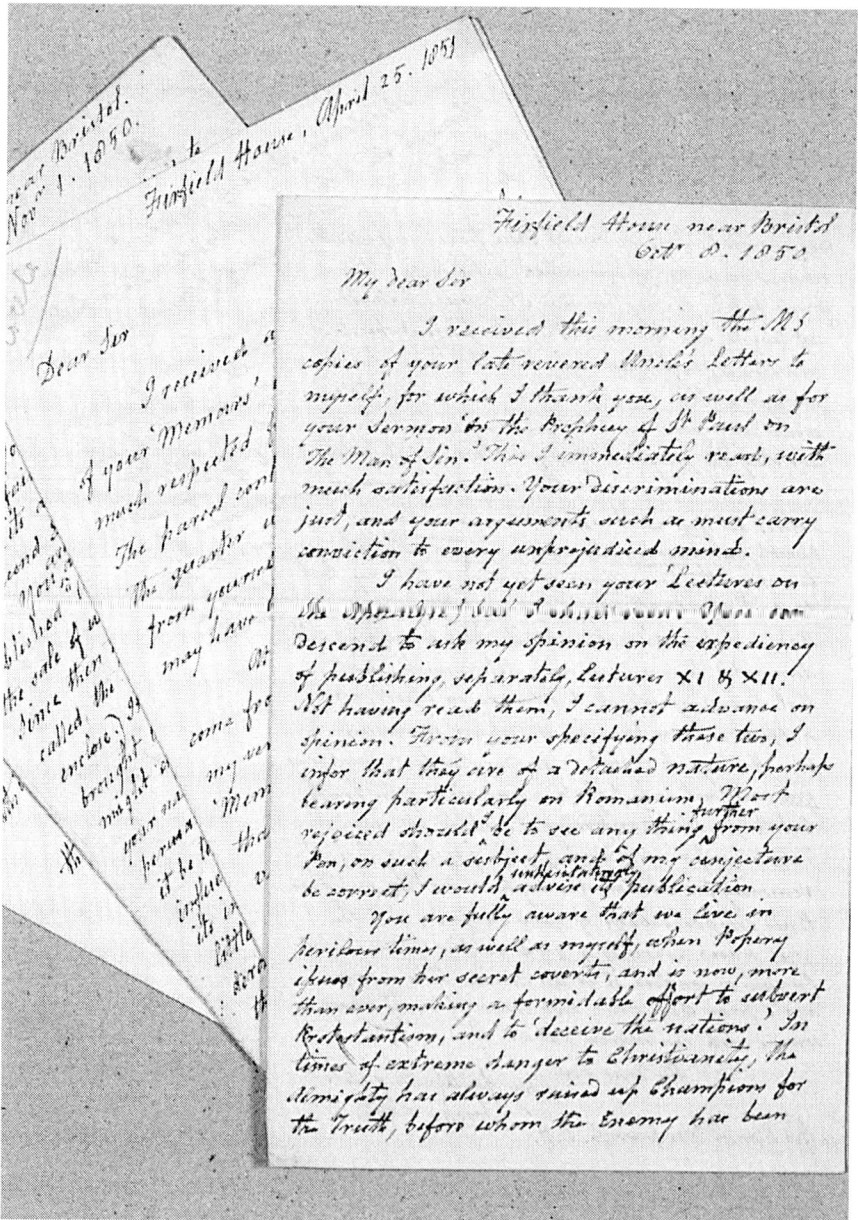

Letters from Joseph Cottle (to Christopher Wordsworth and to a reviewer in the *Times*) written 1850–51 (in the possession of Martin Crossley Evans)

of collecting, five of writing, five of correcting. But most 'Homeridae' begin where Coleridge planned to end, with the composition. Pope, Cowper, Scott, Byron and Crabbe had the right idea; on the other hand, the 'ethical aspirants' are blowing 'penny trumpets in mimicry of one grand and solemn blast … But it is time that we should open the pie of blackbirds, and allow them to sing'. Then they recall Canning's immortalizing of 'these Shallows', and Byron's. Byron, admittedly, attacked Amos for something he couldn't help: the crime of his godparents, which on the title page of an epic poem recalls Tristram Shandy's feelings at his own name. The two Dromios were no harder to distinguish, and Byron did not bother to try, leaving it to the public to fit the fool's cap. As for *The Fall of Cambria*, which Byron mentions, they cannot speak of *its* 'parentage, birth, and death (life there was none to speak of)', but in the matter of *Alfred* Byron nearly 'assigned to Tweelde-dum what belonged to Tweedle-dee'; anyway, the question may properly be left to the department of the antiquarian. 'Alfred Fitz-Joseph was a rickety child – died in infancy – and had long been forgotten'; suddenly, after fifty years, it rises from the dead. Now fifty years ago poetry was languishing, and Cottle's wasn't so conspicuously bad; but since then 'we have witnessed the soaring of the Byrons and Scotts' (not a very sensible remark), so that creeping things *must* now have some originality. Why, then, the revival? It is easy for 'bookseller bards' to 'multiply *editions*', but this is substantially a new work. Thrown in is an anti-papal pamphlet, but the connection is hard to see, since *Alfred* never got on to the Index. They suspect that he here wanted to give the public a really new work, but why did he not reverse the order and slip *Alfred* in 'under the gabardine of the Pope'? The papists are struck with more frenzy than the lyre, but it is all pompous and commonplace and muddled, and his remark on the ubiquity of folly will be cordially assented to! The huge gratuitous prologue is a bad start, too, if Cottle is truly trying to slough his skin. The reviewer then makes the feeble jokes that Abbot Sigbert, with 'weak head' and mangled limbs, must be the author, and that Sigbert's recitation to imps in hell is also autobiographical. There have been four editions, but 'four copies were never seen in circulation by mortal man', and the 3,996 are *somewhere*! But then, Blackmore sang Alfred; so did Pye, 'who did nothing for the King's reputation' (Alfred's or George's? – Pye was the Laureate) 'or his own'; and *now* here is the Warrington attorney John Fitchett … (The papists, by the way, were getting no change out of the Cottle family: in 1852, Robert Cottle, under the pseudonym 'Non Clericus', published in London *Romanism an apostate Church*.)

We have a touching description of Cottle's old age, seen through the eyes of a child.[4] In 1901 his grand-niece, Miss S.E. Green, looked back and remembered his kindness to her and to her cousins, his grandnieces likewise. By this time she owned the 1819 Branwhite portrait, and asserted that it was the artist who insisted on the Byronic collar. In his declining years, she says, Cottle was very lame, 'much bent by age and studious habits', but tall (others, adults, had seen him as short). He had long, silvery hair falling over his coat collar, but he wore a skull cap in winter, and for a time used a wig. His forehead was high and narrow, and his eyebrows grey and bushy, jutting over blue eyes so weak that they were protected by a green shade or blue spectacles; his nose was prominently aquiline, and his very serious mouth 'gave a gentle look to his countenance'. He was of dignified presence, and always dressed in black – long coat, small-clothes, cloth gaiters. He was dear, gentle, kind, patient, and lovable, as far as these children were concerned. He was deeply religious, but he never oppressed them with 'goody' talk. He went on studying right into his old age, and apart from dining with Mrs Hare he lived in his study, where the windows (as in his bedroom) commanded a prospect of gardens and pastures, with Dundry tower in the middle of the hills. Here he sat in an armchair, girt with beloved portraits, reading to himself or reading the Lake Poets aloud to the girls, and using one of them as an amanuensis. Among the portraits was an excellent likeness of Byron, and beneath it he had put the lines:

> O, that face misanthropic, that scowl, and that frown,–
> Take thy genius exalted, thy unhallowed renown;
> Give me the blest forms of the wise and the pure,
> Let me turn to my Milton the nausea to cure.

They knew that he had invented a permanent varnish for oil-paintings, but it 'never came to much'.

Another childhood memory is recorded by Arnold Thomas,[5] whose father David we saw ministering at Zion Chapel and domesticating for two years with Cottle after the death of his first and childless wife, Cottle's niece. Under this roof David came to prefer Foster's *Essays* to the Fathers. Arnold could remember being taken out to Firfield when Hare's 'prim' second wife was there, and seeing the parterres and the rows of tidy little pots of geraniums in the old-fashioned garden, just taken from their winter frames before being bedded out for the summer, and the cold frames covered with bass matting. The Thomas family eventually attained eminence: David's brother Samuel was the father of D.A. Thomas, the great wartime Minister of Food, who became Viscount Rhondda.

J. Morgan, in *A Brief Historical Sketch of Bristol*, published in 1851, mentions 'FIRFIELD HOUSE, Knowle Hill, on the Wells Road, the residence of Mrs. John Hare and J. Cottle, Esq.; a delightful eminence, surrounded by a fine plantation of oak, beech, and lofty waving pine trees; also by fine pasture and arable land.'

There is one last breath of Cottle's poetic life, one last literary pronouncement, but it would have been better unsaid. It concerns Chatterton. On 11 January he wrote to Sholto Vere Hare, stating definitely that the boy's body had been brought secretly to Redcliffe churchyard to be buried by night with his fathers. His ultimate authority was Mrs Edkins, Mrs Chatterton's friend, who had told the secret to George Cumberland, and *he* had called on Cottle with the story about forty years before. We should like to believe it: it has a tearful and tattered majesty. But it is wildly improbable. Why did Cottle say nothing of it in his 1829 note? And did he not remember that Cumberland had already quoted a Mrs Stockwell's evidence for a similar story? Mr John H. Ingram[6] in 1910 invalidated Cottle's account, and we must conclude charitably that the old reminiscer was muddled, or that he was pitying enough to imagine for the boy a decent burial, or that he was just improving on his 1829 story (even as that version had improved on what he said in his edition of 1803).

By 2 June 1853, when Mrs Hare wrote to Pearce the bookbinder, her brother was 'very poorly', but would be grateful if Pearce 'could come about 4 o clock for a couple of hours to stick some sheets of Manuscript together'. After only a few days' illness, Joseph Cottle died at Firfield House on the evening of Tuesday, 7 June 1853. In his last hours 'he was perfectly aware of the approach of death, which he contemplated and spoke of with serenity; and he peacefully ended his long course, having a good hope of eternal life through Jesus Christ'. In these words, the *Bristol Mercury* (who said that he was born in 1769) ended their obituary, and the *Bristol Gazette*, the *Bristol Mirror and General Advertiser*, and the *Bristol Times* and *Felix Farley's Bristol Journal*, likewise on the following Saturday, deplored the death of their venerable fellow-citizen. They saw him in his significant and lasting light, as a friend to people: to Southey, Coleridge, Wordsworth; to some who made nothing of themselves, like Henderson; to an unusual genius like Davy; and, in his maturity, to heavier folk like Mrs More, Hall and Foster. 'He was extensively known', said the *Mirror*, 'by his own literary labours, and throughout his long life was greatly honoured and loved for his distinguished personal worth by all who had the privilege of his acquaintance. He had survived nearly all the friends of his youth and mature life; but there are still left, beside the members of his family, those who will shed a tear over his

345

grave.' 'Advanced as was his age', said the *Mercury*, 'he retained his memory and mental powers with clearness, and employed himself with literary engagements during twelve hours of the day. His temper was calm and cheerful – his life singularly blameless – his character simple and unsuspecting – his heart most warm and generous, and he was throughout life earnestly and consistently religious'. He was 83 years and 90 days old.

He was buried in the Hare grave at Arno's Vale, and two years later Ann followed him thither; she had moved in the meantime, to 5 Buckingham Vale, Clifton. She died on 26 July 1855, at the age of 75, and was buried on 1 August.

In the century that has followed his death, Joseph Cottle has generally been left to sleep the sleep of the petty. A briefly correct notice in the *Dictionary of National Biography*, some censure for his smugness and vanity, some praise for his shrewd and generous gambles before 1799, some mockery for his sillier verses: these have been his lot, and in them no-one need feel that posterity has been unfair. However, it has been falsely assumed by some that a slight man, even in a work of careful scholarship, deserves slight accuracy, and in the course of this narrative I have had reason to correct scholars who have confused him with Amos in their texts and indices, who have called him 'Josiah', who have made him the recipient of letters obviously written to someone else, and who have, by hint or omission, quite misrepresented his little achievements. That Cottle is memorable at all depends on his relations with great men; the more we know of him, the better we shall understand them, especially (I admit) in their relaxed moments. The scholars' mishandling of Cottle makes us wonder how far the other little friends – people like Poole, Wade, Losh, Danvers – have been caricatured or Procrustes'-bedded. Not that I am advocating four more monographs on these gentlemen; material for a life of Cottle has been luckier in its survival than that for others of the group; but there are, for instance, aspects of Poole's influence on Coleridge which have been somewhat belittled. Yet it is in this very material that Cottle has been his own worst enemy, giving us, in two books of memoirs, a tissue of inventions and suppressions, dates wrong by years and letters that are virtually forgeries, white lies and shameless partisanship, preposterous conceit and what sounds very like humbug. One who could have left us with an intimate picture of the shaping of great poets devoted far too many of his pages to trivialities; and incidentally he left to his biographer a heritage of confusion and wrath, which I am not ashamed to have conveyed in these pages.

A few little studies stand apart from the body of shadowy and repetitive criticism. I have already mentioned Professor George Whalley's treatment of

Cottle's library habits and Mr David Foxon's examination of Cottle's part in *Lyrical Ballads*. Mr Edmund Blunden gave Cottle a very respectable article of one large page (albeit garishly captioned 'HERE'S A BOOK WORTH HUNDREDS') in *Everybody's Weekly* of 25 July 1953; and Mr Christopher Morley wrote cheerfully of him in 'Cottle's Pilgrim's Progress', in the *Saturday Review* (New York) of 28 August 1954. In 1930 *The Stuffed Owl*, which I have castigated for its libel on Southey, gave him a fleering paragraph, in which he is called 'a forerunner of what is known in our own time as the Cads' Concert'; this is followed by three quotations from his works, amounting to twenty-six lines. But the sincerest effort to make something of Cottle's position was Carl August Weber's *Bristols Bedeutung für die englische Romantik und die deutsch-englishchen Beziehungen*, published at Halle in 1935. Weber's real hero is Beddoes, but Cottle is given his just place. We see him sympathizing with Savage and Chatterton and Mrs Yearsley, and this is linked with his advocacy of the new young poets; his friendship with Foster associates him with an interesting branch of criticism, and Amos's *Edda* involves him in a movement which the German Weber naturally thinks significant; finally, Cottle had every right to speak out, in his two volumes, on the state of literature in Bristol, marred though his work was by what Coleridge called the 'Bristolism' of his style.

However we may assess Cottle's treatment of greater men, there is no doubt that his long life binds up in itself the life of a great city during critical years, the shaping of a new literature, and the ferments of a revolutionary age. His eighty-three years had swept on from the Gordon Riots to Puseyism, from rebellious New Englanders almost to mutinous Indians, from the death of Chatterton to the appearance of *In Memoriam*, and from the Georgian terraces of Clifton to a Gothic Revival station where Wordsworth was fain to catch a train to Bath.

1   This letter is now in my collection.
2   These three letters are now in my collection. Incidentally, it should be observed that Wordsworth's widow Mary had expressed pleasure (in a letter to Isabella Fenwick on 27 Dec. 1847) that Christopher was undertaking the 'biographical notices', because this might 'prevent indifferent persons' from doing so, 'as poor Cottle and others' did for Coleridge (Mary E. Burton, *op.cit.*, p. 291, No. 136).
3   Vol. XC (1852), No. CLXXX, pp. 333-362.
4   *The Western Counties Graphic*, Vol. II, No. 15, 5 Oct. 1901, in an article by 'The Bookworm'. In Vol. II, No. 11, of 7 Sept. 1901, he says that in Cottle's back parlour Hazlitt met Robert Bloomfield, the 'Farmer's Boy' who briefly stormed the literary world with his verses.

5   See N. Micklem, *Arnold Thomas of Bristol* (London: Allen and Unwin, 1925), pp. 13 ff.

6   J.H. Ingram, *The True Chatterton* (London: T. Fisher Unwin, 1910), Appendix D, pp. 308 ff.

Afterword

In the more than three decades since Basil Cottle finished this biography, there has been a wealth of criticism on some of the figures who pass through its pages, though not much on its principal figure. What has been written and suggested since 1974 neither contradicts the facts of his narrative nor produces new evidence; instead, the literature relating to Joseph Cottle recapitulates the arguments offered and conclusions reached in this book. This critical literature is understandably concerned with the most significant working relationships of Cottle's literary career – the long friendship with Robert Southey, and his more contentious dealings with Wordsworth and Coleridge.

The most famous act of Joseph Cottle's career remains his involvement with the publication of *Lyrical Ballads* in 1798. Basil Cottle's detailed examination of the ambiguities surrounding this episode – to what degree Cottle published the book in Bristol, before selling it to another publisher, and his complicated dealings with Wordsworth – lays out the different scenarios with clarity. He mentions David Foxon's important article of 1954. This has been supplemented by an excellent article primarily on bibliographical questions by Mark Reed, which provides an admirable summary of what Cottle apparently intended to do, even if the resulting Bristol 'publication' might have been restricted to the distribution of a few copies to friends or potential reviewers. The chronology of its publication has also been detailed in the relevant volume of the Cornell edition of Wordsworth's poetry. The editors' reference, though, to 'Cottle's kindly muddleheadedness' suggests the manner in which Cottle is often viewed with regard to the confusions over the publication of *Lyrical Ballads*.[1] The inconsistencies between Cottle's account of the failure of the volume (written much later) and the facts have long been clear, and he has often been seen as either disorganised or even disingenuous. A. D. Boehm goes so far as to claim that he failed to publish the volume at all, due to incompetence. This is an aside in his larger speculation on why Coleridge, Southey and Wordsworth were drawn to Cottle. He suggests that they found in the nonconformist Cottle a 'liberal

349

and humanitarian publisher' more sympathetic to their youthful radical purposes than most, in an argument which perhaps overstates Cottle's interest in politics, and understates the importance of his religion.[2] Basil Cottle's account of his relationship with the budding pantisocrats reminds us of its basis in business, and of the bookseller's suspicions of their wilfulness (pp.30-1).

The span of more than thirty years has produced many changes in fashion in literary criticism, and one of the beneficiaries of these has been the reputation of Robert Southey: critical editions of his poetry, along with biographies and monographs, bear witness to a revisionist trend that rejects the older notion of Southey as the butt of Byron and the mediocre poet who turned his back on youthful radicalism. This has meant more attention for Cottle, albeit indirectly.[3] The Southey scholar and editor Lynda Pratt has produced two articles that examine and print parts of Cottle's unpublished letters to Southey. Their subject is the other great marker in Cottle's account with posterity – the publication of his *Early Recollections* of Coleridge in 1837, which heaped so much opprobrium upon him for his indiscreet revelations of Coleridge's opium addiction. The gossipy and unreliable nature of the *Early Recollections* (and to a lesser extent their reworking in the *Reminiscences* of Coleridge and Southey of 1847) caused Cottle much (avoidable) pain, and has undoubtedly affected his reputation (Basil Cottle spends no little time in distinguishing where Cottle has misdated, elided or selectively edited his materials, or manipulated the 'facts' to support himself).

In examining the evidence for why Cottle needlessly aggravated the family and many supporters of a major literary figure, Pratt is more sympathetic to Cottle than many in the past. She admits that for a long time Cottle has been regarded as unreliable because of his manipulation of materials in his *Early Recollections* and *Reminiscences*, and as a legacy of the offence he caused to Coleridge's reputation. Yet she suggests this is changing, and that 'critics are beginning to realise the length and complexity of Cottle's relationships with his "poets"'.[4] She also speculates, interestingly, on why Cottle's sympathy for and patience with the undeniably difficult Coleridge ended in his publishing revelations about him that could only be harmful. Pratt argues that Cottle's increasing distance from Coleridge was confirmed by the latter's refusal to acknowledge the pivotal role of his Bristol friends (including, of course, Cottle himself) in his account of his intellectual life in the *Biographia Literaria*. Such an omission was one factor behind Cottle's later disastrously candid account of his former friend. This can be aligned with one subtext of Basil Cottle's biography, which is the progressive marginalising of Cottle from the literary world which had been so central to him in the 1790s; the obstinacy with which he pursued his course of action, against the best advice, after Coleridge's death, seems a concomitant to this, a reaction against a cultural establishment which held him in little regard.

In the related piece, Pratt looks at Cottle's letters to Southey in the period leading up to the *Early Recollections*, and absolves Cottle of some blame; after all, the Laureate apparently approved of the manuscript (though Pratt echoes Basil Cottle in saying that we have only Joseph's word for this). She also details interesting contradictions in Southey's apparent dismay at the prurience of contemporary biography (which led to his qualifying his support of Cottle's account of Coleridge), given his own practice in describing William Cowper, for instance.[5] The whole episode, which Basil Cottle details at length, made Cottle appear vain and self-righteous. In Richard Holmes's two-volume biography of Coleridge, Cottle is treated as a necessary part of the great man's early career, but his blunt summary of the *Early Recollections* is that they caused 'endless grief and embarrassment to the surviving family.'[6]

Pratt is also one of the few people to pay any attention to Cottle's poetry. Although Cottle set great store by it, and obviously wanted his verse to make some impression on posterity, Basil Cottle's verdict on the general mediocrity of Cottle's poetic publications is just, and unlikely to be contradicted. His enormous (and often tedious) epic poems were successful in his time only in suggesting bathos and evoking satire. The critical oblivion to which they were long ago confined has only been relieved by attention to their social or ideological aspects; thus, in an essay, Pratt looks at *Alfred* because it is redolent of the English nationalism of its time, considering it alongside the poem on the same monarch by Henry James Pye, another occasional butt of Byron[7] – and the company Cottle here keeps is perhaps a just measure of his talent. Basil Cottle makes plain the vanities and frustrations of a minor poet, but even loyalty to his subject cannot override the critical judgment that prevents him from making exaggerated claims for Cottle's verse. The fact that this verse is only occasionally mentioned, and hardly ever read, is both expected and in no way unjust, given its quality and prolixity.

As well as his dealings with the major Romantic poets, Cottle's biography is sprinkled with cameos from entertaining bit-players. Criticism has sometimes glanced at some of them recently. Tim May has endeavoured to discover where precisely the budding pantisocrats lived in College Street in 1795. Using the same evidence, May reaches the same conclusion as Cottle in this book – the house was number 25, as Cottle shows (p.30).[8] May also provides some touches of local descriptive colour, being, like Cottle, sensitive to the huge changes to the landscape of central Bristol since the Second

World War. Many significant individuals in Joseph Cottle's history are usually now noticed only as part of larger reference works. The online publication of the *Oxford Dictionary of National Biography* in 2004 has revised some of their biographies slightly. Therein the intriguing figure of John Henderson, influential in Joseph Cottle's intellectual evolution, and a man who reportedly conversed with Samuel Johnson in Latin for hours (but who accomplished next to nothing), is summarised by James Sambrook, who describes his potential and its lack of fulfilment. There is an account of the peculiar career of William 'Hurricane' Gilbert in Sally Bushell's revision of Richard Garnett's older *DNB* article. Gilbert is also the subject of an article by Paul Cheshire, which describes the vicissitudes of this strange and unfortunate man, and explicates the heterogeneous and eccentric intellectual context of his only well-known poem.[9] Finally, scholarship on Thomas Chatterton has flourished recently, though little of it is concerned directly with Cottle and Southey's role in his reputation. In his *ODNB* article on the poet, Nick Groom suggests that Chatterton did not take his own life, but died instead from an accidental drug overdose; if so, this will question Basil Cottle's description of the act as suicide, though the most germane point remains that Joseph Cottle thought that Chatterton had killed himself, and he encountered opposition to commemorating the poet within the precincts of a church for this reason (p.305).[10] Such efforts are another reminder of the part played by Cottle in Bristol literary culture for so many years, which Basil Cottle's biography describes with affection, wit, and abiding enthusiasm.

Adam Rounce
Keele University

1   Mark L. Reed, 'The First Title Page of Lyrical Ballads, 1798', *Studies in Bibliography*, 51 (1998), 231-41. *Lyrical Ballads, and Other Poems, 1797-1800*, ed. James Butler and Karen Green (Ithaca & London: Cornell University Press, 1992), pp.14-15.

2   A. D. Boehm, 'Was Joseph Cottle a liberal bookseller?', *English Language Notes*, 32:3 (1995), 32–9, p.35.

3   The latest biography, in which Cottle plays an intermittent part, is W. A. Speck, *Robert Southey: Entire Man of Letters* (New Haven and London: Yale University Press, 2006).

4   Lynda Pratt, 'The 'Sad Habits' of Samuel Taylor Coleridge: Unpublished Letters from Joseph Cottle to Robert Southey, 1813-1817', *Review of English Studies*, 55 (2004), 75-90, p.76. An Appendix lists Cottle's unpublished letters to Southey from 1804-37.

5   Lynda Pratt, 'The Media of Friends or Foes? Unpublished Letters from Joseph Cottle to Robert Southey, 1834-1837', *Modern Language Review*, 98 (2003), 545-62, pp.560-1.

6   Richard Holmes, *Coleridge: Early Visions* (Harmondsworth: Penguin, 1989). *Coleridge: Darker Reflections* (London: Harper Collins, 1998), p.360.

7   Lynda Pratt, 'Anglo-Saxon Attitudes? Alfred the Great and the Romantic National Epic' in *Literary Appropriations of the Anglo-Saxons from the Thirteenth to the Twentieth Century*, ed. Donald Scragg and Carole Weinberg (Cambridge: Cambridge University Press, 2000), pp.138-56.

8   Tim May, 'The Pantisocrats in College Street', *N & Q*, 249 (2005), 456-60.

9   Paul Cheshire, 'The Hermetic Geography of William Gilbert', *Romanticism*, 9 (2003), 82-93.

10 Of Groom's other writings on Chatterton, 'Love and Madness: Southey Editing Chatterton', in *Robert Southey and the Contexts of English Romanticism*, ed. Lynda Pratt (Aldershot: Ashgate, 2005), 41-64, is a discussion of Southey and Cottle's 1803 edition of the poet.

Biography of Basil Cottle

Arthur Basil Cottle was born in Cardiff on 17 March 1917, a fourth generation Primitive Methodist. To the date and place of his birth he attributed his love of all things Celtic, and particularly the history, art, and literature of Ireland and Wales; and to his religious upbringing at Mount Tabor Chapel his detestation of what he perceived as the cultural Philistinism of Nonconformity.

At Howard Gardens' Secondary School, which he loathed, he attracted the attention of Lord Tredegar, who gave him encouragement and the use of his library. At University College, Cardiff, he gained a double first in Latin and English, an upper second in Greek, and trained as a schoolmaster. At the university he was greatly influenced by Professor Nash Williams, whose work on early Christian epigraphy in Wales fired his enthusiasm for the Celtic saints and the archaeology of the Dark Ages, a passion that he was to transmit to generations of students at Bristol. The outbreak of war prevented him from entering the world of museum curatorship.

During the war he rose through the ranks, joining the ENIGMA team at Bletchley Park in 1943, before finally taking over the Albanian section of the Foreign Office in 1945, monitoring the civil war between the Zoggists and the Communists. He learnt the language in six weeks with the help of Stuart Mann (the noted linguist and Bristol graduate, who taught English to King Zog's three unmarried sisters), and he subsequently wrote the internal Foreign Office Albanian grammar.

Demobbed in 1946, Cottle accepted an assistant lectureship in English at the University of Bristol, where he remained until 1980, when (now Reader in Mediaeval Studies) he retired. He taught a large range of subjects, including Middle English, the Greek Lyric (for Professor H.D.F. Kitto), Ancient Irish and Anglo-Saxon Art, and Architecture for the newly-formed course in archaeology and geology, for the Professor of Neotectonics, P.L. Hancock. Cottle was also the University's historian and his *The Life of the University* with J.W. Sherborne (1951, revised 1979) has not been superseded. His play (1976) to mark the centenary of the foundation of University College, Bristol was also much acclaimed.

Between 1946 and his death he did more than anyone else to make Bristolians aware of their eighteenth- and nineteenth-century literary heritage. He led the movement to erect a monument on Fairfax House, Wine Street to commemorate the poet, Richard Savage (c.1698-1743), and to re-cut the inscription to his memory on the south wall of St. Peter's Church on Castle Park, which had been damaged in the blitz. He wrote a short and highly readable biography, *Thomas Chatterton* (1963), for the Bristol Branch of the Historical Association and was responsible for the world première of Chatterton's play *Aella: A Tragical Enterlude*, which he produced in 1970 to mark the bicentenary of Chatterton's death.

In 1942 Cottle was baptised into the Church of England and became an enthusiastic and committed member of that Church. Although a sub-warden at Burwalls, between 1948 and 1973, he attended St. Mary Redcliffe. As one of the historians and church wardens, he led the movement to dismantle the decaying, weathered monument with its 'puppet-statue of a bluecoat boy' erected to Chatterton's memory, which stood opposite Chatterton's birthplace, as being unworthy of the poet. He replaced it with a chaste and elegant tablet within the church itself, receiving for his pains bitter and vituperative letters, a selection of which survive amongst his papers in the University of Bristol's Special Collections.

Cottle became interested in the association of the Romantic poets with Bristol in the late 1940s. It came to his attention that many valuable letters and books associated with the poets were being offered for sale in London. Owing to national austerity, and in spite of his appeals, neither the University of Bristol nor the City of Bristol were willing or able to purchase these items, many of which were subsequently exported to the United States. Notwithstanding his family commitments and his limited salary, he purchased a number of items on his own account. The text of the letters was subsequently interwoven into the chapters of his doctoral thesis *The Life (1770-1853), Writings and Literary Relationships of Joseph Cottle of Bristol* (University of Bristol, 1958), upon which this book is based. In Bristol he formed one of a small group of Romantic enthusiasts and savants, a group which included the late Bertram Davies and Miss Rotha Mary Clay, both subsequently awarded an honorary M.A. by the University.

In 1978 Cottle joined the congregation of Christ Church with St. Ewen's, Broad Street and was elected a Church Warden of St. Ewen's in 1984. (This church was closed in 1788 to make way for the extension to the city's Guildhall and was finally demolished in the early 1820s. The successors to its congregation continue to elect churchwardens annually.) At Christ Church, which was joined with All Saints', Corn Street, Cottle and the late

Vivian George Mildren, with the encouragement of Professor Nicholas Orme of Exeter, subsequently re-formed the mediaeval Guild of Kalendars. Its new centrepiece was the annual Southey Lecture delivered at Christ Church. Many of these lectures were later published as pamphlets in the Bristol Branch of the Historical Association series, including his own *Robert Southey* (1980) and *Joseph Cottle* (1987).

Elected to the Society of Antiquaries of London in 1979, he served as meetings secretary (1978-82) and later President of the Bristol and Gloucestershire Archaeological Society (1987-8), lectured widely on church dedications in Gloucestershire, Bristol and Somerset, and, with the Folk House Archaeological Society in Bristol, took an active role in the excavation and recording of Keynsham Abbey, Somerset. Through membership of the Bristol Diocesan Advisory Committee and the Council for the Preservation of Ancient Bristol, he took an active part in the preservation of Bristol's architectural and archaeological heritage in the 1970s and 1980s.

A gifted lecturer, teacher, philologist, writer, poet, author of *vers d'occasion*, playwright, and heraldic artist, Cottle inspired generations of students at the University and through his extra mural classes.

Following his untimely death on 13 May 1994, a number of volumes of Joseph Cottle's poetry were donated in Cottle's memory to the University's Special Collections, together with Miss Rotha Mary Clay's copy of the 2nd edition of Wordsworth's *Lyrical Ballads*. The lone bell of St. Ewen's Church, cast by Abraham Rudhall of Gloucester in 1698, the sound of which was familiar to Southey during his childhood in Wine Street, also found a permanent home. After the closure of the church and the union of the benefice with Christ Church, the corporation had sold it at auction in the 1790s. It was subsequently hung at Portland Street Wesleyan Chapel. In the 1970s that building was closed and demolished. After a short spell in Victoria Methodist Church, and a longer one in a warehouse, the bell was, through the generosity of the Portland Street Trustees and Cottle's friends, rescued and hung inside his much-loved Christ Church, the jewel of Georgian Bristol. Here it records Cottle's life and achievements. And he has left one other similarly concrete legacy to Bristol's historical heritage: the Paty pulpit, one of the glories of Georgian Bristol, made for Christ Church, City (the church in which Southey was baptized c.1790 and which is often said to be Bristol's answer to St Martin in the Fields) had been removed at the end of the nineteenth century, but was re-assembled from pieces stored in the crypt and returned to its proper place, partly from monies raised in memory of Basil Cottle.

M.J. Crossley Evans